The World beyond Europe in the Romance Epics of Boiardo and Ariosto

JO ANN CAVALLO

The World beyond Europe in the Romance Epics of Boiardo and Ariosto

UNIVERSITY OF TORONTO PRESS
Toronto Buffalo London

Toronto Buffalo London
www.utppublishing.com

ISBN 978-1-4426-4683-4

Toronto Italian Studies

Library and Archives Canada Cataloguing in Publication

Cavallo, Jo Ann
The World beyond Europe in the romance epics of Boiardo and Ariosto / Jo Ann Cavallo.

(Toronto Italian studies)
Includes bibliographical references and index.
ISBN 978-1-4426-4683-4 (bound)

1. Boiardo, Matteo Maria, 1440 or 41–1491. Orlando innamorato. 2. Ariosto, Lodovico, 1474–1533. Orlando furioso. 3. Romances, Italian – History and criticism. 4. Epic poetry, Italian – History and criticism. 5. Geography and literature. 6. National characteristics in literature. I. Title. II. Series: Toronto Italian studies

PQ4117.C42 2013 851′.20932 C2013-902693-2

This book has been published with the assistance of a grant from the Modern Language Association.

University of Toronto Press acknowledges the financial assistance to its publishing program of the Canada Council for the Arts and the Ontario Arts Council.

University of Toronto Press acknowledges the financial support of the Government of Canada through the Canada Book Fund for its publishing activities.

For my children,
Cristina and Alberto

Non se cognosce la virtute intera
se non al tempo che fortuna è fiera.

(Matteo Maria Boiardo, *Orlando innamorato* 2.2.29)

Contents

Acknowledgments

Brief passages from the introduction and various chapters were included in my paper "The World beyond Christian Europe in the Romance Epics of Boiardo and Ariosto," presented at the Austrian Scholars Conference, the Ludwig von Mises Institute, Auburn, AL, 10 March 2012.

Passages from the introduction were included in my paper "Three Approaches to Romance Epic: Global Studies, Popular Traditions, Teaching through Performance," presented at the MLA Annual Convention, Philadelphia, 30 December 2009.

Brief sections of chapters 2 to 6 were included in my paper "Eroi asiatici nell'*Orlando Innamorato* e l'*Orlando Furioso*," presented at the conference "Puppets and Cultures of Asia" held in conjunction with the thirty-first Festival di Morgana, organized by the Museo Internazionale delle Marionette Antonio Pasqualino, Palermo, 8–10 November 2006.

An extended section of chapter 4 was presented as "Theology and Poetry in Boiardo's *Orlando Innamorato*: Agricane's Conversion" at the conference *Tra Amici*: A Symposium in Honor of Giuseppe Mazzotta, University of Mary Washington, Fredericksburg, VA, 27–30 March 2008, and published as "Talking Religion: The Conversion of Agricane in Boiardo's *Orlando Innamorato*" in *Modern Languages Notes* 127 Supplement (2012): S178–S188.

Part of chapter 6 was presented as "Marfisa trasfigurata: Boiardo, Ariosto e Giusto lo Dico" at the conference "L'*Orlando Furioso*: Figure dell'ambiguità dell'epica cavalleresca" held in conjunction with the thirty-fourth Festival di Morgana, organized by the Museo Internazionale delle Marionette Antonio Pasqualino, Palermo, 19–20 November 2009.

Sections of chapter 8 draw on my article "The Pathways of Knowledge in Boiardo and Ariosto: The Case of Rodamonte," *Italica* 79:3 (2002): 305–20.

An abridged version of chapter 11 was presented as "Nur ad-Din to Norandino: The Middle East in Boiardo's *Orlando Innamorato*" at the American Association of Italian Studies, St John's University, Manhattan, 9 May 2009; a fuller version, with the same title, was subsequently published in *Global Perspectives on Italian Literatures, Cinema, and Culture*, edited by Tonia Caterina Riviello (Salerno: EDISUD SALERNO, 2012), 17–37.

Part of chapter 12 was presented as "Crocodiles and Crusades: Egypt in Boiardo's *Orlando Innamorato*" at the Purdue University Renaissance Comparative Prose Conference, 5–6 November 2009, and a slightly abridged version of the full chapter was published as "Crocodiles and Crusades: Egypt in Boiardo's *Orlando Innamorato* and Ariosto's *Orlando Furioso*" in *Arthuriana* 21.1 (2011): 85–96.

Chapters 15 and 17 further develop papers presented at my two-day seminar entitled "Esplorazioni fantastiche e messaggi ideologici in Boiardo e Ariosto" which took place at the Università di Studi di Lecce, Dipartimento di Scienze Sociali e della Comunicazione, 16–17 January 2006. The individual paper titles were "Come si spaventa un'arpia: Il volo di Astolfo alla leggendaria Etiopia (*Orlando furioso* XXXIII, 96–128)" and "Come si bacia un serpente: il coraggio di conoscere l'altro (*Orlando Innamorato* II, XXVI, 1–19)." A revised version of the latter paper was presented as "Come si bacia un serpente: Brandimarte al palazzo di Febosilla nell'*Orlando Innamorato*" at the conference "Boiardo: L'amore, la guerra, la morte" held in conjunction with the thirty-fifth Festival di Morgana, organized by the Museo Internazionale delle Marionette Antonio Pasqualino, Palermo, Italy, and is forthcoming as "How to Kiss a Serpent: Brandimarte's Adventure at the Palace of Febosilla (*Orlando Innamorato*)" in *For a Dangerous Pedagogy: A Manifesto for Italian and Italian American Studies*, edited by Pellegrino D'Acierno and Stanislao Pugliese (New York: Fordham University Press).

A special thanks to Carla M. Bregman for translating the above two seminar papers into English as well as for her unfailingly perspicacious comments on each chapter at various stages. I am also grateful to Charles S. Ross and Karina F. Attar for their detailed and insightful comments on the manuscript. Finally, as I have been teaching this material at Columbia for quite a number of years, I would like to thank the many students who have offered feedback and encouragement. I dedicate this work to my children, Cristina and Alberto, who have not only accompanied me on many intercontinental adventures during their younger years, but who have now set off as intrepid knights errant in the cause of liberty.

The Amministrazione Comunale di Parma, the Pinacoteca G. Stuard-Patrimonio Artistico, and the Comando Provinciale dei Carabinieri di Parma graciously provided permission and made arrangements for the photographing of the fresco detail shown on the book jacket. Noeline H. Bridge compiled the index. Copyrighted articles noted above were incorporated into the current book with the permission of the publishers.

The World beyond Europe in the Romance Epics of Boiardo and Ariosto

Introduction

Just over twenty years separate the publication of the definitive version of the *Orlando innamorato* (1495) and the first edition of the *Orlando furioso* (1516), arguably the two most important romance epics of the Italian Renaissance.[1] Nevertheless, as this study maintains, the poems are worlds apart when it comes to their depiction of the world at large. Writing for a fifteenth-century court society hooked on medieval chivalric narrative but also attuned to the latest current world events, Boiardo charts a complex course in which characters from East Asia, northern Africa, the Middle East, and Europe interact in myriad ways, from armed conflict to friendship and romance. Although Ariosto continues to mix imaginary sites and the geographical reality of a rapidly expanding globe, he increasingly replaces the *Innamorato*'s prevailing attitude of international cosmopolitanism with a more restrictive outlook that brings to bear the crusading ideology characteristic of Carolingian epic.

In an introductory sonnet included in early editions of the *Innamorato*, Boiardo's friend Tommaso Mattacoda alerts readers using their intellect ("gente con ragione") that Matteo Maria's cantos contain "Favole, historie, e comparatione, / Cosmographia con philosophia, / Costumi e usanze d'ogni natione / Et altre cose degne d'armonia" ("Fables, histories, and comparisons, / Geography with philosophy, / Customs and practices of every nation / And other things worthy of harmony") (Harris 1: 107). The poem's geographical tour de force begins in the opening canto when Angelica of Cathay suddenly appears in Paris, disrupting Charlemagne's tournament and eventually drawing paladins from Latin Christendom across the expanse of Asia. There is also movement in the poem towards western Europe from a variety of other directions. Each of the three books, in fact, opens with a foreign ruler determined to reach France:

Gradasso of Sericana covets Ranaldo's horse and Orlando's sword, the North African kings Agramante and Rodamonte seek to conquer Charlemagne's realm, and in the third book the Tartar Mandricardo aims to kill Orlando.[2] At the same time, the interlaced plot introduces additional foreign protagonists whose interests remain beyond the confines of Europe, from the formidable Tartar khan Agricane to the courteous Syrian king Noradino. Regardless of their provenance, Boiardo's characters are motivated by a range of passions – primarily love, ambition, empathy, and the desire for glory or revenge – but not by religious or ethnic differences. The narrative thereby breaks out of the binary opposition of Christians and Saracens typical of Carolingian epic, presenting a broader vision of the globe consonant with a number of ancient, medieval, and fifteenth-century historical and geographical texts that were capturing the attention of the Ferrarese court.

When Ariosto picks up the threads of Boiardo's narrative about a decade after the publication of the 1495 edition, he subjects Boiardo's East Asian and North African protagonists to a process of degradation whereby they lose their earlier positive characteristics, until they are ultimately removed from the poem through physical departure (Angelica) or death (Mandricardo, Agramante, Gradasso, Rodomonte). The only exception to this drastic fate is conversion to Christianity (Marphisa). In the latter cantos, moreover, Ariosto transforms not only the nature of the characters but the epic plot itself. The war between Agramante and Charlemagne, which began in the *Innamorato* as a case of *aviditas dominationis* in which the African king sought to imitate Alexander of Macedonia, increasingly takes on the connotations of a holy war, culminating when the Frankish sack of Biserta evokes the conquest of Jerusalem in the First Crusade. The knight who plays the principal role in this ideological shift is Astolfo, who after a purgatorial experience in the Indian Ocean develops into a *miles Christi*, evidenced by his worship at the Church of the Holy Sepulchre in Jerusalem, his charitable mission on behalf of Prester John in Ethiopia, and finally his participation in the destruction of Agramante's North African kingdom under God's direction. Consonant with this shift is the different treatment of the Middle East in each poem: whereas Boiardo imagines what the region would have been like if the crusades had not taken place, Ariosto anachronistically envisions the Holy Land under European domination.

The distinctive Weltanschauung of the two poems did not escape the attention of the nineteenth-century philologist Pio Rajna, who maintained that whereas in the *Innamorato* "the barriers between the Christian and

Saracen world, if not removed entirely, have largely collapsed," in the *Furioso* "with a bit of the crusading spirit reintroduced and with religious creed placed once again above the chivalric code, it will be sufficient to adore Mohammed in order to be, whether to a greater or lesser extent, portrayed in a bad light."[3] Rajna attributes Ariosto's negative treatment of Boiardo's Asian and African heroes to the younger poet's desire to conform to the demands of his society: "Where Ariosto sees Christians and Infidels, Boiardo did not distinguish except between the valorous and the inept, the courteous and the uncivil. It's not that Lodovico, in his heart, believed more than Boiardo; he's an indifferent fellow who goes to church out of habit, and to preserve appearances, but in any case he goes" (*Le fonti*, 56). Yet rather than analyse the *Furioso*'s disapproving depiction of non-Christians, Rajna simply concludes that "Ariosto was poorly inspired in the portrayal of Saracen characters" (*Le fonti*, 422).

Roughly a century later Antonio Pasqualino, considering the two romance epics in the context of puppet theatre, also found Ariosto's presentation of Boiardo's non-Christian heroes to be less than sympathetic: "[Boiardo] exalts hyperbolically the valour not only of Saracens destined to convert, like Agricane, but also that of Sacripante, Gradasso, Mandricardo, and Rodomonte, heroes whose adventures near the end of the poem are narrated independently of the rest of the plot. [...] No other chivalric text exalts to such a degree Saracen heroes. In the *Orlando Furioso* the same characters are presented in a less favourable light and are judged more severely."[4] To date, however, no study has attempted to account for these perceived differences through a sustained, contextualized comparison of the world beyond Christian Europe envisioned by the two poets.[5] On the contrary, the distinctions on this score are generally blurred or ignored completely. Italo Calvino, who stated that "the *Furioso* is a unique book in its genre and can – I'd almost say must – be read without reference to any other book preceding or following it" (xxxviii), maintains instead that "being 'of two different faiths' does not mean, in the *Furioso*, much more than the different colour of pieces on a chessboard; the time of the crusades, in which the cycle of paladins had attained a symbolic value for the life-and-death struggle between Christianity and Islam, is far away" (xliii).[6] A close reading of the two poems shows on the contrary that while Calvino's assertion rings true for the *Innamorato,* it cannot be applied to much of the *Furioso*.

Nor has Boiardo's precedent been taken sufficiently into account in previous considerations of geography in the *Furioso*. As early as 1923 Santino Caramella maintained that Boiardo "goes beyond the traditional geography of the *Chansons de geste* with his immense new material and offers geographical knowledge not in a descriptive way but in the adventurous progression of the [characters'] travels" (45–6).[7] He drew attention, in particular, to the precedent of Andrea da Barberino for Boiardo's poem: "Boiardo's geographical method is in direct correspondence to that of Andrea [...], and indeed represents here and there an accurate perfectioning" (45). Yet the most extensive recent treatment of the *Furioso*'s geographical focus, Alexandre Doroszlaï's investigation of the use of maps in the poem, looks exclusively to the example of Andrea da Barberino without considering Ariosto's closest predecessor.[8] My comparative reading argues that Ariosto's use of geography does not simply aim to update or surpass Boiardo's references but rather to overturn his worldview.

In short, the present study intends to chart the narratological strategies that Boiardo and Ariosto use to depict characters and places, both imaginary and historical, that represent the world outside Christian Europe in their respective poems. In focusing on interactions of various kinds occurring in the most disparate regions of the globe, I will be addressing issues bearing on the poems' historical and literary context. How did each poet renegotiate the Carolingian epic's traditional backdrop of Christian-Saracen hostilities to reflect contemporary attitudes and political realities? What part did the Ottoman military threat and periodic calls for a renewed crusade against the "infidel" play? How did information about Asia, the Middle East, and Africa from a range of non-fictional works get factored into the fantasy? To what extent was identity created through geographical provenance or religious creed? At issue here is not simply how the geographically and religiously other is portrayed in each poem but rather how, through episodes featuring characters and sites from outside Christian Europe, both poets offered a blueprint for reading their poems and consequently for relating to the geopolitical realities of their day.

A View of the Globe from Fifteenth-Century Ferrara

While it is undeniable, as Margaret Meserve has stated, that "for most fifteenth-century Europeans [...] the countries of Asia were strange and foreign places," it is also true that during this period Ferrara was at the forefront in pursuing knowledge about the world beyond the Italian peninsula through newly translated works of ancient geographers and historians as well as through more recent sources, such as travellers' accounts, merchant activity, and increasingly accurate maps.[9] Donald Lach singles out the Este family among Italian bibliophiles as "the first to begin collecting books on Asia and the overseas world" (vol. 2; bk 2, 48).[10] Jerry Brotton names the Este along with the Montefeltro of Urbino as prime examples of wealthy patrons and power brokers who "were quick not only to commission new manuscript texts but also to allow their names to be associated with new printing initiatives within the field of academic geography" (*The Renaissance Bazaar*, 37).[11] Not surprisingly, both Ptolemy and Strabo figured prominently in the Ferrarese court: Strabo's voluminous *Geography* was translated by the city's preeminent humanist, Guarino da Verona, and an illuminated manuscript of Ptolemy's *Geography* in an early fifteenth-century Latin translation was dedicated to Borso d'Este in 1466.[12] Ercole d'Este kept this precious latter volume in his personal study along with a crucial Bologna edition that was the first to contain a comprehensive cartographical apparatus.[13] These works not only provided factual information – Ptolemy alone described more than 8,000 places – but offered models of open-mindedness in viewing the globe. Brotton explains that the impact of Ptolemy's work "on the world of geography was to revolutionize a certain perception of space itself, which was no longer charged with religious significance but was instead a continuous, open terrestrial space."[14] Strabo explicitly encouraged his readers to adopt an unbiased attitude towards other peoples. Commending a treatise by Eratosthenes as a worthy precedent on this score, he writes: "After withholding praise from those who divide the whole multitude of mankind into two groups, namely, Greeks and Barbarians, and also from those who advised Alexander to treat the Greeks as friends but the Barbarians as enemies – Eratosthenes goes on to say that it would be better to make such divisions according to good qualities and bad qualities; for not only are many of the Greeks bad, but many of the Barbarians are refined" (1: 247–9).

Ancient historians with an interest in foreign cultures also held a prominent place at the Este court – thanks in large part to Boiardo's translations of Herodotus's *Histories*, Xenophon's *Cyropaedia*, and Cornelius Nepos's *De viris illustribus* (*Lives of Famous Captains*). In the preface to his translation of the *Histories*, Boiardo celebrates Herodotus expressly for his global reach: "Si debbe Herodoto tra gli historici nominare Principe e padre, per il quale si ha cognitione della vita & costumi di tutte quasi le nationi che habitano il circuito della terra" ("Herodotus must be called among historians the Prince and father, through whom we have knowledge about the life and customs of almost all the nations that inhabit the circumference of the earth") (2v).[15] Xenophon's *Cyropaedia* surpasses perhaps even Herodotus in its attention to other cultures by portraying a Persian ruler as a protagonist warranting emulation rather than as a threat to the Greeks. Boiardo asserts that Nepos's biographies, moreover, bear witness to the excellence of "alcuni valorosi capitani Greci e Barbari" ("various valiant Greek and foreign captains") in whose lives he can see the reflection of Ercole's own: "io conosco la vita tua per vera forma rappresentarsi in quella di questi illustri" ("I recognize your life to be the true form represented in that of these illustrious men") (1).[16] In this way Ercole is envisioned as embodying exemplary qualities that transcend the purview of his own culture.

The Este court could have also followed an extensive account of European history from ancient Rome up to the end of the thirteenth century in the works of the medieval compiler Riccobaldo of Ferrara (c. 1245–1318). Boiardo composed an expanded translation of Riccobaldo, entitled *Historia imperiale*, extending the material on Europe's foreign affairs to cover periods of both defensive and offensive warfare.[17] After recounting the particularly destructive Saracen incursions in Italy during the ninth and tenth centuries, he turns to the Italo-Norman reconquest of Calabria and Sicily spearheaded by Roger I and his brothers, and subsequently to the early crusades in which, now in the context of a defensive war, the Saracen leaders Nur ad-Din and Saladin emerge as admirable figures.[18]

Medieval travellers' accounts updated and complemented the information provided by historians, shifting the focus from military conflict to peaceful encounters. Among this group, the Venetian merchant Marco Polo (1254–1324) was a privileged witness, having spent several years in the Mongol court of Kublai Khan and journeyed extensively throughout Asia (1271–95). His widely available *Milione* sought to enlighten his contemporaries regarding "le diverse generazioni delle genti e lle diversità delle regioni del mondo" ("the diverse populations and the variety of regions of the world"), specifically "le grandissime maraviglie e gran diversitadi delle genti d'Erminia, di Persia e di Tarteria, d'India e di molte altre province" ("the great marvels and great diversity of the people of Armenia, Persia, Tartary, India, and many other provinces") (*Mil.* 1.1, 2).[19] Marco Polo attempted to convey the reality of foreign lands as objectively as he could, and he often expressed respect and approbation for his Eastern hosts. As Sante Matteo writes, his account "puts on display a different, more humanistic way of looking at the natural world and assessing people's place in it."[20] In the course of the fifteenth century both Latin and vernacular copies of the work are recorded in the ducal library, in Ercole d'Este's private study, and circulating among members of the court.[21]

A number of ambassadors and missionaries who both preceded and followed Marco Polo to the Mongol court also provided accounts of their travels that would have been available to fifteenth-century readers. In 1245 Pope Innocent IV sent the Franciscan friar Giovanni da Pian del Carpine as his emissary to the Mongol khan with the goal of spreading Christianity and gathering information about the empire. The friar's record of his journey, *Historia Mongalorum* (1245–7), not only circulated independently in manuscript form (Olschki, *L'Asia di Marco Polo*, 58n44), but was incorporated into Vincent of Beauvais's encyclopedic *Speculum historiale* and subsequently into the popular *Travels* of Sir John Mandeville, a fictitious travel manual of sorts ranging from the Middle East to India and Cathay.[22] The latter work is mentioned specifically in a letter in which Ercole asks a minister to return a borrowed copy (Milano 90), and is documented in the 1495 inventory as *Giovan de Mandavilla* (Bertoni 242, no. 213). Odorico da Pordenone, another friar who undertook missionary work in the Mongol Empire, wrote a first-hand account of his journeys (1318–30) that was present in the Estense collection both as "Frate hodoricus in latino" (Bertoni 241, no. 178) and through its substantial use in Mandeville's *Travels*. The missionary friar William of Rubruck also documented his experiences among the Mongols (1253–5) in his *Itinerarium*, which became readily available to literate Europeans in the following decades when it was incorporated into Roger Bacon's encyclopedia. In addition, the "Fiore de historie doriente" noted in the Estense library inventory (Bertoni 241, no. 193) corresponds to the title of an early fourteenth-century history of the Mongol Empire by the Armenian noble-turned-monk Hayton of Corycus, *La flor des estoires d'Orient (The Flower of Histories of the East)*.[23] These works would have been the most up-to-date writings available to the Ferrarese court on the Mongol Empire because foreign Christians were expelled after the Mongols were overthrown by native Chinese Ming in 1368. Evelyn Edson notes that in the Catalan-Estense world map of 1450–60, "China is pretty much the world of Marco Polo; the Great Khan is still ruling there" (198).[24]

Extensive land and sea travel during the fifteenth century led to ever-increasing familiarity with various other parts of the world. Given that the Este family were in close contact with both Venice (until the war of 1482) and Naples, contemporary testimonials about eastern regions could have reached the court through merchants and ambassadors from these Italian port cities. Beginning in 1425, in fact, Venetians travelling abroad were required to furnish both an oral and a written account upon their return, and anyone interested in knowing the habits and customs of faraway peoples could consult these reports.[25] Furthermore, Maria Pia Pedani points out that diplomats from Egypt, Persia, the Ottoman Empire, and Albania were a regular presence in Venice, making it "truly an international city, an open door towards the East and the West, where it was possible to tie together the threads of contacts and encounters, open and secret, among Christians and Muslims" (116).[26]

The Estense family assiduously sought the most up-to-date world maps as well as the latest news regarding Portuguese and Spanish attempts to reach India by sea.[27] Ercole d'Este not only possessed a translation of one of Columbus's 1493 letters regarding his purported discovery of India, but his 1494 correspondence regarding Columbus's voyage "demonstrates that the duke's curiosity was based on quite precise geographical ideas" (Greppi, "Luoghi e miti," 448).[28] Lach notes that Ercole followed the progress of Portuguese explorers as they travelled south along the African coast, eventually finding a sea route to India (vol. 2, bk 2, 49).

Imported goods present in Ferrara also served as a window to foreign lands, and the city's access to this material culture was greatly facilitated by, although not limited to, Venice's hegemony in trade with Muslim territories.[29] Giovanni Ricci writes that in the 1460s Borso sent his representatives on various missions to Tunisia to purchase Arabian horses (*I turchi alle porte*, 153).[30] The *Diario ferrarese dall'anno 1409 al 1504* mentions in passing a centrally located "speciaria del Saracino" (Saracen spice shop) in 1471 (69). Oriental carpets were increasingly in demand, and from the middle of the fifteenth century a "tapedo turchesco" was considered a "status symbol" among the Ferrarese (Boralevi 217).[31] In the Salone dei Mesi fresco of Palazzo Schifanoia, painted in the late 1460s or early 1470s, young women view the Palio of St George (April) from balconies draped with four Turkish carpets.[32] In 1490 Ercole d'Este invited an Egyptian weaver and carpet merchant originally from Cairo to establish a workshop near the ducal palace. Ten years later "Maestro Sabadino tapeziero," also referred to as "Syro," "Negro," and "Moro," received as a gift from Ercole two houses for himself and his male descendants (Ricci, *Ossessione turca*, 27–8).[33]

The ducal family's predilection for astrology and esoteric culture also brought them indirectly into contact with different currents originating in the East. This is likewise reflected in the fresco paintings of the Salone dei Mesi, where astrological symbols based on the authority of the Arab astronomer Albumasar (Abu Ma'shar) fill the centre zone. In addition, the earliest Tarocchi known to have circulated in Italy were those of the Este court (1442). Although the exact origin of Tarot cards is unknown, it is thought that they were conceived in Egypt, China, India, or ancient Greece. Boiardo's verses composed to accompany an elaborately illustrated deck attest to their continued popularity (*Tarocchi*).

Pilgrimage narratives, in vogue throughout the fourteenth and fifteenth centuries, were a venue for information specifically about the Middle East. In 1358 Petrarch penned a pilgrimage itinerary that appears to have been translated into Tuscan at the Estense court by Niccolò III d'Este's preceptor.[34] Pilgrimage expeditions from northern Italy to Jerusalem sometimes stopped at Ferrara on their way to or from the port of Venice. The Franciscan friar Niccolò da Poggibonsi, who described his five-year pilgrimage (1345–50) in his *Libro d'oltramare* (*Voyage beyond the Sea*), stayed various months in the "benedetta e gentile" ("blessed and kind") Ferrara upon his return (2: 239). In 1458 the *condottiere* Roberto da Sanseverino (1417–87) visited Borso d'Este in Modena on his way to the Holy Land and then wrote an extensive account of his travels the following year.[35]

The Estense did not need to rely solely on external sources for descriptions of the Middle East, however. In 1413 the marquis Niccolò III d'Este and his entourage, which included Boiardo's grandfather Feltrino, went on what Theodore J. Cachey, Jr, calls "one of the most important and high-profile Italian pilgrimages to the Holy Land of the Quattrocento" (53). Niccolò commemorated the journey through the court chancellor Luchino Dal Campo's detailed account of their various steps, *El viaggio al santo Sepolcro del nostro Signor Gesù Cristo in Jerusalem, el qual fece lo illustrissimo signor marchese Nicolò da Este con altri gentiluomini suoi compagni.*[36] Another member of the Este family to record his voyage to the Holy Land was Milliaduse (1406–52), one of Niccolò's illegitimate sons. His chaplain Don Domenego provides a meticulous account of their experiences during the trip, which took place between May 1440 and February 1441.[37]

Although Ercole did not travel outside Europe, it apparently pleased him to have his court considered the destination of dignitaries from around the world. In the preface to his translation of Herodotus, Boiardo proclaims the global extension of the duke's hospitality: "spesse volte molti principi forestieri ho veduti in quella [corte] ricetare, e di Inghilterra & di Spagna, & di Ungaria, & dalle altre estremita del mondo" ("very often I have seen many foreign princes received in that court, from

England, and Spain, and Hungary, and from the other extremities of the earth") (3r). Since Boiardo does not indicate what he means by the term "other extremities," the duke's avowed cosmopolitanism could have been more an image he wanted to project than documented reality. At the same time, it is worth noting that Ercole could have hosted any number of foreign visitors whose presence is mentioned in court chronicles only by chance. On the occasion of Isabella d'Este's christening, for example, we find that she was baptized by the bishop of Cyprus, who was serving as an ambassador in Ferrara at the time (*Diario ferrarese*, 90).

Some interaction with the Muslim world can be gleaned from the art of the period. The various turbaned figures in the works of the Ferrarese court painter Ercole de' Roberti (c.1451–96) have prompted one recent historian to comment that turbans "radiated out from Ferrara" (Ricci, *Ossessione turca*, 26).[38] And while Ercole de' Roberti was busy depicting a foreign presence in the Estense state, another Ferrarese artist actually took up residence in the Ottoman Empire. Although Gentile Bellini's arrival at Mehmed's court in 1479 is the more commonly cited example of artistic exchange, it appears that the painter Costanzo da Ferrara was sent to Istanbul by King Ferrante of Naples a full year earlier (Babinger 505). In 1485 the Estense orator in Naples informed Ercole that Costanzo was still painting under the patronage of the "Gran Turcho," who had in the meantime dubbed him a knight (Ricci, *Ossessione turca*, 30).[39]

The Este court knew the Ottoman Empire not only for its commercial opportunities and artistic interests, however, but also for its military aggression. As Robert H. Schwoebel remarks, "in the fifteenth century Latin Christendom experienced something entirely new – a direct confrontation with a hostile Moslem Turkish power" ("Coexistence, Conversion, and the Crusade against the Turks," 166). Mehmed II (reigned 1451–81), having captured the Byzantine capital of Constantinople two years after coming to power, continued to extend his dominion into eastern Europe in the following decades. From 1463 to 1479 the Ottomans were at war against Venice for control of the Aegean and Adriatic Seas, and they progressively seized Venetian commercial and military holdings, including Negroponte (Euboea) in 1470, and penetrated into Venetian territory in the Friuli on various occasions.[40] After emerging the victor from this protracted conflict, Mehmed restored commercial relations with the Venetian republic and subsequently proceeded to invade the Kingdom of Naples. In the summer of 1480 his troops attacked Otranto, massacring its inhabitants and effectively establishing a foothold on Italy's southern coast. Only his death in May of 1481 put an end to further plans for expansion and allowed the Neapolitans to regain their territory in September of that year.[41]

The escalation of the Turkish threat during the reign of Mehmed II did not automatically lead to alliances along religious or cultural lines, however. King Alfonso I of Naples (reigned 1442–58) had sought alliances with the Mamelukes and other Muslim rivals of the Ottomans, and his son Ferrante I (reigned 1458–94) was initially friendly to the Ottomans during the latter's war against their mutual enemy, Venice.[42] The Venetians, in turn, not only refrained from intervening on behalf of their southern Italian neighbour when the Ottomans landed at Otranto in 1480, but were suspected of having supported the invasion.[43] Indeed, during the ensuing year in which Ferrante's son Alfonso II d'Aragona was fighting to free their Neapolitan kingdom from Turkish invaders, Venice was preparing to wage a war on Ferrara that they officially declared in early 1482. Although Alfonso II was initially blocked on his way through the Papal States, he arrived in Ferrara the following year in time to confront the Venetian forces that had in the meantime reached the city walls. An irony of history is that Alfonso brought with him not only Greek and Albanian *stradiots* (the latter employed likewise by the Venetians), along with Spanish soldiers, but also five hundred Turkish foot soldiers and horsemen he had captured in Otranto (Rosenberg 126).[44]

The divide became even less clear-cut in the following decades when the Ottoman Empire was involved in European politics not only as a potential threat but also as a useful ally.[45] The 1503 treaty between Venice and the Ottoman Empire marked the beginning of an Ottoman disengagement from Europe that lasted until 1521 (Imber 36), and thus the years corresponding to the composition of the *Furioso* (1505–16) were virtually free of Ottoman aggression.[46] According to Francesco Guicciardini, even after 1517 when Selim I's power grew substantially, the various European states "considered the danger uncertain and very far off" and thus preparations to combat the Ottoman threat were undertaken "only frivolously and, as it were, ceremoniously" (*History of Italy*, 301).[47] Indeed, throughout this period the European sovereigns tended merely to pay lip service to combating the Turks while they were mostly intent on fighting against each other (Housley, *The Later Crusades*, 124–5).[48]

Epic Narrative and the Construction of Group Identity

Multilayered perceptions of the world outside Christian Europe would also have reached the Este court through works of fantasy, especially the epic, the predominant fictional genre of the period. While fifteenth-century humanists promoted ancient Greek culture as the basis of their new educational program, the Italian literary tradition, especially medieval renditions of the Trojan War such as Guido delle Colonne's *Historia destructionis Troiae*, depicted the Greeks negatively as the deceitful enemies of Rome's Trojan ancestors. According to Virgil's *Aeneid*, the ancient epic par excellence in fifteenth-century Italy, these ancestors headed from Asia Minor to Italy after the destruction of their city and subsequently merged with the indigenous peoples of the peninsula.[49]

Movement could also be found from west to east in narratives relating the exploits of Alexander of Macedonia. Alongside earlier, more historical records of Alexander's military expedition through Persia and India, a host of popular legendary biographies appeared with epic and romance episodes that imagined the East as an inexhaustibly fantastic landscape. Leonardo Olschki goes so far as to claim, "Everything that was commonly known in Europe about Muslim and pagan territories outside the restricted limits of geographical experience was in large part from the gests of Alexander the Great which, from the eleventh century onwards, dominated in diverse poetic and fictionalized forms in Western depictions of Oriental lands" (*L'Asia di Marco Polo*, 45). Multiple versions of the life of Alexander are documented in the Estense library.[50]

The medieval period also featured non-Christians as the perennial enemy in its own brand of epic matter, the Carolingian cycle. *Chansons de geste* recounting battles between Christians and Saracens taking place mostly in Spain originally lent moral support to military efforts in the Holy Land by fostering a crusading ideology. The genre continued to circulate and thrive in various guises and languages in the following centuries despite the fact that successive attempts to establish a permanent Latin state in the Middle East ended in failure. Already in the early French tradition, however, stories about Christians fighting Saracens competed with other narrative paradigms, in particular the internal conflicts within the Frankish court and the adventures of its paladins in the Orient.[51] The Franco-Venetian *Entrée d'Espagne* (c. 1320–30), referred to as "the most relevant work of Venetian literature and perhaps of all northern Italian literature up to the Renaissance," combines both patterns.[52] In the context of recounting Charlemagne's exploits in Spain prior to the battle of Roncevaux, the anonymous Paduan author relates that Orlando departs from the Christian camp and heads eastward because of his anger at the emperor. The paladin eventually conquers the Holy Land and surrounding territories, compelling his Saracen allies to convert en masse, after which he returns to Spain and helps bring victory to the Frankish army. The popular fifteenth-century Italian verse redaction of this narrative, *La Spagna in rima*, existed in versions of both thirty-four and forty cantos, including a precious manuscript of the shorter poem elaborately illustrated for Borso d'Este in 1453, the fateful year that the Ottoman Turks seized Constantinople.[53]

Whereas the *Spagna* narratives present Charlemagne on the offensive in a territory long subjected to Muslim rule, the French epic *Aspremont* and its many rewritings imagine the Franks defending southern Italy from a new attack by North African Saracens. Fifteenth-century Italian versions of the *Aspramonte*, in both *ottava rima* verse and in the prose of Andrea da Barberino, provide a respite from the military encounters by relating a romance between a North African female warrior and an Italian paladin that leads to their marriage.[54] Yet this heterogamous union soon ends tragically, and battles dominate the action until the Franks succeed in destroying the entire North African invading army. It is in this epic prequel that the young Orlando makes his debut as a fighter, saving the emperor from death at the hands of the Saracen Almonte and acquiring his sword Durindana and oliphant in the process.

Other popular prose compilations and adaptations by Andrea da Barberino, such as the *Reali di Francia, Ugone d'Avernia,* and *Il Guerrin Meschino*, contain both traditional and novel ways of depicting Saracens in relating the vicissitudes of individual Christian paladins travelling from Spain to the distant East. Referring specifically to the *Guerrino*, Gloria Allaire finds that Andrea combines a disparaging presentation of Islam and Mohammed with a "more detailed and accurate portrayal of Saracen culture than is normally found in chivalric literature" ("Portrayal of Muslims," 245). Antonio Franceschetti similarly contrasts Andrea's depiction of Christian moral superiority in war with a more positive depiction of Saracens during peace ("On the Saracens," 207).[55] Despite this mixed portrayal of Saracens, Juliann Vitullo maintains that a crusading ideology nevertheless informs the plot: Guerrino "becomes the captain of both the Persian and Arab armies against the Turks, precisely because they cannot properly organize themselves. [...] As Guerrino moves closer to discovering his aristocratic genealogy, [...] he uses those same skills to defend Christianity against the Saracens, transforming himself from a merchant into God's knight – the *cavaliere di Dio*" (76).[56]

The most ambitious and successful epic poem to appear in the years immediately preceding the publication of the *Innamorato*, Pulci's *Morgante*, continues this ambivalent attitude towards the non-Christian world. Pulci creatively adds new comic episodes and develops an innovative linguistic register with iconoclastic brio, even bringing upon himself the suspicion of heresy. Nonetheless, his plot follows the same basic storyline of earlier Carolingian works, leading to its culmination in the battle of Roncevaux.[57] Indeed, as Michael Murrin reflects: "If one juxtaposes the poems at either end of this line, the *Roland* and the *Morgante*, one can easily see that the essentials of the story did not change through all the intermediate versions" (*History and Warfare*, 21). Ruggero M. Ruggieri thus sums up the action of the *Morgante* as "a grandiose offensive against Islam" (15).[58]

The storyline invented by Boiardo and brought to a conclusion by Ariosto is situated chronologically between Agolante's invasion of southern Italy in the *Aspramonte* and the fateful Spanish expedition leading to the battle of Roncevaux recounted in the various *Spagna* narratives and the *Morgante*. The *Innamorato* begins with the Christians and Spanish Saracens together in Paris at a peaceful festive gathering, and the *Furioso* ends back in Paris after the Christians have thwarted a massive invasion from all directions and led a counter-offensive destroying the Saracen seat of power in Africa.

Although individual chapters of my study follow the trajectory of events in the two poems, the overall structure is guided primarily by geography rather than narrative chronology. Part One examines a number of prominent East Asian characters created by Boiardo: Angelica of Cathay, Gradasso of Sericana, Agricane and Mandricardo of Tartary, and the Eastern queen Marphisa.[59] Ariosto does not invent any new Asian protagonists of his own; rather, he transforms these characters, often in ways that contradict their development in the earlier poem.

Part Two focuses on Africa and Saracen Spain. The opening chapter examines the historical and literary models of Boiardo's Agramante, the North African king who sets into motion an invasion of France in the opening canto of Book Two. Given that this Tunisian ruler is closely identified with the war right up until the final combat that determines its outcome in the *Furioso*, I postpone my discussion of Ariosto's Agramante until turning to the destruction of Biserta in Part Four. The next two chapters offer a comparative treatment of Agramante's courteous cousin Rugiero and his fellow-overachiever, Rodamonte, across the two poems. Part Two concludes with a consideration of the shifting role of Spanish Saracens in the wake of contemporary vicissitudes involving Venice and the Ottoman Empire.

Part Three turns to episodes taking place within a more finely delineated eastern Mediterranean, from Cyprus and Egypt in the *Innamorato* to Jerusalem and Syria in the *Furioso*. While chapter 10 interrogates the historical and contemporary relevance of Boiardo's courteous King Noradino, chapter 13 traces Ariosto's refashioning of the Syrian ruler into a poor leader and avowed enemy of the Christians. Focusing on Ariosto's Astolfo as he moves from the Indian Ocean to Egypt and Jerusalem before arriving in Damascus, chapters 11 and 12 begin to track his transformation into a *miles Christi* in the latter cantos of the poem.

Part Four keeps the focus on the *Furioso* as we follow Astolfo to the African continent. The English knight takes on an increasingly prominent role as Ariosto superimposes upon Boiardo's chivalric foundation an ideology based on the animosity between Christians and Muslims consonant with the pattern established in the Old French Carolingian cycle. Chapters 14 and 15 examine the major turning point in the poem in this regard: Astolfo's voyage to Ethiopia and the moon followed by his instrumental participation in the destruction of Biserta.

Part Five compares two extended narrative sequences that epitomize the poets' opposing views: in the *Innamorato*, Brandimarte's adventure at Phebosilla's palace projects an irrepressible openness towards the world beyond Europe despite the dangers of facing the unknown (chapter 16); in the *Furioso*, Rinaldo's adventures along the Po River Valley recombine elements from Brandimarte's earlier episode to darken Ariosto's representation of humanity at both a local and a global level (chapter 17).

The present study is outside the scope of Edward Said's concept of orientalism in its stricter sense since the two poems under consideration are not products of colonial-minded imperialist systems.[60] Nevertheless, it is undeniable that the imaginative geography of both romance epics derives from the poets' (and their society's) assumptions, projections, and misapprehensions, as well as from an indeterminate range of fictional and non-fictional sources depicting the various lands outside the Italian peninsula. Likewise, none of us as critical readers can claim a vantage point fully divorced from our perspective on the world we inhabit today. What I do hope to offer, nonetheless, is a nuanced interpretation of the ways of thinking about geographical provenance and identity in two Italian Renaissance masterpieces and perhaps beyond. The following pages thereby aim to move in the direction suggested by Said in the introduction to his classic study: "Perhaps the most important task of all would be to undertake studies in contemporary alternatives to Orientalism, to ask how one can study other cultures and peoples from a libertarian, or a nonrepressive and nonmanipulative, perspective" (*Orientalism*, 24).[61]

PART ONE

Asia

Chapter One

Angelica of Cathay

Boiardo's Angelica

The Innamorato's *Carolingian Prelude: Saracens in Paris*

Counting on his readers' familiarity with the ever-popular Carolingian tradition, Boiardo opens his romance epic by depicting encounters across religious and national lines, thwarting expectations and overturning literary convention even as he prepares the stage for more radical changes to come. As the narrative begins, Charlemagne has proclaimed an international tournament to take place in Paris at Pentecost, the anniversary of the day in which the apostles miraculously spoke in languages they had not learned and were understood by the various foreign visitors gathered in Jerusalem (Acts 2: 6–12). As though to underscore the holiday's implied potential of universal understanding, the tournament is not limited to Christians but is open to those of all nations and faiths. In fact, only apostates and renegades (*OI* 1.1.9) – that is, those who have renounced their original Christian identity – are not welcome. We are told that "una gente infinita" ("numberless people") have arrived in Paris "da ogni parte e da tuti i confini" ("from every region, every nation") (*OI* 1.1.9).[1] Delphia Robinson Eboigbe considers the tournament itself as "the first indication that in Boiardo's universe, religious differences no longer separate men" (130).

As the scene continues, however, we soon discover that the joust's participants are not drawn from the vast lands stretching across the *mappamundi*, but from the narrower space typical of the Carolingian epics circulating in Italy at the time. All the foreigners identified by name turn out to be either Saracens from Spain and Morocco (*OI* 1.1.10) or Christians from Great Britain and Lombardy (*OI* 1.1.14). The Saracens mentioned in the opening sequence – Grandonio (king of Morocco), Feraguto (nephew to King Marsilio of Spain), Balugante (Marsilio's brother), Isolieri (ruler of Pamplona), and Serpentino (Balugante's son) – are all well-known characters from the *Spagna* narratives.[2] This combination of the narrator's initial claim to universality and the limited origin of the named participants creates the impression that the world consists only of these specific regions, a provincial assumption soon to be overturned by the appearance of a princess from distant Cathay.

Already at this preliminary stage, however, the parameters of the familiar Carolingian world have been dramatically altered. The *Spagna*, for instance, opens with Charlemagne's planned invasion of Spain to fight against "ciaschun chi non crede / nel vero Idio, ne la cristiana fede" ("whoever does not believe in the true God, in the Christian faith") (*Spagna* 1.41).[3] Boiardo's Carlo Magno, on the other hand, has welcomed Spanish and North African Saracens as his guests at the tournament's inaugural banquet. Yet the fact that the *Innamorato* brings these two traditionally hostile groups together to break bread rather than cross swords does not mean that the poet feigns ignorance of their conflictual history. The opening narrative oscillates between tension and harmony, placing the focus on both the difficulties of and possibilities for understanding across borders.

The image of Charlemagne sitting among his knights at his "mensa ritonda" ("Round Table") (*OI* 1.1.13) initially suggests an Arthurian setting in which individual characteristics take precedence over collective identity, creating the basis for friendly relations among all.[4] Before the stanza is over, however, we are alerted to the fact that although religion is not a cause for hostile feelings, differences in cultural practice may nevertheless create a disturbance. Employing a derogatory term that Christians and Saracens frequently call each other in Carolingian epic, the narrator announces that the Saracens are lying on their carpets "comme mastini / [...] / Spregiando seco il costume di Franza" ("like hounds / [...] / scorning the customs Frenchmen use") (*OI* 1.1.13).[5] In the initial absence of communication between the groups, an assumption about the other culture's alleged disparagement of French manners goes hand in hand with an attitude of disdain towards them.

Boiardo promptly goes on to expose such assumptions as erroneous by staging a conversation between the Frankish Christian Ranaldo and the Spanish Saracen Balugante, initiated by the latter precisely because of his acute interest in (and ability to understand) the ways of the French court. When Ranaldo is mocked for the poverty of his clothing by Orlando's treacherous stepfather Gano and his clan, the enraged knight "nascose nel petto i pensier caldi, / Mostrando nela vista alegra facia" ("hid his burning thoughts inside / while offering a face that smiled") (*OI* 1.1.16). Balugante is nevertheless able to see through the facade: "in viso il guardava / E divinava quasi il suo pensieri" ("[he] watched his face / and practically divined his thoughts") (*OI* 1.1.17). That Balugante could read Ranaldo's mind demonstrates that an attentive observer can understand a great deal about an individual from another cultural group even prior to any dialogue. Balugante subsequently approaches Ranaldo and, referring to himself as "forestieri / E de' costumi de' Cristian degiuno" ("a foreigner / and ignorant of Christian customs"), has his interpreter ask Ranaldo whether in the French court honour is won "per robba o per vertute" ("by prowess or by wealth") (*OI* 1.1.17). Charles S. Ross suggests that Balugante's "conversational gambit may be read as a first step toward friendship."[6] Whether or not this is the case, Balugante's question concerning the moral values of Charlemagne's court not only opens a channel of communication but points to honour as an essential value common to both Christian and Saracen conceptions of chivalry.

Boiardo's early readers would have been familiar with the character of Balugante from Carolingian narratives. In the *Spagna*, he is repeatedly invoked as one of the principal Saracen enemies along with his brothers, King Marsilio and the sinisterly named Falserone (*Spagna* 1.28). With Charlemagne's invasion imminent, Marsilio sends him to Persia, Alexandria, and Syria to seek assistance (*Spagna* 2.10), and he returns with allies to fight in Saragossa (*Spagna* 27.22).[7] According to an alternative literary tradition found in Andrea da Barberino's *Reali di Francia*, Charlemagne had married Balugante's sister Galerana after having spent time in the court of Saragozza. Andrea does not depict Balugante in a positive light because of this family tie, however, but says of him: "nessuna verità si trovava in lui, crudele contro a' nimici, e degli amici non fu misericordioso" ("no truth was found in him, he was cruel towards his enemies and not merciful to friends") (*Reali* VI.xxi, 475).[8] Balugante and his brothers even plan to kill the young Charlemagne before the latter escapes with his bride (*Reali* VI.xxxvii, 505). In the *Innamorato*, on the contrary, Balugante is not only a relative of the Frankish emperor ("di Carlo parente"; *OI* 1.1.10) and a keen observer of his court, but is the one who makes possible a rapprochement between the two groups. The nature of his question, moreover, lays bare the strained relations among the paladins and thus draws attention to a potentially graver problem internal to Charlemagne's social order.

Ranaldo laughs and replies with good cheer ("con benigno aspetto") that although affection is shown to prostitutes in bed and gluttons at the table, in the end true valour is the only thing that leads to honour: "dove poi convene usar valore, / Dasse a ciascuno il suo debito honore" ("when our valor is on view, / let each receive the honor due") (*OI* 1.1.18). Ranaldo thereby unequivocally affirms his society's adherence to a code of chivalry despite Gano's apparent threat to such values. Thus the first dialogue in the poem – and the only one preceding the appearance of Angelica – demonstrates that erroneous suppositions arising from cultural, political, or religious diversity can be overcome by perceptive individuals from their respective groups who enter into dialogue. In this case, the exchange, revealing a shared chivalric ethos, brings together the Frankish paladin most beloved by the reading public and a figure customarily depicted in a negative guise in Carolingian epic precedents.

The Appearance of Angelica

Once Boiardo has suggested that even within the familiar space of Carolingian epic things are not always what they seem, he is ready to remind readers that the world extends far beyond the homeland of the characters who have initially gathered for the tournament. At the very same instant in which Charlemagne, surrounded by his vassals, golden platters, and enamelled goblets, arrogantly "Tuta la gente pagana disprezza, / Come arena de il mar denanti ai venti" ("scorned all the pagan populace / as ocean sands before the winds"), something new emerges to shatter his self-centred worldview: "Ma nova cossa che ebe ad aparire, / Fè lui con li altri insieme isbigotire" ("But there appeared a prodigy / that left him – with the rest – amazed") (*OI* 1.1.20).[9] The "prodigy" is Angelica who, collapsing the customary framework of Carolingian geography, arrives in Paris from the "fin del mondo" ("ends of earth") (*OI* 1.1.24), referred to in travel time as a two-hundred day journey beyond the Don, the river traditionally considered the dividing line between Europe and Asia.[10]

Angelica goes on to identify her homeland as "Cataio" (Cathay), which she vaguely locates as both between India and Tartary (*OI* 1.1.52) and as part of India (*OI* 1.10.14).[11] In maps of the period "Cathay" corresponded largely to China.[12] Marco Polo equated Cathay more specifically with northern China, drawing attention to its "belle cittadi e belle castella di mercatantie e d'arti, e belle vigne e àlbori assai, e gente dimestica" ("beautiful cities and castles with merchandise and arts, and beautiful vineyards and many trees, and civilized people") (*Mil.* 105.7, 139). In Mandeville's *Travels*, Cathay is referred to as "un grant pays et bel et bon et riche et bien mercheantz" ("a great country, beautiful, rich, fertile, full of good merchandise") (*Le livre* 369; tr. 141).[13] The Armenian historian Hayton likewise underscored the sophistication of its inhabitants: "The kingdom of Cathay is considered the richest and most noble realm in the world. Full of people and incalculable splendor [...] as far as the foot of man has traveled thereabouts, countless luxuries, treasures, and wealth have been observed. [...] People there are creative and quite clever; and thus they have little regard for the accomplishments of other people in all the arts and sciences" (*The Flower of Histories of the East,* bk 1, ch. 1).[14] Among Boiardo's contemporaries, the urge to reach Cathay for commercial purposes was so pressing that the Spanish monarchs financed a highly risky and unprecedented expedition by a Genoese navigator who intended to reach this distant land more swiftly by sailing west across the Atlantic Ocean. Columbus initially presented this audacious plan to the Portuguese crown around the same time that the first two books of the *Orlando innamorato* came out in print.[15]

Cathay would have been known in Ferrara not only for its precious goods and spices, imported through intermediaries by Italian (especially Venetian) merchants, but also for its purported military potential. Ercole's father, Niccolò d'Este, expressed a particular interest in this realm for that reason when he and his entourage travelled to Jerusalem. Following an encounter with a certain "uomo antico, molto pratico e informato delle cose di Levante" ("elderly man, very experienced and informed about things in the East"), Niccolò explicitly instructed his chronicler Luchino Dal Campo to make a record of the immense power of Cathay's emperor, whose many barons could each bring 7,000 horses to the battlefield (112).

Boiardo does not at first direct our attention to the region's commercial or military assets, but to its lovely princess. Odorico da Pordenone had earlier claimed that while the men of India "are of a fair and comely personage, [...] the women are the most beautiful under the sun" (229). Boiardo likewise does not distinguish Angelica by any exotic features in appearance or dress, but simply states that her superior beauty diminishes that of all the other women present (*OI* 1.1.21).[16] Every knight without exception falls in love with her in one fell swoop, thereby providing the first concrete example of the poem's opening assertion of love's universal power (*OI* 1.1.2). This simultaeous enamourment nullifies any ethnic or religious distinctions among the group and thus erases the conflictual themes associated with Carolingian epic. Simona Cremante has in fact remarked that Angelica has the function of enacting "Boiardo's well-known operation of converting Carolingian heroes to Breton values" (5).

Angelica seems equally uninterested in making distinctions between her eastern realm and western Europe. The only explanation she gives Charlemagne for arriving at his court is its reputation for chivalry, which she says reaches "Quanto distende il mare e soi confini" ("as far as seas and shores extend") (*OI* 1.1.24). When proposing a joust against her brother Argalìa with herself as the prize, she includes all those present, whether pagan or baptized ("pagano o batizato"; *OI* 1.1.27). Even after we learn through the Christian wizard Malagise and his demons that Angelica and her brother Argalìa are instruments in their father Galafrone's treacherous plan to capture and imprison knights, this project is never explicitly presented as a Saracen-Christian or East-West conflict. Boiardo, in fact, underscores the desire of Galafrone to have *all* knights ("Tutti i Baron; Ogni [...] Barone"; *OI* 1.1.40) in his grip. Accordingly, both Christians and Saracens hasten to throw their names into the lot, and the first names drawn are those of the Christian Englishman Astolfo and the Saracen Spaniard Feraguto.

The ensuing episode will both recall and refute the poem's Carolingian precedents. In the *Spagna*, Astolfo and Feraù were also the first to fight – albeit, against each other. Astolfo was quickly unhorsed and became a prisoner of Feraù (*Spagna* 3.6–8), who then proceeded to defeat Charlemagne's knights one after another in battles interspersed with verbal exchanges that kept the Christian-Saracen conflict at the forefront. In the *Innamorato*, however, Boiardo ignores religious difference and compares Astolfo and Feraguto in terms of their adherence, or lack thereof, to a code of courtesy. The more chivalrous Astolfo greets Argalìa, formally renews the terms of the joust, and accepts imprisonment without protest when thrown from his horse (*OI* 1.1.60–7). Feraguto, by contrast, disregards the rules of chivalric conduct and acts on impulse: after unceremoniously challenging Argalìa, he does not acknowledge defeat when unhorsed and continues the battle on foot, eventually killing his opponent (*OI* 1.1.68–1.2.16, 1.3.52–67).

The consequent thwarting of Galafrone's plan allows Boiardo to develop the character of Angelica in unforeseen ways. Although she succeeds in returning to Cathay when left to her own devices, she inadvertently drinks from the *Fonte dell'Amore* (Fountain of Love) while still in France and falls hopelessly in love with Ranaldo (*OI* 1.3.38–50). If until this point Angelica was viewed by the love-struck knights as a passive object of desire to be conquered, she now takes on the role of an active pursuer. Indeed, she demonstrates remarkable agency and ingenuity in tracking down the knight she desires, commanding Malagise to lure him away from Barcelona, and erecting by magic the luxurious *Palazo Zoioso* (Pleasure Palace) on an island somewhere in the Indian Ocean where she hopes to enjoy his company (*OI* 1.8.1–14).[17] Although her plan fails because of Ranaldo's intransigence, Angelica nevertheless goes on to save him – a knight in distress! – from the clutches of a monster at the *Roca Crudel* (Castle Cruel) despite his cold rejection of her direct offer of assistance and romance (*OI* 1.9.18–21).[18]

Angelica also occasions the appearance of other new Eastern characters in the poem, most notably her intractable suitor Agricane of Tartaria (chapter 3). Galafrone would have agreed to marry his daughter to Tartary's emperor through fear of his military might, but Angelica overrules her father and adamantly refuses the match. Just as earlier she boldly entered Charlemagne's court proposing a joust on her own terms, she now shows similar aplomb by withstanding Agricane's lengthy siege at the fortress of Albracà near the capital city of Cathay. When her forces are diminished, she travels alone to Dragontina's garden in Circassia (the Caucasus), west of the Caspian Sea, where she frees Orlando from the fairy's spell and leads him and his comrades eastward to take up her defence (*OI* 1.14.23–49). She negotiates command over Orlando's battle against Ranaldo, then, just as he is about to deliver a fatal blow to his cousin, sends him off to the perilous Garden of Orgagna, which may correspond to the realm of Organça (Turkmenistan) on Fra Mauro's world map (Falchetta 609–21). She continues to show inventiveness and an enterprising character in her pursuit of Ranaldo, whether by sending his horse to him by way of messenger or by later convincing the newly returned Orlando to leave Albracà and accompany her to Paris where she hopes to find her love.

Even during moments in which Angelica is in danger – first of rape and subsequently of enslavement and possible death – she quickly manages to take charge of the situation. In the first, Malagise originally intends to place her into a deep sleep through a magic incantation in order to kill her, but then, overwhelmed by her beauty, decides to take advantage of her instead. Since Angelica's ring has the property of breaking spells, she wakes up as soon as he attempts to embrace her and restrains him using her superior physical strength (*OI* 1.1.46–7). After ordering her brother to tie up the wizard, she appropriates his book of spells to conjure up demons and then authoritatively commands them to transport him to Cathay (*OI* 1.1.44–52). Later, as Angelica is travelling alone through Circassia towards Dragontina's garden, she arrives at a river where an old man deceitfully calls out to her for help (*OI* 1.14.26–7). After coming to his rescue, she finds herself locked in a tower and destined to be sent as tribute to Orgagna (ironically, the site to which she will later send Orlando).[19] Angelica easily saves herself, however, by using her magic ring to disappear. On both occasions the maiden remains in complete control, using to her advantage the two distinct properties that Boiardo attributed to her ring.

In sum, when Boiardo's princess appears on the scene from the distant East, she compels Charlemagne's paladins to break out of their parochial view of the world and to take on the guise of Arthurian knights errant. She is responsible for the movement of the poem's principal Christian knights from western Europe to Asia: while Orlando forsakes his duties as a Frankish paladin in order to seek her love, Ranaldo is whisked away involuntarily in an unmanned boat. She also sweeps herself across the globe: from Cathay she travels twice to Paris as well as to imaginary sites in the Caucasus (Dragontina's garden) and along the Indian Ocean (Castle Cruel). In order to attain her goal she can be calculating, deceptive, and pragmatic, yet she is also consistently bold and quick-witted, and capable of self-analysis, heartache, and compassion. Although her cleverness is a weapon that often serves her better than a sword, she is not invulnerable. The reader may thus end up at times commiserating with her unrequited love and admiring her inexhaustible resourcefulness.

Ariosto's Angelica

Ariosto transforms Angelica's character in successive phases, combining features that posit her as both foreign and familiar. In the early cantos, she is repeatedly cast as an erotic object about to be ravished, depicted in naked poses that the author would not have used for the Christian maiden Bradamante. The new importance the character herself attributes to chastity, however, is consonant with the behavioural code expected of Italian court ladies in the period.[20] After examining Ariosto's shifting treatment of Angelica, this chapter takes a closer look at the infantryman she chooses as her lover, husband, and, ultimately, the ruler of her realm. Although geographical provenance seems to play little or no part in Angelica's character, it becomes an essential feature in Ariosto's fashioning of Medoro.

Angelica's agency is curtailed from the first moment she appears in the *Furioso*: no longer in control, she is repeatedly portrayed as a potential victim of rape. While fleeing from the Christian camp in the first canto, she encounters Rinaldo and recoils from him more than a "timida pastorella" ("timid shepherd-girl") would jump back from a "serpe crudo" ("horrid snake") (*OF* 1.11 AC).[21] Still "pallida, tremando, e di sé tolta" ("pale and trembling and quite unstrung") (*OF* 1.13 AC), the frightened damsel ("la donzella ispaventata") (*OF* 1.15 AC) runs into Ferraù, who then crosses swords with Rinaldo over her. As she flees once again, the two knights agree to follow and capture her before continuing their battle. Even the reader is invited to give chase – "ma seguitiamo Angelica che fugge" ("But let us pursue Angelica in her flight") (*OF* 1.32 AC) – as Ariosto describes her terrifying flight through the forest. When she stops to rest, she encounters Sacripante, who expressly states his intention to rape her: "Non starò per repulsa o finto sdegno / ch'io non adombri e incarni el mio disegno" ("I shall not be put off by any repulse or show of anger, but shall carry into effect what I propose") (*OF* 1.58 AC). Fortunately for Angelica, Sacripante is unhorsed by Bradamante as he "s'apparecchia / a dar l'assalto" ("was preparing for his [...] assault") (*OF* 1.59 AC), yet shortly thereafter he is ready to fight the newly arrived Rinaldo for possession of her. In the meantime "la timida donzella" ("the timorous damsel") flees again because she fears "di quel Rinaldo esser rapina" ("falling prey to Rinaldo") (*OF* 2.11 AC).[22]

Before long Angelica becomes the object of two more attempted violations: although she escapes both times, the unsuspecting maiden nevertheless undergoes a form of male sexual aggression. In the first case, an elderly hermit places the maiden into a deep sleep and then proceeds to fondle and kiss her body parts: "l'abbraccia et a piaccer la tocca / [...] / hor le bacia il bel petto, hora la bocca" ("[he] hugged her and felt her at his pleasure / [...] / He planted kisses on her lovely breast and on her lips") (*OF* 8.49 AC). In the second scene, the young Ruggiero fantasizes kissing Angelica's breasts and eyes a thousand times before arriving in a forest "dove ognhor par che Philomena piagna" ("which forever resounded with Philomena's lament") (*OF* 9.101 A; 10.113 C). Yet rather than hint further at the horrific violence Tereus perpetrates upon Philomena in Ovid's *Metamorphoses*, both scenes resort to metaphor for comic effect. The hermit's male organ is likened to ineffectual horses: "Ma ne l'incontro il suo destrier trabocca / [...] / ma quel pigro ronzon non perhò salta" ("But when he came to the impact, his charger stumbled, / [...] / but [he] could not get his flop-eared nag / to jump") (*OF* 8.48–50 AC).

Ruggiero is actually riding a literal, albeit magical, horse through the air, but as he dismounts Ariosto shifts once again to figurative horse language: "Del caval sceso, a pena se ritenne / di salir altri" ("He dismounted, but could scarcely restrain himself / from climbing onto a different mount") (*OF* 9.102 A; *OF* 10.114 C).

Not only do the two episodes share common elements; both also counteract Angelica's agency in escaping threatening situations in the *Innamorato*. In the first case, the hermit's successful incantation evokes and reverses the wizard Malagise's failure to put Angelica into a deep sleep, discussed above. It is only the hermit's own impotence that prevents him from taking advantage of the unconscious maiden. Moreover, whereas Boiardo's Angelica took charge and punished Malagise for his intended transgression by having him "Soto il mar dentro a un scolio impregionato" ("locked inside a deep-sea stone") (*OI* 1.1.53), in the *Furioso* it is Angelica herself who is soon thereafter captured and bound to a sea rock.[23] When Ruggiero's rescue of the maiden ironically turns into another intended assault, Angelica would have been equally helpless if Ruggiero had not relinquished the magic ring. As the knight struggles frantically to remove his armour, the maiden shamefully lowers her eyes over her naked body and only then notices the ring on her finger that allows her to disappear from view.

Both episodes further reduce Angelica to a passive object of male eroticism by suggesting her potential violation at the hands of a mythological god. As Rajna and others have pointed out, Angelica is modelled on Ovid's Europa in the prelude to the first episode in which at the hermit's command a demon enters Angelica's horse and draws it out to sea (*Le fonti*, 196–7). Yet Ariosto reworks some of Ovid's details to better suit his ends. Ovid actually recounts the story twice: in the initial account, the narrator simply tells of Europa's "fluttering dress swelled out in the sea-breeze" (*Met.* 2.874–5), while in Arachne's weaving the girl is more compassionately described as "afraid of the surging waves which threatened to touch her and nervously lifting her feet" (*Met.* 6.106–7). Combining details from both versions, Ariosto relates that Angelica "tenea la veste in su raccolta / […] e trahea i piedi in alto" ("drew up her skirts […] and pulled her feet clear of the water") (*OF* 8.36 AC). Yet while visualizing the maiden in this somewhat compromising position, the poet goes on to privilege aesthetic voyeurism over emotional commiseration by focusing on how her hair hangs loose on her shoulders. Little wonder that even the breeze is caught up with desire and is anthropomorphized into another would-be love-maker: "l'aura le facea lascivo assalto" ("the lascivious breeze caressed [or, more literally, assaulted] her") (*OF* 8.36 AC). Whereas through Arachne's tapestry Ovid captured Europa's distress and censured the gods' abusive power over mortals, Ariosto underscores instead Angelica's irresistible appeal as a sexual object.

In the context of the second episode, Angelica risks becoming the sexual prey of the sea god Proteus. We are told that the custom of sacrificing young women to the Orca began after Proteus violated the king of Ebuda's daughter and is destined to cease when the god chooses one of the exposed women as a worthy replacement (*OF* 8.56 AC). Thus, were Proteus to find Angelica as attractive as his original victim, she would be ravished by him rather than being left as food for the Orca. Although Ariosto does not say whether Proteus had already viewed Angelica before Ruggiero's arrival on the scene, he does not want his readers to miss the chance to glimpse her "così ignuda / come Natura prima la compose" ("as naked as when Nature first fashioned her") (*OF* 9.83 A; 10.95 C). He reveals that not even a veil covered "le polite membre" ("her lustrous limbs") before focusing more specifically on "le crudette poma" ("her unripe apple-breasts") and "l'aurata chioma" ("her golden tresses") (*OF* 9.84 A; 10.96 C).[24]

Despite Angelica's continued eroticization in these early cantos, she loses her own sexual agency and is recast in the role of a chaste virgin. Whereas in the *Innamorato* she expressed erotic desire for Ranaldo at the *Roca Crudel* (Castle Cruel) and brazenly bathed a naked Orlando at Albracà, she now swears to Sacripante that "havea servato il fior virgineo salvo / come ella sel portò dal materno alvo" ("her virginal flower was still as intact as the day she had borne it from her mother's womb") (*OF* 1.55 AC). And lest the reader suspect her of false posturing, Angelica expresses to herself the same concern for her reputation just after having been cast into the role of Europa: "che, se ben con effetto io non peccai, / io do perhò materia ch'ognun dica / ch'essendo peregrina, io sia impudica" ("for though I have committed no fault, yet I give everyone the excuse to hold that, being a wanderer, I must be a loose woman") (*OF* 8.41 AC).[25] Indeed, her subsequent rhetorical question could have come right out of a contemporary manual for proper female behaviour: "C'haver può donna al mondo più di buono, / a cui la castità levata sia?" ("Deprive a woman of her virtue, and what other blessing can she enjoy in this world?") (*OF* 8.41 AC).[26]

Angelica apparently abandons this restrictive stance on female mores when she encounters and initiates a love affair with Medoro, a foot soldier who accompanied King Agramante from Biserta to France. Nevertheless, the same stanza that explicitly announces Angelica's loss of virginity immediately goes on to relate that – "per adombar, per honestar la cosa" ("to clothe what they had done in the trappings of virtue") – the couple arrange a reparative wedding "con cerimonie sante" ("with holy rites") (*OF* 17.33 A; 19.33 C). After a month of "diletto" ("pleasurable enjoyment") in which Angelica is at one point likened to Virgil's Dido, the princess seeks nothing else but to retreat to domesticity in Cathay where she will "Medor coronar del suo bel regno" ("place on Medor's head the crown of her fair kingdom") (*OF* 17.37 A; 19.37 C). We now turn to the importance of geographical provenance in the depiction of the North African soldier on whom this avowed virgin princess so generously bestows her love and her kingdom.

Medoro

Despite Medoro's stated identity as a Moor, Ariosto systematically avoids characterizing him as African and fashions him instead as an heir to ancient Greek culture. The first indication of his classical pedigree is the name of his hometown: he originates from Tolomitta, or Ptolemais (*OF* 16.165 A; 18.165 C), an ancient port in Cyrenaica (modern Libya) that was a Greek settlement from the late seventh century B.C.E. Conquered by Alexander of Macedonia and then controlled by Rome from 96 B.C.E., it remained largely Byzantine from the late fourth century until the Arab conquests of the mid-seventh century. Even beyond its actual history, however, the city's Greek-sounding name recalls the ancient Greek and Byzantine presence in North Africa.

Medoro's physical features likewise classify him as Hellenistic rather than African. When early in the *Innamorato* Angelica rejects the enamoured Spaniard Feraguto, who is dark-skinned ("bruno era molto") with a black, curly head of hair (*OI* 1.2.10), Boiardo adds that she specifically wanted a blond companion. Ariosto accordingly depicts Medoro not only with "la guancia colorita / et bianca" ("lovely fair skin and pink cheeks") but also with a "chioma crespa e d'oro" ("golden head of curls") (*OF* 16.166 A; 18.166 C). Given the youth's resemblance to an angel in a heavenly chorus ("angel parea di quei del summo choro"), the early sixteenth-century reader could have imagined him as one of Raphael's rosy cherubs all grown up. Ariosto soon gives additional relevance to Medoro's golden curls ("chioma d'oro") and lovely face ("bel volto") when a northern European, the Scottish Zerbino, is moved by precisely these features to spare his life (*OF* 17.10 A; 19.10 C). The Cathayan princess subsequently becomes inflamed with love as she gazes upon Medoro's beautiful eyes and blond head ("testa bionda") (*OF* 17.28 A; 19.28 C).

Ariosto further develops Medoro's Greek, as opposed to African, background through a series of explicit Graeco-Roman allusions and references. Medoro's nighttime expedition with his friend Cloridano casts them in the role of Homer's Odysseus and Diomedes, Virgil's Nisus and Euryalus, and Statius's Hopleus and Dymas.[27] Moreover, when Medoro entreats Zerbino to grant him permission to bury his captain, he evokes Creon's negative example from Sophocles' *Antigone* (*OF* 17.12 A; 19.12 C). By measuring Zerbino against Creon, Medoro is suggestively aligning himself with Antigone, who risked her life to bury her brother. The capricious Roman god Cupid is then brought into play to serve as a catalyst by shooting the arrow that causes Angelica to fall in love with Medoro. After the couple declares their mutual desire, they replay the lovemaking of Virgil's Dido and Aeneas in an equally hospitable cave (*OF* 17.35 A; 19.35 C). This allusion to the *Aeneid* also enacts a geographical reversal: while the Cathayan princess plays the part of the North African queen, the Libyan foot soldier is explicitly equated with the Trojan hero who goes on to found Rome.

Even when Medoro prays, it is not as a Saracen evoking Mohammed but as an ancient pagan calling upon the goddess of the moon. This classical reference not only further reinforces his Graeco-Roman origin but specifically follows the precedent of both Virgil and Statius. Yet whereas Nisus and Dymas prayed to Diana (*Aen.* 9.537–47 and *Theb.* 10.360–71, respectively), Ariosto associates the moon with Selene. He then recalls the sexual encounter between the beautiful naked goddess and the shepherd Endymion, foreshadowing that between Angelica and Medoro. Selene is a favourite goddess of love poets, and indeed we soon find out that the classicist Medoro also writes poetry. While Angelica seems capable only of scratching graffiti on trees and stones – names entwined with love-knots – Medoro composes many verses ("parole assai") (*OF* 21.107 A; 23.107 C), including the two-stanza poem that is later read by none other than Orlando (*OF* 21.108–9 A; 23.108–9 C).[28]

The discovery that triggers Orlando's madness also leads to Rinaldo's jealous rage and to the author's sudden refashioning of Medoro as an African Moor. In the episode in which Rinaldo learns of Angelica's sexual activity, Ariosto accentuates the ignominy of her partner in Rinaldo's eyes by referring to him as an African, as a most vile barbarian, and as a Saracen in three consecutive stanzas that represent the successive viewpoints of a demon, of Malagigi, and of Rinaldo himself:

Angelica [...] a un giovine Aphrican si donò in tutto (*OF* 38.35 A)
Angelica [...] s'era posta
d'un vilissimo Barbaro a i servigi (*OF* 38.36 A)
avea del suo amor colto
un Saracino le primizie inante (*OF* 38.37 A)

Angelica [...] had given herself totally to a young African (*OF* 42.38 C)
Angelica [...] had become enthralled
with a barbarian of the lowest sort (*OF* 42.39 C)
a Saracen had forestalled him in gathering
the first-fruits of his love (*OF* 42.40 C)

Angelica's lover may be an African, a vile barbarian, and a Saracen in the estimation of the demon, Malagigi, and Rinaldo, respectively, but Ariosto has taken care to spare his readers the sort of shock experienced by Rinaldo by having first developed the character of Medoro as a fair-skinned, blond, Hellenistic youth with the bravery of Nisus, the loyalty of Antigone, and the passion of Aeneas, and who prays to the goddess Selene and writes love poetry in *ottava rima*.[29]

As Angelica travels to Cathay in the company of Medoro, Ariosto furnishes one last moment of sexual peril. This time the would-be assailant is none other than Orlando himself, who in his mad state does not recognize the woman who has awakened his lust: "così gli piacque il delicato volto, / sì ne divenne immantinente giotto" ("he took a liking to her delicate face and immediately wanted her [or, more literally, became gluttonous for her]") (*OF* 27.61 A; 29.61 C). As Angelica uses her magic ring to elude his grasp, she awkwardly falls off her horse onto the sand with her legs in the air (*OF* 27.65 A; 29.65 C). While the princess is left frozen in this indecorous and vulnerable position, readers may wonder what has happened to Medoro. Riccardo Bruscagli aptly observes: "Of Angelica's young husband there is not even a word. He would also, predictably, have been left on foot: the text ignores him, almost displaying an attitude of indifference" (*Studi cavallereschi*, 79).[30]

Although Angelica no longer appears in the poem, Ariosto goes on to inform us that after an uneventful trip home she does indeed hand over the rule of India to Medoro as she intended (*OF* 28.16 A; 30.16 C). According to Valeria Finucci, "Angelica is worked out of the *Furioso* at exactly its midpoint in order to facilitate the narrative movement toward the providentially dynastic, and therefore normal and normative, plot woven around the emblematic figures of Bradamante and Ruggiero"

(113). Yet with this conclusion to Angelica's vicissitudes, her own story becomes not only "normal and normative" but in some sense dynastic as well. From an individual perspective, her return to Cathay completes her transformation from a feisty wandering princess to a dutiful wifely homebody.[31] From a political perspective, however, it creates a novel situation in which the entire realm of Cathay is conferred upon a North African infantryman.

Medoro's unsought possession of both the body and realm of the Cathayan princess certainly sets him apart from the plethora of knights throughout the two poems who put their lives and livelihood at risk in order to acquire what they cannot attain. But could his meteoric trajectory from foot soldier in Libya to ruler of Cathay have carried any global implications for Ariosto's courtly readers? After all, not only had the Este followed the Portuguese explorations around Africa to India with keen interest, as noted earlier, but both sides of Ippolito's family vigorously pursued a policy of dynastic marriage for political advantage.[32] Medoro's example could show that it is not through the force of arms but through love and wedlock that a lowly African – or European, for that matter – can succeed in attaining dominion over a coveted eastern realm. In this light, the story's finale might have suggested that even the most outlandish cross-cultural dynastic marriage scenario imagined by Ariosto's contemporaries could not be dismissed as implausible. Or perhaps, on the contrary, the fiction's very improbable nature was intended to provide a tongue-in-cheek comment on the other dynastic marriage in the poem – the union between an aristocratic Frankish maiden and an unpropertied North African orphan that had purportedly given rise to the Estense family itself (chapter 7).

Chapter Two

Gradasso of Sericana

Boiardo's Gradasso

Gradasso of Sericana is the second character from eastern Asia whose unexpected appearance in France sets in motion much of what happens in the course of Book One. His introduction as a great king who reigns in the Orient, beyond India (*OI* 1.1.4), conveys the sense that he originates from a realm even more distant than Angelica's Cathay.[1] Gradasso emerges on the scene virtually unstoppable in his aggression and destructiveness as he treks towards western Europe, yet he subsequently demonstrates an unconditional adherence to a universal code of chivalry. As in the case of Angelica, then, his appearance in Paris threatens the existence of Charlemagne's realm, but his underlying humanity is revealed in the course of events.

Gradasso's arrogance stems from his inestimable resources: "Di stato e di richeze sì potente / E sì galiardo dela sua persona / Che tuto il mondo stimava nïente" ("So powerful in wealth and state / and so impressive in his strength / he held the world of no account") (*OI* 1.1.4). Angelica suggests the extent of his vast empire when she states that it comprises the realms of seventy-two kings: "Setanta e dui reami in sua possanza" ("That man has seventy-two domains") (*OI* 2.5.56). Strikingly, this is the exact number of kings that purportedly paid tribute to Prester John, the legendary king believed to have resided in India during the Middle Ages (chapter 14). Since virtually all accounts of Prester John repeat the same number, Boiardo's early readers would have been prompted to equate Gradasso's power with that of a famed Eastern potentate who had captured the imagination of western Europe. In this case, however, the mysterious king is not a potential ally but a hostile invader.

Angelica also reveals that she and Gradasso are related by blood (*OI* 2.5.55), thus evoking the genealogical ties that were believed to exist between the people of Cathay and the Seres.[2] Yet the two characters are related thematically as well: both serve to illustrate the dangerous consequences of unbridled desire for both themselves and those around them. Whereas Angelica demonstrates the overwhelming force of love by awakening desire in every man who catches sight of her (*OI* 1.1.2), Gradasso exemplifies the overreaching ambition of those in power who risk losing their state in the vain attempt to attain something beyond their reach (*OI* 1.1.5). In fact, the poem's opening reflection on those "gran signori / Che pur quel voglion che non pòno avere" ("great lords / who only want what they can't have") (*OI* 1.1.5) is a direct comment upon Gradasso's yearning to acquire Ranaldo's horse, Baiardo, and Orlando's sword, Durindana.[3] In his pursuit of supremacy, moreover, the king of Sericana is so confident in his own valour that he despises the entire world and believes that he could single-handedly "vincere e disfare / Quanto il sol vede e quanto cingie il mare" ("conquer and destroy / all the sun sees, all sea surrounds") (*OI* 1.1.7).

With the 150,000 soldiers he brought from East Asia, Gradasso captures every area he passes on the way to France, including the Indian Ocean, Ceylon, Persia, Arabia, and a faraway land inhabited by black-skinned people (*OI* 1.4.23).[4] Once in Spain, he invades Gibraltar and destroys the kingdom of Granada as well as Seville, Toledo, Valencia, and Aragona, before setting siege to Barcelona. Just as Angelica's beauty inflames every knight she encounters without exception, Gradasso's hostile intentions extend to all of humanity, regardless of social rank, geographical provenance, or religious creed. He does not privilege East over West or Saracen over Christian:

> Con infenita gente ha fatto il passo
> Contra al re Carlo e la gente pagana:
> Cristiani e Saracin mena a fracasso,
> Né tregua o pace vuol con gente humana.
>
> [Gradasso] has crossed the sea with countless troops
> to battle both King Charles and the pagans.
> He ruins Saracens and Christians.
> He wants no peace, he wants no truce. (*OI* 1.4.9)

This ruthless destructiveness may be meant to evoke the hordes of eastern invaders who had threatened Italy and western Europe in the course of the centuries, from Germanic tribes to North African Arabs, from the Mongols to the Ottoman Turks. Yet rather than imbue the king of Sericana with the characteristics of a specific historical group, Boiardo seems interested in accruing suggestive allusions from multiple directions.[5] Gradasso even wears armour that once belonged to the biblical Herculean figure Samson (*OI* 1.4.71).

Once Gradasso is in a position to fight for the symbols of knighthood that prompted his expedition, he takes on an increasingly chivalric guise. In Barcelona he refuses to take advantage of Ranaldo after a day's battle when the latter is surrounded by his troops: "Ma Dio non voglia che tanto difecto / Per mi si facia a un Baron sì galiardo" ("But God prefers that I should do / no ill to such a valiant baron") (*OI* 1.5.8). He proposes instead a one-on-one duel for the following morning, reiterating that if he is victorious he wants only Ranaldo's steed and promising to return east whether he wins or loses (*OI* 1.5.9). The duel never takes place because Malagise sends a demon disguised as Gradasso to lure Ranaldo onto an unmanned ship and eventually to an island in the Indian Ocean where Angelica hopes (in vain) to seduce him.[6] In Ranaldo's absence, Gradasso defeats the Frankish troops with a disparate array of forces and imprisons Charlemagne within his own city (*OI* 1.7.29). Although he had previously expressed an intention to destroy the entire world, now that he has Christendom within his grasp he informs the emperor that he sought only fame: "Io che in Levante mi potea possare, / Sono in Ponente per fama acquistare" ("I could have rested in the East – / I'm in the West to win esteem") (*OI* 1.7.41). He would consequently be content to return home with just Baiardo and Durindana.

If Gradasso demonstrates courtesy to Ranaldo and magnanimity to Charlemagne, his interaction with Astolfo most strikingly reveals his inherently chivalrous nature. Indeed, in the resolution of the episode Boiardo contrasts Gradasso's noble bearing towards Astolfo with Charlemagne's previous iniquitous treatment of the English paladin during the joust that followed Angelica's departure. On that earlier occasion Astolfo, thanks to his unwitting possession of Argalìa's magic lance, defeated not only all the Saracens present but also all of Gano's clan until Anselmo knocked him from the saddle "Con falso inganno e molta tradigione" ("with / much treachery and false deceit") (*OI* 1.3.21). When Gano blamed Astolfo for the ensuing fight, the gullible emperor precipitately condemned the English knight to prison. Ironically, it is only because of Gradasso's victory over Charlemagne that the prisons are opened and

Astolfo is finally released. After the English knight steps forward to challenge Gradasso to a one-on-one combat, Gano paints him as the court buffoon. Rather than give credence to what he hears, however, the king of Sericana forms his own judgment based on observation, expressing his admiration for Astolfo's readiness to face an opponent who has already defeated the entire Christian army. Charlemagne's hasty misjudgment of Astolfo after the Parisian tournament appears even more culpable when compared to Gradasso's ability to perceive the worth of Astolfo regardless of what Gano might claim.

Throughout their contest, both Gradasso and Astolfo observe a universal code of chivalry: they treat each other with mutual courtesy as they make a solemn pact regarding the conditions of the battle. When Astolfo unhorses his opponent against all odds, only the reader knows that it is thanks to Argalìa's magic lance. Gradasso could easily have refused to concede defeat just as Feraguto had done earlier in his battle against Argalìa, especially given the fact that his forces had already overpowered Spain and France. Yet as soon as he rises to his feet, Gradasso nobly declares Astolfo the victor and cedes all the Christian prisoners to him in accordance with their prior agreement (*OI* 1.7.57). Boiardo highlights the camaraderie between the two by depicting them walking hand in hand (*OI* 1.7.58).

In the aftermath of the duel, the mutual understanding between Astolfo and Gradasso is further contrasted to the treachery poisoning Charlemagne's court. With Gradasso's complicity, Astolfo tells Charlemagne that he lost the contest and converted to Islam and that he now intends to serve as Gradasso's court jester thanks to Gano's recommendation (*OI* 1.7.61). This episode takes on a sharper focus when compared to the scene following Orlando's mortal combat against Feraù in some of the *Spagna* narratives.[7] When in the forty-canto *Spagna maggiore* Orlando slyly enters the city of Lazera wearing his opponent's armour, Astolfo "per gran paura" ("out of great fear") states his delight over Orlando's supposed death (*Sp. magg.* 6.26).[8] After offering to accompany the victor personally through Christian territory, he predicts the destruction of Charlemagne's realm and the subsequent Saracen dominion over both France and Italy: "Teco verrò e 'nsegnerotti tutto: / [...] / Carlo Mano per vero fia distrutto: / Parigi e Roma arài a tuo dimino" ("I will come with you and show you everything. / [...] / Charlemagne will truly be destroyed. / You will have Paris and Rome at your command") (*Sp. magg.* 6.37). Indeed, he even declares his readiness to hand over the whole of England to his captor before Orlando finally reveals his true identity.

Although Astolfo claims that he had recognized his cousin all along and only wanted to hear what the traitor Gano would say, the narrator tells us instead that Astolfo is ashamed of his behaviour (*Sp. magg.* 6.39–40).[9]

If in the *Spagna maggiore* it was Orlando who, having just defeated and converted Ferraù, subsequently liberated Astolfo and the other Christians held in Lazera, Boiardo imagines instead that the previously stalwart Orlando has abandoned the emperor and that the ordinarily hapless Astolfo saves not only Charlemagne but all of Christendom as well (*OI* 1.7.69).[10]

The English knight's professed submission to a Saracen opponent on this occasion is motivated not by fear but rather by moral outrage over Charlemagne's previous injustice towards him. The contrast is underscored by the different treatment of the topic of conversion. In the *Spagna maggiore* the otherwise acquiescent Astolfo declares that the one issue not under discussion is his religious belief: "Non crederò però in vostra fé fella: / crederò sempre nel fi di Maria" ("I will not believe in your evil faith: / I will always believe in the son of Maria") (*Sp. magg.* 6.29). In the *Innamorato*, on the contrary, when the Frankish archbishop Turpino exclaims "Ahi, miscredente! / Hai tu lassata nostra fede intiera?" ("You apostate! / Have you completely left our faith?"), Astolfo mockingly proclaims his conversion to Islam: "Sì, pritone, / Lassato ho Cristo et adoro Macone" ("Yes, fat priest, / I have left Christ, and love Mohammed!") (*OI* 1.7.63). What in the epic tradition would have been considered an act of cowardice or villainy here represents the vindication of Astolfo's individual liberty and his criticism of Charlemagne's failure to uphold justice.

This scene also recalls the witty opening exchange between Ranaldo and Balugante prior to Angelica's arrival in Paris in that it likewise censures flaws within the French court while relating a moment of complicity between a Carolingian paladin and a member of a foreign, supposedly hostile, culture. At the same time, the level of both internal criticism and external solidarity has increased: Gano and his clan are the catalyst for the injustice committed in both instances; however, while earlier their mockery of Ranaldo's clothes merely incites his momentary anger, their treacherous treatment of Astolfo leads to his lengthy imprisonment. If in the first case Charlemagne appears simply oblivious to his vassals' offensive behaviour, in the second he is directly responsible for a grievous injury. Indeed, the emperor's actions demonstrate that Ranaldo's confidence in the credit given to honour had been overly optimistic: despite Astolfo's complete victory in the very tournament in which Ranaldo had earlier hoped to get the better of Gano's clan, Charlemagne not only fails to reward the English prince but imprisons him indefinitely on false charges. He is subsequently willing to hand over Baiardo to Gradasso even though, as Astolfo vehemently objects, "Carlo ha a far in quel destrier nïente" ("Charles did not own the steed") (*OI* 1.7.45). In the end, it is not the biased and naïve Frankish emperor who honours valour but the courteous Eastern ruler. Like Astolfo and unlike Feraguto following their respective jousts against Argalìa, Gradasso graciously accepts defeat in accordance with the chivalric code and treats his former opponent with great respect. Maintaining his promise, Gradasso leaves Paris with all his troops that same night (*OI* 1.7.70). Ross aptly sums up the geographical suggestiveness of this episode: "We can conclude that when Boiardo thought of the Chinese maritime, he imagined it not only as a place of sophistication, but as the potential staging ground for an invasion of Europe that eventually ends in reconciliation between Europe and the area that is today the maritime area of China" ("From Asia," 223).

Although this moment seemingly marks Gradasso's definitive departure as the narrative shifts to eastern Asia for the remaining twenty-two cantos of Book One, the king of Sericana returns near the end of the poem. When Angelica asks the Circassian king Sacripante to enlist Gradasso's aid in defending her besieged fortress of Albracà, she claims that he intends to head back to the West to conquer Charlemagne and his people (*OI* 2.5.57). Yet when Gradasso reappears in Book Three, he specifies that the sole purpose of his new expedition to the West is to avenge Ranaldo's inexplicable departure the morning of their scheduled duel outside Barcelona. This time, in fact, he has left behind his innumerable troops and travels alone.

As Book Three unfolds, Gradasso's journey to Paris is marked by a series of romance adventures of the type that generally befall individual knights in the Breton cycle. After Mandricardo frees Gradasso from the magical *Fonte della Fata* (Fountain of the Fay), the two knights set off together and jointly liberate a damsel in distress held hostage by a blind ogre (chapter 4). When they arrive in France they meet up with Brandimarte and Fiordelisa, as well as Rugiero, at the site of the enchanted *Fonte del Riso* (Laughing Stream). Gradasso is chosen by lot to join in rescuing Orlando from the magic fountain, while Mandricardo is excluded and departs. Showing a characteristic weakness for fast horses, Gradasso subsequently falls victim to the enchantment by mounting a flying steed that throws him into the stream. After Fiordelisa and Brandimarte rescue Gradasso, along with Orlando and Rugiero, a dwarf appears to request their assistance. Gradasso initially hesitates, suspecting treachery, but when Rugiero, model of courtesy par excellence, declares his unconditional adherence to the chivalric code, Gradasso readily joins him in the adventure even at the risk of being tricked again (*OI* 3.7.38–55). Thus while Orlando and Brandimarte head to Paris to defend Charlemagne in the upcoming epic battle, Gradasso and Rugiero are last seen following the dwarf to a tower, much like the knights of Arthurian romance.

Ariosto's Gradasso

Whereas in the *Innamorato* Gradasso evolved from an inescapable destructive force into a knight errant, in the *Furioso* he follows a very different trajectory. Ariosto initially reconstructs the character by narrowing in on one particular aspect of his past – his recent proclivity for falling prey to enchanted traps. He is first mentioned in a list of knights held prisoner in Atlante's *palazzo d'aciaio* (*OF* 4.40 AC), the site which Ariosto imagines to be the destination of Boiardo's deceptive dwarf. After Gradasso is liberated along with others by Bradamante, we do not hear about him again until we find him the victim of another of Atlante's enchanted palaces. In this case he is freed from the spell by Astolfo and then flees in terror with the others upon hearing the sound of the magic horn (*OF* 20.20–21 A; 22.20–21 C). In these episodes Gradasso is no longer featured as a protagonist but rather is treated as one among a crowd of victims.

In the course of the poem, moreover, Gradasso progressively abandons his chivalric ethos. He had initially set out in Boiardo's poem to win Ranaldo's steed and Orlando's sword through his own valour; in the *Furioso* he acquires these two coveted prizes (albeit temporarily) without having earned them. In the case of the sword he is not to blame for this failing since Agramante had determined that he would obtain Durindana as a consequence of Ruggiero's victory over Mandricardo. His furtive appropriation of Baiardo in Rinaldo's absence, however, is solely his own doing: breaking an explicit pact he had made with Rinaldo, Gradasso slips away towards India with the steed after discovering it in a cave. He justifies his dishonourable action with a stated desire to avoid battle: "Pazzo è colui che cerca haver con guerra / quel che può haver con pace" ("Crazy is he who seeks to obtain through war / what he can obtain peacefully") (*OF* 30.66 A).[11] Yet attaining such a prize stealthfully is antithetical to Boiardo's original character, who had declared that his greatest pleasure was precisely the challenge of measuring himself against Ranaldo in a contest of arms:

> Che me volesse del Ciel coronare
> (Perché la terra non stimo nïente),
> Non me potrebbe al tutto contentare
> S'io non facesse prova di presente
> Se quel Baron è cotanto gagliardo
> Che mi diffenda il suo destrier Baiardo!
>
> If I were crowned king of heaven
> I still would not be satisfied
> (because I scorn this worthless world)
> until I found out for myself
> if that knight's bold enough to keep
> his horse Baiardo safe from me! (*OI* 1.4.70)

Pio Rajna, calling Gradasso a "breaker of oaths" and "a coward," states that the character who "cravenly declares to himself that he prefers to hold on to it in peace rather than challenge others for it (xxxiii, 94) cannot be the same person who, due to his desire to attain that horse, had set out from India and exposed himself to every danger (*Inn.*, I, I, 5)."[12]

Near the end of the poem Gradasso's character is transformed in an even more drastic fashion when he becomes an avowed enemy of Christianity. When his boat lands on the same island to which King Agramante has retreated after the destruction of Biserta, his proposal to kill Orlando in single combat is couched in religious ideology completely alien to Boiardo's original character: "Morto lui, stimo la christiana Chiesa / quel che l'agnelle il lupo c'habbia fame" ("Once he is dead, the Christian Church may be accounted as so many lambs for a hungry wolf") (*OF* 36.49 A; 40.49 C). It is in the guise of a wolf seeking to devour the sheep of the Christian church that Gradasso takes part in the final contest of three against three on the island of Lipadusa (Lampedusa).[13]

In the course of this battle, Gradasso's character ultimately sinks to a level of degradation beyond recognition: while fighting against Brandimarte, he treacherously wounds his opponent from behind while his back is turned (*OF* 37.99 A; 41.99 C). As if killing Brandimarte in this way were not sufficient to condemn Gradasso to ignominy, Ariosto goes on to depict him as a coward in his final struggle of the poem. After seeing Orlando kill Agramante, Gradasso is so paralysed with fear – "tremò nel core e si smarrì nel viso" ("he quailed, he blanched") – that he is unable even to defend himself (*OF* 38.10 A; 42.10 C). Finding this sudden "mental collapse" inexplicable, Emilio Zanette remarks that the above-cited verse "leaves us incredulous, because it offends the most elemental laws of psychology, and it irritates us because his psychological falsity translates ethically into a flagrant injustice" (346). Gradasso becomes easy prey at the hands of his outraged opponent, who effortlessly stabs him in his side (*OF* 38.11 A; 42.11 C) in a way that reminds Zanette of a "butcher who slits a sheep's throat" (347).[14] With the unceremonious slaughter of this traitor-turned-coward, Durindana and Baiardo return to their rightful owners and Agramante's war comes to a close.

Chapter Three

Agricane of Tartary

Boiardo's Agricane

When Astolfo repudiates Charlemagne's court in canto 7, Boiardo also turns his attention away from France and towards the East, setting the stage for a series of transglobal encounters outside Europe. The first major Asian figure that we come across is King Agricane of Tartaria, who combines within himself the poem's opening reflections on love and power exemplified by Angelica and Gradasso, respectively. Like the king of Sericana, he is a potentate who covets a prize he cannot attain; like those gathered in Paris for the joust, he too has fallen under the spell of the princess of Cathay:

> Né tien altro pensier intro il coraio
> Che de acquistar quela bella fanciula:
> Di regno o stato non se cura nulla.
>
> One single thought consumes his heart.
> He wants to win that damsel fair;
> kingdoms and crowns are not his care. (*OI* 1.10.14)

Angelica and Gradasso, however, originate from the most distant and least-known territories imaginable, whose very vagueness allows the characters to represent universal truths. Agricane, by contrast, is grounded in a specific geo-historical reality familiar to Boiardo's contemporaries through available literature. This chapter argues that Agricane's geographical provenance provides a meaningful context initially for his war against Cathay at Albracà and subsequently for his eleventh-hour conversion to Christianity, both developed in opposition to the crusading ideology of the Carolingian epic.

The War at Albracà

Boiardo could have expected his readers to consider the war at Albracà in relation to previous epic narratives in which Christian knights became involved in military campaigns waged beyond the boundaries of western Europe. The popular *Spagna* narrative once again offers a particularly explicit case for comparison.[1] In the midst of the earlier text's Frankish invasion of Spain, Orlando leaves Charlemagne in anger over an affront to his honour and heads towards Persia, pretending to be a Saracen who escaped when Christians overran his city (*Spagna* 13.6–7). After his ship is blown off course, he lands near "Lameche" ("Mecca") (*Spagna* 13.21), which the elderly king of Persia holds under siege because the sultan has refused to cede his daughter to him in marriage. Orlando initially offers his services as a mercenary soldier but subsequently decides to fight so that the princess will not have to marry against her will. This portion of the *Spagna* narrative accords with Orlando's defence of Angelica from Agricane's relentless siege at Albracà. Yet while in the earlier poem the sultan's daughter desires in vain the Frankish knight (*Spagna* 14.26), in the *Innamorato* it is rather Orlando who is overwhelmed by unrequited love for the beleaguered Saracen princess.[2] Moreover, whereas Boiardo's Orlando seeks no other reward than Angelica, the *Spagna*'s hero eventually conquers Mecca, Persia, Syria, and Jerusalem, finally revealing that the ultimate goal of all his military exploits was to compel these lands to accept Christianity. Indeed, he even forces his Saracen allies to convert upon the threat of dire consequences: "Se çiò non fate, infin a or ve dicho / ch'io ve disfido come mio nemicho" ("If you do not, I tell you right now / that I challenge you as my enemy") (*Spagna* 18.15). Acknowledging that "nissuna potençia à nostro Dio" ("our God has no power") (*Spagna* 18.17), the sultan and his son Sansonetto convert along with all of their subjects.[3] After this successful crusade *avant la lettre*, Orlando leaves his cousin Ansuigi in charge of Jerusalem and eventually returns to Charlemagne's ranks where he continues to destroy Saracens in Spain. Thus an episode that initially appears to be a respite from the poem's ideology of coercive proselytism turns out instead to be its most sensational example.[4]

Boiardo, in contrast, never turns to religious or ethnic difference as a motivating factor in the war at Albracà, and knights on all sides are expected to adhere to an international code of chivalry irrespective of their origin. The few European knights taking part in the battle find themselves on opposite sides for personal rather than religious or nationalistic reasons. The love-struck Orlando enters the fray to defend Angelica, hoping to win her for himself. When Ranaldo arrives he fights for justice, seeking to avenge the torture and murder of the maiden Albarosa by the Babylonian king Trufaldino. Astolfo, who in the meantime has also reached Albracà, initially lends support to Angelica but then changes sides when he learns of Ranaldo's presence and just intentions. Charlemagne's paladins, moreover, leave no mark on the political landscape of the region.[5]

In distancing the war at Albracà from the Christian-Saracen conflict underlying Carolingian narratives such as the *Spagna*, Boiardo brings into play a distinct geo-historical framework.[6] Boiardo's geographical positioning of Tartary (the name given to the Mongol Empire by medieval Europeans) just west of Cathay accords with travellers' accounts and world maps of the time. Giovanni da Pian del Carpine opens his *Historia Mongalorum* situating the neighbouring territories in this way: "There is towards the East a land which is called Mongol, or Tartary, lying in that part of the world which is thought to be most north-easterly. On the east part it has the country of Cathay" (3).[7] The Mongol Empire was the largest contiguous land empire in history, stretching from eastern Europe to the shores of the Pacific. In the *Innamorato* it extends even farther, going beyond southern Siberia and Russia to include Scandinavia (*OI* 1.10.10–13).

That Boiardo wants to evoke the specificity of the Mongol Empire can be seen from his description of the banners raised by Agricane and his allies as they head towards the vast land of Cathay, in India (*OI* 1.10.13–14). As a herald points out for the benefit of Astolfo, Agricane has a black banner with a white horse (*OI* 1.10.9), while King Saritron of Mongolia has a white banner with a gold sun (*OI* 1.10.10). These emblems correspond to the Mongol Empire's most prominent historic flags, which feature either a horse or a white flame sun and a moon. There is even a correspondence with respect to the black, white, and gold colours mentioned by Boiardo: the images on historic Mongolian flags are either white or yellow/gold, and ancient chronicles also speak of the white and black banners of Genghis Khan.[8] The third king singled out by the herald, Radamant, is said to rule "Mosca la grande e la terra Comana" ("great Moscow, and Comanan lands") (*OI* 1.10.10). This inclusion of Russia corresponds to the fact that the Mongols under Genghis's grandson Batu had conquered that territory and established the rule of the

Golden Horde there. In addition, Radamant's emblem of a white lion set on green corresponds to the numerous lions of Russian family heraldry, sometimes used to claim regal descent (Medvedev).

The fourth ruler in the review is King Poliferno of Orgagna (*OI* 1.10.11). This territory, while present in Arthurian narratives (Tissoni Benvenuti, *Inamoramento de Orlando*, 767n), may actually represent a geographical area. Friar William of Rubruck notes that, during his travel from Batu to Mangu Khan, he passed a country that "was once called Organum" whose inhabitants were called "Organa" by the Nestorians (111). Fra Mauro's world map of 1459 contains various inscriptions for Organça and Organza, corresponding geographically to Turkmenistan (Falchetta 606–21).[9] Moreover, Poliferno's red banner with gold moons recalls two Mongol Empire flags depicted in the Catalan atlas of 1375: one with three red crescent moons is found above several cities held by the Grand Khan, while another with a red crescent moon (along with another symbol) is found above various cities of the Golden Horde, including Urgench (Uzbekistan), spelled Organçi in the atlas.[10]

As ruler over this vast domain, Agricane is portrayed as a great khan ("kane" or "cane" in Italian) both through his proper name and his status as "Re de' Re" ("king of kings") (*OI* 1.10.9). Marco Polo, for example, referred to Kublai Khan as the "Grande Kane," which he says means "lo signore degli signori" ("the lord of lords") (*Mil.* 75.1, 96).[11] It is not surprising that Boiardo should have chosen to include a Mongol khan among his examples of great lords who desire what they cannot have (*OI* 1.1.5). Marco Polo described the unbridled acquisitiveness of the Mongol Empire's first khan, Genghis, in the following terms: "Quando Cinghi si vide tanta gente, disse che volea conquistare tutto 'l mondo" ("When Genghis saw so many people, he said he wanted to conquer the entire world") (*Mil.* 64.5, 76). The Mongol khan's next action is to seek to marry the daughter of another powerful ruler; when the latter refuses the union, saying that he would rather consign his daughter to the flames ("io l'arderei inanzi ch'io gliele dessi per moglie"), Genghis sets in motion "la magior battaglia che mai fosse veduta" ("the greatest battle that one had ever seen") (*Mil.* 64.9, 76; 67.1, 78). When in the *Innamorato* a messenger explains to Orlando that the Tartar khan Agricane has asked Galafrone for his daughter's hand, it is now the princess herself who would rather die ("prima vòl morire") than accept his offer (*OI* 1.6.41–2) and who thus finds herself besieged at Albracà.[12]

It is not any specific battle noted by Marco Polo that Boiardo wants to evoke through Agricane's war, however, but rather the larger picture of Mongol expansion in Asia. Victory at Albracà would have extended Agricane's empire into Cathay, which the Mongols actually conquered in the course of the thirteenth century. Giovanni da Pian del Carpine dedicates a short chapter of his travel memoir to "the Many Victories between them and the people of Cathay" (13), writing that Tartar troops "marched with one accord against the Cathayans, and waging war with them a long time, they conquered a great part of their land, and shut up their emperor in his greatest city" (14). The Catalan-Estense *mappamundo* evokes this invasion by picturing Tartars en route to Cathay (Milano 61).[13]

In suggesting a historical precedent for Agricane's war, critics have pointed to the Mongol siege of either Balkh or Bukhara (in today's northern Afghanistan and Uzbekistan, respectively).[14] Yet elsewhere Boiardo indicates actual geographical locations through identifiable names, and none of the variants for either city in Franco-Venetian, Tuscan, or Latin versions of the *Milione* come close to the spelling of this fictitious setting. Moreover, neither of these two cities held out through a lengthy Mongol siege or could be said to lie, like Angelica's fortress, just a single day west of the capital city of Cathay.[15] The magnitude and duration of the war at Albracà seems more likely to evoke the extended siege of Beijing (Marco Polo's Cambaluc), which became the Mongol capital after their victory (Man 134–47).[16] More generally, the episode's inconclusiveness corresponds to Genghis Khan's invasion of northern China: although the Khan died in 1227 while in the midst of extending his dominion over the territory, the offensive continued after his death, meeting with tenacious and sustained resistance before its eventual success in 1279 (Man 147). In the *Innamorato*, the war rages on, with no end in sight, even after Agricane is killed by Orlando.

The gratuitous destructive actions on the part of the Tartars during the war at Albracà call to mind the Mongols' reputation for widespread desolation of territories. The thirteenth-century English chronicler Matthew Paris writes: "Swarming like locusts over the face of the earth, they have brought terrible devastation to the eastern parts (of Europe), laying it waste with fire and carnage. After having passed through the land of the Saracens, they have razed cities, cut down forests, killed townspeople and peasants."[17] In the poem, Agricane's passage through Circassia leaves the area in a shambles (*OI* 1.9.38), and while he is engaged in fighting at Albracà we hear that his son Mandricardo has set the ever unfortunate Circassian realm on fire: "tuto 'l regno come una facella / Mena a roina e mete a foco ardente" ("like a firebrand – all [the] land / he set to flame and ruination!") (*OI* 2.3.10).[18] In addition, the destruction of the besieged town by fire, resulting in the death of all its inhabitants – "La bella terra da ogni parte è incesa / E sono occise tute le persone" ("The fair town flamed on every side. / Every inhabitant was slain") (*OI* 1.14.19) – accords with the assault on Beijing in which the Mongols "ransacked the city, killing thousands" and "part of the city burned for a month" (Man 142).

The characterization of Agricane himself is consistent with descriptions of great khans found in the accounts of medieval travellers. Marco Polo, for example, describes Genghis Khan as a "uomo di grande valenza e di senno e di prodezza" ("man of great valour and wisdom and prowess") (*Mil.* 64.2, 75). Remarking that "to the Mongols disloyalty was abhorrent, even in an enemy," James Chambers quotes Genghis as saying, "A man who is once faithless can never be trusted" (15). Agricane embodies the same combination of military valour and chivalric virtue. Although described as strong and overly audacious ("forte e troppo audace"; *OI* 1.6.41), the Tartar king dismounts from his horse in order to fight without any advantage (*OI* 1.11.22–3). Moreover, he would rather lose the war than employ deceit to secure victory: when the treacherous Trufaldino offers to hand over the fortress of Albracà through an act of betrayal, Agricane is so offended that he threatens to hang the villain: "Né per lo mondo mai se possa dire, / Che alo esser mio sia megio un traditore! / Vincer voglio per forza e per ardire, / Et a fronte scoperta farmi honore" ("Never let it be said on earth / I got my way with help from traitors! / I want to win by force or courage, / to gather glory openly!") (*OI* 1.14.53).

Given, however, that Boiardo is not writing history in a seemingly fictional guise but rather using historical allusions to colour a fictitious narrative, the issue is how these correspondences to the Mongol Empire and to the figure of the Great Khan work thematically and ideologically in the extended episode of the war at Albracà. This brings us to the final scene leading to Agricane's baptism and death. It may at first glance seem incongruous that a war in which religious motives are so conspicuously absent should feature one of the poem's rare instances of conversion. Nevertheless, as I argue below, the significance of Agricane's conversion to Christianity comes into sharper focus if we recognize both its divergence from Carolingian epic precedents and its relation to Mongol history.

Agricane's Conversion

The attempt to convert "pagans" was commonplace in the Carolingian narratives familiar to Boiardo's early readers. Following a pattern established in the *Entrée d'Espagne*, episodes often incorporated debates over the relative merits of Christianity and Islam.[19] The precedent most often cited in connection with the Agricane episode is found in the same fifteenth-century Italian rewriting of the *Entrée* discussed earlier, the *Spagna*.[20] That work begins with Charlemagne calling for a crusade against Muslim Spain and the pope granting plenary indulgences to those who fight against "la fè ria" ("the evil faith") (*Spagna* 1.18). When King Marsilio learns from his messenger that Charlemagne "disffidò ciascun el qual non crede / in Yehsù Cristo Padre omnipotente" ("has issued a challenge to everyone who does not believe / in Jesus Christ, omnipotent father") (*Spagna* 2.5), he calls on Feraù to lead the defence of the city of Lazera.

The ensuing confrontation between Feraù and Orlando in Saracen Spain keeps religious difference at the forefront. Initially Feraù assures his mother of a future Muslim conquest of Rome and the entire West:

E in Roma ne la caxa di san Piero,
in su l'altar mangierà el mio ferante.
La legie di Iesù sença pensiero
abatuta serà, e Trivicante
Apolin e Machon serà più altiero
come signor da Ponente a Levante.

And in Rome in the house of Saint Peter,
my horse will eat upon the altar.
The law of Jesus without effort
will be trampled down, and Trivicante,
Apollin, and Mohammed will be held most high
as lord from West to East. (*Spagna* 3.28)

When Orlando exhorts Feraù to forsake his false beliefs and convert to the true religion – "Deh, rinega la tua fè vile e vana / e torna a Cristo, Padre omnipotente!" ("Come on, renounce your vile and useless faith / and return to Christ, omnipotent Father!") (*Spagna* 3.39) – Feraù adamantly refuses Orlando's demand and maintains the superiority of his own creed. In the ensuing battle in which warfare alternates with sermonizing, the anonymous poet repeatedly portrays the knights as representatives of two opposing belief systems in a bitterly fought contest for dominion over the earth. In this context Feraù's ultimate defeat convinces him that his religion is of no value: "Vegio che non val nulla el paganesmo" ("I see that paganism is worthless") (*Spagna* 5.7). The scene concludes with a mortally wounded Feraù receiving baptism at the hands of Orlando.

The conversion of Agricane is developed in direct contrast to the traditional patterns found in the *Spagna*. Whereas in that poem Orlando and Feraù are depicted as fighting solely "per la fè cristïana et per la fella" ("for the Christian faith and the evil one") (*Spagna* 4.2), in the *Innamorato* the two warriors cross swords over a woman.[21] Indeed, Orlando does not give any indication that he is aware of the religious identity of his opponent beyond the fact that he is not a Christian. Agricane himself never mentions Mohammed, and on the only occasion in which he invokes a higher authority, he refers to his "signore" ("lord") as Trivigante (*OI* 1.14.53), the name given by medieval Italian Christians to a pagan deity of unknown origin that came to be associated with Islam.[22] The narrator frequently refers to the khan as a Tartar but never as a Saracen.[23]

Riccardo Bruscagli, recognizing that Boiardo refashions this episode "in an entirely courtly key and paradigmatically distanced from the ideological and religious contents of the *Spagna*," writes, "It is significant, thinking precisely of the *Spagna* and its epic-religious code, that in the nocturnal conversation between Orlando and Agricane the Christian faith seems more like the vindication of a perfect compatibility between 'culture' and the exercise of military arms than either a theological belief or a distinct ideology" (*Orlando innamorato*, 1: xi).[24] Daniela Delcorno Branca points out further that in distancing his episode from its ostensible model, Boiardo includes various features typical of the Breton cycle: the solitary duel, the fountain, the darkness of night, and the conversation between two jealous rivals for a lady's love (168).[25] In addition, Ettore Paratore has uncovered textual allusions to the *Aeneid* in both the action and the dialogue (361–4).[26]

Boiardo may indeed be using Arthurian romance and Virgilian epic to cut against the grain of the episode's Carolingian precedents; at the same time, however, neither model is sufficiently present to carry its thematic weight. On the contrary, the episode's conclusion opposes the ideology of Arthurian romance by revealing the folly of fighting a rival suitor over a lady: as soon as Agricane is mortally wounded, Angelica is relegated to part of his unworthy past and duly forgotten. Nor can Orlando's personal goal be linked to Aeneas's imperialistic mission since he is fighting solely for love and does not seek to gain any territory. I would like to propose instead that Boiardo shifts the focus away from the perennial clash between Christians and Saracens primarily by developing Agricane's identity as a Mongol khan. I now therefore turn to the question of how –

and why – the Mongol Empire provides a relevant historical context for the episode of Agricane's conversion.

In contrast to Carolingian epic, accounts of Mongol history reveal the total absence of religion as a motivating factor in warfare or statecraft. Chambers credits Genghis Khan with establishing "the first great empire to know religious freedom" (45), and early Western travellers invariably comment on the Mongols' ongoing policy of religious tolerance. Marco Polo, for example, regularly documents the co-presence of Christianity, Islam, and "idolatry" in the Mongol cities he visits, while William of Rubruck records that the capital city of Karakorum housed "twelve temples dedicated to the idols of different nations, two mosques where they observe the laws of Mahomet, and one church of Christians at the far end of the city" (167). Moreover, while the first Great Khan's policy of religious freedom appears to have been linked to his overall indifference to belief systems, some of the subsequent khans not only followed his policy of tolerance, characteristic of shamanism (Jagchid and Hyer, 172–3) but were reported to have been receptive to Christian teaching.[27] Kuyuk Khan's mother was a Christian, and Giovanni da Pian del Carpine was told that the khan himself was close to conversion: "Certain Christians of his family earnestly and strongly assured us that he himself was about to become a Christian" (43). Contrary to such hopes, Kuyuk sent the friar back home with a letter demanding instead the pope's submission to him. Nonetheless, the khan apparently did later convert, as his messenger declared to King Louis IX of France in 1248 when conveying his proposal that the crusaders' invasion of Egypt coincide with the Mongols' planned attack on Baghdad.[28] Kuyuk's death the same year prevented the possibility of a concerted military effort but kept alive in the West the hope of converting a future Mongol ruler.

William of Rubruck writes that he was sent to the Mongol Empire in 1253 by Louis IX when the king heard that Sartak, son of Batu, khan of the Golden Horde, had become a Christian (56). He eventually arrived at the court of the Great Khan Mangu, Kuyuk's successor, where a resident monk tried to convince him of the khan's preference for their faith (139). Although William remained sceptical, he nevertheless records the ruler's visit to the local church and questions concerning Christianity (140–2), and later mentions that the mother of Mangu and Kublai was a Christian (168).[29] Marco Polo notes that Kublai's brother Gigata (Chaghatai), who ruled at Samarkand, also converted to Christianity before his death (*Mil.* 51.4, 60). Hayton goes so far as to claim that Kublai Khan himself had become a Christian: "Qubilai-Khan ruled the Tartars for forty-two years.

He converted to Christianity and built the city called Eons [Beijing] in the kingdom of Cathay, a city said to be greater than Rome" (*The Flower of Histories of the East,* bk 3, ch. 19).[30]

Unlike the *Spagna*'s convention of compelling Saracens to convert at sword point, accounts about the Mongol Empire consistently portray the Christian friars as relying on their power of persuasion. William of Rubruck records his various attempts to convert his Mongol hosts as he is sent from Satrak to Batu and finally to the Great Khan Mangu. He recalls how his first speech to Batu concluded with the following threat of damnation in the afterlife: "Be it known unto you of a certainty, that you shall not obtain the joys of heaven, unless you become a Christian: for God saith, Whosoever believeth and is baptized, shall be saved; but he that believeth not, shall be condemned" (100). The immediate reaction of the khan and his nobles demonstrates the failure of this strategy: "At this [Batu] smiled modestly; but the other Moals [i.e., Mongols] began to clap their hands, and to laugh at us."

William assumes a potentially more productive stance when, near the end of his sojourn at Mangu's court, he responds with humility to the khan's invitation to him and representatives of other faiths to assemble to expound their beliefs.[31] In the ensuing theological debate that takes place on the eve of Pentecost, William's first concern is to prove the existence of God; moreover, in arguing for monotheism over polytheism the Saracens are his allies rather than antagonists (175–8). He recounts that the gathering ended without hostility but also without conversions: "Every one listened without raising the least objection. Yet no one said: 'I believe; I want to become a Christian.' Then the Nestorians and the Saracens sang together in a loud voice; the Tuins said not a word and afterwards everybody drank deeply" (178).[32]

Kublai Khan subsequently sent Marco Polo's father and uncle to the pope requesting that a hundred learned men come to China "che sapessero mostrare per ragione come la cristia[n]a legge era migliore" ("who would know how to show through reasoning why the Christian law was better") (*Mil.* 7.6, 9). Although the pope never actually sent the hundred scholars, missionary activity on the part of Franciscan friars gained momentum in the following decades. Giovanni da Montecorvino, sent to China by Pope Nicolò IV in 1289, reported six thousand baptized converts within a few years and remained to become the first archbishop of Beijing. The Florentine Giovanni Marignolli and fifty fellow Franciscans spent four years in China (1342–7) "converting a good many of the great khan's subjects and even staging Christian ceremonies within the imperial palace – which was next door to the cathedral – for the enlightenment of the emperor" (Silverberg 169).

The *Innamorato*'s conversation between Orlando and Agricane on the outskirts of Albracà, while in contrast to the forced conversions of the Carolingian epic, is in accordance with the spirit of religious tolerance documented by Christian visitors to the Mongol Empire. Rather than hurling insults and threats at each other like Orlando and Feraù in the *Spagna*, Boiardo's two warriors show mutual esteem in their various verbal exchanges. Agricane explains that he wants to preserve Orlando's life because of admiration for his valour as well as gratitude for his earlier courtesy of postponing their battle so that he could aid his troops (*OI* 1.18.34). He therefore offers to let Orlando go free, as long as he will remain clear of the battlefield in the future (*OI* 1.18.35).

In expressing his distress at the thought of killing Orlando, the Tartar king calls upon the sky and the sun as his witnesses: "Ma siami testimonio il ciel e il sole / Che darti morte me dispiace e dole!" ("But let the sun and heavens see / that killing you displeases me") (*OI* 1.18.35). His invocation recalls the Mongolian reverence for the "eternal blue sky" or "heaven" that was believed to keep watch over human events. Walther Heissig writes that "the records of the twelfth and thirteenth centuries, from the time of the political consolidation of the Mongols and the beginnings of the Mongol Empire, give an account of a religious system at the summit of which was the blue or eternal heaven" (6). According to John Man, moreover, Genghis Khan in particular regularly asserted that he was "under the protection of Eternal Heaven" (14).[33] Agricane's evocation of traditional Mongolian belief not only supports the historical context of the episode but keeps the Christian-Saracen binary out of the picture.

In Orlando's reply Boiardo draws attention to both the correspondences and differences between the two knights. If Agricane spoke in a gentle voice ("con voce suave"; *OI* 1.18.34), Orlando also feels compassion ("avea preso già de lui pietate") and responds in a very humane way ("molto umano"; *OI* 1.18.36). And since he too believes in his own certain victory, it is now his turn to express regret over his rival's impending death. In Orlando's case, however, this regret extends to the afterlife: "Quanto sei – disse – più franco e soprano, / Più de te me rencresce in veritate, / Che sarai morto, e non sei christïano, / Et andarai tra l'anime damnate" ("As much as you are bold [or, literally, valorous and outstanding], / so much I grieve, to tell the truth, / that you are not a Christian. When / you die, you'll go among the damned") (*OI* 1.18.36).

Whereas Agricane offered to preserve Orlando's life if he agreed to leave the battlefield, Orlando ups the ante by proposing to save Agricane's body and soul if he consents to be baptized (*OI* 1.18.36). This is Orlando's only reference to the Christian religion in the entire exchange preceding Agricane's conversion.[34]

The reader can well imagine that Orlando's offer is just as unacceptable as the one Agricane presented to him earlier: it is clear that neither knight would be willing to relinquish his values or refuse the battle. On the contrary, Agricane is so elated to have ascertained the identity of his opponent that not only does he show no interest in salvation, but he replies that he would turn down the prospect of ruling paradise itself just for the pleasure of testing himself against the famed Orlando: "Chi me facesse Re del Paradiso, / Con tal ventura non lo cangerei" ("I would prefer to fight you than / to be the king of Paradise") (*OI* 1.18.37). He therefore advises Orlando to cease all talk about the "fàti de' dei" ("works of gods") since his preaching would be to no avail.

Boiardo gives Agricane the last word – indeed, his answer is followed by a succinct "Nè più parole" ("no more words") on the part of the narrator – and returns to the action. Following a battle that lasts from noon until late night, the two knights lie down near each other "Come fosse tra loro antica pace" ("like two men bound by ancient peace") (*OI* 1.18.40). After "ragionando insieme tutavia / Di cose degne e condecente a loro" ("they talked together for a time / of worthy and chivalric matters"), Orlando turns to a higher concern. Pointing to the beauty of the cosmos, he seeks to reach agreement at the most basic level; namely, the existence of a divine creator:

> Questo che hora vediamo è un bel lavoro
> Che fece la divina monarchia:
> E la luna de argento e ' stele d'oro
> E la luce de il giorno e il sol lucente;
> Dio tuto ha fato per la humana gente.
>
> What we see is the lovely work
> that was produced by heaven's monarch.
> The silver moon, the golden stars,
> the shining sun, the light of day –
> God made them for the human race. (*OI* 1.18.41)

Orlando's metaphorical depiction of God as "heaven's monarch" echoes

Agricane's earlier reference to the "king of Paradise." Moreover, he refrains from restricting his discourse to any particular belief and includes all of humanity, rather than just a chosen group, as beneficiaries of God's creative outpouring. Unwilling to discuss religion or science on any level, Agricane confesses his ignorance in the latter subject and recalls how in his refusal to learn he broke the head of his first and only teacher (*OI* 1.18.42). The khan's youthful repudiation of book learning was compensated for by rigorous training in hunting and military exercises, which he claims to be the sole occupations worthy of a knight (*OI* 1.18.43). Respecting Agricane's refusal to discuss theology, Orlando accepts the topic of what gives meaning and fulfilment to human life. Although he expresses his agreement on the primacy of arms, he maintains that learning graces an individual as flowers adorn a field (*OI* 1.18.44).[35] Yet Orlando's defence of letters brings him back to the original topic, and he goes on to assert in metaphorical language that without learning one cannot begin to comprehend the mysteries of the cosmos:

> Et è simile a un bove, a un saxo, a un legno,
> Chi non pensa alo eterno Creatore,
> Né ben si può pensar senza doctrina
> La somma magestate alta e divina.
>
> Not to acknowledge our Creator
> makes you an ox, a stone, a log.
> Unschooled, you cannot well conceive
> the heights of holy majesty. (*OI* 1.18.44)

A few years after the poem's publication, Boiardo's cousin Giovanni Pico della Mirandola would compare one's inner development to diverse forms along the chain of being: "Whatever seeds each man cultivates will grow into maturity and bear in him their own fruit. If they be vegetative, he will be like a plant. If sensitive, he will become brutish. If rational, he will grow into a heavenly being. If intellectual, he will be an angel and the son of God" (225).[36] The possibility of ascension in this scheme depends upon one's state of knowledge. Citing Pico's rhetorical question "For how can we judge or love what is unknown?," Stephen Alan Farmer explains that for Pico the study of philosophy is the necessary preparation for either "earthly rule or the mystical ascent" (33). While Boiardo stops short of refashioning his knight as a mystic, Orlando's speech forcefully upholds the fundamental role of education in the formation of a fully developed human being capable of spiritual contemplation.

Whereas the existence of a divine creator began as Orlando's main point, the discussion has included the interrelated topics of education, proper knightly activity, and spiritual reflection. Contesting his opponent's unfair advantage of superior intellectual training, Agricane refuses to discuss such metaphysical issues and proposes instead the subject of love. Orlando responds willingly to this suggestion, acknowledging that, in contrast to previous battles, he is now motivated exclusively by his desire to obtain the beautiful maiden: "Hor sol per acquistar la bella dama / Facio bataglia, e d'altro non ho brama!" ("Now I fight to win this fair / maiden, and I want nothing more") (*OI* 1.18.48).

Although the knights are in agreement concerning the importance of love, the problem of course is that they are both vying for the same woman. Ironically, whereas the two of them were not estranged by religious or national differences, their rivalry over Angelica impels them abruptly to violence. As they resume their battle in the middle of the night against the traditional chivalric prohibition of fighting in the dark, Orlando even fears treachery on the part of his adversary, whom the poet now coldly refers to as the "pagan" in accordance with Orlando's new hostile attitude (*OI* 1.18.54).

When Agricane finally succumbs after over five more hours of combat, he spontaneously conveys his belief in the Christian God and asks Orlando to baptize him before his death (*OI* 1.19.12). Rather than the triumph of one creed over another, his reasoning shows a shift from a lower to a higher focus: "E se mia vita è stata iniqua e strana, / Non sia la morte almen de Dio rebela" ("If I have led an evil life, / don't let me lose God as I die") (*OI* 1.19.13). Whereas in the *Spagna* Orlando's victory convinced Feraù of his God's superior power, by way of contrast the God evoked by Agricane in his request for baptism is not a promoter of religious warfare but a compassionate and benevolent deity who demonstrates love for mankind through the Incarnation and Crucifixion: "Io credo nel tuo Dio che morì in croce. / [...] / Lui che véne a salvar la gente humana," ("I / believe in your God, crucified. / [...] / The one who came to save mankind") (*OI* 1.19.12–13). This attitude is possible because their combat was not motivated by religious difference.

What could have prompted Boiardo to turn away from the Carolingian model of converting Saracens at sword point and stage instead the voluntary conversion of a Mongol khan? If we consider the episode in the historical context of late fifteenth-century Christian Europe, it emerges not as yet another example of religious propaganda but rather as a thoughtful critique of religious intolerance. The first edition of the *Innamorato* was being prepared for publication during the period in which the Catholic kings in nearby Spain were setting in motion the final phase of the Reconquista, beginning with the invasion of the Muslim kingdom of Granada in 1481. Although the forced conversion or expulsion of Muslims and Jews from Spain could not then have been foreseen, a period of increasing religious dogmatism was already underway with the institution of the Spanish Inquisition in 1478.[37] News of grievous abuses began to reach Italy soon thereafter, and Sixtus IV's Brief of January 1482 cited unjust imprisonment, cruel tortures, and the appropriation of the properties of those executed among the illegal acts committed in Spain under the guise of papal authority. Just over a decade later Giuliano Dati opened his poetic rendering of Columbus's 1493 letter by praising King Ferdinand of Castile's merciless treatment of non-Christians, in this case Jews: "chi altro crede è mal da lui trattato, / come si vede che non è mai sazio / di marrani giudei far ogni strazio" ("whoever holds a different belief is treated badly by him, / as we see that he is never satiated / with torturing renegade Jews") (ottava 10).

At the same time, the fifteenth-century also produced works criticizing attempts at forced conversion as counterproductive and promoting instead the peaceful persuasion of non-Christians. The theologian John of Segovia, in expounding his ideas to the like-minded Nicholas of Cusa in a letter of 2 December 1454, argued against converting Saracens through warfare: "For since one never gives credence to one's enemy, they will not believe their Christian teachers as long as the struggle continues. Their hatred of them, and even more so of Christ, will grow, and they will draw back completely from embracing the latter's faith" (145). Nicholas of Cusa's own *De pace fidei* (On the Peace of Faith, 1453), a treatise composed in the wake of the Turkish invasion of Constantinople, presents the vision of a dialogue among representatives of many divergent faiths and ethnic groups – including Arab, Indian, Chaldean, Jewish, Persian, Turkish, and Tartar – in response to an untenable situation on earth in which "many turn their weapons against each other for the sake of religion and in their power compel men to renounce long observed doctrines or kill them" (I). The vision offers hope "that it would be possible, through the experience of a few wise men who are well acquainted with all the diverse practices which are observed in religions across the world, to find a unique and propitious concordance" (I). According to Cary Nederman, "what distinguishes *De pace fidei*'s idea of religious pluralism is its irenicism; violent persecution and coerced conversion must be replaced with rational debate and proof as the means for realizing the universal truth of Christian doctrine. [...] Once the reasonableness of these doctrines is demonstrated to wise men of other faiths, Nicholas believes, they will naturally and uncontentiously embrace them" (88, 93).[38]

Debates over religion within the Christian church were also taking place in Italy during Boiardo's lifetime. Farmer recalls a heated debate between Dominicans and Franciscans that drew the presence of Florentine intellectuals the likes of Ficino, Poliziano, and Pico della Mirandola (5–6). Pico himself actively advocated an open exchange of religious ideas in order to reach "a universal harmony among philosophers" (Kristeller 216). Whereas Boiardo's Orlando had a single point on which he sought agreement – the existence of a supreme being who created a universe filled with beauty for the sake of humanity – Pico would soon devise 900 theological *conclusiones* that he planned to debate in January 1487. His corollary *Oration* expressed a yearning for "that wished-for peace, most holy peace, indivisible bond, of one accord in the friendship through which all rational souls not only shall come into harmony in the one mind which is above all minds but shall in some ineffable way become altogether one" (231–2).

Glancing ahead to the following decades, we see that Orlando's ecumenical approach anticipates not only Pico's *Oration,* which aims to reconcile other world religions with Christianity, but perhaps even more closely Thomas More's *Utopia*, which seeks to establish a common ground among all religions. In More's imagined society, where everyone is free to observe the religion of his choice, commonalities prevail over differences: "Nothing is seen or heard in the churches that does not square with all the creeds. [...] In these prayers each one acknowledges God to be the creator and ruler of the universe and the author of all good things" (100 and 103). Orlando's non-coercive approach was precisely the one that More would attribute to Utopus, who "prescribed by law that everyone may cultivate the religion of his choice, and strenuously proselytize for it too, provided he does so quietly, modestly, rationally and without insulting others" (94).

Boiardo's fictional scene evoking past examples provided by Mongol history thus offers a positive example of inter-religious dialogue. Agricane's spontaneous conversion results from his friendly conversation with Orlando amid the peaceful beauty of the natural world. When Orlando cannot persuade Agricane of his point of view, he willingly changes the subject. It is not Orlando but Agricane himself who returns to the topic of religion and asks to be baptized. Boiardo has thus transformed the Carolingian epic's stock conversion episode from a case of coercive proselytism into an invitation to communicate even with one's enemy in a spirit of openness and respect for his autonomy.

Ariosto's Agricane

Although Ariosto remembers Agricane on various occasions in the course of the *Furioso*, especially as the father of Mandricardo, he does not creatively imitate the Tartar king's eleventh-hour conversion.[39] Nor does Ariosto offer a coherent picture as to how he imagines events to have played out in the war at Albracà. Early in the poem Angelica claims that Agricane had defeated or killed Galafrone: "il Re di Tartaria Agricane / disfece il genitor mio Galaphrone, / che in India del Cataio era gran Cane" ("Agrican, King of Tartary, defeated my father Galafron, Great Khan of Cathay and the Indies") (*OF* 8.43 AC).[40] Yet Galafrone was last seen in the *Innamorato* alive and still defending his realm many cantos after Agricane's demise, and Ariosto never specifically states when or how the troops of Tartary gained dominion over Cathay. Later in the poem, moreover, he contradicts the substance of Angelica's lament by informing the reader that she returned to Cathay where she offered the realm to her new husband, Medoro. Ariosto is much more interested in Agricane's son, Mandricardo, whom, as I argue in the following chapter, he develops against the grain of Boiardo's original character.

Chapter Four

Mandricardo, Son of Agricane

Boiardo's Mandricardo

Boiardo relates the exploits of Agricane's son, Mandricardo, in a way that echoes the progression of the Mongol dynasty in history. Like the military campaigns of Genghis Khan, Agricane's battles take place entirely in the East and consist primarily of Asians fighting other Asians without posing a threat to western Europe. Mandricardo, on the other hand, will head west and eventually take part in the siege of Paris. Indeed, at the opening of Book Three Boiardo announces to the reader that Mandricardo will emerge as a major threat on a global scale: "pose quasi l'universo al fondo" ("[he] almost ruined all the world") (*OI* 3.1.5). The severity of this forecast suggestively aligns him with Genghis's son and successor, Ogedai (Ogotai, Oktay), who likewise threatened to destroy western Europe. Mongol troops overran Hungary and were poised to continue their attack when Ogedai's death in 1241 forced them to withdraw and return to Karakorum to elect a new ruler. A small reconnaissance mission that appeared about sixty miles north of Venice led Italians to fear a Mongol offensive in the peninsula (Chambers 111). In speculating what the outcome would have been if Ogedai had not died that year, Manuel Komroff remarks: "Certainly Paris and Rome could, at this time, offer little defence" (xiv).

Regarding the issue of religion, we can note that whereas Agricane was not connected to any particular religious practice prior to his conversion, Mandricardo "el Pagano" (*OI* 3.1.6) is specifically introduced as a Saracen (*OI* 3.1.5). This characterization corresponds historically to the gradual spread of Islam in the Mongol Empire.[1] At the same time, Boiardo adds a few details to his depiction of Mandricardo that link him to earlier religious beliefs and practices as well. First, after inheriting his father's kingdom he brutally orders the execution of all adult males unable to fight until a desperate old man yells out to him that Agricane's spirit cannot cross into the otherworld unless his death is avenged. This reference to a supernatural realm, which may recall the afterlife in classical Greek and Latin literature, is also in line with traditional Mongol beliefs. Marco Polo explains how the Mongols contracted marriages for their deceased children and burnt material possessions they believed would reach the newlyweds in the otherworld (*Mil.* 69.30–3, 84–5). Moreover, in China it was traditionally believed that the spirit of someone who died by violence could not be pacified until his assassin was killed in turn; otherwise the deceased victim would himself suffer the pains of hell ("Cina," 174).

Before leaving his homeland to avenge his father's death in accordance with this belief, the chastened Mandricardo carries out a religious act that begs interpretation: "Nel tempio de so' dei ne fo venuto / E sopra al foco offerse la corona" ("[he] sought the temple of his gods / and dedicated to the fire / his crown") (*OI* 3.1.13). This non-Islamic practice is consistent with what Europeans could have heard about the importance of fire in Mongol ritual. On various occasions Marco Polo refers to fire in the context of religious worship, including an end-of-year celebration in which an altar and table were set on fire (*Mil.* 88.11, 115–16).[2] Based on data from the thirteenth century, Heissig cites this yearly fire ceremony and invocations to the fire god in the context of other religious events. In one of these, the community presented "the best things which the nomadic pastoral economy had to offer" to the fire deity, who developed from a protector of the family "into a god to whom was entrusted the increase and prosperity of the people and the princes" (75). Mandricardo likewise offers to the fire his most valuable possession, the crown that symbolizes his kingship.

The setting described by Boiardo may also call to mind a Zoroastrian fire temple. Marco Polo informs us that near the site of the Three Magi there was a "castello de li oratori del fuoco" ("castle of the fire worshippers"), who "tutti li sacrifici che fanno condisco di quello fuoco" ("seasoned all their sacrifices with that fire") (*Mil.* 30.5–31.5, 34–5). Although the worship of Zoroaster decreased with the spread of Islam, such temples were still found in Persia at the time of Tamerlane's conquests (Marozzi 109).[3] Apart from whether Mandricardo's fire temple was meant to recall shamanistic or Zoroastrian practices, Boiardo's evocation of a non-Muslim religious ceremonial despite Mandricardo's designation as a Saracen may suggest the mixing of cultural traditions that resulted from the interaction between the Mongols and neighbouring populations. Marco Polo, in fact, had made a point of noting the contamination of original Tartar customs with those of the conquered lands, in this case Cathay: "quegli che usano au Ca[t]a se mantengono li costumi degl'idoli, e ànno lasciata loro legge; e quegli che usano i llevante tegnono la maniera degli saracini" ("Those who deal with Cathay maintain the customs of the idols, leaving their law intact; and those who deal with the Levant go by the manner of the Saracens") (*Mil.* 69.24, 83–4).

Given the earlier reference to Agricane's distressed spirit in the otherworld, Mandricardo's solemn gesture within a fire temple serves to highlight the gravity of the latter's oath to avenge his father's death. In addition to his public show of respect towards ancestral gods and ritual practices, Mandricardo also swears never to use armour or weapons until he has succeeded in his goal. While extreme vows of this nature are certainly not absent from other epic texts, this particular gesture echoes that of a historical Mongol khan. Marco Polo tells us that when Kublai Khan learned of a rebellious vassal and nephew, "disse che mai no volea portare corona né tenere terra, se questi due traditori no mettesse a morte" ("he said that he never wanted to wear a crown or hold land until he had put these two traitors to death") (*Mil.* 77.1, 98).

After Mandricardo leaves his Mongol homeland, however, his mission takes on the form of a romance adventure. At the enchanted *Fonte della Fata* (Fountain of the Fay) located in or near Syria, he obtains the armour of Hector of Troy by emerging victorious as a result of sheer chance. The fay then abruptly makes him swear to seize Orlando's sword by force of arms:

> E ciò mi giurerai sula tua fede:
> Che Durindana, lo incantato brando,
> Torai per forza de arme al conte Orlando.
>
> On your faith you must swear to me
> that you'll win magic Durindana
> from Count Orlando in a duel. (*OI* 3.2.35)

Mandricardo's vow to accomplish the fairy's command in order to gain an enchanted sword gives new purpose to his original mission to avenge his father's death by killing Orlando.

As Mandricardo continues his journey towards the West, he increasingly takes on the guise of an individual knight errant. When he sets out from the fountain along with Gradasso, whom he had freed from the fairy's spell, the two knights are said to be the most valiant in the entire pagan world: "un par tanto gagliardo / Non fu in quel tempo in tutta Paganìa" ("such a valiant pair / was not then found in pagan lands") (*OI* 3.2.39). They display their chivalric virtue in typical Arthurian fashion when they rush to liberate a damsel in distress, the Cypriot princess Lucina chained to a rock along the Mediterranean coastline (*OI* 3.3.24–54). As the episode develops into an Odyssean-like romance adventure, Mandricardo is singled out for distinction: while running from the blind ogre who holds Lucina and now also Gradasso captive, he tricks his pursuer into running off a cliff and breaking his ribs. Whereas Odysseus had used separate stratagems to blind the Cyclops and to escape from his cave, Mandricardo incapacitates the ogre and frees himself in one fell swoop. He is then able to rescue the others and find safety in Lucina's father's ship before the ogre begins hurling rocks at them in the manner of his Homeric predecessor.

When Mandricardo and Gradasso arrive in southern France following a tempest at sea, they continue to act in quintessential Arthurian fashion. They greet Rugiero "de animo perfetto" ("with courtesy") and show their adherence to the code of courtly love first by telling him that his enamourment is proof of his "gentilezza" ("gentility") and then by offering to come to his aid (*OI* 3.6.36). Even their challenge to each other upon discovering their mutual desire for Orlando's sword keeps them grounded in the world of romance (*OI* 3.6.45–54). As Rugiero laughs at the silliness of their battle, since neither at the time is in possession of Durindana, the reader could ponder how these two powerful rulers from Tartary and Sericana are in France as knights errant fighting over a symbol of knighthood rather than seeking to overtake Christendom with vast armies at their command.

After Mandricardo is excluded from the subsequent Arthurian adventure of the *Fonte del Riso* (Laughing Stream) through a lottery, he is propelled back into an epic arena. In the same stanza in which he loses the draw, the angry warrior reaches Paris and joins the ongoing North African invasion of that city (*OI* 3.7.5). The final completed canto of the poem shows him scaling the walls together with Feraguto and the African kings Agramante and Rodamonte (*OI* 3.8.15), destroying the barrier and gate of a bridge (*OI* 3.8.25), fighting Christians (*OI* 3.8.45), and even rescuing Agramante single-handed (*OI* 3.8.47–8). Likewise drawn into the battle is Orlando, who upon emerging from the Laughing Stream has apparently forgotten Angelica as he rejoins the ranks of Charlemagne's paladins. Orlando's welcome presence in Paris – for the first time since the opening of the poem – also brings the focus back once again to Mandricardo's double goal: to avenge his father's death and to win Durindana by challenging its owner to mortal combat.

Ariosto's Mandricardo

Boiardo's Mandricardo had started out as a ruthless tyrant, a scourge of neighbouring peoples and his own subjects; yet on his way to France he is transformed into a courteous knight errant. His downfall in the *Furioso* comes more quickly than that of Gradasso. Although he is introduced as the strongest and most courageous knight in the East or West (*OF* 12.30 A; 14.30 C), a homage that seemingly goes beyond even Boiardo's celebration of his knightly qualities, Ariosto affords him no room for courtesy. Indeed, by the time of his death in canto 28/30 there seems to be no positive attribute of his left to celebrate, and he is quickly forgotten by both the characters and the poet.

Mandricardo's character is initially defined by his two previous vows: the one made to himself to avenge his father's death by killing Orlando (*OI* 3.1.13–14) and that made to the Fountain Fay to conquer Orlando's sword by force (*OI* 3.2.37). Ariosto singles out in particular the Fountain of the Fay adventure when crediting the knight with many illustrious deeds (*OF* 12.31 A; 14.31 C), and Mandricardo later restates both his promise to acquire Durindana and his oath to kill Orlando (*OF* 21.78–9 A; 23.78–9 C). Nonetheless, Agricane's heir is repeatedly portrayed as a breaker of vows and a usurper of the possessions of others in their absence. When he finds that an unknown knight dressed in black (none other than Orlando) has decimated Agramante's allies, he sets out from camp "e giura non tornare a quelle schiere / se non trova il campion da l'arme nere" ("swearing not to return to the Saracen host unless he found the black knight") (*OF* 12.34 A; 14.34 C). Yet all of his resolve dissipates when a day and a half later he comes upon a convoy escorting Princess Doralice of Granada to Rodomonte. After slaughtering the entire entourage, he kidnaps the lady. He is so happy with "la gran preda" ("the rich prize") that he is no longer in a hurry to catch up with the black knight; indeed, what he seeks instead is "alcun commodo luoco / per exhalar tanto amoroso fuoco" ("some convenient lodging in which to unleash his pent-up amorous passion") (*OF* 12.56 A; 14.56 C). Whereas Boiardo's Mandricardo had just been in Paris fighting alongside Rodamonte, Ariosto imagines the Tartar dishonestly seizing his comrade's bride-to-be.

Mandricardo's subsequent acquisition of Durindana is also in flagrant violation of the chivalric code. When he initially challenges Orlando for the rights to the sword, the latter courteously declares his willingness to place the contested weapon aside:

> Quantunque sia debitamente mia,
> per gentilezza vuo' che si contenda:
> né perché habbi a temer vuo' che mi stia
> al fianco, anzi ad uno arbore s'appenda. (*OF* 21.81 A)

> Mine though it is by right,
> let us stage a chivalrous duel for it;
> and let us hang it from a tree –
> I wouldn't have it be mine any more
> than yours during our combat. (*OF* 23.81 C)

After their bout has been interrupted, however, Mandricardo ends up returning to the tree and taking advantage of his opponent's absence to snatch the weapon. He thus completely disregards both his earlier vows, which required a victory in combat against Orlando, and Orlando's own statement regarding the conditions under which he could attain the coveted object: "Levala tu liberamente via, / s'avien che tu m'uccida o che mi prenda" ("You are free to take it in the event / that you slay or capture me") (*OF* 21.81 A; 23.81 C). Rajna, in fact, wryly observes that "Mandricardo has appropriated Orlando's sword without winning it" (*Le fonti*, 422).

Mandricardo not only takes possession of Durindana against the laws of chivalry, but when Zerbino attempts to defend Orlando's honour in his absence, he ruthlessly overwhelms the disadvantaged knight with the sword he has just usurped. His illicit use of the contested weapon here is especially reprehensible given Orlando's precedent of forsaking his rightful advantage.[4] The nobility of Zerbino's motive further blackens Mandricardo's character. As Marco Praloran remarks, "Killing the English prince who is fighting [...] to defend the armour of Orlando and who represents the figure of the young hero, Mandricardo's *ethos* – even though he is the winner of a perfectly canonical duel – sharpens his negative characterization [and] implicitly opens a demand for vengeance that will reach completion fully in the duel against Ruggiero" (117).[5]

Just as the reader was induced to sympathize with Zerbino in the earlier combat, Ariosto sets up Mandricardo's definitive duel against Ruggiero in a way that unequivocally favours his challenger. Praloran writes: "The identification of the public with Ruggiero, the fear for his death, are sentiments that are easily discernible" (121–2). In the *Innamorato*, Mandricardo had already challenged Rugiero to a duel near the Laughing Stream after noticing that the youth's shield bore Hector's insignia (*OI* 3.6.40). In the deferred contest staged in the *Furioso*, Mandricardo not only fails to win that knight's insignia but simultaneously loses Hector's armour, Orlando's sword, and Rodomonte's Doralice, as well as his own life.

With his death Mandricardo even loses his value in the estimation of others, whether as a fighter or a lover. Agramante's attention is completely absorbed by the victory of Ruggiero, whose worth suddenly grows exponentially in his eyes (*OF* 28.70 A; 30.70 C). Not even Doralice spends time mourning her deceased companion. Ariosto imagines that the Spanish princess might easily have fallen in love with Ruggiero, the very knight who had just killed her lover, if shame had not curtailed her actions. He even goes on to expound her hypothetical reasoning process, dictated by the need for a warm, strong man to satisfy her sexual desires:

Per lei buono era vivo Mandricardo:
ma che ne volea far dopo la morte?
Proveder le convien d'un che gagliardo
sia notte e dì ne' suoi bisogni, e forte. (*OF* 28.73 A)

Mandricardo living was all very well –
but what use was he to her, dead?
For her needs she had to secure a man
who was vigorous by night and day. (*OF* 30.73 C)

Doralice's instantaneous dismissal of Mandricardo provides a conspicuous contrast to Isabella's profound bereavement at the death of her beloved Zerbino.

The characters' overall indifference to Mandricardo's death also invites comparison with the emotionally charged circumstances surrounding his father's demise. In the *Innamorato* Orlando weepingly asked Agricane's forgiveness for the fatal blow:

Egli avea pien di lachryme la facia
E fo smontato in sula terra piana;
Ricolse il Re ferito nele bracia

E sopra al marmo il pose ala fontana.
E' di pianger con seco non si sacia,
Chiedendoli perdon con voce humana.

His eyes were filled with tears as he
dismounted to the level field.
He took the gored king in his arms
and set him on the marble by
the fountain, weeping with him while
he asked for pardon for his deeds. (*OI* 1.19.16)

In the *Furioso*, however, not even Ariosto pays further attention to Mandricardo as his corpse presumably grows cold upon the ground.

Chapter Five

Marphisa, Eastern Queen

Boiardo's Marphisa

Unlike Boiardo's other invented protagonists from beyond Christian Europe, Marphisa is not identified with any specific country or region. When she arrives in Albracà to defend Galafrone against Agricane, Boiardo characterizes her as the greatest warrior throughout the East: "non ha cavalier tutto il Levante / Che la contrasti sopra dela sella" ("not a knight in all the East / could match her in the saddle") (*OI* 1.16.28). This absence of specific geographical markers corresponds to Marphisa's cosmopolitan character: she consistently interacts with others based on a universal code of chivalry that transcends all national and religious barriers.

Marphisa has sworn not to remove her breastplate until defeating three of the world's greatest kings: Gradasso, Agricane, and Charlemagne (*OI* 1.16.29, 1.20.45). Tellingly, her challenge is directed against two rulers from Asia and only one from Europe. In some sense, Marphisa's boundless faith in her own martial prowess recalls that of the poem's first over-reacher, Gradasso. Just as the king of Sericana earlier thought that by himself he could subdue all the earth (*OI* 1.1.7), so this indomitable queen declares her intention to wage war against the entire world after destroying Albracà: "Poi che disfata avrò la roca a tondo, / Vuò pigliar guera contra tuto il mondo" ("When I have razed her citadel, / I want to battle all the world!") (*OI* 1.20.44). At one point she even extends her challenge to the Saracen divinities: when she does not succeed immediately in defeating her opponent, she not only dares Mohammed and Trivigante to descend to earth but threatens to kill them and burn Paradise should she ever find a way to reach the sky (*OI* 1.18.10). Just as

Marphisa's aspirations are not defined by specific geographical boundaries, so she does not form alliances for political expediency. She initially arrives at Albracà as an ally of Angelica's father, Galafrone (*OI* 1.16.28), yet when the king interferes with her battle against Ranaldo, thus breaking the chivalric code, she is so enraged that she switches sides without a moment's hesitation.

Marphisa's ensuing opposition to Galafrone puts into relief her contrast with Angelica, whom she condemns for her manipulative use of sexuality, deceit, and magic (*OI* 1.20.43). Since Angelica is renowned for her beauty, Boiardo could have further underscored the difference between the two female characters by describing Marphisa as ugly, fearsome, or unwomanly, but he chooses not to do so: "Tanto è gagliarda, e ancor non è men bela" ("She / was bold – as bold as she was lovely") (*OI* 1.16.28).[1] Comparing their physical features in juxtaposed stanzas, Boiardo conveys Marphisa's unique combination of beauty and strength:

> Non fo veduta mai cosa più bella:
> Rivolto al capo avìa le chiome bionde
> E gli ochi vivi assai più ch'una stella.
> A sua beltate ogni cosa risponde,
> Destra negli ati e d'ardita favella,
> Brunetta alquanto e grande di persona.
> Turpino la vidde, e ciò di lei ragiona.
>
> She was more fair than any maiden.
> She wore her blonde hair up, and her
> eyes were more lively than a star.
> Everything answered to her beauty.
> Her dextrous movements, confident
> speech, her long legs, her tawny color –
> that's what Turpino says, who saw her. (*OI* 1.27.59)

While Angelica flaunts her feminine attributes in dealing with others, viewing the poem's male knights as either suitors to be exploited (Orlando, Sacripante), objects of desire to be pursued (Ranaldo), or aggressors to be thwarted (Agricane), Marphisa as a knight in armour is defined not by her beauty, but by her valour. Relying on traditionally male weapons to prevail in a world otherwise dominated by men, Marphisa "ha tanta arroganza e sì gran boria / Che vergognata se stima e vilissima / E che beffando ognon dietro li rida, / Se tutto il mondo a morte non disfida" ("had presumption and such pride / she'd think herself disgraced and shamed / and mocked by men behind her back / unless she dared the world to death") (*OI* 1.24.1).

Marphisa's interaction with other knights is not exclusively hostile, however; on the contrary, she readily engages in camaraderie with those who gain her respect. Tellingly, this human side of her character is revealed through her friendship not with a fellow Eastern ruler but with the Frankish knight Ranaldo. When Marphisa turns against Galafrone for interrupting their contest, she quickly finds herself surrounded by his army. Ranaldo's initial reaction is to step aside, assuming it is God's providence that these "pagans" should kill each other (*OI* 1.19.42). Yet this fleeting nod to religious difference only serves to underscore the significance of his subsequent actions on Marphisa's behalf. When the number of her assailants gives them an unfair advantage, Ranaldo's sense of justice wins out over any other considerations, and he offers his aid to the intrepid warrior maiden at the risk of his life: "Io te voglio aiutare, / Se ben dovessi teco esserne morto" ("I want to help, / even if I must die with you") (*OI* 1.19.47). Marphisa's acceptance conveys her sincere esteem for the foreign knight: "Cavalier iocondo, / Poi che sei meco, più non stimo il mondo!" ("Jolly knight, if you're / with me, then I can fight the world") (*OI* 1.19.47). In fact, their joint effort succeeds in thwarting the onslaught.

When Marphisa and Ranaldo subsequently join forces as comrades in arms, they completely transform the nature of the war at Albracà. Whereas until this point the fighting had focused on the rivalry over Angelica, these two new friends team up to eradicate evil personified in the figure of Trufaldino. Ranaldo had already learned of the cruelties of the Babylonian tyrant who "non ha paragone / Di tradimenti, inganni e di mal fiele" ("has no equal / for crime, deceit, and treachery") (*OI* 1.20.43) and had vowed to avenge his torture and murder of the damsel Albarosa. When Marphisa informs him that the perfidious ruler is inside the castle with Angelica, Ranaldo declares his readiness to join her ranks: "Con tieco son contento dimorare, / E star sotto tua insegna e tua divisa, / Sin ch'abi Trufaldino a conquistare" ("I'm happy to enlist with you / and fight beneath your signs and pennants / until you've conquered Truffaldino") (*OI* 1.20.48).

The tandem Marphisa-Ranaldo induces two more knights to switch sides and join their camp, tellingly one a Christian and the other a Saracen. The former is Astolfo of England, who had been defending Angelica since his arrival in Albracà (*OI* 1.10.17) but who changes allegiance when he learns of Ranaldo's presence (*OI* 1.25.33). The latter is "Torindo, il gran Turco" (*OI* 1.20.51), who is originally introduced as a valiant ally of Galafrone along with the king of Media (*OI* 1.10.39–40). After he is treacherously caught in his sleep and imprisoned by Trufaldino, however, upon his release he vows to pay Angelica back for harbouring a scoundrel who would have let him die in chains (*OI* 1.20.54). The bond between Marphisa and Ranaldo, extending to Astolfo the Englishman and Torindo the Turk, demonstrates how representatives of East and West can act in concert through mutual understanding, respect, and esteem, as well as common interests, opinions, and chivalric values. By naming the Turkish ally Torindo, moreover, Boiardo rehabilitates the name of a non-Christian character previously used negatively in Carolingian epics. In the *Storia di Rinaldino di Montalbano*, a "Torindo di Turchia" figures as the protagonist's opponent, unjustly waging war against the neophyte Christian king of Syria in revenge for the latter's marriage to the princess of Persia (230–85). The *Guerrin Meschino*'s Torindo is likewise a less than admirable character: by deceitfully trying to take credit for Guerrino's victory in a joust, the Turkish prince causes his father to declare an untimely war against the Byzantine emperor (*Guerrino* 1.15, 39).[2]

Boiardo portrays Marphisa as a model knight in her unconditional adherence to the chivalric code. When she agrees to a safe-conduct for Angelica to watch the battle between Ranaldo and Orlando, everyone is said to feel safe to move about without danger (*OI* 1.27.43). Moreover, having promised Orlando not to intervene on behalf of Ranaldo (*OI* 1.26.56), she never considers breaking her word even though she fears that the latter has been mortally wounded. Instead, she silently weeps, revealing a hidden tenderness beneath her nerves of steel: "E Marphisa tacendo lacrymava, / Perché pose Renaldo al tuto perso" ("and quietly Marfisa wept / because she thought Ranaldo lost") (*OI* 1.28.27).

There are elements of Marphisa's character and story line that have led readers from the sixteenth century on to associate her with the Amazon queen Penthesilea and Virgil's warrior maiden Camilla.[3] Both prior figures are also known for friendships with male warriors. In Guido delle Colonne's account of the Trojan War, Penthesilea "was closely bound to Hector in friendship on account of the exceeding merit of her valor" (203). She fights at Troy in Hector's memory until she too loses her life at the hands of Achilles. Boiardo explicitly pays tribute to this epic friendship later in his poem when he notes that Hector's sword passed to none other than Penthesilea after his death (*OI* 3.1.28). Virgil's Camilla fights as the friend and ally of the noble warrior Turnus. Virgil describes her character as that of "a warrior girl whose hands / Were never deft at distaff or wool baskets, / Skills of Minerva, she was hard and trained / To take the shock of war" (*Aen.* 7.1107–10). Marphisa likewise despises such traditionally feminine tasks since she scornfully threatens to reduce Agricane to spinning thread inside the fortress after she has defeated him (*OI* 1.17.65).

Marphisa does not share the distinguishing characteristics of either the Amazons or Virgil's Camilla, however. While the mythic women warriors engaged periodically in intercourse for the purpose of procreation while living in an all-female community, Marphisa, by contrast, has no relations with men beyond friendship and shows no solidarity with other women. She loathes Angelica, later insults the maiden Fiordelisa, and never encounters the poem's other *donna guerriera*, Bradamante. Nor does Marphisa share Camilla's complaints about the limitations prescribed by her gender, since she knows no such bounds. Whereas Virgil's female warrior fights primarily from a distance using the bow and the javelin, Marphisa fights up front and close with her sword. In the end, moreover, both Penthesilea and Camilla die in battle after a relatively brief episode while Marphisa will eventually leave the epic arena behind her and move on to further adventures.[4]

Whereas Boiardo does not provide Marphisa with a personal history, Niccolò degli Agostini anticipates Ariosto by revealing in his 1505 continuation of the *Innamorato* that she is the daughter of the North African female warrior Galicielia and the Christian knight Rugiero (*OI* 4.10.73).[5] The tragic vicissitudes of this couple are related in Italian rewritings of the old French *Aspremont*.[6] In Andrea da Barberino's prose version (*Aspramonte*, 1.8.5–6, 11), Galiziella, the daughter of the North African king Agolante and an Amazon warrior, is raised among her mother's clan and subsequently welcomed into her father's family despite her illegitimate birth. Highly esteemed for her military prowess, she will only wed a man who can best her in a show of arms. When Riccieri defeats her, she converts to Christianity in order to marry him, and the couple live in Reggio Calabria until the treachery of Riccieri's brother Beltramo brings their happiness to an end. According to Pio Rajna, Boiardo had already intended for Marphisa to emerge as the long-lost daughter of this heroic couple (*Le fonti*, 510), but there is no clear textual evidence in the *Innamorato* supporting such a parentage.[7]

Whatever Boiardo's intentions regarding Marphisa's genealogy, Andrea da Barberino's Galiziella is not a sufficient literary model for his Eastern queen any more than Penthesilea, Camilla, or the various women warriors of the medieval epic tradition.[8] Moreover, whereas Galiziella, like Pentesilea and Camilla, is restricted to a single episode, Marphisa breaks out of the confines of the war at Albracà when Brunello steals her sword. Her exasperated chase of the little trickster thief, which has both comic and serious moments, moves Marphisa from the battlefield of epic to the open space of romance adventure. She is last seen in the poem as she encounters two unidentified knights who, Boiardo announces, will eventually lead her to France (*OI* 2.19.15). Although this development suggests that Marphisa would have played a major part in Agramante's war, it is not clear which side she would have taken, given her previous friendship with Ranaldo on the one hand and her vow to challenge Charlemagne on the other – not to mention her readiness to switch alliances when offended.

Ariosto's Marphisa

Although Marphisa figures prominently in the *Furioso*, her character changes substantially in the latter part of the poem. Pio Rajna, who maintains that Marphisa, "as she is represented by Boiardo, is worthy even of being declared the most ingenious creation ever produced in Italian romance epic poetry," speaks of a "lowering of tone" in Ariosto's treatment of her (*Le fonti*, 53–4). Yet the differences go well beyond a question of tone: while Marphisa initially continues to play the part of the intrepid warrior who is nevertheless ready to bond with worthy knights regardless of their religion, after her conversion in the final cantos of the poem Ariosto turns her into a zealous Christian crusader and blatantly rewrites her prior history in the process.[9]

When Marphisa appears in the *Furioso* in canto 16/18, Ariosto seems ready to cast her in the role of an Arthurian knight by claiming that she travels about seeking glory by fighting knights errant:

> e 'l dì e la notte armata sempre andava
> di qua e di là cercando in monte e in piano
> con cavallieri erranti riscontrarsi,
> et immortale e gloriosa farsi. (*OF* 16.99 A)

> Day and night she was always armed,
> always on the prowl, up hill and down dale,
> alert to measure herself against knights errant
> and foster her immortal fame. (*OF* 18.99 C)

Following up on Boiardo's announcement of the chance encounter with two knights who will lead Marphisa to France, Ariosto imagines that she has met up with Astolfo and Sansonetto on their way to a tournament in Damascus. Recognizing the English prince as her former comrade at Albracà, Marphisa joyously embraces him ("con gran festa ad abbracciarlo venne"; *OF* 16.101 A; 18.101 C). Indeed, the poet seems keen to confirm that the bond the warrior queen had developed in the *Innamorato* with Ranaldo and Astolfo has been carried over to this new situation. When Marphisa declares her intention to join the two knights in the upcoming tournament (*OF* 16.102 A; 18.102 C), they are overjoyed at the prospect of her company: "Sommamente hebbe Astolfo grata questa / compagna d'arme, et così Sansonetto" ("Astolfo was highly pleased to have Marphisa for companion at arms, and so was Samsonet") (*OF* 16.103 A; 18.103 C). Ariosto subsequently refers to the trio as friends and good companions ("amici e buon compagni"; *OF* 16.132 A; 18.132 C).

If earlier Boiardo's Marphisa had remained distant from the characteristics of the Amazons, who regularly served as the prototype for virago figures, Ariosto provides his character with an occasion to demonstrate even more concretely that she has little in common with this female warrior type. Marphisa and her male companions eventually set sail for France, but a storm at sea blows them off course and they are forced to land "nel golfo di Laiazzo invêr Sorìa" ("in the Gulf of Alexandretta, towards Syria") (*OF* 17.54 A; 19.54 C) where they are met by six thousand women armed with bows and decked out for war. They have in fact arrived at the land of the "femine homicide" ("killer-women") (*OF* 17.57 A; 19.57 C), a society composed of women warriors as hostile to men as the mythical Amazons. Throughout the episode Marphisa acts in solidarity with her male companions against her supposed female counterparts. In order to save her friends from death, she takes up the challenge to fight ten knights in mortal combat by day and then satisfy ten women in bed at night. Remarking that for the second task she would use her sword just as Alexander cut the Gordian knot, Marphisa famously dismisses gender distinctions just as she ignores difference based on geographical provenance and religion.

When Marphisa later encounters Ruggiero, Ricciardetto, and Aldigier, she joins them in rescuing the latter's brothers Malagigi and Viviano from Saracens who planned to hand them over to the murderous Maganza clan in exchange for gold, clothing, and other precious goods (*OF* 24.7 A; 26.7 C). This joint undertaking of two Saracen and two Christian knights without any thought to religious difference is reminiscent of the collaboration between Marphisa, Torindo, Ranaldo, and Astolfo at Albracà in opposition to the treachery of Trufaldino. The adventure also serves to initiate the camaraderie between Marphisa and Ruggiero that matches, and eventually surpasses, the personal friendship and military alliance between Marphisa and Ranaldo in the Albracà episode. Indeed, whereas Boiardo's Marphisa had cried in silence when she believed Ranaldo to be mortally wounded, Ariosto's character will now take it upon herself to nurse Ruggiero back to health (*OF* 30.30 A; 32.34 C).

The bond between Marphisa and Ruggiero, aside from prompting Bradamante's unfounded jealousy, prepares the reader for the subsequent disclosure that they are long-lost twins. At the same time, however, when the spirit of Atlante reveals Marphisa's identity in order to stop her battle against Ruggiero, it is not her role of sister but rather that of daughter which claims our attention. Identifying Marphisa's parents as Ruggiero II and Galaciella, Atlante rewrites events from the *Aspramonte* and the *Innamorato* in order to shift the blame to the African side. The earlier narratives had singled out the Christian Beltramo as the most blameworthy for having treacherously handed over Reggio Calabria to the North African Almonte out of jealous spite when the warrior maiden preferred his brother to him. In Andrea da Barberino's prose version, Galiziella herself cries out to the treacherous Beltramo: "Tu ài morto te medesimo, e il tuo padre, e' tuoi fratelli, e la tua città, e' tuoi cittadini e la tua patria" ("You have murdered yourself, and your father, and your brothers, and your city, and your fellow citizens and your fatherland") (*Asp.* 1.42.31–3, 41). After killing Riccieri and taking over the city, Galiziella's brother Almonte has Beltramo thrown into a fire to punish him for his villainous act (*Asp.* 1.44.12–13, 43). According to Andrea, Galiziella was subsequently either burned at the stake or secretly sent back to be imprisoned in North Africa, where she possibly gave birth to a son and a daughter (*Asp.* 1.44.13–16, 43).

Although Boiardo does not link Marphisa to this earlier narrative, as noted above, he keeps the focus on Beltramo's treachery when relating the origins of Rugiero. The King of Garamanta explicitly states that his father, Rugiero II, was betrayed ("fu tradito"; *OI* 2.1.72) and that his mother Galaciella returned to Africa ("a nostra gente") to give birth. Their son Rugiero later provides a more in-depth account of the circumstances:

La voglia di Beltramo traditore
Contra del patre se fece ribella,

E questo fu per scelerato amore
Che egli avea posto alla Gallacïella,
[...]
Morto fu poscia con extremo oltragio,
Né magior tradimento vide el mondo,
Perché Beltramo, el perfido inhumano,
Tradìte el patre e il suo franco germano.
Riza, la terra, andò tutta a roina,
Arse le case, e fu morta la gente

Beltramo's lust made him rebel
against his father. His betrayal
arose from his illicit love
for Galaciella
[...]
That knight's betrayal and his murder
were the world's most unnatural.
Inhuman, infamous Beltramo
sold out his father and his brother.
He let the enemy take Reggio,
burn its homes, slay the population. (*OI* 3.5.31–4)

After unequivocally blaming Beltramo for the death of his father and brothers and for the ensuing destruction of Reggio, Rugiero then relates that Galaciella escaped to give birth on the shores of Africa before expiring.

In Niccolò degli Agostini's continuation, Marphisa's account of her birth closely follows Boiardo's precedent, underscoring the treachery of Beltramo even to the point of omitting the role of the North African invaders: "Et fu mia madre la Galicielia, / la qual poi che Beltramo el traditore / occise a torto la persona fella, / l'amato sposo suo pie di valore, / sendo fugita alla marina quella, / ivi mi parturì con gran dolore" ("And my mother was Galaciella / Who, after Beltramo the traitor, / The evil person, unjustly murdered / Her beloved husband full of valor, / Fleeing to the marina / She there gave birth to me in great pain") (*OI* 4.10.73). And just as earlier Rugiero had converted to Christianity out of love for Bradamante, Marphisa now converts wholly out of love for her newfound brother: "Et scieppe si ben dire el cavaliero / che per suo amor si fece christiana" ("And the knight knew how to speak so well / that out of love for him she became a Christian") (*OI* 4.11.3). There is no trace of hatred against the Africans or desire for revenge against non-Christians in this episode.

In the *Furioso*, Atlante's summary of events, while acknowledging Beltramo's betrayal, focuses instead on the murderous deeds of the Africans. This time, moreover, it is not Almonte alone, but Galaciella's unnamed "fratelli" ("brothers") who are said to have killed her husband and deliberately sought her death by placing her in an unmanned boat (*OF* 33.64; 36.60 C). In addition, following Atlante's revelation Ruggiero identifies Agolante's sons as both Almonte and the father of Agramante ("padre d'Agramante"), and then relates that "Agolante e i figli iniqui e felli" ("Agolant and his cruel, evil sons") (*OF* 33.78 A; 36.72–4) set Galaciella in the boat to die at sea. This new account not only takes agency away from the woman, who in Boiardo's version set sail on her own initiative, but specifically accuses Agramante's absent father, Troiano, of these iniquitous actions. Ariosto reinforces his revised version by repeating it for a third time, now from the point of view of Marphisa when she hears "ch'el padre d'Agramante e l'avo e il zio / Ruggiero a tradigion feron morire, e posero la moglie a caso rio" ("[of] the treacherous murder of their father by Agramant's father, grandfather, and uncle, and [of] the ordeal inflicted upon their mother") (*OF* 33.80 A; 36.76 C).

Ariosto's thrice-repeated summary of the story thus holds Agramante's father, Troiano, and grandfather, Agolante, responsible for the death of both Marphisa's parents. This flies in the face of literary history, since in previous versions neither took part in the surreptitious attack on Reggio negotiated by Beltramo and Almonte.[10] Nevertheless, it may sound familiar to readers given that earlier in the poem, as Bradamante lamented Ruggiero's delay in joining her, she imagined addressing him thus: "Fu morto da Troian (non so se 'l sai) / el padre tuo; ma fin a' sassi il sanno" ("Your father was slain by Trojan [can you not realize this? – the very stones know it!]") (*OF* 30.83 C). Rather than recalling the precise events at this time, Bradamante's assertion simply claims universal recognition in a way that could compel the unwary reader to take its veracity for granted.[11]

Pio Rajna, in noting how in this version of events "Almonte's merciful act [of sparing Galaciella from death] is converted into a kind of fratricide," posits a possible motivation on Ariosto's part that would explain his inclusion of Troiano at the same time: "I imagine that it was desirable to add new reasons for Ruggiero and Marphisa to hate the family of Agolante and embrace the Christian faith" (*Le fonti*, 517). In fact, stunned by the news of her origin, Marphisa declares:

Io fo ben voto a Dio, che adorar voglio
Christo Dio vero ch'adorò mio padre,
che di questa armatura non mi spoglio
fin che Ruggier non vendico e mia madre. (*OF* 33.82 A)

I swear to God that I mean to adore
Christ as true God, just as my father did,
and not to take off this armour till
I have avenged him and my mother. (*OF* 36.78 C)

Thus, in the same breath that she converts to Christianity she also swears to avenge her parents by killing Agramante.[12]

Although Marphisa's new vow to the Christian God echoes her initial oath to Mohammed and Trivigante, there is a notable difference in her motivation. While her prior intention to challenge the world's three greatest kings would have demonstrated her valour as a knight, her present aim is exclusively that of revenge. Moreover, since she identifies with her Christian father and considers Agramante to be her enemy, her animosity and loyalty are now determined solely by religious difference. In this light, Marphisa's earlier collaboration with Christian knights, while seeming to show her lack of concern for religious creed as it did in Boiardo's poem, now appears to have been a foreshadowing on Ariosto's part that she was destined to join the ranks of Christendom's foremost warriors.

Ariosto proceeds to rewrite Marphisa's entire past in the ensuing scene at Charlemagne's court. When she is baptized by the bishop Turpino and "reborn" as a Carolingian paladin, Marphisa relates startling new information about her life both prior to and concurrent with the *Innamorato* narrative. Elaborating on Atlante's earlier disclosure that she had been kidnapped at a young age by "una masnada / d'Aràbi" ("a band of Arabs") (*OF* 33.67 A; 36.63 C), Marphisa reveals to Charlemagne that she was subsequently sold as a slave in Persia where she became the intended sexual prey of the king, whom she killed to preserve her virginity. Without pause she goes on to tell how she slaughtered the entire court, drove out all the ruler's wicked progeny, and seized seven more kingdoms to boot. This envisions the Orient stereotypically as a dangerous site of corruption and lechery. Yet what is most shocking about Marphisa's autobiographical account is not the lecherous sultan or her own disproportionate response but rather the new hostility she espouses towards the religiously other. She "confesses" to Charlemagne that she had previously envied his fame because he was of another faith:

E (per narrarti il ver) sola mi mosse
Invidia, e sol per farti guerra venni,
acciò che sì potente un Re non fosse
che non tenesse la legge ch'io tenni.
Per questo ho fatto le campagne rosse
Del christian sangue; et altri fieri cenni
ero per farti da crudel nemica,
se non cadea chi mi t'ha fatto amica. (*OF* 34.13 A)

And, truth to tell, my sole motive has been envy:
I came only to make war on you – for there was to be no king,
however mighty, but must hold to the law I held.
To this end I have dyed the fields red with Christian blood;
and I was all prepared to manifest further tokens
of my cruel hostility had I not fallen in with one
who has made me your friend. (*OF* 38.13 C)

In her new calling as a paladin of Christ, Marphisa not only belies her own history in the two poems by claiming a prior attitude of envy and hatred towards Christendom but, accusing Troiano as well as Almonte of the crime against her parents, she transfers all of her supposed hatred to Agramante:

e quella invidia e quel odio protervo
ch'io t'hebbi un tempo, qui tutto depono;
anzi pur contra il Re d'Aphrica il servo,
e contra tutti quei che scesi sono
da Troiano e d'Aimonte, che fur rei
de l'empia morte de' genitor miei. (*OF* 34.17 A)

And the jealousy, the insolent hatred
I felt against you I now put by –
or rather I reserve it all for Agramant and for
all those who [descended from Troiano and Almonte, who]
were guilty of my parents' death. (*OF* 38.17 C)

Her desire to become a Christian is tied not only to her mission to kill Agramante, however, but to a new large-scale military agenda:

E seguitò, voler christiana farsi,

e poi che haverà extinto il Re Agramante,
voler, piacendo a Carlo, ritornarsi
a battizar il suo regno in Levante;
et indi contra tutto il mondo armarsi,
dove Machon s'adori e Trivigante;
e con promissïon, ch'ogni suo acquisto
sia de l'Imperio e de la fé di Christo. (*OF* 34.18 A)

She wished to become a Christian, she continued.
Then, after dispatching Agramant,
she proposed, if Charlemagne agreed,
to go back to her Eastern kingdom and baptize it.
This done, she would make war against any part of
the world where Mahomet and Trivigant were worshipped:
her every conquest, she promised, would be a gain
for the Holy Roman Empire and for the Christian Faith. (*OF* 38.18 C)

Marphisa's plan to arm herself exclusively against Islam for the greater glory of the Holy Roman Empire and the Christian faith brings resoundingly into play the rhetoric of the crusades. Her individual transformation from an independent *donna guerriera* to a fanatical *miles Christi*, moreover, corresponds to a general shift in the treatment of Agramante's war, to which we turn in the second part of this study.

PART TWO

Out of Africa

Chapter Six

Agramante of Biserta (Tunisia)

Boiardo's Agramante

The opening of Book Two shifts the poem's geographical focus from eastern Asia to northern Africa, where Agramante of Biserta has convened a council to announce his planned invasion of France. Like Gradasso and Agricane, Agramante also suffers from an insatiable – and ultimately futile – desire to gain something he does not possess. However, while the king of Sericana coveted a Frankish sword and horse and the khan of Tartary craved a Cathayan princess, Agramante seeks nothing less than the entire realm of Charlemagne. He is thus the first ruler with openly territorial ambitions and represents a much graver threat to western Europe than Gradasso, who did not intend to occupy France even after defeating the Frankish troops and imprisoning the emperor.

Agolante

Another factor that sets the king of Biserta apart from Book One's overreachers is his association with a specific genealogical line and a precise imitative model. Boiardo imagines him to be the grandson of the North African king Agolante, whose invasion of Calabria was recounted in the French *Aspremont* and its various Italian redactions, most notably Andrea da Barberino's *Aspramonte*.[1] Although this epic narrative, like the *Spagna*, centres on a war between Christians and Saracens, in this case Charlemagne is not attacking a long-standing Muslim state in Spain but rather defending southern Italy from a North African ruler who seeks to extend his dominion farther into Europe.[2] Thus whereas Book One worked against the *Spagna*'s example of military expansion, as argued in previous chapters, Book Two's epic plot is aligned with the *Aspramonte*'s positive model of defensive warfare.

This defensive paradigm would have corresponded, moreover, to the situation of the Italian peninsula in the early Middle Ages. In the *Historia imperiale*, Boiardo states that, from the time of Ludwig II to Berengarius II, "steteron in Italia oltro a trecento milia de Saracini, cum e' quali fu sempre combatuto da' Italiani soli sancia aiuto di alchuna foriestiera natione" ("over three hundred thousand Saracens were in Italy, against whom the Italians always fought without help from any foreign nation") (119r).[3] He goes on to relate that after destroying southern Tuscany, Saracens from Africa attacked Rome and desecrated St Peter's Church.[4] Although the invaders were thereafter forced out of the city, they nevertheless succeeded in occupying large sections of southern Italy and all of Sicily:

> E presa dapoi Capua e Napoli et in breve tute le citade de Italia, e' populi de le quale abandonandoli per li monti ne le pichole castellette se erano diversamente disterminati, passò alfine in Cicilia e quella integramente summesse a sua iurisdictione. (119r-v)

> And having then taken Capua and Naples and in a short time all the cities of Italy – whose people having abandoned them for the mountains were exterminated in various ways in the small castles – they eventually passed to Sicily and placed it entirely under their command.

In the *Innamorato* Boiardo places this Muslim occupation of southern Italy in the context of their military actions against other parts of western Europe: "E preser Spagna con tanta aroganza, / Parte de Italia e tempestarno in Franza" ("[they] conquered Spain with arrogance, / divided Italy, stormed France") (*OI* 2.1.13). Moreover, he links these historical events directly to the poem by claiming that "Dela casa affricanna: e gran segnori / Che fèrno a' Christïan cotante offese" ("the mighty lords of Africa / who caused the Christians much mischance") (*OI* 2.1.13) are actually the ancestors of King Agramante of Biserta.[5]

The genealogical nexus between the historical North African Muslims who invaded Italy and the *Innamorato*'s Agramante brings us back to Agolante. The account of this North African ruler's incursion into Calabria, well-known through the various *Aspramonte* narratives, was also considered historically authentic in texts available to fifteenth-century readers. Two popular Third Crusade chronicles, Amboise's Old French verse *Estoire de la guerre sainte* and the anonymous Latin prose *Itinerarium peregrinorum et gesta regis Ricardi*, recount that Agolante attacked Reggio Calabria. Whereas the former simply states that Agoland "seized Reggio by force" (11), the latter claims that Charlemagne himself had engaged in battle against the North African sovereign: "There was no disagreement between comrades when [Charlemagne] advanced through Rome to encounter the most powerful Aguland and meet him in battle – Aguland had landed near Reggio, a city in Calabria, with a very strong force of Saracens which was almost invincible to human strength except with God's aid" (300).[6]

Boiardo himself refers to this war as a factual occurrence in the *Historia imperiale* despite the fact that it is not mentioned in any of Riccobaldo's extant works (Rizzi, *The "Historia imperiale,"* 1: 173n).[7] Consistent with the basic outlines of the epic account, a climactic battle in the mountains of Aspromonte is said to have ended in the deaths of Agolante, his oldest son, Almonte, and 140,000 others (120v). In this light, Agramante's connection to historical precedents not only gives his upcoming war a greater sense of verisimilitude but may also suggest a link back to contemporary reality. Before pursuing this thread, however, let us examine more fully Agramante's other genealogical and thematic ties.

Alexander of Macedonia

In the *Aspramonte* Agolante's right to rule the world is occasionally reinforced through his proclaimed descent from Alexander of Macedonia.[8] The *Innamorato* brings Agramante's same genealogical claim to the forefront by opening Book Two with a double biography of Alexander: the first, a historical background provided by Turpino, includes a sequel regarding his sons that leads up to the ruling house of Africa; the second, painted on the walls of Biserta's great hall, celebrates the conqueror's most famous exploits. During the council scene, Agramante presents his plan to invade France more as a way of emulating his Macedonian ancestor than of following his North African grandfather. For the better part of three stanzas he urges his fellow kings to win renown in the manner of Alexander, whereas the aim of extending Mohammed's law, so central to Agolante, is simply tacked on in the final verse (*OI* 2.1.35–7).

Like Boiardo's various fictitious overreachers, the historical Alexander could be seen to illustrate the poem's opening statement regarding the inordinate desires plaguing powerful figures. His early biographers already concur in characterizing him as "bent upon action and glory"

(Plutarch, *Life of Alexander*, 6), "for ever insatiate of conquest" (Arrian 7.19.6), and with "ambitions knowing no bounds" (Curtius Rufus 10.1.17).[9] Boiardo's Turpino accentuates the negative aspects of his military conquests by singling out the character trait of arrogance ("sua arroganza") and by noting not his victories but rather the suffering he caused in the world: "ebe il mondo tuto quanto aflitto" ("having afflicted all the world") (*OI* 2.1.5).[10] In the end, his bellicose actions are not only destructive but entirely in vain. After Alexander is poisoned by someone he trusts, his unstable empire falls to pieces amid global chaos: "Onde convien ch'il mondo si commova: / E questo un pecio e quel' un altro piglia, / Il mondo tuto a guera se ascombiglia" ("The earth was stirred by turmoil then. / The warring world was overwhelmed / as different men grabbed different realms") (*OI* 2.1.6).

Alexander of Macedonia is not the only classical precedent evoked at the opening of Book Two, however. As Giovanni Ponte and Michael Murrin have pointed out, Agramante's council recalls parallel scenes in both Herodotus and Livy.[11] In the former case Agramante would be a new Xerxes invading the vulnerable and divided Greeks, while in the latter he is akin to Hannibal attacking Rome. Boiardo makes a direct reference to these ancient histories near the end of Book Two when he remarks that neither Xerxes nor Hannibal had assembled an army as large as Agramante's (*OI* 2.29.1–2). According to Murrin, "The kind of history Boiardo imitated signals the Renaissance and separates him from his quattrocento contemporaries north and south. True to his humanist education, the poet looked to Livy and Herodotus rather than to medieval chronicles, thus lending dignity to his romance" (*History and Warfare*, 58).[12] At the same time, Boiardo's classical allusions do more than dignify his poem. Like Alexander, Xerxes and Hannibal provide examples from ancient history corroborating the *Innamorato*'s pattern of overreaching rulers bent on global conquest in a context that is completely unconnected to the crusading ideology of the episode's Carolingian precedents. The suggestive linking of Agramante to these figures thus serves to reinforce the negative connotations of his aggressive military expedition.

Within this disapproving account of imperialistic ambition, Boiardo inserts an original sequel to Alexander's history that offers a very different paradigm. According to Turpino, while in Egypt Alexander fell in love with a woman named Helidona who, in the turmoil following his death, courageously boarded an unmanned boat that took her to foreign shores where she gave birth to triplets (*OI* 2.1.7–9). This narrative does not have any known source in the many stories that accrued around the figure of Alexander in historical and legendary versions of his life.[13] What Helidona does have in common with Alexander's actual wives, however, is her status as a foreigner. Alexander first married Roxane, a noblewoman from Bactria (now northern Afghanistan), and then wed Statira, daughter of the Persian king Darius, in a ceremony at Susa three years later.[14] Not only did his own marriages thus constitute culturally mixed unions, but on the occasion of his second wedding Alexander took the unprecedented step of arranging marriages between eighty of his companions and Persian noblewomen. This collective event included the official legitimization of the unions between Macedonians and foreign women that had already taken place.

Ancient authors offered different perspectives on Alexander's stated policy of empire consolidation through intermarriage. The Roman historian Quintus Curtius Rufus disparages the ruler's marriages as a consequence of his unruly lust, remarking that "control over his appetites was weakening amid the indulgences of Fortune, against whom mankind is insufficiently armed" (8.4.24). He thereby questions the sincerity of Alexander's political justification for the mixed marriages, wryly commenting that Alexander "fell in love [...] with such abandon as to make a statement that intermarriage of Persians and Macedonians would serve to consolidate his empire" (8.4.25). The Roman historian further deflates the ruler's professed aim of removing all distinctions between the two peoples by having Alexander underscore the subjugated status of his foreign wives, referring to them as captive concubines in his speeches.[15]

In contrast to Curtius Rufus's scepticism regarding Alexander's intentions, Plutarch extols the king's nuptials as a highly adept political strategy. He depicts Alexander's marriage to Roxane as a love match that is at the same time in accordance with the king's goal of intermixing Macedonian and Persian culture (*Life of Alexander*, 46). Plutarch even imagines the exclamation he would have shouted out had he witnessed the mass marriage at Susa: "O dullard Xerxes, stupid fool that spent so much fruitless toil to bridge Asia with Europe; it is not by beams or rafts, nor by lifeless and unfeeling bonds, but by the ties of lawful love and chaste nuptials and mutual joy in children that they join the nations together" ("De Alexandri Magni fortuna aut virtute," 401).[16] Of course, Plutarch does not suggest that Alexander's marriages or his other attempts to reconcile Asiatic and Macedonian customs were due to an enlightened concept of multiculturalism but rather presents them as sheer realpolitik: "It would be wiser to depend upon the good-will which might arise from intermixture and association as a means of maintaining tranquility, than upon force and compulsion" (*Life of Alexander*, 46).[17]

The *Innamorato*'s presentation of Alexander's love life can be seen in relation to the positions taken by both classical historians. Like Curtius Rufus, Boiardo attributes an exclusively personal rather than political motivation to Alexander's union with a foreign woman. At the same time, however, he steers clear of Curtius Rufus's moralistic terminology regarding the appetites. While Turpino's biography gives the basic facts of Alexander's enamourment (*OI* 2.1.5), the ekphrasis in the royal palace employs the language of the courtly love lyric:

Dapoi che vinto egli ha ben ogni cosa,
Védese lui che è vinto dal'amore,
Perché Helidona, quella gratïosa,
Con soi begli ochi e' gli ha passato el core.

After he'd conquered everything,
he found that love had conquered him,
since Elidonia, that mild lady,
had pierced his heart with her bright eyes. (*OI* 2.1.29)[18]

Moreover, by choosing the setting of Egypt, Boiardo distances this episode from the context of war. Historians commonly noted that Alexander did not occupy this land militarily but rather was welcomed by the local inhabitants. As Curtius Rufus explains: "The Egyptians had long been opposed to the power of the Persians, believing that their rule had been avaricious and arrogant, and Alexander's prospective arrival had inspired them to hope" (4.7.1). Alexander, in turn, "settl[ed] administrative matters without tampering with Egyptian traditions" (4.7.5). Given the absence of warfare in Egypt, readers would not have any reason to view Helidona as a captive.

Boiardo follows Plutarch, on the other hand, by drawing a connection between exogamy and the peaceful merging of diverse populations. Yet whereas the Greek biographer hailed the mixed marriages as part of a political strategy that did not see fruition because of Alexander's early death, in the *Innamorato* an effective intermixing does indeed occur through the birth of triplets. The three brothers eventually extend their dominion throughout the territory because of their good nature, which "tirava ad obedirli ogni persona" ("prompted men's obedience") (*OI* 2.1.11). Indeed, unlike their arrogant father, who had subdued other states through conflict, the brothers find that "ogni terra e ciascadun paese / Di gratia gli veniva a dimandare" ("every city and each realm / approached them to request their rule") (*OI* 2.1.12). As a result, they came to rule all of Africa without violence.

Alexander's enamourment has another consequence that likewise leads to a fruitful mixing of peoples: his love for Helidona inspires him to found the city of Alexandria (*OI* 2.1.5). Both early biographies and later romances celebrate this act as a benefit to future civilization. According to Plutarch, for example, the augurs told Alexander that "the city he was about to build would not only abound in all things within itself, but also be the nurse and feeder of many nations" (*Life of Alexander*, 27). The *Romance of Alexander the Great* by Pseudo-Callisthenes – a legendary biography that originated in Alexandria some time prior to the fourth century C.E. and gave rise to most of the Alexander stories circulating in the Middle Ages – anticipates Boiardo's Turpino in asserting that Alexander's lasting glory was due not so much to his territorial conquests as to the founding of this city. In this work Demosthenes is quoted as saying, "Not one of the Greek kings has entered Egypt except Alexander; and he did this not for making war but in order to ask an oracle of the gods as to where he should build a city to immortalize his name. And then he laid its foundations and built it" (81).[19] In subsequent centuries Alexandria was renowned as a site of cultural exchange through both learning and commerce. Its library held writings from all over the known world, and both Strabo and Ptolemy conducted their research there about a century apart.[20] The Este were not only well acquainted with the accomplishments of these geographers, as noted in the introduction, but were also familiar with the city's commercial fame, given that Italy's maritime powers had had extensive trade through Alexandria since the early Middle Ages.

The two acts of creation resulting from Alexander's love for Helidona – the birth of sons and the founding of a city – have far-reaching consequences. The first, however, went awry when his later descendants, from the Saracens who attacked western Europe in the ninth and tenth centuries to the current ruling house of Africa, reverted back to the military arrogance that he exhibited prior to his enamourment rather than following the example of his good-natured sons. The city of Alexandria, on the other hand, continued to thrive as a major commercial centre at a global level, "the classic meeting point of east and west, even the far east" (Tangheroni 139). In the *Historia imperiale* Boiardo includes an authorial aside noting the prominence of Alexandria in the late fifteenth century: "Questa città fu dal grande Alessandro in Egitto collocta, & è ancora tra le principali di quella regione di maritimi commerci, e d'ogni mercatanzia molto frequentata" ("This city in Egypt was founded by the great Alexander, and is still among the principal cities for maritime commerce and is very full of activity with every kind of merchandise," col. 406).[21] In the *Innamorato* itself he likewise remarks that it had survived right up to his own day: "et anchor si trova" ("and it still stands") (*OI* 2.1.6). He makes the same point, moreover, with respect to the Libyan birthplace of Alexander's three sons, which is said still to bear its original name of Tripoli (*OI* 2.1.9).

The continued existence of Alexandria and Tripoli in the historical present is contrasted with the foretold destruction of Biserta in the course of the upcoming war:

> Era in quel tempo gran terra Biserta,
> Che hogi è disfatta al litto ala marina,
> Però che in questa guerra fo diserta;
>
> Biserta was a large town then,
> though crumbling on the shore today,
> since in this war it was destroyed. (*OI* 2.1.19)

Biserta's destiny to suffer the same destruction as nearby Carthage in ancient times (*OI* 2.27.45) may be not only an allusion to the classical antecedents of Agramante's war but also a warning to any future would-be imitators of Alexander and Hannibal.

Mehmed II

Some medieval works celebrated Alexander as a model for the emperor Charlemagne and his intrepid paladins.[22] In the *Innamorato*, however, the Macedonian conqueror is imitated instead by a North African overreacher doomed to failure. While this may discourage the reader from identifying with such an imperialistic attitude, it also serves as a reminder that Alexander was similarly used as a model in Muslim societies. The contemporary ruler of the Ottoman Empire, Mehmed II, "the Conqueror," envisioned himself as both the rightful heir to the Graeco-Roman empire and a modern-day Alexander.[23] Just as the ancient Macedonian conqueror was proclaimed "King of Asia" after overthrowing Darius's Persian Empire (Plutarch, *Life of Alexander*, 35), so Mehmed adopted the title of Roman Caesar after conquering Constantinople and thereby toppling the eastern Roman Empire. Yet his goal was to conquer Rome and proclaim himself ruler of the western Roman Empire as well (Babinger 494).

Mehmed's ambitions both to imitate Alexander and to invade Italy were well known in the peninsula in the aftermath of the 1453 fall of Constantinople.[24] In 1454, the Negropontian humanist Niccolò Sagundino delivered an oration on the Turks to the Neapolitan king Alfonso of Aragon, alerting him to the danger of an impending attack on the Italian coastline (Pertusi 474). Meserve notes that Sagundino's report underscored the sultan's "emulation of Alexander the Great and interest in Roman and Greek history, his ill will toward Christendom, his sadism and sexual perversions, and his elaborate schemes for the conquest of Italy" (*Empires of Islam*, 112).

Boiardo himself shows attentiveness to Ottoman aggression in Europe as early as his youthful Latin *Pastoralia* (1463–4). In the opening verses of the first eclogue, the god Pan explains that he was forced to abandon Arcadia because of war (I.4–8), which Stefano Carrai finds to be "an evident allusion to the recent Turkish invasion of the Morea" (*Pastoralia*, 3). The fourth eclogue of the collection alludes to Mehmed II's unremitting warfare by referring to the ruler metaphorically as a "caedibus hydram / crescentem innumeris" ("hydra growing through innumerable slaughters") (*Pastoralia* IV.49–50). As if to leave no doubt as to the referent, Boiardo equates the hydra with Mehmed in his own gloss to the eclogue: "hydra insigne regis Turchorum" ("the hydra [is] a symbol for the king of the Turks") (Carrai, *Pastoralia*, 41n). It would therefore not have escaped the *Innamorato*'s first readers that Agramante's planned conquest of France, while drawing from the history of earlier centuries, also corresponded to ongoing military aggression on the part of contemporary Ottoman armies.[25]

In reading Agramante's war as an allusion to the Turkish campaigns, Murrin has pointed out that the height of the threat to the Italian peninsula coincided with the period in which Boiardo was writing the *Innamorato* (*History and Warfare*, 70). Tissoni Benvenuti's revised dating of the poem's composition allows for even greater precision: if, as she convincingly argues, the opening of Book Two corresponds to the onset of Ercole's reign in 1471, then it also coincides with the aftermath of the Turkish capture of Negroponte (1470), an event that alerted the Italian states to their collective vulnerability.[26] Humanist poems and vernacular *lamenti* written following the fall of Negroponte associated

Mehmed with various ancient historical conquerors, including Alexander, Xerxes, and Hannibal (Meserve, "News from Negroponte," 462–4). Boiardo's translation of the medieval historian Riccobaldo of Ferrara, which Andrea Rizzi dates to the period between August of 1471 and April of 1473, contains a historical precedent for the peninsula under attack from Saracen forces in the medieval period (*The "Historia imperiale,"* 1: xxxiv). Ottoman pressure throughout the 1470s in the context of their war against Venice, notably their various incursions into Friuli, caused alarm in all the cities of the Po Valley. These current events would have certainly given heightened relevance to the epic plot developed in the course of Book Two.

Through the examples of Agramante's various ancestors, combined with allusions to the historical Muslim invasions of Italy during the early Middle Ages, Boiardo draws a sharp distinction between offensive and defensive warfare. While Alexander's history and its sequel ultimately discourage aggression in favour of the peaceful uniting of peoples, Agolante's attack on the Italian peninsula underscores instead the need for military readiness to ensure the survival of one's own state. To put it another way, while the former suggests that falling in love and founding cities are far worthier enterprises than warmongering, the latter warns that one must be prepared to thwart foreign invasion if need be. Erasmus would express a similar distinction between unwarranted belligerence and necessary self-defence in his *Consultatio de bello Turcis inferendo* (1530): "For while it is true that not every war against the Turks is just and pious, it is also the case that non-resistance to the Turks is nothing other than betraying Christianity to its most savage foes, and abandoning our brothers to a servitude which they do not deserve" (178).

Ariosto's divergent treatment of Agramante and the disastrous conclusion of the war in the final cantos of the *Furioso* will be the subject of chapter 15. At present we turn to two additional African protagonists invented by Boiardo who serve to further develop the poem's vision of international relations. While Rugiero puts into practice the example offered by Alexander's three courteous sons, Rodamonte is propelled forward by even more extreme ambitions than those of Alexander himself.

Chapter Seven

Rugiero (Atlas Mountains, Northern Africa)

Boiardo's Rugiero

At the conclusion of Book One, Boiardo announces the appearance of Rugiero, "d'ogni virtù il più perfeto / Di qualunque altro ch'al mondo si vanta" ("blessed with all virtues, who surpassed / all other men the world has known") (*OI* 1.29.56). Such a depiction effectively places him above every other character in the poem, including Charlemagne's famous paladins. The following pages examine his elaborate genealogy, his symbolic associations both with historical personages of the distant past and with the current ruling family of Ferrara, and his future intercultural marriage to Bradamante, as well as the mixed family tree of his bride-to-be. I shall argue that these various aspects would have had political relevance at a global level for the poem's early readers.

Rugiero's Ancestry

Boiardo imagines his new hero to be the son of Rugiero and Galaciella, whose tragic story is related in Italian versions of the *Aspramonte* narrative. As noted earlier, Boiardo imagines that Galaciella escaped to the North African coast and gave birth to twins before expiring. He identifies only one of the twins, however – the new Rugiero, who was raised in isolation by the magus Atalante on the Mountain of Carena.

Taking his cues from the *Aspramonte*, Boiardo further develops the figure of Rugiero through genealogical and historical ties that take him well beyond the immediate context of this medieval narrative. During the council in Biserta that opens Book Two, we learn that through his maternal grandfather Rugiero is – like his cousin Agramante – a descendant of Alexander of Macedonia. His character, however, will consistently show not the unbridled aggressiveness of Alexander but rather the good nature attributed to his sons.[1] This association is evident right from his birth narrative, in which his pregnant mother's precipitate departure from Reggio Calabria on an unmanned boat to give birth on a foreign shore replays the actions of Alexander's beloved Helidona, and is reinforced when Rugiero sails from Africa to France at the head of troops from Tripoli, the city appropriately named in honour of Helidona's triplets according to Boiardo.

Near the end of the poem we learn that Rugiero's paternal line also reaches back to an illustrious classical figure – Hector of Troy. In tracing his genealogy for his future wife, Bradamante, Rugiero recounts that Hector's son Astyanax escaped the destruction of Troy to become the ruler of Messina (*OI* 3.5.23). He then married the queen of Syracuse, who after his death due to treachery set out alone from Messina to Reggio Calabria (*OI* 3.5.26) where she gave birth to their son Polidoro in circumstances as dire as those of Alexander's Helidona and Rugiero's own mother, Galaciella. Whereas Helidona's son Argante eventually gave rise to the ruling house of Africa, Polidoro's descendants remained in Europe, eventually splitting between France and Italy. While one branch of the family led to Charlemagne, Rugiero's ancestors eventually made their way back to Polidoro's birthplace of Reggio Calabria, where his father and grandfather ruled with justice until they were treacherously murdered (*OI* 3.5.30).[2]

In the course of Rugiero's intricate genealogy, both sides of his family have an important geographical tie to the city of Reggio Calabria. As noted above, Astyanax's Sicilian widow arrives there to give birth to their son, and later Rugiero's grandfather Rampaldo rules the city; his own mother, Galaciella, resides in Reggio with his father until his uncle Beltramo's treachery drives her back to Africa. The centrality of Reggio Calabria in these genealogies, with its connections to Sicily and North Africa, brings to mind a historical figure whose relevance for Rugiero has gone largely unnoticed. Building on an association that was already implicit in the *Aspramonte*, Boiardo links his newly invented character by name and geographical location to the Italo-Norman leader Roger I (1031–1101).[3]

Roger I

After his arrival in southern Italy in the mid-1050s, Roger I helped his brother Robert Guiscard gain control over the region and subsequently shared with him the rule of Calabria. From his base in Reggio, Roger launched the reconquest of Sicily, whose rulers were nominally subject to the sultan of Tunis. His thirty-year campaign definitively ended more than two centuries of Muslim rule on the island. A closer look at the historical Roger may explain why Boiardo would have evoked him as a model for his fictional hero and in turn for his Este patrons.

Roger's battles in southern Italy and Sicily are reported most extensively by the Benedictine monk Goffredo Malaterra, whose *De rebus gestis Rogerii, Calabriae et Siciliae comitis, et Roberti Guiscardi ducis, fratris ejus* covers Italo-Norman history up to 1098.[4] Malaterra introduces Roger as "a most handsome youth, lofty in stature with an elegant body. He was eloquent in his speech, shrewd in his deliberation, thoughtful in his arrangement of things to be done, cheerful and affable toward everyone, mighty and fierce in war. On the basis of these talents he became, in a very short time, worthy of every grace" (1.19). In examining the onset of the Sicilian expedition, Malaterra informs us that Roger conceived of conquering the island after having secured Calabria (2.1) but did not take action until an exiled Sicilian emir named Betumen arrived in Reggio and implored him to provide assistance. Malaterra writes, in fact, that "with repeated entreaties, [Betumen] encouraged the count to attack Sicily" (2.3).[5]

There is a later portrayal of Roger I that is of even greater relevance for the character of Rugiero. It is the one provided by Boiardo himself in the section of the *Historia imperiale* devoted to the Normans in southern Italy and Sicily. There Roger (Rigieri) is introduced as a younger brother of Robert Guiscard, yet "di bellezza, di gagliardia e di virtute non solo de li fratelli ma de tuti li homini de il suo tempo superiore" ("in beauty, valour, and virtue superior not only to his brothers but to all the men of his time") (202). Boiardo's explanation of how Roger came to govern all of Sicily and part of the North African coast concurs with the general outline of Malaterra's account but imbues the episode with the ideals that inform the fictional world of the *Innamorato*:

> Bethumi per il soldano de' Saracini la isola governava, et essendo in quella la fama de Rigieri che a Regio dimorava trapassata cum grandissimo nome di la sua virtude e piacevolecia e gagliardia e prudencia e liberalitate, la quale da lui oltro al suo picholo potere era usata, etiandio verso de ogni natione istraniera, se rivolssero a lui non solo li animi de' Ciciliani ma de' Saracini anchora, [<]né de altrui se ragionava, non pure in Cicilia, ma per tuta la barbaria de Affrica che de Rigieri. Per questo temendo Bethumi di univer-

> sale rubellione e favorendo forsi anchor lui sì come tutti li altri a la virtutue di quel giovinetto[>], passato nascosamente il mare li propose il modo di acquistare la isola. (202)

> Bethumi governed the island for the sultan of the Saracens, and having passed into that land the fame of Rigieri who lived in Reggio – with the exceptional reputation of his virtue and gracefulness and vigour and prudence and liberality, which was shown by him not only in his small domain, but towards every foreign nation – the souls not only of the Sicilians but also of the Saracens turned to him, nor did they speak about anyone else but Rigieri, not only in Sicily, but throughout all of the barbarian lands of Africa. For this reason Bethumi, fearing a universal rebellion and perhaps esteeming the virtue of that young man as did all the others, crossed the sea secretly and proposed to him the way to conquer the island.

Whereas in Malaterra Betumen's appeal to Roger stemmed solely from his need for external military support in a conflict that had led to his expulsion from the island (2.3), in the *Historia imperiale* the emir's plea is based less on his political vulnerability than on his appreciation of Rugiero's chivalry.[6] And whereas Malaterra repeatedly characterized Roger (and his fellow Normans) as hungry for territory, Boiardo replaces the *aviditas dominationis* attitude with one of disinterested courtesy.[7] This emphasis on action inspired by virtue takes us beyond Malaterra's history to the *Innamorato* account of Alexander's three good-natured sons who came to rule all of Africa by popular demand. By creating a narrative parallel between Rugiero's medieval namesake, Roger I, and the sons of Alexander the Great, Boiardo establishes a precedent for Rugiero's unconditional courtesy involving figures linked to both sides of his family. Furthermore, since the *Historia imperiale*'s account of Roger I follows the report of successive waves of Saracen attacks throughout the Italian peninsula and Sicily beginning in the ninth century, it is not a naive refusal to acknowledge historical reality but rather, like that of Alexander's sons, an envisioned alternative to a situation of violence.

Boiardo's early readers, moreover, would have recognized this model of governance by popular consent as the very image that Este rulers cultivated about themselves throughout their own family's history. In 1240 the citizens of Ferrara chose Azzo d'Este as their leader (Folin, *Rinascimento estense*, 59). At his death twenty-four years later, his grandson Obizzo II d'Este, "in a move without precedent, […] was elected *signore* of Ferrara for life by plebiscite, and the office was made hereditary" (Gundersheimer 25). Obizzo provided an even closer precedent for Alexander's sons when the neighbouring towns of Modena and Reggio Emilia invited him to rule over them: "In 1288, an embassy from Modena, which for years had been rent by a virtual civil war among its magnates, invited Obizzo to accept the lordship of that city. [...] Not long thereafter Reggio [...] also elected Obizzo as *signore*" (Gundersheimer 39).[8] Between 1430 and 1451, thus closer to Ercole's time, the Garfagnana region in the Apennines southwest of Reggio Emilia willingly ("liberali animo") came under the domain of the Este without any threat of armed intervention on their part (Folin, *Rinascimento estense*, 112). The elaborate way in which Boiardo works this paradigm into the legendary account of the family's origins shows his interest in asserting the wisdom and antiquity of this manner of consensual governance.

Continuing to recount the exploits of Roger I in the *Historia imperiale*, Boiardo imagines that he rules in tandem with his brothers Roberto, Guiscardo, and Guglielmo. Glossing over the many obstacles that according to Malaterra the brothers had to overcome to establish their leadership in Sicily and southern Italy – not the least of which were conflicts among themselves – Boiardo asserts that this arrangement led to eighteen continuous years of prosperous fortune (142v). This unusual circumstance of shared rule among brothers echoes the *Innamorato*'s fictional sequel to its own version of Alexander's story in which his sons came to jointly govern all of Africa.

The collaborative rule among brothers also recalls another crucial moment in Estense history: in the turbulent period following the death of Azzo VII d'Este in 1308, Ferrara was controlled alternately by the outside forces of Venice and the Papal States until Aldobrandino d'Este's three sons, Rinaldo, Obizzo III, and Niccolò I, initially along with their cousin Bertoldo, assumed joint rule in 1317. According to Jane Fair Bestor, "the cousins' cooperation in the struggle to regain the city and its district affirmed their identity as co-equal members of the house and underscored the importance of family unity to the preservation of the dynasty" (561). This arrangement not only consolidated their rule and "strengthened their descendants' claims [...] to a share of the patrimony," but eventually led Pope John XXII to give the Este family full powers of jurisdiction over the Ferrarese state in 1329 "in the first bestowal of an apostolic vicariate in the history of the papacy" (Bestor 561).[9]

Another feature of the Normans' early history in Italy that would have a bearing for the poem's hero Rugiero is rapid integration into their new homeland. Although the Normans were initially foreign to the Italian peninsula, they readily assimilated its language, culture, and religion, whereas the Byzantines and North Africans who had invaded the land before them had not. The Normans became papal vassals in 1059, and Malaterra records that in 1098 Pope Urban II appointed Roger as "legate of St. Peter over all of Sicily as well as over the territory he controlled in Calabria" in a decree that refers to him as the "count of Calabria and Sicily" (4.29). Boiardo relates the Normans' conversion to Roman Catholicism and their alliance with the pope in the same chapter in which he had described the devastation in southern and central Italy caused by the African Saracens: "E' Saracini de Affrica [...] guastarno di là da Roma tuta Italia, occidendo li populi, ardendo le citade e deruchando le chiesie e, tra le altre, quella del beato Benedetto nel Monte Cassino deruparno da li fondamenti" ("The Saracens of Africa [...] destroyed all of Italy up to beyond Rome, killing the populations, burning the cities and demolishing the churches and, among others, that of the blessed Benedict in Monte Cassino they hurled down from its foundations") (121r). This juxtaposition underscores the role of the Normans as defenders and protectors of the Italian peninsula in the face of a real and continued danger.

At the same time, it is important to note that the eventual victory of the southern Italian Normans over the sultans of Sicily did not lead to the death or forced conversion of local Muslim inhabitants as recounted in crusading chronicles and Carolingian epics such as the *Spagna* narratives, discussed above. Malaterra often points to Roger's interaction and collaboration with Muslims on various levels: he not only formed alliances with Sicilian and Tunisian emirs (2.3–4, 2.18, 2.20, 2.22, 4.3), but used Muslims in his own forces (3.18, 3.20, 3.30, 4.22). Betumen remained loyal to Roger and assisted him in the expansion of his dominion (2.22), and most of the island's cities capitulated under terms that allowed Muslim inhabitants to stay and live according to their own law (2.13, 2.45, 4.16).

Roger II

The figure of Roger I's son and heir may also have served as a precedent for Boiardo's fictional hero. Roger II (1095–1154) not only ruled Sicily but furthered his reach to the coastline of North Africa. Although Malaterra's chronicle leaves off before Roger II becomes king, certain notions about the Sicilian sovereign's character and policies are reiterated in various sources. The consolidation of his power over the North African coast across from Sicily won for him the unofficial title of "King of Africa" (Houben 7). The medieval chronicler Hugo Falcandus indicates that "he subjugated Tripoli in Barbary [...] and numerous other barbarian cities through many personal efforts and dangers" (cited in Houben 178). This situation provides a historical connection to the two moments in which the city of Tripoli is featured in the *Innamorato* narrative: that is, its founding in the name of Alexander's three sons and Rugiero's command over its troops.

Roger II was especially commended by his contemporaries for establishing peace and order in the land he ruled. Peter the Venerable, abbot of Cluny, credits him with creating "a peaceful and very pleasant kingdom like that of the peacemaker Solomon" (cited in Houben 5). Romuald I, archbishop of Salerno, wrote that Roger II "established peace and good order in his kingdom, and to preserve that peace instituted chamberlains and justiciars throughout the land, promulgated laws which he had newly drafted and removed evil customs from their midst" (cited in Houben 135). This perception of Roger as a peacemaker is combined with his reputation for tolerance and even openness to different creeds, races, and languages. He employed both Arabs and Byzantines at his court in Palermo, where he intermingled Western, Byzantine, and Arabic elements in court ceremonial. His standing army, like that of his father, included Muslims, and for a period he managed to be the "guarantor of the peaceful coexistence of Greek, Arabic and Latin cultures in Palermo" (Houben 112).[10]

Contemporary Relevance

In the *Historia imperiale*, Boiardo recounts that Roger II, referred to alternately as Rigieri and Regieri, "seguendo la fortuna che a favorirlo parea disposta, prese tuta Calabria e tuta Puglia. E già non più Conte di Cicilia ma re de Italia se apellava" ("following Fortune who seemed ready to favour him, took all of Calabria and all of Apulia. And he was already calling himself not simply Count of Sicily, but King of Italy") (154r). This history would have had particular resonance for the designated descendants of the poem's hero Rugiero. The land that officially came under the rule of Roger II in 1139 when Pope Innocent II proclaimed him *rex Siciliae ducatus Apuliae et principatus Capuae* corresponded to the two kingdoms of Naples and Sicily that were rejoined when the Aragonese king Alfonso the Magnanimous conquered Naples in 1442. Ercole d'Este, after growing up at the Neapolitan court, eventually married Alfonso's granddaughter, Eleonora d'Aragona. Roger II was thus in a very real way the political ancestor to Eleonora and Ercole's children (albeit via the Aragonese rather than the Este line).

The parallels could not have been missed, since not only were Eleonora's family the political heirs of the two Rogers but her father, King Ferrante of Naples, was threatened by a Muslim invasion as Boiardo was writing Book Two. The greatest danger to his kingdom came when Mehmed II's planned conquest of Italy began at the Adriatric coast with the capture of Otranto in August 1480. Having established a base on the peninsula, the Ottomans raided Brindisi, Taranto, and Lecce, and Otranto itself "immediately became a market for Christian slaves" (Hibbert 66).[11] Historians maintain that at this moment the Italian peninsula risked falling under Turkish rule: the vizier in command "returned to Rumelia to collect a large army for the invasion of Italy" (Inalcik 29). After Mehmed's death in May 1481, however, Ferrante's son Alfonso d'Aragona was able to recover Otranto that September. Alfonso also claimed a title held by both Roger I and II – that of duke of Calabria.[12]

These Neapolitan events were of particular importance to the Estense family for two principal reasons: first, Duke Alfonso d'Aragona was Eleonora's brother and Ercole's brother-in-law; second, his victory over the Turks freed him to lend military support to the Este during the Ferrarese-Venetian War. As they awaited the arrival of Alfonso's allied forces, Ercole was confined to bed with a fever and Eleonora ruled the besieged city. Boiardo interrupted his romance epic and wrote five eclogues regarding the ongoing war that featured Alfonso as both the liberator of Italy from the Turks and, it was hoped, of Ferrara from Venice.[13] Alfonso was eventually able to make his way up the Italian peninsula and lessen Venice's grip on Ferrara, leading to an end of the war in 1484. The current duke of Calabria was thereby responsible for thwarting invasions by both the Ottoman Turks and the Venetians. Just such a role is prophesied for Rugiero in the *Innamorato* when his guardian Atalante foresees that he is destined to take up the defence of the Frankish empire against the North African invaders and their Spanish Saracen allies. Thus if, as seems likely, Boiardo had Mehmed's expansionist ambitions in mind when depicting Agramante's enterprise at the opening of Book Two, he was not devising a vague historical allegory but rather linking his narrative to a contemporary context that would soon threaten the existence of Ercole's extended family.

Bradamante's Parentage

Given the centrality of genealogy in the creation of Rugiero, it is worth taking a closer look at the family ancestry that Boiardo fashions for his hero's future wife. Bradamante presents herself as the sister of Ranaldo and a descendant of the houses of Chiaramonte (Clermont in French) and Mongrana.[14] Since the historical house of Clermont already traced its origins back to Troy, this connection would grant her the same illustrious origin as Rugiero without the need to invent another foundation myth. In this way, moreover, the couple would be rejoining a Trojan line that had earlier been divided into two branches.

Boiardo may also have wanted to suggest through this intricate genealogy that the uniting of two Trojan branches into one house was replayed in the duke and duchess of Ferrara themselves. Like Bradamante, Eleonora was descended from the house of Chiaramonte/Clermont: her mother was Isabella di Chiaramonte, eldest daughter of the French-born noble Tristan de Clermont. Thus, just as within the poem the character Bradamante is on a par with Rugiero, the duchess of Ferrara could effortlessly claim the same Trojan origin that Boiardo goes to such lengths to create for Ercole.[15]

This double genealogy joining two branches that could ultimately be traced back to Troy had political implications as well. First, by proclaiming both Ercole and Eleonora as descendants of Hector, Boiardo imaginatively frees Ferrara from its current status as a papal vicariate. As Marco Dorigatti points out with reference to Rugiero, "His Trojan ancestry allows Boiardo to assign the origins of the House of Este to a time pre-dating the Papacy, thereby implying its autonomy and validating its claim to full sovereignty."[16] Yet this genealogy not only distances the Este from the Papal States, it indirectly links them to the French crown, since some medieval genealogies had claimed that the Frankish emperor himself united the two branches stemming from Troy. The twelfth-century chronicler Godfrey of Viterbo (in his *Pantheon*, written c. 1185–7) asserts that the Trojan refugees led by Aeneas and Antenor were originally split into two groups (the Italian and the Teutonic) that eventually came together in the person of Charlemagne (Meserve, *Empires of Islam*, 54).[17] Although Boccaccio was sceptical of any claim to Trojan ancestry other than the Roman one, both Brunetto Latini and Giovanni Villani accept Godfrey's genealogy (Meserve, *Empires of Islam*, 54–5).

Boiardo does not cast doubt on Charlemagne's Trojan heritage, but he elaborates an alternative lineage to accommodate his narrative. Like the Frankish emperor, Rugiero and Bradamante descend from the worthiest of the Trojans, Hector himself (*OI* 3.5.29). Yet whereas Charlemagne's line separated at Floviano's son Constante, the poem's dynastic couple descend from Buovo d'Antona through Floviano's other son, Clodovaco

(*OI* 3.5.28–9).[18] Rugiero and Bradamante, and by extension their descendants Ercole and Eleonora, are thus not only related to Charlemagne, but their progeny will replace him as the restorer of a Trojan line that had separated into two. Such genealogical ties indirectly asserted the ducal family's symbolic parity with the French state, under which it held Modena and Reggio Emilia as imperial fiefs.

Mixed Marriages

Despite Rugiero's destiny as Christian knight and progenitor of the Este family, his lineage is developed through a complex genealogy that often involves distinct, and sometimes opposing, ethnicities and creeds. Heterogamy is the very touchstone of his ancestry right from the union of the Trojan Astyanax and the queen of Syracuse on his father's side and of the Macedonian Alexander and the Egyptian Helidona on his mother's. One of Rugiero's historical namesakes provides a precedent for cross-cultural marriage in the specific context of medieval Muslim-Christian relations. Roger II's first wife, Elvira, was a daughter of Alfonso VI, King of Castile and León, and of "a Moorish woman called Zaida, who at her wedding in 1098/9 had taken the Christian name of Isabella" (Houben 35). Even Rugiero's immediate genealogy is mixed: his mother was born of an Amazon warrior and a North African king, while his father was one of the southern Italian Christians at war with the North Africans at the time. The fact that his parents belonged to different sides of the conflict did not prevent them from falling in love and marrying. Looking ahead to the poem's storyline, Rugiero's complicated heritage means that he has roots on both sides in the ongoing war between Agramante and Charlemagne.

Bradamante, no less than Rugiero, is the product of a mixed union. Although she does not refer to her maternal family history in the poem, she was born to a pagan mother in the Rinaldo cycle in which her character originates. Vitullo explains that the female warrior Bradamante, or Braidamonte as she is first called, "appears in several anonymous fourteenth- and fifteenth-century versions of the rebellious vassal story, Rinaldo da Montalbano. Like Galaziella, she too is a *bastarda* since her father is the French Duke Amone who had an affair with the pagan queen Balialta and left her pregnant when he returned to France" (68). Margaret Tomalin finds that with the exception of one fifteenth-century *cantare*, all the other versions depict the *guerriera* initially under the wing of a Saracen mother before she shifts loyalties and identifies with her father (56).

How would Boiardo's patron, Ercole d'Este, have reacted to the news that his progenitors were the product of an ethnic and religious mix? Perhaps any account would have been more welcome than a pseudo-genealogy in circulation that traced the Este family to the arch-traitor of Roncevaux, Gano di Maganza.[19] At the same time, however, Boiardo's new genealogy may not have seemed all that strange given that dynastic marriages are by definition the union of members from disparate groups. After all, Ercole I, born of a Ferrarese father and a mother from Saluzzo, wedded the Aragonese Eleonora, whose family tree encompassed France, Spain, and Sicily and whose power extended across the Mediterranean. Nor is the idea of marriage across larger territories unprecedented. Ercole's ancestor Beatrice d'Este had briefly been the Queen of Hungary in the thirteenth century, and Eleonora's sister Beatrice d'Aragona married Hungary's current king Matthias Corvinus in 1476. Nor were the marriage proposals limited to greater Europe. Eleonora's grandfather, King Alfonso I of Naples, had offered the sovereign of Ethiopia an alliance cemented through intermarriage of the royal families (Pistarino 121).[20] Boiardo gives the practice a new twist by imagining a mixed marriage based on romantic love that leads to a political dynasty.

When Rugiero and Bradamante meet, they are technically mutual enemies, since Rugiero is part of the invading force attacking Bradamante's sovereign, Charlemagne. Nevertheless, they exercise unconditional courtesy towards each other, treating one another first and foremost as individuals. Rugiero initially acts chivalrously by offering to take Bradamante's place when her opponent Rodamonte will not give her leave to follow Charlemagne's retreating army. Although Bradamante at first accepts his offer and departs, she soon regrets her decision and returns to find Rugiero waiting for Rodamonte to recover from a stunning blow before resuming their duel. The youth's identity as a North African Saracen is not a hindrance in the least to the Frankish *donna guerriera*, who admires him because of his exemplary actions. It is somewhat remarkable that the purported founders of Ferrara's ruling family are able to meet and fall in love precisely because both have placed codes of universal chivalry and individual honour above the interests of their political leaders. This, however, accords with the emphasis throughout the poem on a code of behaviour that transcends national and religious boundaries.

The ensuing love story of Rugiero and Bradamante recalls and goes beyond the literary precedents that provide the background for both characters. The *Historia di Bradiamonte*, for example, took for granted the impropriety of mixed marriages. The eastern king Almansor, having learned of the great beauty of Bradiamonte, a *donna guerriera* who would only marry someone who could best her in a duel, travelled to France to win her hand. The maiden, however, kills him in the course of their combat, and the Christians then go on to attack and defeat the "pagans." Eleonora Stoppino points out the lack of scruples on the part of the Christians in this episode: "Christians prove to be treacherous in this second part of the poem: Almansor comes in peace, to form an alliance with Charlemagne, probably through the marriage; once he is killed, the Christians seize the occasion to wage war against an army without a leader and far from its territory" (27).[21] She also notes how the anonymous author plays up Almansor's racial alterity: "When Bradiamonte sees his face for the first time, she remarks that it looks like charcoal [...], and is upset by the fact that he, who seems a devil [...], aspires to her 'sovereign body'" (28–9).

Although the chivalric tradition was not lacking in episodes describing relations between Saracen women and Christian paladins, these were typically short-lived, even when they led to progeny, and mostly due to the lustful appetites of the former and vulnerability of the latter when finding themselves far from home.[22] Boiardo's choice of the *Aspramonte*'s Galiziella and Riccieri as a thematic and genealogical precedent is apt, since it is not the case of another wayward Christian hero dallying in the East but rather of the marriage for love of a male and female knight from two distinct cultures in conflict with each other. His variations on the model, however, are worth pointing out. First of all, in the *Innamorato* it is a Frankish Christian woman who feels both admiration and physical attraction for a North African Saracen man. Second, although Bradamante falls in love in part because of the knight's prowess, thus recalling Galiziella's situation, Rugiero demonstrates his valour not in a show of arms against her but rather in a combat undertaken on her behalf. Indeed, the overwhelming trait that characterizes Rugiero and sparks her enamourment is his unconditional courtesy. Third, whereas in the *Aspramonte* "the possibility of an alliance by marriage is rejected by the text, which does not even mention this alternative" (Stoppino 41–2), in Boiardo's poem the heterogamous match provides the very foundation of Ferrara's ruling family.

In sum, Rugiero's genealogy and virtuous actions, in contrast to the arrogant imperialism demonstrated by both Alexander of Macedonia and the present king of Biserta, represent the possibility of moving beyond war to an alternative model of relations among peoples. On a personal level, the culturally mixed unions of his distant ancestors as well as that of his parents prefigure his own future marriage to Bradamante. On a collective and political level, the good nature of Alexander's three sons, which leads to the voluntary submission of all of Africa, anticipates Rugiero's unparalleled courtesy, which is acknowledged by those he benefits. His association with the historical figures of Roger I and II further suggests his foretold conversion to Christianity and his potential to rule over various peoples in a harmonious coexistence. At the same time, the Christian connotations that Boiardo gives to his character are not those connected to fighting the enemies of one's faith but rather those showing benevolence to everyone he encounters.[23] One of the most striking consequences of Rugiero's honourable conduct, in fact, is the moral conversion of the fiercest of all Africans, Rodamonte, discussed in the next chapter. Boiardo thus avoids identifying Rugiero in a dogmatic way with any one creed, highlighting instead his unconditional adherence to a code of chivalry that transcends cultural and religious difference.

Ariosto's Ruggiero

Commenting on the change in Ruggiero's character as he passes from the *Innamorato* to the *Furioso*, Rajna remarks: "In Ariosto that freshness and that fragrance are unfortunately gone; one would say that Ruggiero has aged at least ten years" (*Le fonti*, 55). Notwithstanding the hero's sudden aging (assuming we agree with Rajna), it becomes clear from the early cantos of Ariosto's poem that he is no longer the ideal knight who saves others from peril but is more akin to a helpless boy who falls into traps and needs to be rescued by others. Of the three enchantments devised by Atlante in rapid succession to keep Ruggiero away from his destiny – the *castello d'acciaio*, Alcina's island, and the *palazzo incantato* – the one that has elicited the most critical attention has been the central one.[24] What still bear examining in the context of the present study, however, are the ideological implications of the episode's global context. The following pages focus on how Ariosto creates a negative portrait of both Ruggiero and Alcina by equating luxury and moral degeneracy specifically with the East. The chapter then addresses the geo-politics behind the transformation of Ruggiero's consort, Bradamante, from an independent warrior maiden of mixed heritage to a conventional Christian maiden of legitimate birth.

Alcina's Island

Although Alcina's precise location remains vague in the *Innamorato*, she is clearly a northern fairy with no connection to the Far East. Boiardo informs us that Alcina "dimorava al regno degli Atarberi, / Che stano al mar, verso Tramontana" ("dwelt with the Atarberies / who lived up north beside a sea") (*OI* 2.13.55). Bruscagli deduces that her territory lies on the (northern) edge of the Caspian Sea because that is the only body of water the knights could have encountered on their westward journey (*Orlando innamorato*, 2: 761n). In the *Furioso*, however, Alcina's realm has been furtively relocated to an island off the eastern coast of India, specifically "dove il mar orïental la bagna" ("where it is washed by the Eastern Sea") (*OF* 9.58 A; 10.70 C).[25] Ruggiero reaches the fairy's island from Europe by first travelling south to the Tropic of Cancer and then, in anticipation of Christopher Columbus, heading due west across the ocean (*OF* 4.50).

In line with its new oriental placement, Alcina's palace exudes a luxuriousness specifically associated with southern and eastern regions of the globe.[26] The gardens display palm trees as well as "Cedri et Naranci, c'havean frutti et fiori / contesti in varie forme et tutte belle" ("[citron] and orange-trees whose fruit and blossoms were disposed in sundry harmonious ways") (*OF* 6.21 AC).[27] Palm trees are native to tropical and sub-tropical regions, while citrus trees originated in southern China, India, and southeast Asia.[28] The gate wall is described as being entirely covered with "le più rare gemme di Levante" ("the rarest jewels of the Levant") (*OF* 6.71 AC). In addition, the sumptuousness of Alcina's table is compared to that of Ninus's Assyrian successors and the Egyptian queen Cleopatra (*OF* 7.20 AC).

The fairy inhabiting this oriental world is not simply dangerous and magical but is portrayed as the very embodiment of moral depravity. Astolfo calls Alcina and her twin sister, Morgana, "inique e scelerate / et piene d'ogni vitio infame et brutto" ("a wicked, pernicious pair [...], surfeited with every sort of ugly infamy") (*OF* 6.43–4 AC), and he reveals to Ruggiero, moreover, that they were born of incest.[29] He then goes on to disclose that Alcina had previously had a thousand other lovers that she had transformed into both animate and inanimate objects upon discarding them "perché essi non vadano pel mondo / di lei narrando la vita lasciva" ("to prevent their spreading about the world the story of her wanton ways") (*OF* 6.51 AC).

This combination of oriental luxury and moral decadence spills over into the portrayal of Ruggiero when he becomes Alcina's lover (*OF* 7.27 AC). Indeed, in describing the first sexual encounter between the knight and the fairy, Ariosto evokes the fragrances of India and Arabia: "cogliendo il fior del spirto su le labbia, / che più suave non esce di seme /

ch'India nutrisca in l'odorata sabbia" ("drawing from each other's lips pollen so fragrant that it will be found on no flower which grows in the scented Indian or Arabian sands") (*OF* 7.29 AC). When Merlin's handmaiden Melissa subsequently finds Ruggiero lounging in idleness at a riverbank, Ariosto's lengthy description of him explicitly equates foreign fashion with depravity:

Il suo vestir delitïoso e molle
tutto era d'otio e di lascivia pieno,
che di sua man gli havea di seta e d'oro
tessuto Alcina con sottil lavoro.

Di ricche gemme un splendido monile
gli discendea dal collo in mezo il petto;
in l'uno e in l'altro già tanto virile
braccio girava un lucido cerchietto;
gli havea forato un fil d'oro sottile
ambe l'orecchi,' in forma d'annelletto;
e due gran perle pendevano quindi,
qual mai non hebbon li Arabi né l'Indi.

Humide havea le ben nodate chiome
de i più suavi odor che sieno in prezzo;
tutto ne' gesti era amoroso, come
fusse in Valenza a servir donne avezzo;
non era in lui di sano altro ch'el nome,
corrotto tutto il resto, e più che mèzzo. (*OF* 7.53–5 A)

The delicious softness of his dress
suggested sloth and sensuality;
Alcina had woven the garment with her
own hands in silk and gold, a subtle work.

A glittering, richly jewelled necklace
fastened round his neck and hung to his chest,
while his two arms, hitherto so virile,
were now each clasped by a lustrous bangle.
Each ear was pierced by a fine gold ring
from which a fat pearl hung,
such as no Arabian or Indian ever boasted.

> His curly locks were saturated in perfumes,
> the most precious and aromatic that exist.
> His every gesture was mincing, as though he
> were accustomed to waiting on ladies in Valencia. (*OF* 7.53–5 C)

While references to Ruggiero's clothing could suggest the Tyrian purple cloak that Aeneas was wearing in Carthage at Mercury's arrival, Ariosto's scathing depiction of the knight's debauchery specifically names Arabia, India, and Valencia. Moreover, later in the episode, as the reformed Ruggiero is suffering from thirst, heat, and exhaustion on his way to Logistilla's island, the damsels from Alcina's court who try to entice him away from his path are said to be reclining upon "tapeti Alessandrini" ("Egyptian rugs") (*OF* 9.25 A; 10.37 C).

Since the degenerate Alcina is associated with an opulent East, it is telling that Ariosto distances her righteous half-sister not only morally, but geographically as well. Logistilla, who "vivendo in castitate, / ha posto in le virtuti il suo cor tutto" ("has steeped her heart in all that is virtuous, and lives in chastity") (*OF* 6.46 and 44 AC), is protected by a natural formation that Ariosto likens to the British Isles: "sì come tien la Scotia et l'Inghilterra / il monte et la riviera separata" ("similar to the mountain and the firth which separate England from Scotland") (*OF* 6.45 AC). Through an ingenious geographical analogy, Logistilla escapes the connotations of oriental decadence that characterize her half-sister and joins instead the company of good fairies of Celtic stock.

Bradamante

Many scholars have noted that in the course of the *Furioso* Bradamante is transformed from an autonomous *donna guerriera* to a docile daughter and then wife.[30] Whereas in the *Innamorato* she commanded Charlemagne's troops in the absence of Ranaldo, in Ariosto's poem she does not participate in the Christian victory over Agramante's army. Indeed, for several cantos she remains confined to her familial home, racked by jealousy over Ruggiero's apparent betrayal.[31] When she does enter the Saracen camp at Arles, it is not to help Charlemagne's cause but to enact a private revenge against her future consort. And although she earlier defeated Rodomonte at his perilous bridge, in the poem's final scene she recedes into the background as passive spectator while Ruggiero's battle against the king of Algiers takes centre stage. As Finucci aptly puts it, "In time the empowered, phallic woman warrior entering the scene in Canto

1 with a lance, a pennant, and a horse turns into the swooning bride exiting the epic forty-six cantos later, aghast at the thought that her husband is locked in combat with a knight whom ironically she herself, as well as her mate, bested earlier" (230).

With respect to the dynastic couple's genealogy, Ariosto emphasizes their sameness while erasing signs of their diversity. First of all, he does not lose any time in refashioning Bradamante as legitimate. When she is reintroduced into the narrative in the second canto (following her canto I defeat of Sacripante), Ariosto identifies her as the daughter not only of Duke Amone but also of his wife, Beatrice (*OF* 2.31 AC), effectively negating the character's Saracen heritage on her mother's side.[32] Not only are Bradamante's parents both Franks, but Ariosto also emphasizes that she and Ruggiero share the same Trojan as well as French lineage. Already in Merlin's cave Melissa informs Bradamante of their future blending of Trojan blood: "L'antiquo sangue che venne da Troia, / per li duo miglior rivi in te commisto" ("The blood deriving from ancient Troy, in its two most perfect streams, is to be blended in you") (*OF* 3.17 AC).

Later in the poem Ariosto underscores that Ruggiero and Bradamante belong to the same French houses of Mongrana and Chiaramonte. He twice names both of these families with respect to Ruggiero's twin sister as well, initially when Ruggiero tells Marphisa of their common origin (*OF* 33.79 A; 36.75 C) and subsequently when she officially enters the Christian community as an adopted daughter of Charlemagne (*OF* 34.20 A; 38.20). In the final canto Ariosto draws attention yet again to their common French lineage by noting the joy of the two illustrious houses that are rejoined by their wedding: "Si rallegra Mongrana e Chiaramonte, / di nuovo nodo i dui raggiunti rami" ("Mongrana and Clairmont rejoiced at the new bond uniting the two branches") (*OF* 40.44 A; 46.67 C). Thus, although Ariosto follows Boiardo's genealogical tree closely when it comes to claiming the identical European origins of the dynastic couple, at the same time he eliminates any material that pointed instead to their equally essential diversity.

Chapter Eight

Rodamonte of Sarza (Algeria)

Boiardo's Rodamonte

Rodamante of Sarza, introduced in the context of Agramante's invasion of France, provides a point of comparison with his fellow African king. While not motivated by religious difference, Agramante is nevertheless depicted as a respectful follower of Mohammed. By contrast, Rodamonte demonstrates a derisive stance towards all religion, including Islam: "Ch'una vil foglia il suo Macon non stima, / E meno ancor se acosta ad altra fede" ("[he] believed / Mohammed was not worth a leaf. / And he thought less of other faiths") (*OI* 2.5.66–7). Whereas Agramante asks the help of his fellow Africans in the planned military action against the Frankish state, Rodamonte is ready to invade France with or without Agramante. And if the king of Biserta would like to cap his conquest of the earth with an invasion of Paradise – "Ancor nel Paradiso io vuò far guera!" ("I'll want to war in Paradise") (*OI* 2.1.64) – the king of Sarza plans not only to single-handedly subjugate the world (*OI* 2.5.67) but to invade hell as well as heaven (*OI* 2.1.65). This expressed readiness to overpower the very cosmos, with no apparent preference for either of the latter two otherworldly locations, underscores both his condescending attitude towards religion in general and his uncontainable desire for domination.

Boiardo invites further comparison between the two African rulers through their respective genealogies. Rodamonte's father is said to be Ulieno di Sarza, the son of Agolante's sister in Andrea da Barberino's *Aspramonte* (3.90, 214).[1] Although this family tie would thus make Rodamonte, no less than Agramante, a descendant of Alexander of Macedonia, Boiardo prefers to link him to a different ancestor, Nimrod, here characterized as a fierce giant who first challenged the gods at Thessaly and then constructed the Tower of Babel in order to destroy heaven (*OI* 2.14.33). This association between the mythical Gigantomachy and the biblical Tower of Babel could be found in *Inferno* 31, where Nimrod is imagined to be one of the giants guarding the entrance to Cocytus.[2] Yet while Dante focuses on God's punishment in this scene through Nimrod's unintelligible speech, Boiardo underscores the pride ("quel soperbo") and arrogance ("la sua arroganza") that motivated his acts of defiance (*OI* 2.14.33) – the very character traits epitomized by Rodamonte.

Boiardo might also have chosen Nimrod as Rodamonte's forebear because of his connection to Africa. Although the Tower of Babel was traditionally situated in ancient Babylon, Nimrod himself was linked to the peoples of Africa via his grandfather Cam or Ham, the son of Noah, who was purported to have emigrated there. Riccobaldo accepts both the genealogy and the geography, explaining in his *Compilatio chronologica* that "Cham generated Chus, who generated Nimrod [...]. The generation of Cham held Africa" (col. 195).[3] Thus Rodamonte could claim not only a more ancient genealogy, dating back to Greek mythology and the Bible, but a prior link to the African continent as well.

The Council of Biserta

While Rodamonte surpasses Agramante in overreaching ambition, at the opening council scene he comes into direction opposition with the three rulers who speak out against the proposal to invade Charlemagne's realm. King Branzardo responds to Agramante's opening speech by turning a problem of action – whether or not to attack France – into a question of knowledge. Explaining that there are three ways to arrive at an understanding of all things – "per ragione, / O per exempio, o per experïentia" ("by reason or / example or experience") (*OI* 2.1.39), he argues that all three modes of knowledge lead to the conclusion that their military expedition would end in failure. King Sobrino, having already fought Charlemagne's paladins in the context of Agolante's war, supports Branzardo's argument based on his personal experience (*OI* 2.1.51).[4] The unnamed king of Garamanta agrees with their assessment because of the disposition of the stars: "Saturno, ch'è signor del'ascendente, / Ad ogni modo ci farà perire" ("the planet Saturn is ascendent, / so we will perish anyway") (*OI* 2.1.68).[5] When the latter king reveals that a young man named Rugiero who could defeat Charlemagne is hidden out of sight in the mountains, Agramante places the seer's credibility above Rodamonte's incredulity and decides to delay the invasion while searching for the youth. Boiardo also tips the scales in favour of Rodamonte's adversaries: Branzardo is said to be known as the most prudent ("il più prudente"; *OI* 2.1.38), Sobrino is credited with having much wisdom ("ha molto sapere"; *OI* 2.1.44), and the king of Garamanta is a "Sagio [...], / Incantator, astrologo e indivino" ("sage [...], / astrologer, enchanter, seer") (*OI* 2.1.57) whose previous astrological predictions regarding "Divicia, guerra, pace e caristia" ("wealth, war, peace, and want") have always been correct (*OI* 2.1.76).

Using concepts drawn from scientific observation, Rodamonte argues for sense perception as the exclusive basis for determining reality. His refutation of the first two kings begins by positing a "truth" based on natural phenomena: "In ciascun loco / Ove fiama s'acende, un tempo dura / Picola prima, e puo' si fa gran foco; / Ma come vien al fin sempre s'oscura, / Mancando dil suo lume a poco a poco" ("In every place / where one ignites a fire, the flame / is small at first, and then it gains. / But as it nears the end it wanes / and gradually it loses light") (*OI* 2.1.53). This statement then becomes the basis of an analogy that purportedly describes human nature: "E cossì fa l'humana creatura, / Che poi ch'ha di sua età passato il verde, / La vista, il senno e l'animo se perde" ("And human beings do the same, / since when their age has passed its prime / they lose their courage, sense, and sight") (*OI* 2.1.53).[6] Rodamonte focuses on sight once again to relate his general statement regarding humankind to the circumstances at hand: "Questo chiaro si vede nel presente, / Per questi doï ch'adesso han parlato" ("At present, this is clearly seen / in these two who've just spoken") (*OI* 2.1.54).

The limits of sense perception, however, were pointed out by philosophers at least as far back as Plato's *Theaetetus*, in which Socrates derided the "uninitiates," that is, "people who don't think there is anything other than what they can grasp firmly in their hands" (155e). Indeed, in the course of this dialogue Socrates' interlocutor moves from his original proposition that "knowledge is nothing but perception" (151e) to the opposite conclusion: "It has now become absolutely clear that knowledge is something other than perception" (186e).[7] In his works of speculative philosophy, Nicholas of Cusa likewise outlined a trajectory of knowledge acquisition that moved from the senses to the higher faculties of reason and intellect.[8] He believed, moreover, that even knowledge attained by reason was no more than approximate or conjectural and that, especially in the quest to know God, philosophy must be supplemented with the higher science of theology.

Boiardo could have expected the early readers of his poem to favour the three (wise) kings over Rodamonte not only because of the rational arguments of the first two rulers but also based on the astrological explanation of the king of Garamanta. His use of Saturn accords with the astrological studies of the ninth-century Arab astrologer/astronomer Albumasar (Abu Ma'shar), who posited Saturn and Jupiter as "the makers of history" since their conjunction was responsible for changes in "religion, prophecy, empires, kingdoms, dynasties" (De Armas 157).[9] Albumasar singled out Saturn as "the most powerful and the most malefic" of planets (De Armas 154). His works were highly esteemed at the Este court, which was in the vanguard of astrological scholarship during the reigns of both Borso and Ercole.[10] Indeed, the thirty-six decan-gods that cross the middle zone of the Sala dei Mesi frescoes in Palazzo Schifanoia are based on his *Introductorium in astronomiam*.[11] When, years later, Pellegrino Prisciani, the humanist intellectual behind the Schifanoia commission, exhorted Eleonora d'Aragona to pray during a favourable conjunction involving Jupiter, he still cited Albumasar as an authority.[12]

The king of Garamanta's assertions are a reminder that while Italian scholars of the fifteenth century translated tracts of moral philosophy and natural science directly from Greek sources and thus no longer relied on medieval Arab intermediaries, those interested in astrology still turned primarily to Arab works sanctioned by Italian tradition. Moreover, in this light the entire opening council scene – from its explicit and implicit references to Alexander of Macedonia, Herodotus, and Livy discussed in the previous chapter, to its use of Greek philosophy and Arab astrology in the present debate – brings home the fact that classical history, literature, philosophy, and science were a shared heritage across the larger Mediterranean.[13] The inherited commonalities between the Muslim and Christian worlds that emerge in the opening council scene could have thereby suggested that Agramante's North African realm was not to be envisioned simply as a polar opposite of western Christendom.

The Search for Rugiero

The debate over the acquisition of knowledge continues even after the conclusion of the council scene. When the king Mulabuferso fails to find Rugiero on Mount Carena, he claims that the youth is not there simply because he has not seen him:

> Visto ho l'ultimo dì quel che 'l primero;
> Onde io t'acerto e affermo in iuramento

Che là non se ritrova alcun Rugiero.

I saw the same first day and last.
And I assure you – this I swear –
that no Rugiero lives out there. (*OI* 2.3.18)

Echoing Rodamonte's utter reliance on sense perception, Mulabuferso then states his belief that the Rugiero he has not seen was never even born (*OI* 2.3.18).

Rodamonte subsequently turns the alleged non-existence of Rugiero into a general maxim about humanity: "Mal agia l'homo che dà tanta fede / Al ditto d'altri e a quel che non si vede!" ("It is not good to give such credence / to others' words, to what's not seen") (*OI* 2.3.20). He then abruptly changes the argument from the dubious existence of one individual to that of the gods themselves. Although Rodamonte admits his ignorance of whether any god exists or not ("io nol sciò certo" ["I don't know"]), he again takes for granted that sight is the only way to obtain such knowledge: "Homo non è che l'abia visto o experto" ("There's no one who has witnessed him") (*OI* 2.3.22). Asserting that belief in a supernatural divinity is based simply on fear, he proclaims that his own personal "god" amounts to his weapons, horse, and valour:

Io de mia fede vi ragiono aperto,
Che sol il mio bon brando e l'armatura
E la maza ch'io porto al destrier mio
E l'animo ch'io ho son il mio dio.

I'll tell you my faith openly:
[That only] my armor, my good sword,
my horse, the club I carry, and
the heart I have [are] my own god! (*OI* 2.3.22)

The king of Garamanta, while reaffirming his greater ability to discern and convey the truth ("il vero"), attributes to Rodamonte a faulty manner of seeing: "Comme vedeti, egli ha il [viso] perduto / Benché mai tutto non l'avesse intiero" ("He's lost perspective, as you see, / though he was never all that sound") (*OI* 2.3.25).[14] Agramante, thus invited to share his fellow king's superior mode of perception through his own power of sight ("comme vedeti" ["as you see"]), accordingly decides to continue the search for Rugiero.

In France

Rodamonte, in the meantime, refuses to wait any longer and sets out for France with his troops. Once he comes into contact with the world beyond his homeland, however, he begins to realize his own limitations.[15] His vulnerability is first exposed when a storm at sea leads to the loss of two-thirds of his men before he even steps ashore onto French territory. Yet it is not the forces of nature but the single knight Ranaldo who leads him to reassess the position he held at the council in Biserta. After testing Ranaldo's valour at first hand, Rodamonte exclaims that King Sobrino had indeed spoken truthfully (*OI* 2.15.30). His "Io l'ho provato" ("I've fought him") (*OI* 2.15.29) is a direct echo of the king's earlier "Io gli ho provati" ("I tried them") (*OI* 2.1.51). In fact, he is so impressed by the veracity of Sobrino's statement that he virtually goes from one extreme to the other – whereas earlier he had remarked that one should never lend credence to another's words, he now declares that "Sempre creder si debe a chi ha provato" ("you [always] have to trust [another's] experience") (*OI* 2.15.30).

Rodamonte's character undergoes an even more substantial transformation through an encounter with his fellow African knight, Rugiero, who in the meantime had been found and drawn into Agramante's campaign. When Rodamonte refuses to allow his opponent Bradamante to join Charlemagne's retreating forces, Rugiero offers to take her place in the ongoing battle and then courteously waits for Rodamonte to recover from a blow and retrieve his sword rather than acting on his advantage. Moved by such exemplary chivalry, Rodamonte uses the terminology of sight to acknowledge his opponent's superiority: "Ben chiaramente hagio veduto / Che cavalier nonn è di te migliore" ("I've seen and it is clear / no one can win fame fighting you") (*OI* 3.5.12).

Ironically it is Rugiero, whose existence he had doubted and whose importance to the invasion he had dismissed, who provides Rodamonte with greater knowledge of the world and of his (smaller) place in it. Rugiero's greatness in both arms and courtesy leads the king of Sarza to humble himself and promise unconditional obedience: "E sempre quanto io posso e quanto io valia / Di me fa el tuo parere in ogni banda, / Come el magiore al suo minor comanda" ("Anywhere you see fit you may / order my services – always. / Masters command subordinates") (*OI* 3.5.13). Although the poem is interrupted before Rodamonte meets Rugiero again and can act on his declaration, the outcome of this initial encounter suggests that the future relations between the two knights might have continued to develop both Rugiero's unconditional courtesy and Rodamonte's ongoing enlightenment.

Ariosto's Rodomonte

Ariosto introduces Rodomonte not simply as the king of Sarza but as the "Re d'Algieri / [...] e di Sarza" ("king of Algiers / [...] and of Sarza") (*OF* 12.25; 14.25), and he privileges the new title in subsequent references. This change may be due to the fact that Sarza, the Italianized form of Chercel (also Sharshal and Cherchell), would not have sounded particularly African.[16] Algiers, on the other hand, was a recognized North African city that had recently grown in size and importance when Moors expelled from Spain settled there. Rodomonte is referred to in less formal ways as well, not only through the common terms of Saracen, pagan, and African but also as "il barbaro" ("the barbarian") and "il Moro" ("the Moor").[17] This also represents a departure from Boiardo, who had not used either of the latter two terms for Rodamonte.[18] Ariosto also has recourse to adjectives such as "crudel" ("cruel") (*OF* 27.11; 29.11) and "brutto" ("ugly") (*OF* 27.13; 29.13) that reinforce Rodomonte's negative characterization.[19]

With respect to religion, as noted above, Boiardo's Rodamonte was sceptical of the belief in any divinity and refused to worship a god he had not seen (*OI* 2.5.66–7). Ariosto turns scepticism into outright enmity, making Rodomonte "d'ogni legge inimico e d'ogni fede" ("hostile to every law, to every faith") (*OF* 26.100 A; 28.99). At the same time, however, his hostility is given a religious focus that it did not have in the *Innamorato*: all the force of his violence is now directed specifically against those of the Christian faith. Whereas in the *Innamorato* Rodamonte intended to conquer the entire earth and then move on to heaven and hell, in the *Furioso* he desires instead to burn down Paris and level "Roma santa" ("sacred Rome") (*OF* 12.65 A; 14.65 C), the capitals of the Holy Roman Empire and the Catholic church, respectively. Carlo Dionisotti remarks that the ideology behind this statement was foreign to Boiardo's poem.[20] It was, however, common enough in earlier Carolingian epics such as the *Spagna*, where Feraù expresses his desire to destroy Rome, specifically St Peter's Church (*Spagna* 3.28).

In Paris

The transformation of Rodomonte's character from a quintessential overreacher who scorned all religion to a sworn enemy of Christendom can be seen in the episode of the attack on Paris, where he evinces a "grande odio" ("great hatred") (*OF* 14.27 A; 16.27 C) of Christians in general and a brutality towards everyone in the city regardless of age or gender. Referring to Rodomonte as the "empio Re, capo e signor de li empi" ("impious king, master and chief of all the wicked") (*OF* 14.26 A; 16.26), Ariosto brings religious difference to the fore when recounting the atrocities committed against the Christians by both the king of Algiers himself and by "the Turks and Moors" as a group:

Deveano allhora haver li excessi loro
di Dio turbata la serena fronte,
ch'ogni lor luoco scórse il Turco e 'l Moro
con stupri, uccisïon, rapine et onte:
ma più di tutti li altri danni, fôro
gravati dal furor di Rodomonte. (*OF* 15.6 A)

The Christians' excesses must have vexed
the serene face of the Almighty,
for the Turks and Moors had overrun all their lands,
committing rape and murder, pillage and outrage.
But at no one's hands did they suffer worse
than at those of rabid Rodomont. (*OF* 17.6 C)

Ariosto later uses Rodomonte's blasphemous attitude as an occasion to denigrate the African continent as a whole: "non ha timor né reverentia / di Dio o di santi; e nel mancar di fede / tutta a lui la bugiarda Aphrica cede" ("he neither feared nor respected God and the saints – when it came to breaking faith, the whole of deceitful Africa yielded to him") (*OF* 27.18 A; 29.18 C).

Doralice and Isabella

With regard to the nature of belief, Ariosto actually reverses the problem presented by Boiardo. Whereas in the *Innamorato* Rodamonte initially did not give credence to anything he could not verify with his own eyes, in the course of the *Furioso* he reverts into the very picture of credulity through a zigzagging succession of mistaken assumptions. First, the Algerian king believes that the Spanish princess Doralice will remain enamoured of him while he spends all his time away at war. Reeling from disillusionment when she chooses to remain with her abductor, Mandricardo, he immediately believes *all* women to be false. While this is presented as a case of disbelief (that is, he does not believe in the fidelity of any woman), it is actually one in which a single instance serves as the basis for a universal claim: "Io credo ben che de l'ascose / feminil frode sia copia infinita" ("I do believe there is no limit to woman's wiles") (*OF* 26.76 A; 28.75 C). Yet another Spanish princess will soon prove him wrong.

When Rodomonte subsequently meets the beautiful widow Isabella of Granada, he shows his own fickleness by forgetting his previous disdain for women and immediately becoming inflamed with desire for her. Realizing that Rodomonte intends to rape her, Isabella devises a plan that will preserve her honour at the cost of her life. She tells him about a magic potion that will make him invulnerable and invites him to test it out on her body first. Her explanation focuses specifically on the question of knowledge and belief:

> Acciò che paia
> che mia parole al vento non ho mosse,
> quella ch'el ver da la bugia dispaia
> et può far dotte ancho le genti grosse,
> te ne farò l'esperïenza adesso,
> prima che in altri, nel mio corpo istesso. (*OF* 27.23 A)

> Lest you should think my words are just air,
> I shall give you what it takes to distinguish truth
> from deceit and convince the dullest mind –
> I shall give you proof, here and now,
> and on my own person, not upon another's. (*OF* 29.23 C)

Paradoxically, Rodomonte's willingness to test the potion's efficacy denotes his extreme gullibility, since he needs to believe in magic in order to go through with an experiment that requires putting an axe to Isabella's desirable neck. When he unwittingly beheads the maiden, his error is said to be precisely that of his credulity: "Quel huom bestial [...] le credeva" ("The brute believed her") (*OF* 27.25 A; 29.25).[21]

Ariosto suddenly describes Rodomonte as an observer of Islamic law in this scene: "Non era Rodomonte usato al vino, / perché la legge sua lo vieta e danna" ("Rodomont was unaccustomed to wine, which Moslem law forbids and condemns") (*OF* 27.22 A; 29.22 C). This religious restriction would not have been news to Ariosto's readers. Yet while Boiardo had noted in the *Historia imperiale* that "i Saracini non bevono vino per divieto di lor legge" ("Saracens do not drink wine because their religion outlaws it") (col. 381), neither he nor Ariosto had previously intruded upon the fictional world of their poems with this kind of doctrinal explanation. That Ariosto should do so at this point is surprising since until now Rodomonte had acted outside all rules, whether human or divine. Even more unexpected, therefore, is Ariosto's assertion that with the exception of drinking wine, "the Saracen" followed Moorish custom in all other matters: "ch'el Saracin nel resto alla Moresca, / ma vòlse far nel bere alla Francesca" ("Rodomont was Moorish in all things else, but [he wanted to be French in his drinking]") (*OF* 25.129 A; 27.130 C). This aside identifies him as previously a strict follower of Muslim practice rather than as the archetypal overreacher dismissive of all religion that he was in Boiardo's poem.

Having unintentionally beheaded Isabella, Rodomonte reacts by building a tomb for her and challenging knights to cross swords with him on a nearby bridge. This new role completes his degradation from a major epic hero to a minor figure of romance. Whereas his earlier attack on Paris placed him in the category of Boiardo's Agricane, Virgil's Turnus, and Statius's Capaneus, he is now reduced to a rather dismal copy of Zambardo at the Bridge of Death (*OI* 1.5.78–6.14) or any number of evildoers who present obstacles to Arthurian knights travelling through wild forests in the Breton cycle. Despite this shift from epic to romance, however, Rodomonte continues to make religious distinctions: whereas he simply despoils Saracen opponents, he sends defeated Christians as prisoners to Algiers (*OF* 27.39 A; 29.39 C).

The End of Rodomonte

Ariosto's reversal of Rodomonte's character extends to his relation with the ideal knight Ruggiero. The battle between the two that takes place in the last canto of the *Furioso* recalls their duel near the end of the *Innamorato*. Yet here we find not the enlightened Rodamonte of *OI* 3.5, who declares himself subordinate to the courteous Rugiero, but rather the insolent Rodamonte of *OI* 2.1, who wanted to live and die as a god unto himself. When Rodomonte "s'aventa a Ruggier che nulla sente; / in tal modo intornata havea la testa, / in tal modo offuscata havea la mente" ("flung himself on his dazed opponent while his head was so benumbed, his brain so clouded") (*OF* 40.96; 46.124 C), he was refusing to show the same civility that Rugiero had extended to him in Boiardo's poem. In the end, Ariosto brings the battle, and indeed the entire poem, to a close with Ruggiero conquering Rodomonte – this time not through a demonstration of courtesy but by a fatal blow that sends him reeling down to Hades.

Zanette takes issue with Ariosto for the transformation that Rodomonte's character undergoes in the *Furioso*: "We were right to say that it was for him a tremendous misfortune to pass from the hands of Boiardo to those of Ariosto, who with that serious air of one who is simply and scrupulously writing a story – extraneous from its quirks since whatever happens in it does not depend on him – ruins a hero for you forever" (363).[22] At the same time, however, Ariosto's degradation of Rodomonte is in keeping with the fate that befalls Boiardo's entire cast of non-Christian characters not destined for conversion.

Chapter Nine

Saracen Spain

Spanish Saracens in the *Orlando innamorato*

Boiardo portrays Spanish Saracens alternately as friends and enemies, gallant heroes of romance adventure and fierce epic warriors. Whereas in the opening canto of his poem they break out of the antagonistic role that epitomized their presence in Carolingian epic, in the latter cantos of Book Two they suddenly threaten Christendom as allies of the North African invaders. The poem's variable treatment of Spanish Saracens, as I argue below, may be linked to contemporary events during the period of the poem's composition.

Book One

From the poem's opening canto the Spanish Saracens, no less than the Frankish Christians, are quick to divest themselves of any association with Carolingian epic in order to enter the world of romance. Feraguto, following his duel against Argalìa, acts like an Arthurian knight when he comes upon Orlando in the Arden Wood and challenges him for the rights to Angelica. Viewing Feraguto as a pagan counterpart to Orlando, since both are nephews of their sovereign and poorly suited for the role of courtly lover, Denise Alexandre points out that his indifference to religion and his enamourment run contrary to literary tradition: "Whereas in the *Spagna* Ferraù still fights a religious war, praying continuously to Mohammed, Apollino, and Trivigante, and, until defeated, tries to convert Orlando to Islam, in the *Orlando innamorato* he fights in singular combat (jousts or duels), whether these be against Christians or coreligionists (against Orlando, but also against Argalìa and Rodamonte) when love commands him" (130–1).[1]

Although champions from both sides have abandoned Paris to follow Angelica, Charlemagne's tournament nevertheless takes place as scheduled. Boiardo uses the occasion to imagine how the remaining members of these traditionally antagonistic groups might interact when brought together in the context of a joust. The first participant to take the field is Balugante's son Serpentino, who in the *Spagna* figured as a "campion de la fè pagana" ("champion of the pagan faith") and who was killed by Orlando after refusing to convert (*Spagna* 26.29–30). Presently, as Serpentino defeats one Christian opponent after another, everyone in the crowd is said to applaud his valour: "Di tal valor si mostra e di tal nerbo / Che ciascadun ben iudica ala vista / Che altri che lui quel pregio non aquista" ("He showed such valor and such force / that everyone who watched agreed / no one but he would win the prize") (*OI* 1.2.34). He is eventually defeated by the Dane Ogieri, who then takes on Feraguto's brother Isolieri. The latter knight, while a formidable enemy in the *Spagna*, is here refashioned as "il giovene Isolieri: / Ben è possente e destro cavalieri" ("youthful Isolier, / strong and agile cavalier") (*OI* 1.2.45).

After defeating Isolieri, the Dane Ogieri also bests his fellow Christian Gualtiero da Monleone. He then invites his fellow Christians to refrain from jousting among themselves, pointing out how his defeat of Gualtiero has led the Saracens to laugh at them: "Che io vedo caleffarci a' Saracini, / Perché faciamo l'un l'altro tapini!" ("I see the pagans mocking us / for giving one another trouble!") (*OI* 1.2.47). His statement draws attention to the fact that the joust was not categorically divided along religious lines a priori while providing a practical motivation to establish this procedure. The explicit new alignment transforms the joust from a test of individual valour to a collective contest between two rival groups.

The introduction of the Moroccan king, Grandonio, into the arena further transforms the tournament by turning it into a deadly combat (Tissoni Benvenuti, *Inamoramento de Orlando*, 1: 82n). As Grandonio defeats the same Christian knights that Ferragù had overcome in the *Entrée* (Sberlati 180), the old Christian-Saracen antagonisms that had been put aside now come to the fore. Yet before long Astolfo and his magic lance will come to the rescue to save Charlemagne's honour and to prevent the episode from slipping too far into the Carolingian pattern of an outright battle. When the typically luckless English knight defeats the fearsome king of Morocco, Boiardo looks for a moment beyond his poem to acknowledge the ultimate destiny of both knights at Roncevaux: Grandonio, "(sì comm'io odo) / Occise Astolpho al fin per tal ferita, / Ben che anchor lui quel dì lasciò la vita" ("I've heard, / murdered Astolfo in revenge / but died as well that fatal day") (*OI* 1.3.7).[2]

The poet then regains a lighter touch as he goes on to describe Astolfo's easy victory over other Saracen characters familiar from the Carolingian narratives. While in the *Spagna* Astolfo was the first to be defeated and imprisoned by Feraù, now he is the one who saves the day, taking on the role that Orlando had assumed in the earlier narrative. The treachery that leads to Astolfo's imprisonment by Charlemagne despite his victory will be devised by Gano and his clan without the complicity of the Saracens.

After the conclusion of the Parisian joust, we do not hear any more about the Spanish Saracens until Marsilio's kingdom is invaded by Gradasso. This emergency provides the occasion to bring Feraguto back into the epic arena. When Marsilio's daughter Fiordespina brings news that their realm is under attack, Feraguto immediately breaks off his fight against Orlando for Angelica and heads back to Spain (*OI* 1.4.10–11). Unlike the hopelessly love-struck paladin, the Spanish Saracen shows himself capable of putting aside his private passion and joining in the collective effort to save his homeland – not from Charlemagne's army as in the *Spagna* but from a new external threat.

Whereas the traditional Carolingian epic pictured Marsilio as the perennial enemy of the Christians, Gradasso's attack provides the occasion for an alliance between Latin Christendom and Saracen Spain. Dismissing King Marsilio's religious difference as irrelevant, Charlemagne considers instead the potential danger to his own state and his obligation to his brother-in-law:

> Io odo ragionare
> Che quando egli arde il muro a noi vicino
> De nostra casa debiàn dubitare:
> Dico che, se Marsilio è saracino,
> Ciò non attendo; egli è nostro cognato
> Et ha vicino a Francia gionto il stato.
>
> I've heard it said
> that when the wall beside us burns
> we ought to fear for our own house.
> Marsilio is a Saracen:
> that does not matter. He is our [brother-in-law]
> and rules the country next to France. (*OI* 1.4.14)

Charlemagne thereby decides to send troops led by his champion, Ranaldo, to assist the Saracen sovereign.

Although Saracen Spain may not have been identified with Venice at this early point in the poem, Charlemagne's reasoning would nevertheless have had resonance with Boiardo's contemporaries in the context of the Ottoman-Venetian War. After the Venetian Senate voted for war in late July of 1463, Cardinal John Bessarion of Trebizond, as Pope Pius II's legate in the Venetian dominions, included the same arguments of neighbourly concern and preventive self-defence in his instructions for preachers in order to encourage military engagement against the Ottomans: "In vain do they expect mercy from God, who do not show it to their neighbour," and "if we are unmoved by love for religion and calamity [in the East], let us be moved by our country, our homes, our children, our family, and our wives" (149). And although the Este were not historically proponents of crusading ventures, Pius II persuaded Borso to send two galleys to Ancona for the expedition against the Turks that was scheduled to set out in August 1464.[3] The difference in the poem is that the neighbours to be defended are the traditional Saracen enemies of the Carolingian epic.

The subsequent progression of Gradasso's military expedition shows how all sense of self and other in the political arena of the poem is contingent upon circumstance. During the ensuing siege of Barcelona, forces on both sides of the war are Saracen with the exception of Ranaldo's 50,000 Frankish troops supporting Marsilio (*OI* 1.4.37). After Ranaldo inexplicably disappears at dawn prior to his decisive combat against Gradasso, Feraguto and Serpentino are captured in the battle of Barcelona, and the remaining Christians flee, there is no one left to defend Spain against "Gradasso furïoso" (*OI* 1.6.57). Marsilio, in view of his utter helplessness as well as Ranaldo's apparent betrayal of his cause, cedes defeat and is compelled to join forces with the king of Sericana against Charlemagne (*OI* 1.6.59). Like the Italian states of Boiardo's day, Marsilio shifts alliances on the basis not of ideology but of sheer necessity. His troops are listed as the fourth of five formations that attack Paris, yet they are no match for Charlemagne's army and are put to flight (*OI* 1.7.18–19). Marsilio returns to Spain after Astolfo's victory over Gradasso (*OI* 1.7.71), and we hear nothing more about the Spanish Saracens for the remainder of Book One as the focus shifts to events occurring in Asia.

Book Two

During the council at Biserta, King Sobrino anticipates that the Spanish Saracens can be counted on to join in the war effort because Marsilio is

Agramante's relative (*OI* 2.1.48). Earlier in the poem, as noted above, parentage was given as one of the reasons that Charlemagne had sent his forces to defend Marsilio against Gradasso. In canto 17, Boiardo indirectly confirms that Marsilio rates his ties to the African Agramante above those to his neighbour Charlemagne when he notes that Marsilio has not only granted passage to Agramante's troops but is gathering his own troops as well (*OI* 2.17.3). Nevertheless, apart from these two brief references, Boiardo pays no heed to Saracen Spain in the first twenty-one cantos of Book Two. Moreover, the only Spanish Saracens who enter the narrative – Feraguto and Isolieri – appear outside their realm in the guise of Arthurian knights. Feraguto, who had not been active since Gradasso left Paris early in Book One, re-enters the poem replaying Orlando's earlier departure from Paris by abruptly deciding to leave Spain in disguise ("travestito") in order to search for Angelica (*OI* 2.15.33). Upon encountering Rodamonte, he capriciously engages him in a duel over Doralice, princess of Granada, even though he admits that he no longer loves her (*OI* 2.15.35–41). This episode not only draws the North African Rodamonte into the territory of romance but goes back to the poem's opening cantos in which Feraguto had crossed swords with Orlando over the absent princess of Cathay. Feraguto's brother Isolieri, who had not been seen since the tournament of Paris, resurfaces as the "gioveneto ardito" ("daring youth") guarding Narcissus's tomb on behalf of Queen Calidora (*OI* 2.17.65). Boiardo leaves no doubt as to his character's romance colouring in this episode: "Insin di Spagna al'India era venuto / […] / Amor l'avea conduto e ritenuto" ("He'd come to India from Spain. / […] / Love brought him and Love kept him there") (*OI* 2.17.66).

Canto 22 opens with a shift to epic and an ensuing review of the African troops who prepare to invade France.[4] Yet when we receive news of a new invasion (Rodamonte had earlier sailed directly to France), it is led not by Agramante but by Marsilio. A Christian messenger interrupts the ongoing combat between Feraguto and Rodamonte over Doralice to inform them that Spanish Saracens are besieging Ranaldo's homeland of Montalbano. The scene recalls the moment in which Feraguto's cousin Fiordespina had interrupted his earlier battle against Orlando, but the affiliation of this courier with the Christian side allows for a critique of the "perfido Pagano" ("treacherous pagan") who has destroyed the territory: "E quel paese è in gran distrutïone, / Ché tuto intorno l'han arso e robato" ("The whole domain now lies in ruin. / Spaniards have robbed and burned it all") (*OI* 2.22.38–9). In both cases, the duels are immediately suspended so that Feraguto may enter the war in support of Marsilio. Now, however, the military action is offensive rather than defensive, and rather than go their separate ways, the two former opponents join forces against Ranaldo's homeland.

When Feraguto and Rodamonte reach Marsilio's camp at Montalbano, Boiardo explicitly names warriors from the Iberian peninsula and Morocco, including Marsilio's brothers Balugante and Falcirone, Grandonio, Serpentino, and Isolieri (*OI* 2.23.5–9).[5] The latter knight, however, was last seen guarding the Narcissus fountain. Boiardo never explains how or why Isolieri left India, but his inclusion in this grouping creates the sense that the upcoming epic battle has taken precedence over any individual romance adventures.

Yet it is not simply the abruptness with which the Spanish troops are placed in France but their unprecedented centrality that warrants our attention. The new prominence of Balugante and Grandonio, in particular, brings into play allusions to the Carolingian epic that the poem had previously resisted. Balugante was last seen in the second canto of the poem watching his son Serpentino at the tournament, and although he was later mentioned in passing as one of the Spanish knights who had been either captured or killed by Gradasso during the siege of Barcelona (*OI* 1.4.22), he was not mentioned at all during the ensuing invasion of Paris. The Moroccan king, Grandonio, did make it to Paris in the context of that earlier war, yet he had virtually no role in the fighting and was only mentioned once as he fled in retreat alongside Marsilio and the Spanish army (*OI* 1.7.19). Presently, by contrast, not only are both characters heavily involved in the battle at Montalbano, but Grandonio conjures up explicit connotations of the Carolingian epic as he defeats one Christian warrior after another. His seeming invincibility even prompts Oliviero (Orlando's close companion in the Battle of Roncevaux throughout the literary tradition) to call upon God to lend him strength against this Saracen in defending "la tua Fede santa [...] e 'l tuo culto divino" ("your holy faith and sacred doctrine") (*OI* 2.23.37).

Why would characters who were Charlemagne's guests at the poem's opening – and who only joined Gradasso's invasion when defeat left them no other option – return explosively in the final cantos of Book Two to inject Carolingian overtones into the Battle of Montalbano? The new aggressive role of Saracen Spain in cantos 22 to 31 prompts us to inquire whether historical circumstances could have played a part in transforming Charlemagne's neighbours into mortal enemies. Might the unforeseen ferocity of the Spanish Saracens in the final ten cantos have been coloured by the growing hostilities towards Ferrara on the part of the Venetians? After Venice made peace with the Ottomans in 1479, the state was viewed by many as "the devious accomplice of the Turk in a perspective in which even an Ottoman occupation of the Italian peninsula could occur" (Cardini 131). When Mehmed II turned his military might against Otranto in 1480, Venetian ships stood by and allowed the Ottoman ships to attack the southern Italian coastline rather than come to the aid of the Neapolitan kingdom. A dispatch sent from Rome to Ferrara immediately following the Turkish attack on Otranto pointed the finger at Venice: "Se tiene per certo che la venuta de questi Turchi in el Reame sia stata opera de Venetiani" ("It is deemed certain that the coming of the Turks to the realm is the work of the Venetians") (cited in Ricci, *I turchi alle porte*, 71). Noting that "the suspicion of having favoured the Turkish invasion of Otranto weighed on Venice," Dionisotti adds that while the republic now acted "neutral in the Orient, she became ever more threateningly powerful in Italy" ("La guerra d'Oriente," 474). Even as Alfonso d'Aragona strove to recover Otranto from the Turks, Venice was preparing to attack Ferrarese territory. Venice officially declared war against the Estense state in 1482 and, as noted earlier, succeeded in pushing the defending troops right up to the walls of the ducal city itself.

While Agramante's North African troops are depicted in such a way as to evoke Mehmed's Ottoman Empire, the concomitant aggression of Marsilio's troops against Charlemagne's realm sounds very much like the corollary military action of Venice against Estense Ferrara during this period. Boiardo decries both aggressors in his *Pastorali* written between 1483 and 1484: in the first eclogue, Italy is said to be "ripiena di spietati Turchi" ("filled with ruthless Turks") (I:143), while a "magior monstro mai non fo veduto" ("greater monster was never seen") than Venice itself (I:164); in the second, he refers to the invading Ottoman army as "un drago sì crudel" ("a dragon so cruel") (II:41), while Venice still figures as "quel monstro" ("that monster") (II:38).

When Rodamonte and Feraguto lead an assault that overpowers the Christian defenders despite their best efforts, Boiardo conveys a sense of desperation and pending disaster: "Come iudichi il Ciel quel giorno a morte / L'Imperator e la sua real corte" ("Heaven, it seemed, doomed Charlemagne / and his whole court to death that day") (*OI* 2.24.10). Despite Charlemagne's prayer for divine aid (*OI* 2.24.18), the Christians continue to lose ground: "La nostra gente tutta se sbaraglia, / Perché adosso gli sónno e Saracini / Che gli tagliano tutti a pezi e a fetta" ("Our soldiers scattered every place, / with Saracens pursuing them, / who cut them into chunks and pieces") (*OI* 2.24.22). The situation becomes even more dire for the Christians after the arrival of Agramante's troops (*OI* 2.29.23). As the tide of battle shifts back and forth, there are moments of utter devastation for Charlemagne's forces: "Il crido è grande e' pianti e la roina / Di nostra gente morta con fracasso, / Cresciendo ognor la folta saracina" ("Great was that massacre. Our troops / scattered in discord or lay moaning. / The swarm of Saracens kept growing") (*OI* 2.30.10).

Boiardo brings his chivalric fiction and historical reality together at the conclusion of Book Two when he suspends the poem's epic action with a reference to the contemporary Venetians as "anime fele / Che fan guera per sdegno e per furore" ("villains who fight from spite and rage") (*OI* 2.31.51). The publication of the first two books between April 1482 and February 1483 coincides with the bleakest period of the Ferrarese-Venetian war.[6]

Book Three

Boiardo resumes the poem some time after the "infernal tempesta / Dela guerra spietata è dipartita" ("infernal storm / of heartless war has gone its way") (*OI* 3.1.2) and, indeed, opens Book Three imagining the Este court as once again in full bloom. In the poem's fiction, however, the war initially rages on. As the Venetians had brought their attack right to the walls of Ferrara, now the combined Saracen forces chase the retreating Christian army to the gates of Paris (*OI* 3.4.46). Yet the timely arrival of Brandimarte and Orlando in the penultimate completed canto of the poem brings new hope and ensures the survival of the city despite the great losses incurred.

Notwithstanding the centrality of the Spanish Saracens in the invasion and the resulting Carolingian overtones, Feraguto and Isolieri are not permanently removed from the space of romance. Feraguto's retreat from the battlefield after his defeat at the hands of Ranaldo leads him back into the forest where he inadvertently drops his helmet into a stream (*OI* 2.31.4). His attempt to retrieve this piece of armour that originally belonged to Angelica's brother Argalìa brings us back to the opening cantos of the poem in which he borrowed it from the dying knight with the promise to return it. Nevertheless, he is last mentioned taking part in the siege of Paris (*OI* 3.8.15 and 47), and it seems likely that he would have continued to traverse both romance and epic terrain if the poem had not been interrupted.[7] Isolieri also returns briefly in the context of a romance adventure, albeit in a minor role: although present at the siege of Montalbano, he is later found among those imprisoned by the Fountain Fay and liberated by Mandricardo (*OI* 3.2.38).

Near the end of the poem, Boiardo devotes greater attention to Feraguto's cousin Fiordespina. No longer simply acting as a messenger, the Spanish princess becomes the unrequited lover in a saucy new romance episode. She unwittingly falls in love with Bradamante, whose hair had been shorn by the hermit tending her wounds after a battle that separated her from Rugiero. The fact that Fiordespina mistakes Bradamante for a male warrior may confirm Charlemagne's earlier comparison of her to Ranaldo in "ardir e forza" ("strength / and daring") (*OI* 2.6.23). Yet despite the warrior maiden's knightly appearance, Bradamante playfully remarks on her inability to satisfy Fiordespina's sexual desire:

> Qualche una malcontenta
> Sarà de noi, e ingannata alla vista,
> Ché gratugia a gratugia poco acquista!
>
> One of us won't be happy! She's
> deceived by what she sees. Small gain
> comes when grates grate on grates, not cheese! (*OI* 3.9.11)

Bradamante's espousal of diversity over sameness, while here referring exclusively to gender, is also suggestive in a more general way, since her future husband, Rugiero, is not only of the opposite sex but is a foreign other who is at present fighting on the enemy side and adhering to a different religion.

We will never know how Boiardo intended to resolve this tale of the "vano amore / Di Fiordespina ardente a poco a poco" ("hopeless love / of simmering Fiordespina") since, just as he is about to say what it was that Bradamante lacked, his attention is drawn out of the fiction and into the historical reality of "la Italia tutta a fiama e a foco" ("all of Italy on fire") (*OI* 3.9.25–6) that brings the poem to a halt. In Niccolò degli Agostini's continuation, Fiordespina indicates her interest in marriage to the handsome stranger ("ch'altro mia mente non brama et desia / se non potermi teco maritare" ["Since my mind yearns for and desires / Only to be able to marry you"]) (*OI* 4.4.37) and anticipates her readiness to convert should this prove necessary: "e per tuo amor faromi christiana, / come per Carlo fece Gallerana" ("And for your love I will become a Christian / As Galerana did for Charles") (*OI* 4.4.39). Her recourse to the example of her father's sister evokes a model of conversion for love that Agostini will shortly thereafter adopt for Ruggiero and Bradamante. Indeed, as though eager to propel the dynastic plot forward, Agostini promptly narrates Rugiero's arrival on the scene and Fiordespina's subsequent departure "sconsolata" ("unconsoled") and "quasi piangendo per desperatione" ("almost crying out of desperation") (*OI* 4.4.48).

Saracen Spain in the *Orlando furioso*

Princess Fiordispina of Spain (Saragossa)

When Ariosto picks up this episode several cantos into the *Furioso*, he substitutes Bradamante with her (now twin) brother, Ricciardetto, who, upon hearing of her strange adventure, decides to impersonate her in order to gain access to Fiordispina's bed. While this narrative strategy removes the problem created by the sameness of gender, Ariosto introduces a new focus – the difference of religion. Ricciardetto, in fact, specifies that the Spanish princess prayed to "suo Machon e a tutti i dèi" ("[her] Mahomet and all the gods") that the object of her desire would change gender (*OF* 23.42 A; 25.44 C). Despite the episode's romance patina, moreover, it serves in the poem's larger epic scheme as a reminder of the Saracen invasion of Christendom. Ricciardetto reaches the fortress housing Fiordispina with ease because her father, Marsiglio, has penetrated deep into French territory. The setting is explicitly identified as "una terra / ch'el Re Marsiglio in mezo Francia tenne, / di man di Carlo tolta in quella guerra" ("a stronghold of Marsilius in the middle of France, one which he had seized from Charlemagne in the course of the war") (*OF* 23.5 A; 25.7 C).

Boiardo had earlier set in motion the story of mutual love between the Christian Bradamante and the Saracen Rugiero in the course of the same war. Yet the autobiographical novella that Bradamante's brother relates to her future spouse provides not a parallel but a contrast to their union. Whereas the future of the dynastic couple holds in store conversion, marriage, and progeny, Ricciardetto's quickly consumed affair with the Spanish princess focuses exclusively on sexual gratification in the present without any thought to the future. In opposition to the reciprocal courtesy demonstrated by the two Este forebears, Ricciardetto readily admits that his ploy to dress as a woman by day in order to sleep beside Fiordispina at night was a simple adventure of questionable merit (*OF* 23.49 A).[8] His tale repeatedly emphasizes the sheer physicality of his desire: he first remembers how Fiordispina's eyes and cheeks had initially whetted his "appetito" (*OF* 23.47 A; 25.49 C); he then recalls his offer of sex to the maiden as he guided her hand to his male organ (*OF* 23.63 A; 25.65 C); and finally he remarks how "il piacer" ("the pleasure") continued for some months before his ruse was discovered (*OF* 23.68 A; 25.70 C). For her part, Fiordispina cannot wait to arrive at the enjoyment afforded by the bedroom and, unlike Agostini's character, expresses no interest in marriage.

Rajna mentions a possible precedent for this story of cross-dressing in an episode from the *Tristan* in which the knight dresses as a woman in order to enter Isotta's bedchamber. After three days of bliss, the couple are discovered in their subterfuge and condemned to die. Tristan flees as he is being led to the stake, and Isotta is rescued while on her way to a leper colony (*Le fonti*, 367–8). If Ariosto had this or a similar episode in mind, then Ricciardetto's lack of interest in Fiordispina at the tale's conclusion is even more striking. As he departs in the company of Ruggiero, he is completely oblivious to the fate of the woman he has left behind imprisoned in a fortress (*OF* 20.40 A; 22.40 C). Finucci notes that not even the poet gives any further thought to the Saracen princess: "Fiordispina is literally abandoned by the author in her father's dungeon, crossed out of the story without even a stroke of the pen" (207).

In the end, the plot is in line with neither Boiardo's dynastic couple nor the grand Breton-style lovers who could have inspired the cross-dressing plotline but rather with late Carolingian narratives in which lusty Saracen princesses desire paladins who pass through their land and sometimes have love affairs with them but do not establish lasting, legitimate ties.[9] Thus, while agreeing with Finucci that in this episode "Ariosto constructs, by way of apparent transgressions, socially correct gender identities" (202), I would further argue that the poet seeks to reinforce socially correct national and religious identities as well.

Princess Isabella of Granada

Between the call for help on the part of one of Fiordispina's servants (*OF* 20.38–41 A; 22.38–41 C) and Rugiero's rescue of Ricciardetto (*OF* 23.16 A; 25.18), Ariosto inserts the central component of another episode of requited love between a Christian knight and a Spanish Saracen princess that nevertheless ends badly – that of Zerbino and Isabella. Like Ricciardetto's frivolous account, this latter, dramatic rendering of an interfaith relationship is set against the normative example of Bradamante and Ruggiero. By this point in the poem, Bradamante finds herself at home in the role of an obedient Christian daughter. In contrast, the Saracen Isabella has disregarded her society's restrictions and abandoned her family in order to elope with the Christian Zerbino. She is reunited with him in canto 21/23 only to be shortly thereafter separated from him by death when he is killed by Mandricardo in the following canto.

The couple was introduced several cantos earlier when Orlando rescued Isabella from thieves who had sold her to a merchant planning to take her to the sultan "in Levante" ("in the East") (*OF* 11.31 A; 13.31 C). As she relates her vicissitudes to Orlando, Isabella explains that Zerbino was compelled to abduct her precisely because interfaith marriage was prohibited:

E perché vieta la diversa fede
(essendo egli christiano, io saracina)
ch'al mio padre per moglie mi chiede,
per furto indi levarmi si destina. (*OF* 11.10 A)

As we were of different faiths
(he a Christian, I a Saracen),
he could not ask my father for my hand,
but had to resort to abducting me. (*OF* 13.10 C)

Her reference to their "diversità de leggi" ("difference of religion") in the following stanza as well keeps the heterogamous nature of their relationship at the forefront of the unfolding story.

When Mandricardo kills Zerbino in canto 22/24, the couple's tragic tale seems to have reached an endpoint that fixes it at the opposite pole from Bradamante and Ruggiero's foretold dynastic union; yet Ariosto nevertheless continues to invite comparison between the stories by introducing the theme of conversion. Although Ruggiero's baptism is the necessary condition for gaining his beloved's hand in marriage (*OF* 20.36 A; 22.36), he delays his conversion indefinitely while continuing to fight out of a sense of loyalty to Agramante. Isabella, on the other hand, having lost the hope of becoming Zerbino's wife, nevertheless converts spontaneously when a hermit "le fece veder come non fusse / alcun, se non in Dio, vero contento, / e ch'eran l'altre transitorie e flusse / speranze humane, e di poco momento" ("had her see that there was no true happiness except in God, and that all human hopes were transient and mutable and of little moment") (*OF* 22.88–9 A; 24.88–9 C). Her subsequent desire to "tutta dicar al servigio di Dio" ("dedicate the rest of her life to the service of God") and to sequester herself from the world in a convent (*OF* 22.89 A; 24.89 C) is now set against Bradamante's unwilling confinement to her family home.

If initially it seemed that the bawdy tale of Ricciardetto and Fiordispina bracketed the emotionally wrought love story of Zerbino and Isabella, it turns out to be the other way around. A few cantos after Ricciardetto leaves Fiordispina behind and sets off together with Ruggiero, Isabella reappears in the narrative and fatefully encounters Rodomonte as she is on her way to a convent in Provence. If, as discussed earlier, this episode brings Rodomonte's (newly invented) Muslim manners to the forefront, at the same time it also refashions the neophyte Isabella as a Christian martyr who prefers death to the violation of her chastity.[10]

Isabella and Zerbino thus die as the heroic victims of the virtual sword-thief Mandricardo and would-be rapist Rodomonte. These endings not only reflect negatively on the two Saracen knights, as discussed earlier, but also prevent the possibility of marriage and progeny for characters who had dared to disregard the prohibition against interfaith marriage. By way of contrast, it could be noted that Zerbino's sister Ginevra has much better luck when she chooses to marry the Italian knight Ariodante (*OF* 4–5 AC). It may not be coincidental that the characters who choose a partner within the alliance system of Christian Europe will live happily ever after while the couple who most openly defy religious and societal norms for the sake of love meet a tragic end.

Indeed, the same pattern is borne out in the case of Angelica and Orlando. Whereas the princess of Cathay is granted a happy ending through marrying someone of her own religion and retiring to her distant homeland to play the part of a ruler's consort, the love-struck paladin – in the midst of the juxtaposed stories discussed above – loses both his mind and his humanity. As we later find out, in fact, Orlando's madness is nothing less than God's punishment for his illicit desire for a pagan woman. In Part Four we will look more closely at Orlando's compulsory renunciation of the Saracen princess and dutiful return to the battleground of Carolingian epic. First, however, we turn our attention to the third geographical region that plays a decisive part in determining the ideological underpinnings of both poems.

PART THREE

The Middle East

Chapter Ten

Boiardo's Noradino in Cyprus

Whereas some of the *Innamorato*'s East Asian and North African rulers harbour ambitions that threaten the existence of Latin Christendom, the poem offers an entirely different paradigm when the action moves to the eastern Mediterranean and what has come to be known as the Middle East. In particular, Boiardo's depiction of Syria and Cyprus creates the impression of a sophisticated Saracen courtly society completely uninvolved with the affairs of western Europe. This chapter examines an international jousting tournament that takes place in the Cypriot capital of Nicosia, focusing in particular on Orlando's interactions with Saracen Syrians and Christian Byzantines (*OI* 2.19.50–2.20.43). My contention is that Boiardo develops this episode against the crusading ideology of its Carolingian precedents, exemplified in the *Spagna* and the *Storia di Rinaldino di Montalbano*, drawing instead on a more positive vision of the region found in a number of chronicles and travelogues well known in Estense Ferrara.

The *Innamorato* narrative moves westward from Cathay when Orlando, leaving the Tartar siege at Albracà to rage on, escorts Angelica towards France where the princess secretly hopes to woo the intractable paladin Ranaldo. Although they initially travel in the company of the knight Brandimarte and his damsel Fiordelisa, the couples are separated after escaping from a group of hungry Lestrigons.[1] Orlando and Angelica continue the journey alone from this dangerous site, traversing two territories that gave rise to great civilizations: "Già il paese de' Persi avìa passato / E la Mesopotamia che confina" ("[They passed] through Persia's land and then / Mesopotamia, its neighbor") (*OI* 2.19.51). Yet that ancient world, which Boiardo describes so vividly in his translations of Herodotus's *Histories* and Xenophon's *Cyropaedia*, here serves only as a transitional space between the vaguely etched lands of Cathay and Tartary and the more sharply delineated eastern Mediterranean.

As Orlando and Angelica leave Armenia on their right and travel through "Soria" (Syria) to the coast, Boiardo suddenly draws attention to their surroundings: "E tuto questo e rico e bel paese / Passò sanza trovar guere o contese" ("a wealthy, splendid realm where they / encountered neither wars nor battles") (*OI* 2.19.51). This depiction of Syria as both beautiful and tranquil is in contrast not only with the besieged Albracà but also with the neighbouring territory of Circassia, which was dangerous to travellers because of the negligence of the ruler, Sacripante, and vulnerable to assault by Mongol armies.[2] The Middle East thus offers, for the first time in the poem since the opening joust in Paris, a region in which individuals and groups from all over the globe may come together in harmony and safety.

Although Orlando is not the first knight to pass through Syria in a chivalric narrative, he is quite possibly the first ever to find this region at peace. In the fifteenth-century prose *Storia di Rinaldino di Montalbano*, the eponymous hero arrives in Syria only to find the country racked by war as Giliastro attacks his brother Alipandro at Antioch (88). Rinaldino comes to the aid of the latter, who confirms the correctness of this choice by converting to Christianity upon discovering the newcomer's identity (93). Thanks to Rinaldino's valour, the neo-Christian Alipandro gains control not only over all of Syria but, in a subsequent war, over nearby Armenia as well. Yet peace does not reign for long, and Rinaldino is later compelled to return to Antioch to save the city from an onslaught by the Turks (230). In this epic sequence, discussed below, the invading army is defeated and forced to return to Turkey (285). This wish-fulfilment fantasy of a progressive Christianization of the Middle East apparently leaves the anonymous author no time to take notice of the Syrian countryside.

Boiardo's contemporaries could have found references to the loveliness of the Middle Eastern landscape outside the medieval epic, however, notably in travelogues about the Holy Land. Mandeville's fictional *Travels*, for example, extol the beauty of a valley near Beirut: "Le val de Bochar qe est moult bele vallee et mout fructuouse, et gist entre les montaynes, et y ad des bele riveres et des pretz et des grantz pasturages pur les bestes" ("the Vale of Bochar [...] is a fine fertile valley, producing all kinds of fruit. It is surrounded by hills. There are in it lovely rivers and broad meadows and noble grazing for cattle") (*Le livre* 256; tr. 100). Poggibonsi describes the delightful view from Damascus: "Verso ponente gli stanno grande montagne, e verso il levante grande pianura, con belli e molti giardini" ("Towards the west are great moutains, and towards the east a great plain, with many beautiful gardens") (2: 10). Moreover, both the Marquis Niccolò III d'Este and his son Milliaduse had personally travelled through both Syria and Cyprus during their respective pilgrimages of 1413 and 1440. The latter's chronicler, Don Domenego, points out the "giardini bellissimi" ("very attractive gardens") between Damascus and Jerusalem (84) as well as the beautiful plains in Cyprus (68). Yet whereas Boiardo comments on the absence of warfare or conflict in the region, the travel account simply observes that the once-magnificent cities have decayed and the countryside is unpopulated.[3] During the trip from Nicosia to Famagusta, for example, the chronicler remarks: "mai non vidi più bella pianura, ma è inabitata" ("I never saw a more beautiful plain, but it is uninhabited") (68).

Nur ad-Din

Boiardo's suggestive correlation between the beauty of the land and its state of peacefulness prefaces his introduction of the country's current ruler, the benevolent and courteous king Noradino of Syria, who first appears in the narrative as he is travelling from Damascus to Cyprus.[4] The king's name is the Italian rendering of Nur ad-Din (1118–74), the Muslim leader who was generally known in the Arab world as a figure of military courage, piety, and modesty, celebrated for uniting his people in the defence of their land against Frankish invaders.[5] Despite the losses that the crusaders incurred at his hands, he was also generally portrayed in positive terms by Christian chroniclers, who referred to him in Latin as Noradinus.[6]

In the *Historia imperiale*, Boiardo describes "Noradino" as a Syrian sultan "che di valentigia non avea pari in tutto l'Oriente" ("whose valour was unequalled in all the East") (col. 351) and who defended his homeland against French and German armies led by Louis VII and Conrad III in the Second Crusade. In drawing the outlines of this war, Boiardo refrains from siding with the Western invaders against their Middle Eastern foes; rather, he contrasts northern and southern Europeans. The French and Germans are said to look disparagingly upon Spaniards and Italians, considering the former to be half-Saracens and the latter to be "mercatanti, & uomini civili" ("merchants and non-military men") (col. 351).[7] Boiardo censures the arrogance of the German crusaders, whom he refers to as barbarians ("Barbari"), and he faults Conrad in particular for his boast to fill oriental rivers with Saracen blood and cover France and Germany with Asian gold and precious gems. The failure of his troops, in fact, is seen as God's inevitable punishment for their pride and avarice:

"Dio solo, il quale sdegnando la superba alterezza di questi Barbari, ridusse in vano la loro gonfiata & incomportabile elazione" ("Only God, disdaining the haughty pride of these Barbarians, reduced to emptiness their puffed-up and insufferable elation") (col. 351).

As Boiardo continues his account of the war, we find that God defeated the Christians not through direct intervention but via the acumen of the Muslim leaders.[8] When the sultan of Persia sought the support of the Saracens of Syria, King Dodequin of Damascus (the historical Toghtekin, who ruled Damascus from 1104 to 1128) sent for none other than Noradino, who subsequently "fece maravigliosa difesa" ("carried out a remarkable defence") of the city (col. 353). Boiardo goes on to say that Noradino died in Damascus "dopo molte imprese fatto con grandissimo onore contro a' Cristiani" ("after many deeds undertaken against the Christians with the greatest honour") (col. 375).

Both the crusading chronicles and Boiardo's *Historia imperiale* devote much greater attention, however, to Nur ad-Din's successor, Saladin (c. 1138–93). D.S. Richards, who translated Baha' al-Din Ibn Shaddad's influential biography of Saladin, notes that "the fundamental premise of the whole book is that Saladin's life provided a model fit to be set alongside the great figures from Islam's earlier history" because of both his military achievements and his "moral excellencies" (4). His fame crossed religious and ethnic boundaries, transforming him into a figure of legendary status even in western Europe. As Christopher Tyerman writes: "Saladin's reputation as a noble adversary of honour, chivalry, clemency and justice, invented in the immediate aftermath of the Third Crusade (1188–92), became a staple image of crusading from the vernacular cycles of crusade epics and romances of the thirteenth century into the pulp history of the twenty-first" (350–1).[9]

Referring to Saladino as Noradino's son, Boiardo likewise portrays him as the embodiment of virtue, underscoring his courteous and chivalric qualities: "Era in Damasco molto amato il Saladino, perchè in quella Cittade avea fatta lunga dimora, e con animo liberale e graziosa affabilitade avea a se tratti gli animi di tutti i Soriani" ("Saladin was very much loved in Damascus since he had lived long in that city and treated all the Syrians with a liberal spirit and gracious affability") (col. 377). Boiardo quotes Saladin as saying that he aimed exclusively to acquire "gloria" ("glory") and not "Provincie" ("territory") (col. 392), and praises him for loving and honouring "virtù" in his enemies (col. 392). His reputation was "per clemenza e bontà magnificato" ("magnified by his clemency and goodness") (col. 421), and "corse la fama di questa bontade per tutta l'Asia" ("the fame of his good nature spread throughout Asia") (col. 392–3).

Given that in his romance epic Boiardo would have been interested in evoking an exemplary Middle Eastern figure but not in establishing a strict historical identification, Saladin's outstanding fame would have made his name too familiar. The name of Noradino, on the other hand, could have evoked other praiseworthy figures from the period in addition to Saladin's predecessor. In the *Historia imperiale* Boiardo briefly mentions that another Noradino, this time Saladin's son, "per sua virtù si fece dappoi grandissimo nelle parti d'Oriente" ("because of his valour later became very great in the East") (col. 422).[10] If such virtuous and courteous individuals could emerge in the midst of a war, one might wonder what they would be like if their land were not under attack. In my view, Boiardo is imagining just such a scenario in the *Innamorato*'s Middle Eastern episode.

When Orlando and Angelica encounter Noradino at the port of Baruti (Beirut), they become the immediate beneficiaries of his hospitable nature. Fostering the idea of a chivalric and courtly ethos transcending all national and religious barriers, Noradino immediately recognizes Orlando's worth on sight, exclaiming:

> "Se costui non me inganna nel'aspeto,
> Debbe esser cima e fior d'ogni valente,
> Se l'apparenza al'animo non mente."
>
> "If that man's form does not deceive,
> he has to be the flower of knights.
> His looks and spirit do not lie!" (*OI* 2.19.57)

Pointedly, Noradino invites Orlando to join his entourage on its way to a tournament in Cyprus even before asking his name, rank, and nationality (*OI* 2.19.57–8). Without hesitation Orlando states his readiness to serve ("servire") Noradino whether in a joust or in battle, identifying himself as a homeless knight from Circassia who has lost everything in war. Boiardo has thus created a situation in which Charlemagne's foremost paladin finds himself in the Middle East not to fight a holy war but to participate in a tournament under a Muslim king's banner.

Although it does no credit to our Christian paladin to subject himself to Noradino disguised as a Saracen, it was not uncommon for Christians to conceal their identity while travelling through the region. According to

Luchino Dal Campo, Niccolò d'Este visited the Holy Land anonymously under the name of Niccolò Contarini, while Don Domenego tells us that Niccolò's son Milliaduse actually dressed as an Arab ("a la rabesca") on his way from Damascus to Jerusalem and then again from the latter city to Cairo (79). The latter's disguise allowed him to pass through the area with greater ease; it did not lead, however, to any real interaction with the local culture. When stopping to rest for the night, Milliaduse's men were careful to remain silent in order not to give themselves away. Orlando, on the other hand, not only speaks Arabic well enough to fool Noradino (albeit this is a poetic licence typical of chivalric epic) but will participate fully in the major activities of his host country by entering a joust.[11]

The Eastern Mediterranean

Having departed from Damascus and encountered Orlando at the port city of Beirut, Noradino and his retinue cross the sea with "optimal northeast winds" ("Intra Levante e Greco, ottimo vento"; *OI* 2.20.2), land at Famagusta, and then ride on to the royal city of Nicosia.[12] Boiardo's early readers would have had information about these sites from a range of sources. Damascus was known as a hub for trade between East and West in the fifteenth century. In a description of potential use to both merchants and pilgrims, Mandeville's *Travels* called it a "moult bele cité, et moult noble, et plaine de toutes marchandises" ("lovely city full of good merchandise") and located it at a three-day journey from the sea and five days from Jerusalem (*Le livre* 254; tr. 99).[13] Petrarch, judging Damascus "noteworthy for its aspect and its antiquity," considered the city "more illustrious and also much more ancient" than Antioch (*Itinerarium* 16.1). Milliaduse's chronicler Don Domenego, who stayed there with his patron for almost two months, remarks on the city's extensive trade with Italian merchants (73–4). In the *Historia imperiale*, Boiardo himself notes that Damascus was considered by his (unnamed) source to be the world's most ancient city (col. 353), maintaining that it was "grandissima" ("very great") not only in antiquity but also right up to the present day (col. 341). He later goes on to claim that the closest one could get to the beauty of Damascus in the West was Naples, which he says Saladin used to call "la piccola Damasco" ("the little Damascus") (col. 382). This analogy might have helped Ercole to better visualize the splendour of Damascus, given that he had lived for several years at the Neapolitan court.

The Este might have been particularly interested in Beirut as the site where St George had purportedly killed the dragon, since this warrior saint was the patron of Ferrara. After recalling the legendary feat, Don Domenego reports having actually entered the dragon's cave with Milliaduse (70).[14] He also draws attention to the city's importance as a commercial centre despite the fact that its moment of grandeur had passed, noting that Venetian, Genoese, and Catalan ships and galleys arrived regularly at the port (70). Mandeville likewise describes Beirut as a "bone ville et bon chastel et fort" ("good town, with a fine castle"), noting that pilgrims regularly travelled by sea from there to Cyprus (*Le livre* 257; tr. 100).

Boiardo depicts the island of Cyprus as Saracen, thus predating its conquest by Crusaders in 1190. The Ferrarese court would have known even more about Cyprus than about Damascus. Cyprus had remained under Latin rule since the Third Crusade, and after the Muslim reconquest of Acre in 1291 its port cities of Famagusta and Paphos became central for trade between Syria and western Europe. Cyprus's pivotal role in commerce made it a crossroads for merchants of diverse cultures and creeds. Mandeville draws attention, in fact, to Famagusta's multiethnic environment: "Y ad une de principaux portz de mer qe soit en mounde. La arrivent christiens et Sarazins et gentz de toutes naciouns" ("There is the world's best harbour. Christians and heathen and men of all nations land there") (*Le livre* 122; tr. 55).

The Este family, moreover, could have claimed a privileged perspective on this island through their own connections to it. Niccolò d'Este's chronicler, Luchino Dal Campo, records that the travellers, among them Matteo Maria's grandfather Feltrino Boiardo, were honoured guests there on their way back from Jerusalem in 1413. After sailing to Cyprus from the port of Beirut, the same route Noradino was to take, Niccolò journeyed by horse to visit King Janus of Cyprus at Nicosia, where he was met outside the gates by a "grandissima compagnia di cavalieri, e lo ricevettero tanto graziosamente e con tanta allegrezza che fu maraviglia" ("very great company of knights, and they received him so graciously and with such pleasure that it was a marvel") (Dal Campo 131–2). For his part, Milliaduse not only visited Nicosia but actually escorted the daughter of the marquis of Monferrato there in 1440 on the occasion of her marriage to Janus's son John II of Lusignano, the current Cypriot king. As bride-to-be, the princess Amadea had travelled down the Po from Saluzzo and was hosted in Ferrara by Ercole I's mother, Ricciarda of Saluzzo, before joining Milliaduse (14).

Events that occurred during the composition of the *Innamorato* increased the ties between the Italian peninsula and Cyprus, leading in fact to Venice's eventual appropriation of the island. In 1468 the Cypriot king James II of Lusignano married the Venetian Caterina Cornaro, who relocated to Cyprus in 1472. James died a few months later, amidst suspicion that he might have been poisoned by agents of Venice. During Caterina's ensuing reign, the island was controlled by Venetian merchants, and in 1489 Venice would force the queen to abdicate, officially turning Cyprus into a colony.[15] The *Innamorato* episode, without the slightest reference to Venice's machinations, imagines it governed by a worthy Saracen king named Tibiano.

As the episode unfolds, the Cypriot capital, a cosmopolitan city steeped in court culture, is portrayed with a wealth of detail that renders it more concrete than any of the poem's previous settings. Its festive atmosphere is enhanced by the sound of various instruments – "Gnachere e corni e tamburini e trombe" ("Castanets, trumpets, horns, and drums") (*OI* 2.20.16) – a detail sure to have interested the Ferrarese court, one of Europe's most important musical centres under Ercole d'Este.[16] Boiardo also draws attention to the luxuriousness of the public decorations and the sophistication of the participants' dress: all sides of the tribunal were adorned with "seta e drappi d'or" ("silk drapes / and cloth-of-gold") (*OI* 2.20.14), while every knight was "a maraviglia adorno" ("marvelously dressed") (*OI* 2.20.12) and "ciascun è forbito, / Con riche sopraveste e con cimeri" ("each man shone / in his rich overvest and crest") (*OI* 2.20.15). If Turpino is to be believed, moreover, the ladies present were all wearing make-up – a practice said to be prevalent in the poet's own day as well (*OI* 2.20.13–14). Boiardo thus evokes a stylish aristocratic society in the eastern Mediterranean whose cultural and aesthetic sensibilities could have been appreciated by Ferrara's courtly readers.

Boiardo imagines that King Tibiano has organized a tournament in Nicosia to determine the future husband of his daughter Lucina. Noradino, described as "Ardito e forte e di nobil aspeto / Quanto alcun altro fosse in quel confino" ("noble, strong; he was / as bold as any in that land") (*OI* 2.19.53), explains that he is on his way there to "dimostrar nel'arme il suo valore / Per una dama a cui portava amore" ("demonstrate his worth in arms, / all for a lady whom he loved") (*OI* 2.19.52). The fact that he intends to win Lucina's hand in this way takes him definitively out of the context of the crusades and places him in the midst of a romance setting. He is thus associated not only with an international chivalric ethos but most closely with knights from the Breton cycle who participated in jousts where they could win a princess as their bride.[17]

The absence of external threats and his own lack of military aggressiveness free him from warfare and allow him to act like a knight of the Round Table. We should perhaps not be too surprised to find the Syrian king in this guise, since the proem of the previous canto had emphatically affirmed the superiority of Arthurian over Carolingian narratives: whereas Charlemagne's court "tiéne ad Amor chiuse le porte / E sol se dete ale bataglie sante" ("closed its gates to Love / and only followed holy wars"), King Arthur's knights "Mostrarno in più batalie il suo valore, / Andando con lor dame in aventura" ("displayed their worth in many battles / and sought adventure with their ladies") (*OI* 2.18.1–2).[18] In the present episode Boiardo corrects this disparity not only by having Orlando, the quintessential Carolingian hero, participate in an Arthurian-style joust in the company of his delectable beloved but by imagining a Middle East dominated by Saracen characters equally imbued with the values of Arthurian romance.

The *Storia di Rinaldino di Montalbano* also takes us to Nicosia – not for a festive occasion, however, but for a war between Christians and Saracens. While Charlemagne is off fighting in Spain, the Saracen Atrasse, who held half of Cyprus, attacks the Christian queen, Laura, who governed the other half (15), and the Frankish empress sends Rinaldino to help the queen "acciò che la fede nostra si conservi, e disperga ogni saraino" ("so that our faith may be preserved, and every Saracen dispersed") (29). With Rinaldino's crucial aid the Christians successfully defend Nicosia and then proceed to take over all of Cyprus, expelling "tutti e Saraini dell'isola, chi non si volle battezzare" ("all the Saracens from the island who refused baptism") (83).

When the anonymous author of the *Storia di Rinaldino* does relate a joust outside western Europe, the episode espouses a crusading ideology despite its initial romance plot. Rinaldino and Alipandro take part in a tournament organized by the king of Persia to marry his daughter (120). After Rinaldino's predictable victory over the Turk Torindo and many others, he cedes the Persian princess Elisena to the neo-Christian Alipandro upon the condition that she also convert. The ensuing marriage provokes the ire of Torindo, who subsequently lays siege to Antioch (230). Thus the Turk's earlier bout against Rinaldino in the Persian joust was simply a prelude to an extensive war that once again pits Christians against Saracens in the Middle East. Even the queen of Cyprus arrives in Antioch with her troops in support of its newly Christian king. The defeat of the Turkish invaders effectively establishes and expands Christian rule throughout the region, thus imaginatively refashioning crusading history (285). The prominence of Antioch in this epic echoes the city's importance in both the early Christian church and the context of the crusades.

The Tournament in Cyprus

At the *Innamorato*'s Cypriot joust, in opposition to the *Storia di Rinaldino*'s Middle Eastern adventures, alliances are not based upon religious affiliation. We are told that Greeks arrive in Cyprus together with pagans ("Greci insieme co' Pagani"; *OI* 2.20.3). In fact, in the same stanza Boiardo singles out "Basaldo e Costanzo e Morbeco" as the three most esteemed knights present, informing us that two are Turks while the one named in the middle is Greek. The verse's positioning of the Greek Costanzo, son of the Byzantine emperor Vatarone, in between the two rulers from Anatolia not only indicates the interfaith nature of the gathering but suggests a Byzantine-Turkish alliance. Indeed, when the tournament gets underway we find that the Turks Morbeco and Basaldo join the team captained by Costanzo against that led by their fellow Saracen, Noradino (*OI* 2.20.15). This presents a new situation even with respect to the poem's opening joust in Paris where Christian and Saracen knights, even though not initially differentiated according to religion, ended up on opposing sides. Moreover, like the war at Albracà from which Orlando and Angelica have just escaped, the Cypriot joust presents rival groups from outside the boundaries of western Europe. In both cases, individual Frankish paladins find themselves fighting against each other for personal reasons that have nothing to do with religious difference. As the armies involved in the war at Albracà reflected the geo-political realities of Mongol history, the current joust distinguishes the realm of Syria from that of Anatolia and Byzantium.[19]

At Albracà Orlando fought in the company of the brothers Grifone and Aquilante to defend the treacherous Trufaldino against his cousin Ranaldo. He now finds himself unwittingly pitted against the same two knights. Boiardo takes this occasion to inform us that the brothers, who were raised separately in Spain and Greece, have recently travelled through "diversi paesi e gente istrane" ("different lands with different races") to arrive at the joust (*OI* 2.20.6). He specifically notes that they made their way south from King Manodante's *Isole Lontane* (Faraway Islands) to the port of Blancherna (the harbour outside Constantinople), then, en route to Cyprus in the company of Costanzo, passed the site in which the river Xanthus reaches the sea (*OI* 2.20.8). Such detailed information offers a parallel to the trajectory Noradino had travelled from

Syria to Nicosia and is consistent with the sense of greater geographical precision conveyed throughout this episode. At the same time, by referring to the Xanthus, the river flowing beneath Troy, Boiardo elicits the reader's memory of an ancient epic war in which the Greeks were the enemies of Rome's purported Trojan ancestors.

At first Grifone and Aquilante do not recognize Orlando because he is in disguise and they have adopted Costanzo's insignia. Even after they identify the Frankish paladin, however, the brothers continue to show their allegiance to the Byzantine leader. Grifone initially suggests that they depart rather than suffer defeat but subsequently declares himself ready to undertake any action for Costanzo's sake: "Griphon ripose a lui che per suo amore / Quel che potesse far, tuto farìa" ("Grifone answered that by his / love for Costanzo he would do / all he could") (*OI* 2.20.36). Costanzo devises a deceitful plan to send Orlando away: he tells the paladin that a messenger sent by Gano has arrived with orders to seize him and that King Tibiano is consequently arming his men. This creates an ironic situation in which Orlando flees a hospitable (Saracen) Middle Eastern setting because of a (Greek's) rumour of treachery involving his (Christian) homeland. Costanzo's scheme succeeds only because Gano is considered capable of such evildoing. In this way Boiardo turns the spotlight back on the internal discord and injustice within Charlemagne's court, as he did in the poem's opening cantos both prior to and following the Parisian joust. In the first instance, Gano and his Maganzan clan had provoked Ranaldo's anger by mocking his inferior clothing (*OI* 1.1.15–16). In the second, the Maganzans' perfidy led to the imprisonment of the joust's victor, Astolfo (*OI* 1.3.10–30). At present the situation is such that the very mention of Gano is sufficient to cause Orlando's immediate departure from Cyprus.

The Greeks do not fare particularly well in this episode, either. Costanzo's deceitfulness discredits his character and places him in a bad light vis-à-vis the exemplary Noradino. Boiardo attributes this trait not only to the individual but to his cultural group at large: "Il Greco, [...] era di malicia pieno / Come son tuti, d'arte e di natura" ("The Greek was full of intrigue [both / blood and upbringing make Greeks crafty]") (*OI* 2.20.37). A hostile attitude towards Greeks can be traced back to Roman history and epic poetry, most famously Virgil's *Aeneid*. The acrimony between the two territories separated by the Adriatic Sea continued after the fall of Rome, when for centuries Byzantium subjected portions of Italian territory to its rule. In addition, crusade chroniclers regularly blamed the Greeks for luring them to fight Muslims and then deceiving them at every turn. William of Tyre refers to the Byzantine emperor Alexius as "a wicked and crafty man" (1: 123) and has Godfrey of Bouillon state that "with inexorable hatred the crafty race of the Greeks ever ardently desires to persecute our people" (1. 130).[20] In his pilgrimage guide, Petrarch actually cautions against stopping in Cyprus because "there Gallic extravagance, Syrian ease, and the frauds and enticements of the Greeks are brought together in a single island" (*Itinerarium* 15.1).[21] In the present episode, Boiardo's disapproving portrayal of the devious Costanzo prevents us from privileging the Greeks over the Syrians. Indeed, it seems that only Noradino escapes moral censure in this turn of events.

Boiardo's positive representation of a Saracen Middle East can be seen even more clearly if we compare the Cypriot joust to Orlando's eastern exploits in the *Spagna*. In the earlier poem, the Frankish knight initially fights in disguise with Saracens from Mecca to wrest Jerusalem from the allied Greeks and Persians. However, when he recognizes his opponent as his fellow paladin Ugone, he identifies himself to him in confidence and the two devise a plan requiring Ugone's rupture with his current allies (*Spagna* 17.30–5). Once the Holy City has been captured thanks to the friends' secret complicity, Orlando publicly reveals his true identity and demands that the sultan and his people convert to Christianity or face his enmity (*Spagna* 18.15). In this manner Orlando, with the collaboration of a friend discovered among the enemy forces, succeeds not only in capturing Jerusalem but also in forcing a mass conversion to the Christian faith. Only after having completely transformed the political and religious structure of the Middle East does the triumphant Orlando return to western Europe and reconcile himself to Charlemagne.

The entire *Innamorato* episode can be read as an alternative to the hostilities depicted in works like the *Storia di Rinaldino* and the *Spagna*. Departing radically from the ideological underpinnings of these Carolingian epics, Boiardo's Middle East comprises people of diverse cultures who display their rivalries in the context of a joust while the territory itself remains free of warfare and safe for travel. Orlando's (disguised) presence does not have any consequences for the land, since he leaves the political composition of the state untouched. The anticipated marriage between Noradino and the Cypriot princess Lucina will unite the Saracen realms of Syria and Cyprus without recourse to combat. Even Costanzo's disposal of the outsider Orlando through a false story is not such an evil deed when compared to the extreme acts of treachery and cruelty witnessed elsewhere in the poem and in history. In the end, although Syrians and Byzantines have distinct and competing group identities, they are not out to conquer each other's land, and they can express their aggressive drives in the accepted form of a tournament.

The *Innamorato*'s idealistic presentation of a multicultural civil society in the Levant is more consonant with attitudes that can be found outside the Carolingian epic. As noted above, chronicles from the Second and Third Crusades praised Nur ad-Din and his successor, Saladin, as courteous rulers despite the fact that they were in the enemy camp, and Boiardo himself followed this line in his own brief account of these two crusades in the *Historia imperiale*. Moreover, later pilgrim travelogues, such as those relating the journeys of Niccolò and Milliaduse d'Este, show that travellers could reach the Holy Land precisely thanks to the absence of war. Although Niccolò's group occasionally feared a hostile presence at sites along the coast and were once hit with stones when inadvertently passing a Muslim army against regulations, there is no sense of an ongoing religious conflict that could disturb or hinder their act of devotion. The latter work, even as it notes the physical deterioration of Middle Eastern cities, consistently acknowledges their past splendour as well as the continued coexistence of many different cultural groups.[22] The Middle East portrayed in Boiardo's poem goes even further to elicit our interest in and respect for the foreign other, using the freedom afforded by fiction to imagine a universal chivalry crossing religious and regional boundaries.

Looking ahead a few decades we find a comparable attitude in Castiglione's *Libro del cortegiano* (*Book of the Courtier*). At the beginning of the third evening, Federico Fregoso states his desire to include a discussion of the court of the "Gran Turco" ("Great Turk") as well as that of the Sophi, king of Persia. Referring in particular to the Persians, whose ceremonies, use of arms, and customs in amorous matters he would like to discuss, Fregoso adds that merchants long familiar with the region find:

> gli omini nobili di là esser molto valorosi e di gentil costumi ed usar nel conversar l'un con l'altro, nel servir donne, ed in tutte le sue azioni molta cortesia e molta discrezione e, quando occorre, nell'arme, nei giochi e nelle feste molta grandezza, molta liberalità e leggiadria [...]. (258).

> that the noblemen there are of great worth and of gracious customs, and that in their intercourse with one another, in serving their ladies, and in all their actions, they observe much courtesy and discretion, and, when it is called for, much magnificence, great liberality, and elegance in arms, games, and festivals. (203)[23]

Although the courtiers do not go on to discuss the topic, the passage nonetheless suggests an openness towards international chivalric practices transcending religious difference not unlike the viewpoint conveyed in the Noradino episode. With this in mind, we could see Boiardo's alternative scenario of a multicultural society free from warfare under Saracen rule as a deliberate move away from old stereotypes found in Carolingian epic and a desire to focus on common values linking his Ferrarese readership to the world beyond Christian Europe.

The Rescue of Lucina

After the interruption of the episode with Orlando's sudden departure the reader may not expect to hear anything further about these Middle Eastern events, yet in Book Three Boiardo supplies an unexpected sequel to the joust. When the Tartar king Mandricardo succeeds in winning Hector's armour at the Fountain of the Fay, this enchanted site is at first identified only vaguely as west of "gli Armeni et altre regïone" "Armenia and some other realms" (*OI* 3.1.15). After the victorious hero sets out from the fairy's castle with his new companion Gradasso, however, Boiardo notes more specifically that the two first pass through Syria: "Sorìa, Damasco, quel paese bello / Senza travaglia già passato aveano" ("they'd / already passed through Syria – / Damascus and that [beautiful] region – safely") (*OI* 3.3.23). This depiction recalls the way that Syria appeared when Orlando arrived there with Angelica: beautiful and without conflicts or obstacles.

When the two friends reach the coast, however, they encounter a maiden chained to a rock. The damsel, as noted in chapter 4, is none other than the Cypriot princess Lucina, held hostage by a blind ogre. The appearance of a Cyclops-like creature seemingly pulls us away from geographical reality and back into another fictional Odyssean site like that of the Lestrigons. Yet while Homer's Polyphemus lived in complete isolation from human civilization, the ogre's huge cliff-side cavern is on the contrary "riccamente d'oro [...] lavorata" ("adorned with gold, luxurious") (*OI* 3.3.51). When Mandricardo frees Lucina and Gradasso, the poet adds that within the cave are to be found "veste" and "ricche zoglie" ("expensive gems and clothes") (*OI* 3.3.51). These signs of commercial wealth may serve to suggest that, unlike Syria's peaceful cities and surrounding inland territory, shorelines were plagued by pirates and other predators. In fact, when Niccolò d'Este and his entourage reach Syria during their travels, they do not disembark until assured of their safety (Del Campo 116).

The conclusion of this episode brings us back once more to a world of precise geographical locations. As fortune would have it, Tibiano's ship is nearby undertaking a search expedition as the two knights and the princess reach the shore. We now discover that Lucina's father is the king not only of Cyprus but also of Rhodes and many other lands (*OI* 3.3.53). After the overjoyed king takes Lucina, Gradasso, and Mandricardo on board and heads out to sea, a tempest blows them off course to Acquamorta (Aigues-Mortes), the port city in southern France where Agramante's invasion is underway. While the two knights set off to investigate their new environment, Lucina and Tibiano remain on the ship (*OI* 3.4.10). We hear no more about events in Cyprus or Syria before the *Innamorato* is interrupted five cantos later.

Ariosto picks up the episode's narrative thread in Damascus, but he takes the reader there only after first passing through Egypt and Jerusalem. The following two chapters therefore focus on these sites before turning to a consideration of how Ariosto reconstructs both the character of King Norandino and the nature of his Syrian realm.

Chapter Eleven

Egypt: From Damietta to Cairo

Egypt in the *Orlando innamorato*

The previous chapter looked at how Orlando's foray into the Middle East to participate in a joust as a Saracen knight under the king of Syria's banner contrasted with episodes of conquest and forced conversion found in popular Carolingian epics of the period. We now follow two Christian knights who participated in that tournament, the brothers Grifone and Aquilante, as they subsequently arrive in Egypt where they encounter an Arthurian-type adventure.[1] In order to keep them out of France until an unpropitious astrological conjunction has passed, their fairy guardians have devised an enchantment in the form of a seemingly invincible magician named Orilo and his fierce crocodile, placed along the Nile near the port city of Damiata (Damietta). Whereas in the Cypriot joust Boiardo had written holy war out of the Middle East by imagining a multicultural courtly society at peace, I would like to propose that in this Egyptian episode he brings the history of the crusades to the forefront – albeit in a way that expressly distances his poem from the ideology typical of the Carolingian narratives.[2]

Orilo and the Crocodile

The first hint that the geography of Egypt is relevant to a reading of this episode is the presence of a creature that – unlike the dragons of Arthurian romance and fabulous beasts found elsewhere in the *Innamorato* – is a product of the natural world and native to the Nile River. Boiardo gives a detailed factual description of the animal that includes information about its longevity, size (albeit overstated) and amphibious nature, hunting and eating habits, resemblance to an enormous lizard, coloration, and, finally, its impressive upper jaw with rows of long thick teeth.[3] Since its skin is virtually impenetrable, the knights have no success in trying to overcome it until one brother leaps on top of it while the other thrusts his lance through its mouth into its tender underbelly (*OI* 3.3.3–16). Boiardo continues to emphasize the crocodile's biological reality not only by relating the practical strategy that the brothers use to overcome it but also by following up with an explanation of why their method worked: "Però che sotto al corpo e nele aselle / El cocodrillo ha tenera la pelle" ("All crocodiles have tender hides / where their legs join their undersides") (*OI* 3.3.16).

The Crusades in Egypt

The episode's narrative context suggests, however, that the Egyptian location is meant to evoke more than its zoological peculiarities. The brothers' most fearsome opponent turns out to be not the crocodile but the wily magus Orilo, who reattaches his severed body parts at will each time he is injured or dismembered and springs back to fight with renewed vigour. It is this same pattern of ineffectual struggle against a resilient opponent that characterizes the various crusading expeditions aimed directly at the Nile delta. Indeed, Boiardo could probably not have found a better example of fruitless warfare than the crusading campaigns in Egypt.[4]

Egyptian territory was considered a prime military target from the 1160s, when the Franks in Jerusalem reoriented their military strategy, to the disastrous Fifth Crusade (1217–21), right down to the ill-fated Seventh Crusade under Louis IX of France (1248–50). On each occasion Christian advances were consistently reversed by Muslim troops or the forces of nature. Nor did the failure of these expeditions dissuade others from focusing on the same location in the future. Referring to the period following the Seventh Crusade, Tyerman writes: "As after 1221, instead of arguing that an Egyptian strategy was impossible, the legacy of Louis's campaign stirred planners, strategists and propagandists to examine how exactly Egypt could be conquered" (802).[5]

The fact that Boiardo's Egyptian adventure takes place at Damietta, moreover, accords with the centrality of that city in these expeditions. Oliver of Paderborn called it "the key to all Egypt" (88), a designation iterated in other crusading chronicles and recent histories alike.[6] Beginning in September 1163, the Christian king Amalric I of Jerusalem led five unsuccessful invasions of Egypt over the course of six years, often clashing with Nur ad-Din and the younger Saladin. The last of these was aimed exclusively at Damietta and definitively foiled by Saladin, at that time Egypt's new vizier (Tyerman 349). In the context of the Fifth Crusade, in accordance with the Lateran Council's decision in 1215 to focus on Egypt, allied Christian armies narrowed in on Damietta as their first objective (Tyerman 628–9; Runciman 3: 150). Despite their quick success in establishing camp upon landing there in May 1218, the crusaders were repeatedly blocked in their attempt to conquer the city. Although they eventually entered Damietta in November of the following year, they were forced to retreat two years later after several additional vicissitudes culminated in a failed operation against Cairo. Their unremitting efforts in this region over the course of three and a half years made this, according to Tyerman, "the longest static campaign in the history of the eastern crusades" (629). In the Seventh Crusade, Louis IX of France aimed his attack specifically against Damietta, arriving there in June 1249 and capturing the city in the course of a day's battle. His easy victory was only illusory, however, since his inability to make further progress after almost an additional year of fighting led to the unconditional surrender of Damietta in April 1250 (Runciman 3: 261–70).

Both the chronicles of the Egyptian expeditions and the *Innamorato* episode convey a strong sense of fruitless effort combined with staunch determination. Oliver of Paderborn recounts the seeming impossibility of overtaking the city during the Fifth Crusade, even following initial successes:

> The more often they made an attack afterward, so much the more were the walls strengthened by wooden towers and palisades; the defenders resisted the oncomers even more vigorously and efficaciously, and thus the ladders, injured by fire and several times repaired, were forced to the bank, and the attempt was fruitless. And so it was truly understood that by divine power alone would Damietta be delivered into the hands of the Christians. (81)

Even their eventual, albeit temporary, occupation of the city did not lead to a definitive victory. Oliver of Paderborn goes on to lament that although they had success against crocodiles – "we found and killed crocodiles at Damietta" (98) – they were unable to make further progress and risked dying of starvation. Nevertheless, on various occasions during the stalemate they refused the Egyptians' offer of "peace or a truce" (Oliver of Paderborn 84; also 85–6, 124).

In the *Innamorato*, the brothers' battle against Orilo similarly presents a futile activity extended potentially *ad infinitum*. When Aquilante initially hears from the white fairy that Orilo is invincible – "Se in mille parte l'avesti a dividere, / E più menuto el tagli che el panìco, / Non lo potrai veder de il spirto privo: / Speciato tutto, sempre sarà vivo" ("If he were in a thousand parts, / milled finer than ground millet is, / you would not see his spirit give. / Even divided thus, he'd live") (*OI* 3.2.57) – he expresses his intention to continue the battle unconditionally:

> "E' non fia mai sentito
> Questo nel mondo, o tal vergogna intesa
> Che ogni mio assalto non abi finito,
> Se ben me consumase in fiama accesa.
> E ben che a questo non veda partito,
> Fino ala morte seguirò la empresa:
> Fia de mia vita poi quel che a Dio piace,
> Ma' con costui non vo' tregua ní pace!"

> "Such disgrace
> and failure will not be my fame,
> for I won't stop attacking him,
> even if I'm consumed by flames.
> Although I see no end to this,
> I will keep trying till I die.
> Let God do what he wants with me,
> I won't accept a truce or peace!" (*OI* 3.2.58)

After several more failed attempts to overcome Orilo, however, Aquilante begins to question the nature of the undertaking itself: "Io non sciò certo anchora / Che honor ce seguirà questa aventura" ("I'm not sure [...] / that this adventure leads to fame") (*OI* 3.3.19).

Having chosen Damietta as the site of the Orilo episode, Boiardo is mindful of the geographical specificity of the terrain, most prominently the expanse of water surrounding the city. This characteristic is regularly noted in the chronicles, and Boiardo's own brief account of Amalric I's Egyptian campaign in the *Historia imperiale* also refers to the "profonde paludi, che sono intorno a Damiata" ("deep swamps that surround Damiata") (col. 375).[7] In the *Innamorato*, when Aquilante throws Orilo's arms half a mile into the river, Boiardo explains that "Grande in quel loco è il Nilo, asembra un mare" ("there, wide / as any sea, the Nile extends") (*OI* 3.3.13).

Two additional features of the *Innamorato* adventure are associated with the practical difficulty of conquering Damietta according to the crusading chronicles: a tower and a chain. In the various campaigns directed against the city, crusaders aimed to take over a seventy-foot-high tower that stood in the Nile midway between the Christian camp and Damietta, but a great chain stretching across the river prevented Christian ships from passing, while local boats could bring supplies indefinitely to the garrison. Oliver of Paderborn recounts that during the Fifth Crusade this Tower of Chains, as it was called, could not be captured by normal means "for this was attempted for many days," and it was only finally overcome thanks to the construction of an elaborate floating fortress which he himself had designed (64–8).[8] In the *Innamorato*, Orilo is stationed at a tower on the Nile (*OI* 3.2.46) and, as the brothers continue their fruitless combat, a knight appears leading along a giant with nothing other than a chain (*OI* 3.3.21). Yet just at this moment of heightened suspense Boiardo switches topics, in keeping with his technique of *entrelacement*.

Since the Orilo episode remains incomplete when the poem is abruptly interrupted six cantos later, it is not possible to know how the historical reality of the Egyptian campaigns might have coloured its resolution. At the very least, it would appear that by situating this adventure in Damietta, Boiardo used his knowledge of crusading history to underscore the hopelessness of the brothers' effort. Yet such an allusion implies a disenchanted view of holy war that accords with both his presentation of the early crusades in the *Historia imperiale* and his stated preference for Arthurian over Carolingian material.[9]

Egypt in the *Orlando furioso*

Although Ariosto seems to have detected an allusion to the Egyptian campaigns in the Orilo adventure, he did not share Boiardo's detached position. On the contrary, he brings the crusades resoundingly to centre stage in both his conclusion to this episode and in additional adventures set in the surrounding territory. Aquilante and Grifone are also present, but the knight who takes the lead is invariably Astolfo.[10]

Astolfo's Earlier Itineraries

Prince Astolfo of England is already a world traveller in the *Innamorato*, setting out from Paris across the expanse of Eurasia into Cathay, then heading on a circuitous journey that takes him west to Morgana's Lake, to the extreme north at Manodante's realm, and then in a southwesterly direction to the shores of Alcina's kingdom. He continues to traverse the globe in the *Furioso*, travelling by sea, land, and air, from the easternmost reaches of Asia through the Middle East and to Africa, eventually reaching even the terrestrial paradise and the moon. Given that he is the protagonist of most of the episodes that take place outside western Europe in Ariosto's poem, he will figure prominently in the remainder of Part Three and all of Part Four of the present study.

In expanding Astolfo's trajectory, Ariosto also transforms his character. Boiardo's Astolfo is distinguished by his fierce individualism and adherence to a universal code of courtesy rather than by membership in a religious or ethnic group. Much less skilful as a knight than his cousins Orlando and Ranaldo, he unwittingly gains possession of Argalìa's magic lance early on and wins many unexpected victories as a result. He saves Christendom on two occasions, first from embarrassment during Charlemagne's joust and later from subjugation in the context of Gradasso's war (*OI* 1.7.69). At the same time, he is also the only character to openly criticize the emperor. As discussed earlier, he leaves Paris in protest against injustice at the Frankish court and travels to the East in search of Orlando. During this journey he befriends the Saracen Brandimarte out of admiration and a shared code of courtesy. At Albracà he initially defends Angelica but then joins Ranaldo under Marphisa's banner in the interest of justice (*OI* 1.25.33–4). Yet Astolfo is not without his shortcomings, most notably his vainglorious nature and his partiality towards beautiful women. As he is once again heading west with the intention of defending France from Agramante, he is drawn off course by the enchantress Alcina (*OI* 2.13.51–66). Portraying Astolfo as literally swept away by the *fata*, Boiardo announces that he will play a major role in the adventures to come: "Di lui poi molte cose avremo a dire" ("We'll have much more to say of him") (*OI* 2.14.8). The poem is interrupted, however, before the narrative returns to his predicament.

Astolfo reappears in the *Furioso* when Ruggiero stumbles upon him in the form of a myrtle bush on Alcina's island. After summarizing the *Innamorato* episode in which he was tricked into stepping upon the *maga*'s whale and led away, the repentant knight explains that he subsequently became her lover for more than two months. Astolfo's present state of suffering is viewed as a form of "estrema disciplina" ("most rigorous penitence") to purge his sin (*OF* 6.49 AC). Once he has regained his original body thanks to Merlin's handmaid, Melissa, he is sent to Logistilla for moral instruction. The "pudica et santa" ("chaste and [holy]") fairy (*OF* 6.46 AC) then sends him on his way with a book that explains how to protect oneself from enchantments and a horn that puts to flight those who hear it. The English knight will repeatedly use these two gifts, allegorized as moral virtues by sixteenth-century commentators, to carry out a series of exemplary actions in various historical and invented sites beginning in Egypt.[11]

En Route to Egypt

As Astolfo travels westward, Ariosto focuses his attention on the knight's itinerary, highlighting the religious importance of the places passed along the way. Making his way up the coastline of India, Astolfo gazes upon "la terra di Thomasso" ("the land of Thomas") (*OF* 13.16 A; 15.16 C), meaning the site near Madras where according to maps of the day the apostle Thomas was martyred for his faith. The mention of this early missionary calls to mind the spread of Christianity across the globe as well as the extreme sacrifices that this vocation sometimes entailed. When Astolfo arrives at the Persian Gulf, Ariosto makes a reference to "gli antiqui Maghi" ("the ancient magi"), thus evoking the Magi who according to Christian tradition travelled from Persia to Bethlehem to pay homage to the baby Jesus.[12] As the knight continues across Arabia Felice, Ariosto mentions first its incense and myrrh, a direct reference to the gifts brought by these emblematic figures (Matthew 2:11), and subsequently the mythical phoenix, a popular Christian symbol of the Resurrection. Astolfo's journey next brings him to the Red Sea, identified through its avenging role in the Bible:

> sin che l'onda trovò vendicatrice
> de Israhel, che per divin consenso
> Pharaone summerse e tutti i suoi. (*OF* 13.20 A)

> Next he reached the sea which once
> avenged Israel when by divine consent
> it drowned Pharaoh and all his army. (*OF* 15.39 C)

After Astolfo has passed the "terra de li Heroi" ("Land of the Heroes") (*OF* 1320 A; 15.39 C), a city on the Suez Canal known as Heroopolis, he encounters his first Egyptian adventure. The fact that this occurs even prior to his reaching Damietta creates the impression that the region harbours multiple dangers for travellers.

Caligorante on the Nile

When Astolfo approaches the mouth of the Nile River, a hermit warns him that a giant kills every knight and wayfarer who happens to approach. As it turns out, however, Caligorante is deemed a threat not simply to travellers in a generic sense but specifically to those passing through Egypt on a pilgrimage. The hermit describes how this giant habitually uses fierce cries and threats to trap the terrified pilgrims ("li spaventati peregrini"; *OF* 13.25 A; 15.44 C), whom he then cannibalizes in the most gruesome manner:

o lo scana o li schiaccia le cervella,
sel mangia, e l'ossa restano al deserto;
e de l'humane pelli intorno intorno
fa il suo palazzo horribilmente adorno. (*OF* 13.26 A)

He eats their flesh, sucks their brains and blood,
and abandons their bones to the desert;
and his house is hideously adorned
with human skins hung all about. (*OF* 15.45 C)

Astolfo hopes to have God's assistance in his mission to kill Caligorante: "Ma quando Dio sì mi drizzasse l'armi / che colui morto, et io restassi vivo, / a mille renderei la via sicura" ("But if God directs my arms, and the giant dies while I remain alive, I shall make the road safe for thousands") (*OF* 13.28 A; 15.47 C). The hermit then gives Astolfo his blessing and expresses his wish that God will send the Archangel Michael to his aid. Although Caligorante expects to catch Astolfo in his net the same way he captured other pilgrims ("altri peregrini"; *OF* 13.33 A; 15.52 C), thanks to Logistilla's horn Astolfo sends the giant fleeing into his own trap. Ariosto risks redundancy by telling us that the road is now safe for pilgrims: "ch'ir possa hormai sicuro il peregrino" (*OF* 13.42 A; 15.61 C).

In contrast to the seemingly endless struggle undertaken by Grifone and Aquilante, Astolfo's bout is both quick and decisive. In this light, if the inexhaustible energy of Boiardo's Orilo evoked the futility of the crusading effort in Damietta, Ariosto's first Egyptian episode suggests on the contrary the need for military intervention abroad to ensure the safety of pilgrims to the Holy Land. The fate of Caligorante testifies to this shift in perspective: Astolfo triumphantly pulls him along through Egypt as a captive by using the net as a chain (*OF* 13.41–2 A; 15.60–1).[13] This new role for Caligorante will undergo a further development, to be discussed in the next chapter.

Cairo

As Astolfo continues on his journey past the pyramids and the tombs of Memphis, the reader's attention is directed once again to ancient history. Yet when the knight arrives at Cairo, Ariosto abruptly announces a shift to the condition of the city in his own day. After offering some preliminary descriptive information, he discloses the alarming news that the sultan of Cairo maintains fifteen thousand vassals all of whom are renegade Christians: "son christiani rinegati tutti" (*OF* 13.45 A; 15.64 C). Ariosto is referring to the Mamelukes, a military group that ruled Egypt from about 1250 until 1517, when they were defeated at the hands of the Ottoman Turks. Historically, they were Christians enslaved at a young age, forced to convert to Islam, and trained as soldiers to serve in high army and government posts. In 1440, Milliaduse d'Este's chronicler had estimated that ten thousand Mamelukes served the sultan in Cairo and that another four thousand could be found in Alexandria (Don Domenego, 112 and 122). Pilgrimage narratives sometimes referred to the Mamelukes as Christian renegades without polemical intention.[14] In the epic, however, renegade was a derogatory term used to insult one's opponents. Renegades, in fact, were the only ones not welcome at Charlemagne's joust at the opening of the *Innamorato* (*OI* 1.1.9), and Charlemagne calls Orlando a "rinegato" (as well as "traditor bastardo" ["base traitor"] and "figliol de una putana" ["son of a whore"]) because of his inexplicable absence during that joust (*OI* 1.2.64–5). Thus, Ariosto's blunt characterization of Mamelukes as "all Christian renegades" without any further explanation has a jarring effect. It not only brings to the fore a centuries-old Christian-Muslim conflict but creates the worrisome impression that in his day thousands of Christians were freely renouncing their religion en masse and joining forces with the Egyptian sultan.[15]

Horrilo

It is at this point that Ariosto picks up the threads of the Orilo episode, imagining that the unidentified knight announced by Boiardo was actually Astolfo, who had been leading Caligorante in chains across Egypt. Ariosto takes the geographical location and topographical characteristics from the *Innamorato* (*OI* 3.2.46, *OI* 3.3.13, and *OF* 13.46–7 A; 15.65–

6 C); his Horrilo, however, is not simply a magician but rather a thief who harms both his own countrymen and unwary pilgrims ("a paesani e peregrini nuoce") between Damietta and Cairo (*OF* 13.46 A; 15.65 C). Moreover, whereas in Boiardo's poem the victimized travellers were simply identified through the chivalric marker of knights and damsels (*OI* 3.2.47), Ariosto specifies that Horrilo had habitually fed wayfarers and pilgrims ("vïandanti e peregrini") to his crocodile (*OF* 13.49 A).[16] These continual references to pilgrims, following those in the Caligorante episode, keep the focus on this region as a route to the Holy Land.[17]

For a second time Astolfo's intervention will save future pilgrims from falling prey to a danger lurking in Egypt. Whereas previously the paladin used Logistilla's gift of the horn to prevail over Caligorante, he now succeeds in killing Horrilo thanks to her book, which explains that he must remove a particular strand of hair from the magician's head. Rather than attempt to ascertain the exact strand, Astolfo beheads Horrilo and literally shaves off his hair while holding onto the nose. Displaying his victim's severed corpse, he then invites Aquilante and Grifone to accompany him to France in order to defend the Roman Empire and the Holy Church. Ariosto confirms the brothers' readiness to join in this enterprise, underlining that they do not need to be prodded:

> Il Duca, come al fin trasse l'impresa,
> confortò molto i nobili Garzoni,
> ben che da sé v'havean la voglia intesa,
> né bisognavan stimuli né sproni,
> che per difender de la santa Chiesa
> e del Romano Imperio le ragioni,
> lasciasser le battaglie d'Orïente,
> cercando miglior fama in la lor gente. (*OF* 13.72 A)

> Having accomplished this exploit,
> the duke exhorted the noble youths
> to leave off fighting in the Orient
> and seek honour among their own people
> by coming to the defence of Holy Church
> and the Holy Roman Empire; the brothers
> required little prompting or encouragement,
> for their thoughts were already turned that way. (*OF* 15.91 C)

The political and religious overtones of this passage are especially clear when seen in relation to two similar moments in the *Innamorato* (*OI* 2.9.44–8, 2.13.50–1). On both earlier occasions, Orlando refused to follow the path of duty because his desire led him towards Angelica. In the more developed scene, his fellow paladin Dudone explained that a North African king was poised to invade France (*OI* 2.9.44) and urged his comrades to return west "ala diffesa di Christianitate" ("in defense of Christianity") (*OI* 2.9.45). While Ranaldo "incontinente se dispose / Sanza altra indugia in Franza ritornare" ("soon made up his mind / to go to France without delay"), the love-struck Orlando preferred to return to Albracà to seek the fair Angelica (*OI* 2.9.46–8). In contrast to Boiardo's rather humorous scenario, Ariosto adopts a serious tone when considering service to Charlemagne as a high moral calling that cannot be ignored.

In sum, Ariosto's conclusion to Boiardo's Orilo adventure brings home his very different position on the crusades. In the *Innamorato*, the foxy magus may represent not only the seemingly magical resilience of Damietta but in a broader sense all those overcome by crusading armies who nevertheless managed time and again to recover their land. It is therefore telling that the episode does not involve any of Boiardo's foremost paladins but rather two secondary characters, raised separately in Constantinople and Spain, who during the war at Albracà had defended the treacherous Trufaldino against Ranaldo and at the Cypriot joust had been aligned with the devious Byzantine prince Costanzo against the courteous Syrian ruler Noradino.[18] Their ineffectiveness despite their tenacity suggests the futility of the exercise – apart from their guardians' stated purpose of keeping them safely out of France.

In the *Furioso*, by contrast, a hero no less than Astolfo engages in armed combat to render the route through Egypt safe for pilgrims. Ariosto thus uses the same Egyptian setting to insinuate that the crusades are both necessary and potentially successful. As if this were not enough, the emphasis on both crusades and pilgrimage is continued beyond the confines of the episode. Having rid the route through Egypt of threats to pilgrims, Astolfo takes Grifone and Aquilante with him on a pilgrimage of his own to Jerusalem before heading back to France.

Chapter Twelve

Jerusalem

Jerusalem in the *Orlando innamorato*

Although the historical Charlemagne had never been to the Middle East, many literary works available in fifteenth-century Ferrara link him to Jerusalem: in some he is said to have visited as a pilgrim while in others he plays the part of a conqueror.[1] In the *Amorosa visione*, for example, Boccaccio suggests that the emperor has successfully undertaken a crusade by depicting him "di verde alloro e de' triunfi ornato / ch'egli acquistò sopra le terre sante" ("decorated with green laurel and with the triumphs / which he won in the Holy Land") (11.62–3). In the *Dittamondo*, Fazio degli Uberti supports this tradition by noting succinctly that Charlemagne "oltra mar Ierusalem conquise" ("conquered Jerusalem across the sea") (2.21.24).

Other works combine the themes of crusade and pilgrimage with regard to Charlemagne's paladins. As discussed earlier, the *Spagna* imagines that Orlando conquers Jerusalem. In the *Storia di Rinaldino da Montalbano*, Rinaldo's son visits the Holy Land with the king of Syria and a giant, both recent converts to Christianity, only to discover his father there doing penance. The eponymous heroes of Andrea da Barberino's *Guerrin Meschino* and *Ugone d'Avernia* both pass through Jerusalem as they are carrying out their individual missions.[2] In the former work, Guerrino spends a night there in prayer while he is in the course of a campaign against the Turks on behalf of the sultan (*Guerrino* 3.24, 212). In the latter, Ugone arrives in Jerusalem while a crusade is in progress and becomes the captain of a multinational Christian army (*Ugone* 1:147–8). He fights against an allied Saracen force to conquer both Syria and Jerusalem, killing the unnamed king of Damascus ("lo Re di Domasco"), the king of Persia, the Saladin of Babylon, and the king of Africa. After entering the Holy City and baptizing its inhabitants, he prays in the Church of the Holy Sepulchre (*Ugone* 1:149–173).

In the *Historia imperiale*, Boiardo rejects the tradition depicting Charlemagne and his paladins in the Middle East in any guise whatsoever. Following Einhard's *Vita Caroli* (*Life of Charlemagne*), he simply records that the emperor sent alms yearly to the impoverished Christian pilgrims serving God under Saracen domination in Syria, Jerusalem, Egypt, and Africa (Einhard 33; *Historia imperiale*, 1: 165). Like Einhard, moreover, he also notes that Charlemagne was on friendly terms with the caliph of Baghdad, Harun-al-Rashid: "Grande e precipua amicitia hebe cum Arone re di Persia et da lui hebe molti e preciosi doni" ("He had a great and excellent friendship with Aaron, the king of Persia, from whom he received many precious gifts") (Einhard 26; *Historia imperiale* 1: 163). This suggests a situation of mutual respect between leaders from vastly different cultures, in contrast to the crusading ideology underlying narratives relating Charlemagne's purported conquest of the Holy Land.

Although Boiardo refuses to lend credence to the spurious accounts of Charlemagne's presence in Jerusalem, his *Historia imperiale* does focus on the city's fate during two critical moments of crusading history: its conquest by Christian forces in 1099 and its recapture by Saladin in 1187. In the first case, by commenting that all the city's inhabitants were killed "cum pari feritate a la soprascritta presa di Antiochia" ("with the same ferociousness as the above-mentioned taking of Antioch") (*Istoria imperiale*, col. 341), Boiardo takes us back to his earlier description of a barbarian army mercilessly attacking a defenceless civilian population: "E certamente parea, che la voce de' miseri uccisi, e l'orribile grido de' Barbari vincitori, da diversi idiomi mescolati, avesse i sensi e gli animi dementati, e rivolti in tutto da pietade" ("And it certainly seemed that the voices of the unfortunate victims and the horrible shouts of the victorious Barbarians, mixing diverse languages, had their senses and their hearts demented, and utterly devoid of compassion") (*Istoria imperiale*, col. 337).[3] Saladin's victory, in contrast, is characterized not by indiscriminate slaughter but rather by an act of devotion: "Entrò la santa Città di Gerusalemme, e fece nel gran Tempio divota preghiera a Dio, e a Maometto datore della sua Legge" ("He entered the holy city of Jerusalem, and prayed devotedly to God in the Temple, and to Mohammed the provider of his Law") (*Istoria imperiale*, col. 405).[4] The reference to Mohammed as a lawgiver, moreover, works against the tendency in medieval Latin Christendom to vilify the prophet.[5]

In the *Innamorato*, despite close attention to the Middle Eastern landscape, Boiardo does not mention either Jerusalem or Antioch, the city featured in the *Storia di Rinaldino*. The Holy Land is referred to on just one occasion, in an ekphrastic scene unrelated to the purported exploits of Charlemagne's paladins. Painted on the walls of the fairy Phebosilla's palace, along with other highlights of Este family history, one finds a reference to Niccolò d'Este's historical pilgrimage:

Poi se vedea da Conti e da Baroni
Acompagnato, con le vele al vento,
Andar cercando con devocïone
La Sancta Terra et altre regïone.

Next he was shown accompanied
by counts and barons setting sail
upon a sacred course to see
the Holy Land and other realms. (*OI* 2.25.52)

This brief description underscores the accessibility of Jerusalem and the surrounding states, which the group reached with their sails to the wind.[6] It also accords with the prevailing view of Jerusalem in the late fifteenth century as a site for pilgrimage divorced from crusading aspirations. James Hankins notes that, "The Holy Land in the fifteenth century was in the hands of the Mamluk sultans of Egypt, who presented no particular military threat to the Latin West and with whom the commercial powers of Italy had worked out a mutually beneficial *moyen de vivre* with regard to trade" ("Renaissance Crusaders," 113).

Jerusalem in the *Orlando furioso*

As anticipated at the end of the previous chapter, Ariosto brings Jerusalem to centre stage by sending Astolfo there as a pilgrim. Having travelled from Egypt following a popular pilgrimage route, the English prince and his companions arrive in the city to find that it is governed by a knight from Mecca they knew named Sansonetto (*OF* 13.76 A; 15.95 C). This character would also have been familiar to the poem's early readers, since in the *Spagna* he appears as the son of Mecca's sultan during Orlando's eastern travels. Thus Ariosto not only disregards the *Innamorato*'s precedent of keeping Jerusalem out of the poem's fictive landscape, but he treats as authoritative a text that Boiardo had been working against in his episodes of the war at Albracà and the joust at Cyprus. As noted earlier, in the *Spagna* Sansonetto and his father are forced to embrace Christianity after Orlando's conquest of Jerusalem and are baptized at once along with all their people. The young neophyte then accompanies Orlando to Pamplona, still under siege by Charlemagne's troops, where he fights against Spanish Saracens and becomes as prolific a proselytizer as any Christian-born knight. Indeed, in trying to persuade his opponent Isolieri to convert, Sansonetto declares:

Tu se' perduto s'tu non te provedi,
[...]
perché con gli altri tapini tu credi
in quel malvasio e falso Machometo.
In fè de verità, Isolïer, vedi
che Ihesù Cristo è pur signor perfecto.
Rendite a lui; Carlo perdonerati,
in Cristiantà terre magior darati.

You are lost if you don't see to this,
[...]
because with the other wretches you believe
in that evil and false Mohammed.
In true faith, Isolier, see
that Jesus Christ is a perfect lord.
Give yourself to him; Charles will pardon you,
he will give you greater land in Christendom. (*Spagna* 21.35)

In the ensuing battle Sansonetto forces Isolieri to accept Christianity, and when the city is sacked those who refuse to convert are put to death without hesitation (*Spagna* 23.40).

In designating Sansonetto as Jerusalem's ruler, Ariosto explains that he was converted and baptized by Orlando and then appointed by Charlemagne as governor of the Holy Land (*OF* 13.76–8 A; 15.95–7 C). And lest the reader forget, he repeats the same information a few cantos later: "gli diè battesmo Orlando, et Carlo (come / v'ho detto) a governar la Terra Santa" ("Orlando baptized him; Charlemagne [as I have said] appointed him Governor of the Holy Land") (*OF* 16.97 A; 18.97 C).[7] Ariosto also alludes to the city's continued danger of attack by noting that Sansonetto is building up his defences against the sultan of Egypt:

Quivi lo trovan che disegna a fronte
del Soldano d'Egytto una fortezza;
e circondar vuol il Calvario monte
di muro di duo miglia di lunghezza. (*OF* 13.77 A)

They found him planning fortifications
to resist the caliph of Egypt;
he meant to enclose the hill
of Calvary with a two-mile wall. (*OF* 15.96 C)

We are thus transported to the period following the onset of the crusades in which the Latin West sought to consolidate its holdings in the Middle East. Moreover, the precise reference to Mount Calvary as in need of protection prompts the reader to consider simultaneously the sacred site of Christ's Passion and the crusaders' attempts to secure and maintain possession of the Holy Land.

Astolfo offers Caligorante as a gift to Sansonetto to use in his construction works, given that he "a portar pesi gli varrà per diece / asini o muli, tanto era robusto" ("could replace ten beasts of burden, such was his strength") (*OF* 13.78 A; 15.97 C).[8] In this way a romance-type giant is forced into manual labour as a slave, a fate that befell prisoners on both sides in crusading history. In reciprocating Astolfo's present, Sansonetto bequeaths to him nothing less than the belt and spurs of St George. The acquisition of holy relics was an integral part of narratives concerning Charlemagne's purported visit to Jerusalem. In the twelfth-century *Voyage de Charlemagne à Jérusalem et à Constantinople*, the emperor and his paladins receive a number of relics, including St Simeon's arm, St Lazarus's head, and St Stephen's blood (vv 112–203).[9] Sansonetto's gift of the belt and spurs is not quite as spectacular as these but may still have had a resonance for readers in the Este circle. Not only was St George the patron of Ferrara, but Luchino Dal Campo recounts that when Niccolò d'Este knighted five of his companions in Jerusalem's Church of the Holy Sepulchre, he personally bestowed upon each of them a set of golden spurs (125).

The main overtones of the current episode, however, are religious. Astolfo is no longer the independent knight who left Paris after having jokingly claimed conversion to Islam but a repentant sinner reborn as a paladin of Christ. Ariosto relates how the English knight and his companions purify themselves spiritually before they enter the holy temples.

It is a short step from describing the diligence of their worship to imprecating against the unholy Saracens who shamefully usurp Christian temples in the present day:

Purgati de lor colpe a un monasterio
che dava di sé odor di buoni exempi,
la passïon di Cristo e ogni mysterio
contemplando n'andâr per tutti i tempî
c'hor con eterno obbrobrio e vituperio
a' Christïani usurpano i Mori empi. (*OF* 13.80 A)

They purged their sins in a monastery
fragrant with the odour of good example,
and, contemplating the mysteries of Christ's passion,
they visited every shrine – Christian shrines now,
to their eternal shame and degradation,
usurped by the impious Moors. (*OF* 15.99 C)

Ariosto concludes the stanza lamenting that "L'Europa è in arme, e di far guerra agogna / in ogni parte, fuor ch'ove bisogna" ("Europe is in arms and aches to do battle everywhere, except where battle is needed") (*OF* 13.80 A; 15.99 C). Astolfo's visit to the temples of Jerusalem thus occasions the poem's first call for a continuation of the crusades in the historical present.

The need for Christians to cease internecine warfare and seek combat in the Holy Land is a familiar topos found as far back as accounts of Pope Urban II's First Crusade exhortation to "turn the weapons which you have stained unlawfully in the slaughter of one another against the enemies of the faith and the name of Christ" (William of Tyre 1: 91) and expressed in poetic terms by Dante and Petrarch (*Inferno* 27.85–90; "Trionfo della Fama," 139–44). Militant popes, Italian statesmen, and humanist poets iterated similar pleas at regular intervals in response to the encroaching Ottoman threat.[10] At the same time, however, we cannot assume that Ariosto's call for renewed crusading efforts in the Holy Land voiced a widely shared aspiration during the period of the poem's composition. On the contrary, Ricci argues that the failure of Pope Pius II's crusading plans in 1464 definitely marked the end of the medieval model of crusade: "From then on [...] for Christians it was about organizing individual defensive undertakings to block Turkish expansion towards the West. The difference with respect to the dream of marching on Jerusalem is not negligible. [...] Nobody thought seriously any longer about freeing the Holy Land or converting infidels" (*I turchi alle porte*, 68–9).

An upcoming tournament in Damascus provides the knights with the occasion to move out of the genre of pilgrimage narrative and back into romance epic mode. As the next chapter shows, however, this ostensibly chivalric setting will provide an additional platform for Ariosto to advance his plea for another crusade.

Chapter Thirteen

Ariosto's Norandino in Damascus

Whereas in the *Innamorato* the action moved from Syria to Cyprus to Egypt, Ariosto takes Astolfo to Egypt and Jerusalem before introducing Syria into his poem. By this time, moreover, the narrative has come full circle. Whereas Boiardo's Noradino had initially departed from Damascus in order to win Lucina's hand at Tibiano's Cypriot joust, Ariosto's character returns there to hold a tournament of his own in celebration of her delivery from the ogre and safe return (*OF* 15.23–5 A; 17.23–5 C).[1] Although Ariosto does not refer specifically to the outcome of the events in Nicosia but simply mentions that Norandino had wed Lucina after many years of devotion (*OF* 15.26 A; 17.26 C), the current joust brings to mind aspects of the earlier one. As Rajna points out, both are instituted because of Lucina and feature Norandino in a principal role (*Le fonti*, 281). Despite these basic correspondences, however, Ariosto radically transforms both the Middle Eastern setting and the character of the Syrian king.

Considering the geography, Ariosto seemingly goes along with Boiardo's precedent of conveying the concrete reality of the Middle East but then uses this greater precision to a different end. His initial overview of Damascus repeats several of the city's physical and societal characteristics reported in medieval travelogues. As in Poggibonsi's *Libro d'Oltramare* (1345–50), for example, Ariosto notes its location on a plain near a hill, the two rivers supplying water to extensive and beautiful gardens and the general abundance of running water, its huge population, wealth, remarkable ornamentation, carpeted streets, and richly decorated houses, its importance as a centre for East–West trade with its readily available precious metals, jewels, and spices, as well as its geographical relation to Jerusalem (*OF* 15.18–21 A; 17.18–21 C).[2] However, when he turns to the procession of knights, he draws attention to a peculiarity not found in Poggibonsi. The Syrians, he asserts, have adopted emblems on their crests and shields in imitation of western European usage, most likely as a result of the French presence in the region:

> Sorïani in quel tempo haveano usanza
> d'armarsi a questa guisa di Ponente:
> forse ve l'inducea la vicinanza
> che de' Franceschi havean continuamente,
> che quivi allhor reggean la sacra stanza
> dove in carne habitò Dio omnipotente (*OF* 15.73 A)

> In those days the Syrians were accustomed
> to wear armour after the Western fashion;
> perhaps this was due to the vicinity
> of the French settled there as rulers
> of the holy places where Almighty God
> dwelt in human flesh. (*OF* 17.73 C)

This apparently offhanded aside about how the style of armour in Syria mimicked French fashion contradicts the fact that Westerners who remained any length of time in the Levant acclimated to life there by adopting Arab dress.[3] Furthermore, by claiming that Frankish Christians had already occupied territory in the Middle East by this time, Ariosto once again affirms his adherence to the fictional account of the *Spagna* outlined earlier against Boiardo's presentation of the region as free of European interference.

Having indirectly evoked the crusades by noting French-style armour among the Syrians, Ariosto abruptly bewails how Christians of his own day have left Jerusalem's holy sites in the hands of (Muslim) dogs: "c'hor li superbi e miseri christiani, / con biasmo lor, lasciano in man de' Cani" ("Christians, the arrogant wretches, leave these places in the hands of dogs") (*OF* 15.73 A; 17.73 C). This lament comes rather unexpectedly considering the current festive gathering to commemorate Lucina's return and marriage to Norandino. Yet the most shocking verses are still ahead. Ariosto's sudden shift to the present in the above-cited couplet leads to a six-stanza impassioned appeal for a new crusade (three of the stanzas are cited below):

> Dove abbassar devrebbeno la lancia
> in augumento de la santa fede,
> tra lor si dàn nel petto e ne la pancia

a destruttion del poco che si crede.
Che fate qui, gente di Spagna e Francia?
Volgete altrove, e voi, Svizari, il piede,
e voi, Tedeschi, a far più degno acquisto;
che quanto qui cercate è già di Christo.

S'esser voi Christianissimi volete,
e voi altri Catholici nomati,
perché di Christo li huomini uccidete?
perché de' beni lor son dispogliati?
Perché Hierusalem non rïhavete,
che tolto è stato a voi da' rinegati?
perché Constantinopoli e del mondo
la miglior parte occùpa il Turco immondo?

[...]

Se 'l dubbio di morir ne le tue tane,
Svizer, di fame, in Lombardia ti guida,
e tra noi cerchi o chi ti dia del pane
o, per uscir d'inopia, chi te uccida,
alle ricchezze d'Asia pon le mane;
d'Europa il Turcho, o almen di Grecia snida:
o del lungo digiun potrai sfamarti,
o cader con più merto in quelle parti. (*OF* 15.74–5, 77 A)[4]

They ought to be setting their lances
for the greater spread of our Faith; instead,
they are running each other through
the breast or belly and wreaking destruction
on the few who already belong to the Faith.
You men of Spain, you Frenchmen, you Swiss and Germans,
turn your steps elsewhere, make worthier conquests:
what you covet here is already Christ's.

If you wish to be called Most Christian,
if you wish to be called Catholic,
why do you kill Christ's men?
Why despoil them of their possessions?
Why do you not retake Jerusalem, seized from you by renegades?

Why is Constantinople and the better part
of the world occupied by unclean Turks?

[...]

You Swiss, if it is fear of starving to death
in your lairs which tempts you down to Lombardy,
and if you come among us looking for someone to give you bread
or else release you from famine by slaying you:
the riches of the Turk are not far to seek –
drive them out of Europe, or at least dislodge them from Greece.
Thus you shall be able to escape hunger or at any rate
meet a more meritorious end in those regions. (*OF* 17.74–5, 77 C)

As Tobias Gregory notes, "Ariosto employs the same line of exhortation used by Urban II in preaching the First Crusade: for God's sake, leaders of Christian nations, stop attacking each other and go attack Muslims" (132). This new call for a crusade, however, like the one prompted by Astolfo's visit to Jerusalem, is not dictated by current events since, as noted in the previous chapter, this period was one of decreased danger from the Turks. As Murrin states, "The Ottomans did not at present menace Europe. The new sultan had turned east, attacking Persians and Mamluks" (*History and Warfare*, 84).[5] Like the comment regarding the armour in Damascus as an imitation of French style, moreover, this plea to take up a crusade against the infidel occurs before the onset of the tournament. While the first remark imagined that the upcoming fictitious event would take place in a Middle East dominated by Western Christians, the second urges renewed military action in the historical present. In this way, Ariosto keeps the Christian-Muslim conflict at the forefront even while professing to relate a festive occasion.

In the course of the episode, Ariosto follows Boiardo's precedent by including accounts of mistaken identity and of cheating through trickery, but the implications are vastly different. In the *Innamorato*, Orlando disguised himself and was subsequently deceived by a Greek prince. He left for France without creating any disturbance, and we later find out that Noradino was still able to win Lucina as his bride. In the *Furioso*, Ariosto introduces a new character, the villainous Martano from Antioch, who dons Grifone's armour in order to take credit for his exploits. While Boiardo's Noradino was quick to assess Orlando's merit at first glance and was not implicated in the later act of trickery either as perpetrator or victim, Ariosto's character is completely deceived by Martano's ruse. He ends up acting improperly, first by honouring the wily coward and subsequently by mistreating the real hero, Grifone. Ariosto even makes a point of telling us that Norandino's overhasty judgment soiled his good name and led to the demise of his own men: "ei denigrò sua fama più che pece, / et si diè causa che sue genti messe / a morte furo" ("he merely blackened his reputation worse than pitch. Thanks to him his people suffered death") (*OF* 16.3 A; 18.3 C).

As if this incident were not bad enough, Norandino makes the same mistake again when he sends his men to fight Marphisa after she has reclaimed her armour. Seeing the still unidentified warrior easily defeat her assailants, Norandino is described as the embodiment of uncontrolled anger: "di veneno / havea le luci inebrïate et rosse" ("blood-shot and dilated the king's eyes were with sheer venom") (*OF* 16.117 A; 18.117 C). Even after the withdrawal of the initial group, Norandino pursues her with new troops "tutti pronti alla morte o alla vendetta" ("all of them ready to be avenged or die") (*OF* 16.121 A; 18.121 C). The revelation of Marphisa's identity, however, is enough to produce an instantaneous change of heart in the Syrians. Although Ariosto remarks that it is the men's ire that is turned into fear, the king is nevertheless implicated in the passage describing the terror that Marphisa's name causes throughout the region:

> Come Re Norandino ode quel nome
> così temuto per tutto Levante,
> che facea a molti ancho arricciar le chiome,
> ben che fusse da lor spesso distante (*OF* 16.126 A)

> When King Norandin heard this name,
> which was so feared throughout the Levant
> that it made people's hair stand on end
> even when she was nowhere near (*OF* 18.126 C)

Norandino immediately pays homage to Marphisa by insisting that she keep the armour she has already seized. We later hear that he gave her the best horse in Damascus as well (*OF* 17.76 A; 19.77 C). Thus Ariosto's Syrian king is no longer a paragon of courtesy who perceives valour at a glance but is revealed to be an overly rash, undiscerning tyrant who cuts a cowardly figure when confronted by a superior warrior maiden.

Although the narrative does not return to the Middle East after canto 17/19, Ariosto evokes Norandino later in the poem in the context of Agramante's war. Following the fall of Biserta, Sobrino tries to brighten the African king's spirits by calling to mind his allies. After noting that the neighbouring sultan of Egypt could be relied upon for money and troops, Sobrino expresses his confidence that "verrà con ogni sforzo Norandino / per ritornarti in regno, il tuo parente" ("your kinsman Norandin will make every effort to restore you to your kingdom") (*OF* 36.39 A; 40.39 C). The king of Damascus is thus revealed to be not only Agramante's trusted ally but his blood relative as well. This passage, moreover, occurs at a time in which the conflict had assumed the guise of a holy war. Pivotal in that transformation is the figure of Astolfo, to whom we now turn in Part Four.

PART FOUR

Back to Africa

Chapter Fourteen

From Ethiopia to the Moon

Following his departure from Damascus, Astolfo acts on two successive occasions to liberate his fellow knights from traps with the aid of Logistilla's gifts. First, he frees himself and his friends from a horde of killer women using the horn whose terrifying sound sends everyone fleeing. Then, travelling alone after the ensuing dispersal, he rescues those imprisoned within Atlante's magic palace thanks to the combined use of the horn and the book that explains how to break the enchantment. As a consequence of this action, he finds himself in possession of the mythical hippogriff, lost earlier by Ruggiero and left behind by Atlante. Yet in order for Astolfo to soar to new heights on this flying horse, he must find somewhere to leave his current steed, Rabicano. When Bradamante fortuitously appears, the knight gives her both Rabicano and his magic lance. This practical situation of needing to do away with extra "baggage" has a symbolic significance as well. Both the horse and the lance originated in the first canto of the *Innamorato*, which has served as the *Furioso*'s principal basis for creative imitation until this point. After Astolfo takes flight on the hippogriff in canto 30/33, however, Ariosto looks primarily to sources outside Boiardo's poem. This shift in narrative procedure away from the *Innamorato* corresponds to a greater ideological distancing as well. The present chapter explores these changes in the context of Astolfo's subsequent travel to Ethiopia.

Ariosto begins by tracing Astolfo's itinerary from Europe to Africa, pointing out the various locations he passes along the way. This mini-travelogue brings the early sixteenth-century reader face to face with contemporary reality, providing an aerial view of Spain and Portugal, the two countries vying for supremacy in global exploration. Because of the hippogriff, Astolfo now not only surpasses the achievements of these realms in the velocity of his transportation, but he treats them in turn as territories to explore, flying from the Pyrenees over Lisbon and every city in Spain before reaching the pillars of Hercules (*OF* 30.68–70 A; 33.96–8 C). He then circles northern Africa from the Atlantic to Egypt, appropriating with his gaze a series of cities whose names would have been familiar to the poem's early readers from the most recent maps (*OF* 30.70–3 A; 33.98–101 C). Astolfo is no longer seeking absolution as he was in Jerusalem. Nor, however, is he either sightseeing for pleasure like Ruggiero (*OF* 9.60–1 A; 10.72–3 C) or forging new trade routes like the Iberian explorers of Ariosto's day. As we shall soon learn, he is about to assume the new role of religious, mythical, and ultimately military hero.

Prester John

In due course Astolfo's hippogriff lands in the midst of Ethiopia, at the court of the emperor Senapo, who is said to be known to Europeans as "Prete Ianni" ("Prester John") (*OF* 30.77 A; 33.106 C).[1] This figure was the purported author of an apocryphal letter from around 1165 in which he depicted himself as an incomparably rich and powerful Christian king: "Si vero vis cognoscere magnitudinem et excellentiam nostrae celsitudinis et in quibus terris dominetur potentia nostra, intellige et sine dubitatione crede, quia ego, presbiter Iohannes, dominus sum dominantium et praecello in omnibus divitiis, quae sub caelo sunt, virtute et potentia omnes reges universae terrae" ("If you indeed wish to know wherein consists our great power, then believe without doubting that I, Prester John, who reign supreme, exceed in riches, virtue, and power all creatures who dwell under heaven") (*La lettera del Prete Gianni*, 52–4; Silverberg 42).[2] He claims, moreover, that his vast realm is to be found near the earthly paradise, and that it contains the Tower of Babel, a river of gems, and many other marvels. Nor does he leave out the various local resources, such as gold and balsam. To give an idea of the dimensions of his court, Prester John asserts that he feeds thirty thousand men at his table daily and that he is served by seven kings, sixty-two dukes, and three hundred and sixty-five counts on a rotating basis. As a Christian ruler, moreover, he not only protects followers of this religion in his territory but has vowed to lead an army to Jerusalem to wage war against the enemies of Christendom: "In voto habemus visitare sepulchrum domini cum maximo exercitu, prout decet gloriam maiestatis nostrae humiliare et debellare inimicos crucis Christi et nomen eius benedictum exaltare" ("We have made a vow to visit the sepulcher of our Lord with a very great army, as befits the glory of our Majesty, to wage war against and chastise the enemies of the cross of Christ, and to exalt his sacred name") (*La lettera del Prete Gianni*, 54; Silverberg 42).

This letter became one of the most widely read documents of medieval Europe and, with the introduction of print, appeared in innumerable editions in several languages. As copies of the letter circulated, additional passages were inserted, including an early interpolation relating how Prester John's father built a palace for his unborn son following a dream vision in which an angel advised him that whoever entered such a dwelling would never suffer hunger or disease. Moreover, "si validissimam famem quis habuerit et infirmetur ad mortem, si intraverit palatium et steterit ibi per aliquam moram, ita exiet satur, ac si de centum ferculis comedisset, et ita sanus, quasi nullam infirmitatem in vita sua passus fuisset" ("if someone ever entered the palace starving and deathly ill, he would later exit as satiated as if he had eaten one-hundred dishes and as healthy as if he had never been sick in his life") (*La lettera del Prete Gianni*, 84).[3]

The attempt to make contact with Prester John had already begun in the late twelfth century. In 1177 Pope Alexander III wrote a letter to "Joanni, illustro et magnifico Indorum regi" ("John, illustrious and magnificent king of the Indies") explaining that he was sending someone to instruct him in the Catholic faith and warning him against excessive pride: "The more nobly and magnanimously you conduct yourself, and the less you boast of your wealth and power, the more readily shall we regard your wishes" (cited in Silverberg 61). The interest in the priest-king was not merely academic, since Western Europeans sought him as a military ally in their fight against Muslims. Nor were some of them above claiming that he had already joined forces with the crusaders. As the Fifth Crusade headed towards failure, Jacques de Vitry, as bishop of Acre, wrote to Pope Honorius III and others in 1221 claiming that Prester John's son or grandson commanded a vast military contingent that had taken up arms against its Muslim enemies in the East and was soon to aid his fellow Christians in the Holy Land (Silverberg 71–3).

In the fourteenth century the location of Prester John's purported realm was transferred from Asia to Africa. Robert Silverberg traces this shift to 1306 when thirty Ethiopians travelled to Europe seeking an alliance with the Spanish rulers of Castile and Aragon against Muslim domination in their lands. After they visited Avignon and Rome (and possibly reached Spain), these envoys stopped to await sea passage in Genoa, where they met the geographer Giovanni da Carignano. The latter subsequently compiled a treatise on their government, customs, and religious practices, identifying their Christian king as Prester John (Silverberg 164–5).

Africa was, in fact, a logical place to situate the elusive Christian king given that historically many Christians lived in Nubia, a region in the Nile Valley that was also sometimes referred to as Ethiopia (from the ancient Greek Aithiopia).[4] As a result of the efforts of Egyptian missionaries in the sixth century, Christianity had flourished in Nubia for hundreds of years, and Nubian religious influence extended westward over much of the neighbouring territory. Muslim invaders conquered this region and established Islam as the official religion in the 1300s, but Christian communities persisted and were tied to the Coptic Christians of Egypt. Thus when the Armenian monk Hayton tried to convince Pope Clement V to embark on a new crusade in 1307, he could argue that the king of the Nubians would want to join in the venture: "I truly believe that these Nubians, for the honor of Our Lord and out of reverence to Your Holiness, would make war against the Sultan and his men and would cause harm and damage to their power, creating great trouble for the Sultan and his men" (*The Flower of Histories of the East,* book 4).

The expectation of finding Prester John was sustained by relations between Europeans and Ethiopians that developed during the following two centuries, including the exchange of ambassadors and correspondence.[5] Following the above-mentioned visit documented by Carignano, in 1428 two Ethiopian messengers arrived in Valencia to offer King Alfonso the Magnanimous of Aragon an alliance that included a double royal marriage. A subsequent delegation was sent to the Council of Florence in 1441, awakening interest on the part of humanist historians of the stature of Poggio Bracciolini and Flavio Biondo.[6] In 1450 ambassadors purportedly sent by Prester John returned to the Aragonese king Alfonso, now residing in Naples, under the guidance of Pietro Rombolo, an Italian who had lived in Ethiopia since 1407.[7] The Ethiopian envoys who arrived in Rome in 1481 would have found an increasing number of their own priests in the city, where by the end of the century a hospice had been founded for them (Milanesi 44).

Italian ambassadors, merchants, artisans, friars, and adventurers likewise travelled to Ethiopia during this period, and some of their accounts gained wide circulation. The Venetian Nicolò de' Conti (c. 1395–1469), who stopped in Ethiopia after more than two decades in Asia, related his journey in 1437 to the Spanish traveller Pero Tafur and in 1439 to Poggio Bracciolini, at that time papal secretary, both of whom provided written accounts.[8] Poggio's version became the fourth book of his *De varietate fortunae* (manuscript completed by 1448), which also made use of Carignano's earlier work on Ethiopia. This fourth book was published in Milan in the fateful year of 1492 as *India recognita* (*India Rediscovered*) (Breazeale 103). Both Carignano and Bracciolini found their way into Jacopo Filippo Foresti of Bergamo's *Supplementum chronicarum*, an appendix to his universal chronicle (Milanesi 45).[9]

Although more accurate information was thus available about Ethiopia during the fifteenth and early sixteenth centuries, the legend surrounding Prester John continued unabated. First, the supposedly non-fictional accounts nevertheless incorporated fabulous materials.[10] Second, the priest-king himself began to make appearances in the genre of fiction. In Andrea da Barberino's *Ugone d'Avernia* and *Guerrin Meschino*, the eponymous heroes chance upon Prester John's kingdom in the course of their travels.[11] The priest Giuliano Dati (1445–1524), better known for his poetic translation of Columbus's 1493 letter concerning his transoceanic voyage, also composed a *cantare* shortly thereafter entitled "La gran magnificentia de Prete Ianni signore dell'India Maggiore et della Ethiopia."[12] These and other writings about the legendary priest-king served to keep his memory alive in the collective imagination well into the sixteenth century.

Nor did the active attempt to contact Prester John show signs of subsiding. On the contrary, one of the principal motives for Portugal's African explorations in the fifteenth century was precisely to reach his kingdom in order to secure both a commercial treaty for the spice trade and a military alliance against a common Muslim enemy. In the 1480s King John II of Portugal organized two expeditions, one heading southeast overland and the other sent around the African coast, for the express purpose of seeking out this prospective ally, now believed to reside in the heart of the continent.[13] Francesc Relaño notes that when Vasco da Gama arrived in Mozambique in 1498, he wrote in his logbook that Prester John was nearby (60). The Portuguese commander Afonso de Albuquerque, upon reaching the eastern coast of Africa in 1506, also sent messengers to make contact with Prester John.[14] When an Ethiopian envoy found his way to Albuquerque in 1512, the latter sent him to King Manoel of Portugal, who in 1514 informed the pope that Prester John's ambassador was "offering in the name of his monarch, as one Christian to another, all possible aid and everything necessary for a war against the enemies of the Catholic faith, such as soldiers, arms, and supplies, especially if our fleet should penetrate the Red Sea, on which his domains border and where the forces of both can be most conveniently joined" (quoted in Silverberg 214).

The Este court not only had access to a range of medieval works dealing with the Prester John legend but was well informed about the various ongoing attempts to reach the priest-king. Ercole I would have been able to follow in person King Alfonso's relations with the Ethiopians, since he was educated at the Neapolitan court from 1445 to 1460 and then married Alfonso's granddaughter Eleonora after inheriting the dukedom of Ferrara. He owned a copy of Jacopo Foresti da Bergamo's recently published *Supplementum chronicarum* (Bertoni 250, no. 45), mentioned above, and even stationed an agent in Lisbon to report on Portugal's latest discoveries. In 1502 this agent, Alberto Cantino, gave a Portuguese cartographer twelve gold ducats for a map that he then smuggled at the risk of death to Ferrara for the duke's personal library. According to Brotton, this map, known today as the Cantino Planisphere, was "perhaps the most comprehensive and up-to-date visualization of the Portuguese seaborne discoveries" (*Trading Territories*, 23). Like previous world maps, it showed Prester John, "senyor de les Indies," seated in front of tents in the area designated as Nubia (Milano 61–4).[15] Ariosto was serving under Ercole at this time and subsequently resided at court after joining Ippolito's entourage the following year. He would therefore have expected his courtly readers to comprehend the magnitude of Astolfo's achievement: as soon as the paladin sets foot in Africa, he chances upon a figure who had eluded Europeans for centuries and who was at that time being doggedly sought after by the Portuguese.[16]

Although Astolfo is not the earliest hero of romance to stumble upon Prester John, Ariosto is the first poet to exploit the full implications of his legend. As mentioned above, the heroes of *Ugone d'Avernia* and *Il Guerrin Meschino* both arrive in the land of Prester John during their journeys; however, in both cases the knight's sojourn there constitutes a self-contained episode. For Ugone, this realm represents the farthest reaches of human civilization, which he briefly visits before resuming his mission on behalf of the Frankish ruler Charles Martel (*Ugone* 2: 311–16). Guerrino successfully defends Prester John and his people from a ferocious group of attackers (*Guerrino* 3.30–3, 229–38) but then continues on his own, more personal quest. By contrast, as discussed below, Astolfo's encounter with the emperor of Ethiopia is a crucial phase in the development of Ariosto's poem, with far-reaching consequences for its epic plot.[17]

Because of the precedent offered by these two narratives, Pio Rajna maintained that the figure of Prester John in general had no importance for Ariosto: "But to us it is not Prester John in general that can matter, but rather the Prester John of chivalric romance" (*Le fonti*, 529). Rajna further steered readers away from investigating the Prester John legend in the *Furioso* by arguing that Senapo had only a superficial resemblance to the "holy and venerable pontiff" and was modelled instead on Alexander of Macedonia (*Le fonti*, 533).[18] His statement, however, is misleading. Although the kindly priest-king briefly encountered in *Ugone d'Avernia* and *Il Guerrin Meschino* fits Rajna's description of an ethical model, the boastful claims in Prester John's epistles recall instead the Macedonian conqueror. Indeed, historians have found that these letters actually drew from material circulating about Alexander.[19] As discussed below, Senapo's previous Alexander-like ambitions as a world conqueror as well as his future role as a military ally align him with the legendary Prester John rather than with the saintly figure who appears in the two chivalric romances cited by Rajna.

While the *Furioso*'s description of Senapo's realm generally accords with the Prester John letters (*OF* 30.77 A; 33.105 C), the depiction of the ruler himself centres on his religious faith. First of all, Ariosto chooses to refer to him by a purported proper name that emphasizes his holy calling, since it stems from an Arabic title meaning "servant of the cross" (Silverberg 224; Relaño 68). Ariosto underscores this connection by pointing out that Senapo "in luoco tien di settro in man la croce" ("wields the Cross instead of a sceptre") (*OF* 30.74 A; 33.102 C). The same stanza affirms that he adheres to the Christian sacrament of baptism, noting that the Ethiopians use fire when practising the rite. The most significant marker of Senapo's Christianity, in terms of its further development in the poem, is his ongoing battle with the Muslims outside his realm. Indeed, Ariosto prefaces his introduction of Senapo by stating that the Christians of this land are always ready to engage in war against their Saracen neighbours across the border: "Questi Christiani son, quei Saracini; / e stan con l'arme in man sempre a' confini" ("the former a Saracen town, the latter Christian, and they keep a constant armed watch at their border") (*OF* 30.73 A; 33.101 C). While reflecting the historical plight of Christians in Africa following the Muslim invasions referred to above, this reference to local religious conflict also anticipates the Nubians' later role in the poem's Christian military offensive.[20]

Once Ariosto has firmly established Senapo's connection with the Prester John legend, he goes on to reverse his personal situation. Whereas the priest-king claimed to live in a palace which fed thousands daily and to own a second palace built by his father which sated any traveller's hunger or thirst, Senapo, by contrast, "quantunque ricchissimo se chiame, / cruciato era da perpetua fame" ("for all his reputed wealth, [...] was tortured by perpetual hunger") (*OF* 30.78 A; 33.107 C). In addition, he suffers from physical blindness. Although these two afflictions liken him to Phineus in the story of the Argonauts recounted by both Valerius Flaccus and Apollonius Rhodius, the cause of his plight is markedly dissimilar. Whereas the Greek gods punished Phineus for revealing too much of their business to mortal men, the Christian God has stricken Senapo for attempting to scale a nearby mountain leading to the earthly paradise in order to subjugate its inhabitants (*OF* 30.81 A; 33.110 C).

The Ethiopian sovereign's unbridled hubris and imperialist aspirations take us from Phineus back to the Prester John legend through both his Alexander-like quest for domination and the geographical extension of his kingdom. The various Prester John letters claim, in fact, that a river found in one of his pagan provinces originated in "paradiso" (*La lettera del Prete Gianni*, 56; Silverberg 42). Mandeville's fantastical *Travels* (*Le livre* 467; tr. 183) and Poggibonsi's empirical *Libro d'Oltremare* (2: 68) note the Garden of Eden's relation to Prester John's realm and Ethiopia, respectively.[21] Mappamundi, such as the Catalan-Estense map of 1450–60, situated both sites in Africa.[22]

Given the persistence of allusions to Prester John beneath the Phineus parallel, it may be that details from the medieval legend actually led Ariosto to the Argonaut episode in the first place. For example, although the harpy is a distinctly classical creature, various exotic and monstrous animals, such as enormous serpents with two horned heads and blazing eyes, can be found in later redactions of the Prester John letter (*La lettera del Prete Gianni*, 162–74). Old French versions and their Italian translations describe in particular griffons strong enough to carry oxen to their nests and alerions red as fire with razor-sharp wings, as well as another species of bird that makes war on a race of small people.[23] This latter phenomenon is presented explicitly as God's retribution: "Et ceste pestillense leur douna Nostre Sires pour les pechiés que leur ancisseur fisent" ("And Our Lord gives them this pestilence for the sins of their ancestors") (*La lettera del Prete Gianni*, 162). Moreover, although Phineus is also guilty of a transgression, a much closer match for Senapo are the giants who "vorrent abatre le ciel pour le tour que fonda Babiel qui estoit leur sires" ("wanted to bring down the heavens through the tower built by their ruler, Babel") and whose descendants are thereby obliged by God to labour in the fields of Prester John's realm (*La lettera del Prete Gianni*, 176).[24]

In the *Furioso*, God responds to Senapo's crime not only by punishing the ruler but also by annihilating the hundred thousand men who had accompanied him to the mountain. This is in line with the Genesis episode behind the account of Prester John's giants, in which both Nimrod and his people were forever dispersed as punishment for attempting to construct the Tower of Babel. The earliest extant letter of Prester John already suggested a connection to Nimrod by asserting that his domain extended to Babylon "iuxta turrim Babel" ("near the tower of Babel") (*La lettera del Prete Gianni*, 54).

Senapo's ambition also calls to mind the *Innamorato*'s foremost African kings, Agramante and Rodamonte, who in turn claimed descent from Alexander of Macedonia and Nimrod, respectively. Anticipating Senapo, in fact, both African kings had intended to cap their conquest of the earth with an invasion of paradise (*OI* 2.1.64–5). However, whereas these two Saracen overreachers meet their death later in the *Furioso*, the Christian emperor's trajectory will lead instead to moral and physical regeneration.

The first step of Senapo's journey to salvation is his contrition. Upon Astolfo's arrival, the ruler addresses the unknown knight as "Angel di Dio, Messia novello" ("Angel of God, new Messiah") (*OF* 30.85 A; 33.114 C) and then proceeds to confess his prior offences to God using the terms of sin, forgiveness, and repentance:

> ben che *perdon* non mertino *mie offese*,
> mira che proprio è a noi *peccar* sovente,
> a voi *perdonar* sempre a *chi si pente*. (*OF* 30.85 A; emphasis added)

> if I do not deserve *pardon* for so great *offences*,
> remember that it is our nature to *sin* often,
> yours ever to *pardon* those who *repent*. (*OF* 33.114 C)

Senapo, moreover, simply beseeches Astolfo to liberate him from the harpies and refrains from seeking a cure for his blindness because he recognizes the justice of God's punishment: "Del mio error consapevole, io non chieggio / né chiederti ardirei li antiqui lumi" ("Conscious of my transgression I do not ask – I dare not ask – for the eyes I used to have") (*OF* 30.86 A; 33.115 C).

When Astolfo accepts the undertaking, he acknowledges his own human failings in equally religious language: "son mortal e *peccatore* anch'io / di tanta *gratia* a me concessa indegno" ("I too am a mortal man and a *sinner*, unworthy of the [*grace* given to me]") (*OF* 30.88 A; 33.117

C, emphasis added). The English knight, however, exemplifies a sinner who has already taken concrete steps to reach redemption. As we recall, he had earlier repented of his amorous indiscretions while suffering in the form of a plant on Alcina's island and contritely confessed his failings to Ruggiero; after embracing virtue with the help of Logistilla and purging his sins in Jerusalem, he then used his newfound gifts in a series of penitential acts – freeing pilgrimage routes from danger, rescuing friends from killer women, and liberating countless knights and damsels from Atlante's palace. His encounter with Senapo places him in a position to continue performing good deeds by assisting in the Ethiopian emperor's ultimate reconciliation with God, discussed below.

Astolfo's actions recall the steps taken by previous mythical heroes in confronting the harpies.[25] In the classical Greek version, Calai and Zete, sons of the wind Borea, intend to kill the harpies, but the goddess Iris advises them against such violence and promises that Phineus will no longer be disturbed. Changing their mind, they then chase the monstrous birds to the Strophades in the Ionian Sea. In the *Aeneid*, the harpies twice ruin Aeneas's feast when his crew inadvertently land on their island (*Aeneid* 3.210). The effort of the Trojan warriors to kill the birds not only fails to achieve the desired result but prompts the harpy Celaeno to pronounce a dreadful prophecy. Astolfo's initial attempt to kill the harpies is similarly futile (*OF* 30.93 A; 33.122 C). Changing strategy, he uses Logistilla's gift of the horn to chase the harpies away from Senapo's table and into a cavern (*OF* 30.98 A; 33.127 C).

The substitution of a faraway island with a cave takes us back once again to the Prester John legend. At the outermost reaches of his realm one finds, in fact, a very deep "caverna" harbouring "infinita milia draconum terribilium" ("infinite thousands of terrible dragons") that – like Ariosto's harpies – molest the inhabitants of nearby provinces (*La lettera del Prete Gianni*, 62). In the *Furioso*, moreover, the cave turns out to be the entrance to hell, an association exploited earlier in both *Ugone d'Avernia* and *Il Guerrin Meschino*. Astolfo's ensuing exploration of this infernal cave, in fact, dissociates him from the Boreades, who returned promptly to Phineus after their labour, and links him instead to Ugone and Guerrino, who also preceded him in visiting the realm of Prester John.

Inferno

Both earlier chivalric heroes travel through an infernal setting where they learn about sin and divine punishment. Guerrino reaches hell after first visiting St Patrick's purgatory. Moving from the lower depths where he sees a black-winged Satan submerged in a frozen lake (*Guerrino* 6.18–19, 413–15), he traverses in Dantesque fashion a series of circles in which each of the seven deadly sins is punished. Ugone's goal from the start of his journey is precisely to reach hell, where Charles Martel has charged him with exacting tribute from Lucifer. After losing a bout with "una grandissima brigata d'uccelli [...] i quali uccelli puzzavano di un puzzo velenoso e cattivo" ("a huge swarm of birds [...] that reeked of a poisonous and bad stench"), he arrives at a large cave within a great mountain (*Ugone* 2: 4, 5). Coming upon a hellish scenario where "sentiva grandissime strida; e vedeva entrare e uscire della fiamma e delle putride acque molte anime" ("he heard very great shrieks; and he saw many souls entering and exiting the flame and putrid waters"), he discovers from a "messo di Dio" ("messenger from God") that it is indeed a branch of hell (*Ugone* 2: 11). Later in the poem he travels for seven days through hell proper, under the guidance of Aeneas and St William of Orange, where he witnesses the suffering of Saracens and Christians alike. Among the latter, Tristano and Isotta are characteristically punished for their "disordinato amore sanza ragione" ("irrational, immoderate love") (*Ugone* 2: 156) while King Arthur and many others from the Round Table are condemned for vainglory (*Ugone* 2: 154–6), the two sins later exemplified by Ariosto's Astolfo and Senapo, respectively. The episode's doctrinal focus accords with the work's overall religious underpinnings. As Luisa Meregazzi has observed: "Ugo's entire journey has very little to do with the aimless wanderings of errant knights; it is instead a voyage of penitence, of exploration, of religious apostleship" (7).

Ariosto clearly had these two precedents in mind while composing the *Furioso*'s infernal episode, as Rajna has noted (*Le fonti*, 531), but he eschews the traditional deadly sins to focus on one offence in particular – ingratitude. In an autobiographical novella removed in spirit from Astolfo's Ethiopian journey and the immediate setting's Dantesque overtones, Lidia, the Anaxarete-like princess of Lydia, relates her cruel and ungrateful actions towards her suitor, Alceste.[26] Lidia's alternation between holding out false hope and rejection led the knight to fight a series of battles both on behalf of and in opposition to her father until, learning definitively of her scorn, he falls ill and dies. Astolfo's lack of response to Lidia's Boccacesque tale seems to indicate that there is no connection between the novella's vicissitudes and the knight's undertakings. Indeed, the vanity of Alceste's reckless violence, in which countless lives are lost for frivolous motives, provides an a priori negative exemplum that sets in greater relief the ideologically charged mission upon which Astolfo is about to embark. Moreover, Lidia's ungratefulness could be contrasted to the gratitude that Senapo will be expected to show after his suffering is relieved.

The Earthly Paradise

After listening to Lidia's tale, Astolfo is forced by dense smoke back to the earth's surface, where he washes himself from head to foot in a stream in order to remove the terrible stench (*OF* 31.47 A; 34.47 C). The symbolic sense of this cleansing will soon become apparent: just as the knight had earlier purged himself of sin before contemplating Christ's Passion in the temples of Jerusalem, he now purifies himself before moving to the next step of his journey, the earthly paradise. As Rajna has noted, this site was also previously visited by both Ugone d'Avernia and Guerrino, who were each instructed by the patriarch Enoch and the prophet Elijah.[27] Astolfo's journey to the earthly paradise, while echoing those of his chivalric counterparts, is nevertheless most directly developed in contrast to Senapo's earlier expedition: whereas the overbearing African king wanted to subdue its inhabitants, the English prince wanders up the mountain spurred on by "il desir [...] del veder" ("his urge to explore") *OF* 31.48 A; 34.48 C). Like Ugone and Guerrino, he is furnished with a guide who discourses on moral virtue, but his interlocutor is neither Enoch nor Elijah (who are nevertheless said to inhabit the site), but St John the Evangelist (*OF* 31.57–9 A; 34.58–9 C).[28]

If earlier Logistilla had tutored Astolfo in a humanistic and secular spirit, now St John will expound divine truth in the guise of a religious authority. Indeed, the saint diminishes the fairy's importance by referring to both the horn and the hippogriff as indirect gifts from God: "Che né il tuo corno, né il cavallo alato / ti valea, se da Dio non t'era dato" ("neither your horn nor the winged horse would be of any use to you had not God given them to you") (*OF* 31.56 A; 34.56 C). Moreover, he asserts, "per voler divino / sei nel terrestre paradiso asceso" ("by God's will [you] have ascended to the earthly paradise") (*OF* 31.55 A; 34.55 C). This further explains why Astolfo has arrived with such ease at a site that had proved inaccessible to Senapo and any others who had previously attempted the journey on their own.[29]

According to St John, moreover, God has been guiding Astolfo's journey ever since he left Europe: "pur credi che non senza alto mystero / venuto sei da l'Artico hemispero" ("your arrival here from the Northern hemisphere is, believe me, not without highly-placed help") (*OF* 31.55 A; 34.55 C). Ariosto had already hinted as much at both Astolfo's departure from France and his arrival in Ethiopia. On the first occasion, when Astolfo's flight to Africa was made possible by his unexpected encounter with Bradamante, noted above, "parvegli che Dio gli la mandasse" ("her arrival truly seemed to him a godsend") (*OF* 21.11 A; 23.11 C). Once in Ethiopia, the knight told Senapo that if he were to rid his kingdom of the harpies, his success would be due to God, who had led him there precisely to help the beleaguered ruler ("che per tuo aiuto qui mi drizzò il volo"; *OF* 30.88 A; 33.117 C). St John's disclosure thus confirms Astolfo's own prior assumptions about God's involvement in his chivalric destiny.

St John shows further that Providence has been controlling more than just Astolfo's movements: indeed, he reveals that even the poem's central action – Orlando's descent into madness – was decreed by God. Although the account of Orlando's loss of sanity was framed in purely psychological terms in canto 21/23, the saint now informs Astolfo that his cousin's affliction is nothing less than a divine punishment: "Sappi che 'l vostro Orlando, perché torse / dal camin dritto le commisse insegne, / è punito da Dio" ("Your Orlando has misappropriated the standards committed to him, and God is punishing him") (*OF* 31.62 A; 34.62 C). He goes on to explain that although God had given Orlando special attributes "perché a difesa di sua santa fede / così voluto l'ha constituire" ("in order thus to constitute him defender of His holy Faith") (*OF* 31.63 A; 34.63 C), the knight was so blinded by his illicit love for a pagan woman that he not only forgot his higher calling but even attempted to kill his cousin Rinaldo.[30]

Orlando's penalty, like Astolfo's earlier suffering as a myrtle bush and Senapo's tribulations as a famished blind man, is for a limited period of time and thus corresponds to a purgatorial rather than an infernal punishment: "Sol di tre mesi dal voler divino / a purgar questo error termine è messo" ("the divine will has imposed a period of only three months to purge his sin") (*OF* 31.66 A; 34.66 C). And as St John reveals, God has chosen Astolfo to help his fellow paladin make the transition from sin to salvation. Just as he had earlier ended Senapo's perpetual hunger, the English knight is now divinely charged with relieving Orlando's insanity:

> Né ad altro effetto per tanto camino
> salir qua su t'ha il Redentor concesso,
> se non perché da noi modo tu apprenda
> come ad Orlando il suo senno si renda. (*OF* 31.66 A)

And if our Redeemer has permitted you
to arrive up here after so long a journey,
it is quite simply so that you may learn from us
the way to bring Orlando to his senses. (*OF* 34.66 C)

As discussed below, Orlando will also need to make amends for his sinful behaviour by using his regained faculties to further the Christian cause.

The Moon

Astolfo's divinely willed mission requires him to travel to a location beyond the range of both Ugone and Guerrino: the moon. Although this site is outside the sphere of knight errantry, it is nevertheless linked to Prester John, since medieval writers not only associated his realm with the earthly paradise but also sometimes added that the latter was to be found upon a mountain high enough to approach the moon's circuit (Silverberg 168).[31] Mandeville accounts for this purported geographical connection in the following way: "Paradis terrestre dit homme ceo est la plus haute terre de mounde, et est si haute qe elle touche près de cercle de la lune par quel la lune fait soun tour" ("The Earthly Paradise, so men say, is the highest land on earth; it is so high it touches the sphere of the moon") (*Le livre* 468; tr. 184). In locating the *Furioso*'s earthly paradise at the top of a high mountain near Senapo's land, Ariosto likewise remarks that "non lontan con la superna balza / dal cerchio de la Luna esser si stima" ("it was generally believed that the orb of the moon stood not far from its highest peak") (*OF* 31.48 A; 34.48 C).

As if to underscore his status as God's instrument, Astolfo no longer rides the hippogriff but flies to the moon in a celestial chariot driven by St John (*OF* 31.68 A; 34.68 C). Before obtaining Orlando's wits, moreover, he receives a miraculous gift from God that surpasses those he had been given earlier by Logistilla: with the authorization of the saint he inhales "gran parte" ("a good portion") of his own brain previously lost through his folly (*OF* 31.84–6 A; 34.84–6 C). Notwithstanding the comedic overtones in this action – or the satirical thrust of the episode as a whole – Astolfo's resulting reacquisition of his intellectual faculty marks another transition in the evolution of his character. From this point on in the poem, he will more actively and knowingly carry out God's will on a personal and collective level.[32]

Astolfo's miraculous cure of Orlando will bring about a transformation in the latter's character as well, since it will cause him to direct his thoughts solely to the Christian cause. Zanette remarks that "while in Boiardo's poem the story of his enamourment was completely independent of and extraneous to any religious or moralizing interpretation, in Ariosto's epic [...] the paladin, purified of his misdeeds, returns to being the Roland of the old French cycle, the austere defender of Faith and of Christianity" (330).[33] Indeed, in the final phase of the war both Orlando and Astolfo take on the role of religious as well as military leaders:

> Come veri christiani Astolfo e Orlando,
> che senza Dio non vanno a rischio alcuno,
> nel exercito fan publico bando
> ch'oratïone sia fatta e digiuno. (*OF* 36.11 A)

> As true Christians who never affronted
> danger without God's aid, Astolfo and Orlando
> gave orders that all hands should
> turn to prayer and fasting. (*OF* 40.11 C)

At the same time that Orlando regains his legendary moral stature, however, he relinquishes his individuality. As Dorigatti remarks, "He becomes a wholly Carolingian figure once again, but there is something sad, something unresolved about him. [...] After he has recovered his wits there is not much scope for Orlando; he is back on his way to Roncesvalles, where death awaits him" ("Reinventing Roland," 123–4).

Before restoring Orlando's sanity, Astolfo will first cure Senapo's blindness. To this end, St John gives him a herb "di virtù excellente" ("of outstanding virtue") (*OF* 34.24 A; 38.24 C) when they pause at the earthly paradise upon their return from the moon. At the same time, the saint explicitly states that the Ethiopian ruler is expected in turn to provide an army to attack Biserta – "Acciò per questi e per li primi merti / gente gli dia con che Biserta assaglia" ("so that, for this and his earlier benefaction, the king should give him men with whom to attack Bizerta") (*OF* 34.25 A; 38.25 C) – thus connecting his personal recovery to God's greater plan of leading the Christians to victory. When Astolfo completes his task, the grateful king not only furnishes him with the number of soldiers requested but adds an extra hundred thousand and offers his own person to boot (*OF* 34.28 A; 38.28 C).

If we compare the conclusion of Astolfo's Ethiopian adventure to either the classical tale of Phineus or the chivalric episodes of Ugone and Guerrino, we find a huge divergence in the range of consequences. Phineus simply predicts the successful finale of the Argonauts' mission and explains to Calai and Zete how to avoid a danger en route. Prester John offers to share the rule of his kingdom with both Ugone and Guerrino, but each knight declines the offer and continues on his way. Senapo, on the other hand, puts a vast army at Astolfo's disposal. Indeed, in the following cantos the Christian Ethiopians will seemingly spring out of nowhere to attack the kingdom of Agramante. Ariosto's poem thus brings to fruition Christian Europe's great wish-fulfilment fantasy of finding a powerful ally in the heart of Africa to help defeat the Muslims. In the end, Astolfo's haphazard arrival in Ethiopia, initially fashioned as an isolated romance narrative, becomes the catalyst for the total destruction of Biserta. It is to this topic that we turn in the next chapter.

Chapter Fifteen

The Destruction of Biserta

Boiardo's Agramante exemplified an overreaching ruler destined to lose his kingdom in a reckless attempt to acquire something he did not possess. He not only looked to Alexander the Great as his explicit model but also echoed the aspirations of Xerxes and Hannibal. Boiardo had foretold that his invasion of France would fail, leading to the destruction of Biserta as well. Although Ariosto brings this prophecy to fruition, he transforms the ideological context along the way. While Boiardo had distanced his poem from the Christian-Saracen hostilities animating Carolingian epic, Ariosto brings back the ideology of religious conflict with a vengeance. Indeed, he not only calls for another crusade in narrator's asides, as discussed earlier, but, by the final cantos of the poem, he transforms Agramante's *aviditas dominationis* pattern into a holy war narrative. The African king thus comes to represent an enemy of the Christian faith who must be converted or annihilated.

Ariosto's new emphasis on religion in Agramante's war is apparent from the moment he picks up the threads of the battle in Paris. In the *Innamorato*'s final allusion to the African king's attack, a storm and an earthquake temporarily interrupt the fighting outside the city walls. Boiardo speculates as to whether these were caused by the people's prayers or by some unknown fate (*OI* 3.8.51). Referring to this moment eight cantos into his own poem, Ariosto maintains that it was God Himself who suspended the battle in response to Charlemagne's just lament (*OF* 8.70 AC). This gives the impression that divine intervention predates the *Furioso*'s continuation of the war, setting the stage for God's increased involvement in determining its outcome.

With Paris again under attack, Ariosto's Charlemagne seeks divine aid in a prayer that lasts four stanzas (*OF* 12.69–72 A; 14.69–72 C). His claim that "Li pagani diran che nulla puoi, / che perir lasci i partigiani tuoi" ("the pagans will say that you are powerless, leaving your own followers to perish") (*OF* 12.70 A; 14.70 C) is an indirect challenge to divine power no less than that of Iarbus to Zeus in *Aeneid* 4. Gregory aptly remarks that "Charles's accents are those of a client addressing a prince: self-abasement, a heavy dose of flattery, and an appeal to his lordship's own best interests" (117). Yet when the emperor goes on to remind God of the Christians' past services, he evokes the religiously charged context of the crusades:

> Difendi queste genti, che son quelle
> ch'el tuo sepulchro hanno purgato e mondo
> da' brutti cani, e la tua santa Chiesa
> con li vicarii tuoi spesso difesa. (*OF* 12.71 A)

> Defend your faithful, then; they are the ones
> who have cleansed your sepulchre and purged it
> of brutish dogs; many a time have they defended
> your holy Church and her vicars. (*OF* 14.71 C)

Using stereotypically derogatory language for the Saracen enemy, Ariosto once again alleges that the Christian capture of Jerusalem occurred prior to the poem's fictional present. Crusading ideology also comes through in the stated motivation of Charlemagne's troops, who are said to be "per Christo e pel suo honor a morir pronti" ("ready to die for the honour of Christ") (*OF* 12.102 A; 14.102 C). Rajna, in fact, notes the importance given to the Christian faith in this episode not only through Charlemagne's prayers but also in detailed references to the celebration of mass and to the sacraments of confession and communion (*Le fonti*, 240).

If in canto 8 Ariosto had simply commented on the wisdom of turning to God for help – "Savio chiunque a Dio sempre se volse; / ch'altri non puoté mai meglio aiutarlo" ("Wise is the man who always turns to God: for no one else can give him better assistance") (*OF* 8.70 AC) – here he demonstrates at first hand the efficacy of Christian devotion by bringing God into the poem as an actual character. After Charlemagne's guardian angel carries his prayers, together with those of all the other faithful, up to heaven, God decides to send the archangel Michael to obstruct the Saracens and assist the Christians (*OF* 12.73–7 A; 14.73–7 C). The archangel's ensuing quest to locate Discord and Silence begins as a criticism of corruption within the church but then slips into a depiction of the world outside Christendom as a morally bankrupt universe. Whereas Discord dwells within a monastery, Silence, found previously among the virtues, "fece alle sceleraggini traghitto" ("forsook his virtuous propensities") (*OF* 12.89 A; 14.89 C) and ultimately ended up at the House of Sleep. Although this site can also be found in Ovid's *Metamorphoses* and Statius's *Thebaid*, Ariosto transforms it from a moral locus into a geographical one by situating it "in Arabia" (*OF* 12.92 A; 14.92 C).[1] The fact that Silence is found lying between fat, indolent Sloth and inert Laziness carries over the moral censure of the previous scene, suggestively presenting idleness as a distinct characteristic of the Orient.

Despite the satirical tone of Michael's quest, in the end his efforts do bear fruit, leading to the first miracle of the poem. Silence and the angel fly to Rinaldo's troops in Picardy and cause them to reach Paris in a single day without being heard (*OF* 12.96–8 A; 14.96–8 C). The intervention of Discord, while less marvellous, is even more far-reaching, since it results directly in the death of Mandricardo and the extended absence of Ruggiero from the battlefield on the Saracen side and, indirectly, in the permanent departure of Rodomonte and subsequently Sacripante from the war. Ponte even views the later conversion of Marphisa as one of the "very grave" consequences of Discord's action ("La discordia," 10).

In the final cantos of the poem God intervenes with greater immediacy and success, having chosen Astolfo as his new intermediary. After the rehabilitated paladin has returned to earth with Orlando's wits and his own, he performs a series of miracles that ensure a Christian victory. First, following St John's instructions he captures the South Wind in a wineskin, which permits him to cross the desert with Senapo's troops undisturbed. Next, he throws down an enormous quantity of stones that miraculously grow into horses, a feat that is said to thereby transform 80,102 "pedoni" ("foot-soldiers") into outright "cavallieri," that is, knights (*OF* 34.33–5 A; 38.33–5 C). Finally, he tosses leaves into the sea, and these become a fleet of ships sufficient to hold 26,000 men (*OF* 35.37–40 A; 39.26–9 C). All three miracles reveal an awareness of conditions in Africa recorded in writings of the time: the wind-swept desert, the oft-noted scarcity of horses in Prester John's realm, and the lack of ships. Yet it is not simply the greater realistic detail that separates these events from the various marvels of the *Innamorato* and of medieval romance in general. Although one can find precedents in secular literature, the episode's distinctly religious tone directs the reader to sacred sources.[2] The latter two miracles, in fact, recall biblical episodes associated with the figures of Moses (e.g., the metamorphosis of his rod into a snake, Yahweh's transforming the waters of the Nile into blood) and Jesus (e.g., the multiplication of bread and fish, the changing of water into wine).

Ariosto draws attention to God's active role in bringing about the miracles. Before hurling the stones from the mountain, Astolfo kneels to pray to St John: "inchinando le ginocchia, fece / al santo suo maestro oratïone, / sicuro che sia udita la sua prece" ("kneeling to invoke his holy patron, confident that his prayer was heard") (*OF* 34.33 A; 38.33 C). The ensuing miracle elicits the poet's proclamation of God's power to help those who believe in Christ: "Oh quanto a chi ben crede in Cristo, lece!" ("Ah, what shall be denied to the man who truly believes in Christ!") (*OF* 34.33 A; 38.33 C). After the metamorphosis of leaves into ships, the poet again expresses his awe of God through exclamatory verses: "Oh felici e dal ciel ben dilette alme, / gratia che Dio raro a' mortali infonde! / Oh stupendo miracolo che nacque / di quelle frondi, come furo in l'acque!" ("O fortunate souls, beloved of Heaven! O bounty seldom conferred by God upon mortals! O sublime miracle produced on those leaves when they were in the water!") (*OF* 35.37 A; 39.26 C). Readers have discerned parody in the miracles (Rajna, *Le fonti*, 549) and irony in the overblown exclamations (Gregory 114), yet within the fiction of the poem they underscore God's participation in a Christian victory that is anything but funny.[3] In the midst of retelling the battle of Roncevaux, Pulci had likewise exclaimed: "O Dio, quanti miracoli hai mostrati! / Quanto è felice chi in te pon sua speme!" ("Dear God, how many miracles You showed! / Happy the men who place their hope in You!") (*Morg*. 27.211).[4]

Now that Senapo has regained God's favour and the harpies no longer desecrate his table, it is his own troops who wreak havoc on neighbouring territories. Indeed, it is specifically with the Nubian "cavalry" that Astolfo "scòrse Aphrica intorno, / facendo prede, incendi e prigionieri" ("scoured Africa, pillaging, burning, and taking prisoners") (*OF* 34.35 A; 38.35 C). These new recruits are described as "d'ogni indugia impazïenti, / da la speranza del guadagno tratti" ("impatient of all delay and lured by the hope of booty") (*OF* 36.18 A; 40.18 C).

The increased emphasis on religion in this final stage of the war is accompanied by greater ferocity among the troops. In the same stanza in which Astolfo and Orlando order collective prayer and fasting prior to the battle in Biserta, Ariosto anticipates the general freewheeling sack of the city that is expected to follow their victory:

e poi, ch'el terzo Sol, dal mar spuntando,
ritruovi in arme apparecchiato ognuno

per expugnar Biserta, che data hanno,
vinta che s'abbia, a fuoco e a saccomanno. (*OF* 36.11 A)

Three days hence, at the given signal,
everyone must be ready
to storm Bizerta, which, once captured,
was to be given up to fire and pillage. (*OF* 40.11 C)

The unrestrained violence culminates in the ensuing destruction of Biserta, described at great length and in particularly harrowing detail:

D'huomini morti pieno era per tutto;
e de le innumerabili ferite
fatto era un stagno più scuro e più brutto
di quel che cinge la città di Dite.
Di casa in casa un lungo incendio indutto
ardea palagi, portici e meschite;
de pianti e strida e man percosse ai petti
suonano i vuoti e depredati tetti.

Li vincitori uscir de le funeste
porte vedeansi de gran preda onusti,
chi con bei vasi e chi con ricche veste,
chi con rapiti argenti a' Dèi vetusti:
chi trahea i figli, e chi le madri meste:
stupri infiniti e mille altri atti ingiusti
commessi fur, di che gran parte intese,
né lo puoté vietare, il Duca inglese. (*OF* 36.33-4 A)

The dead lay all about.
Countless bloody gashes had produced
a swamp darker and more foul
than the one which rings Hades.
A trail of fire spreading from house to house
burnt down palaces, arcades, and mosques.
The empty, ransacked houses echoed with cries
and shrieks and the thud of beaten breasts.

The victors could be seen emerging from the doorways
of the ill-fated homes laden with rich spoils:
some carried fine vases, others costly garments,

others silverware stolen from the ancient household gods.
Some men dragged out the children,
others the grieving mothers;
[infinite rapes] and a thousand other crimes
were committed, which [...] Astolfo in great part
knew of but [was] unable to prevent. (*OF* 40.33–4 C)[5]

This combination of religious piety and uncontrolled rapaciousness recalls chronicles of the First Crusade. William of Tyre notes that a fast and a procession preceded the capture of Jerusalem, which then became a scene of "frightful carnage" no less than Ariosto's Biserta:

> Everywhere lay heaps of severed heads, so that soon it was impossible to pass or to go from one place to another except over the bodies of the slain. [...] So frightful was the massacre throughout the city, so terrible the shedding of blood, that even the victors experienced sensations of horror and loathing. [...] Wretched survivors [were] dragged out into public view and slain like sheep. Some formed bands and broke into houses where they laid violent hands on the heads of families, on their wives, children, and their entire households. (1: 370–2)

Having incorporated crusading ideology in his continuation of Agramante's war, Ariosto reproduces even the most gruesome and troubling aspects of the First Crusade chronicles.[6] Like William, he reports the violent scene with a sense of dismay over the excesses.

The Battle of Lipadusa

The sack of Biserta does not spell the end of the war, however. Although all is already lost for the Saracens, the final outcome is decided by a three-on-three duel on the island of Lipadusa (Lampedusa). The Saracen side, comprising Agramante, Sobrino, and Gradasso, initially has some advantage in weaponry. Because of prior narrative twists and turns, Gradasso is in possession of both Orlando's sword, Durindana, and Rinaldo's horse, Baiardo. Thanks to divine intervention, however, an unmanned boat miraculously arrives on the island bringing assistance to the Christian warriors in the form of Hector's armour, the magic sword Balisarda, and the horse Frontino. Orlando takes the sword for himself while giving the armour and horse to Oliviero and Brandimarte, respectively.

This final battle brings religious difference to the forefront. The Christian pedigree of Orlando and Oliviero is evident, especially since both knights traditionally had a prominent role in the battle of Roncevaux. Ariosto reaffirms the Christian identity of Brandimarte by having him attempt to convert Agramante. Unlike the conversation between Orlando and Agricane in the *Innamorato*, but like the discussions between warriors in the *Spagna* and other Carolingian epics, the debate contrasts Christianity and Islam. Brandimarte debases Mohammed when relating his own conversion to Agramante: "Io mi conversi a Christo, e Machon stolto / e mendace connobbi" ("I knew Christ for God, Mahomet for a dupe [and mendacious]") (*OF* 37.39 A; 41.39 C). Predictably, the king is not any more persuaded than the countless Saracens in Carolingian narratives who were presented with the same simplistic argument.[7] Brandimarte's sole attempt at religious proselytism thus ends in failure, and he is not given an occasion to return to the topic in the way Orlando did with Agricane in the earlier poem. Indeed, as soon as he delivers a fatal blow to Agramante, Gradasso stabs him from behind.

The three who remain alive following the battle are Orlando, Sobrino, and Oliviero, who is unable to walk as a result of his injuries. When they encounter a hermit, referred to as "el servo del Signor del paradiso" ("the servant of the Heavenly King") (*OF* 39.187 A; 43.190 C), Orlando explains to him that Oliviero was critically wounded "pugnando per la fé di Christo" ("fighting for the Christian cause") (*OF* 39.188 A; 43.191 C). The holy man then miraculously cures the knight simply by blessing him "in nome de le eterne tre persone, / padre e figliuolo e spirto santo" ("in the name of the three Eternal Persons, Father, Son, and Holy Spirit") (*OF* 39.189 A; 43.192 C). Ariosto's immediate cry of "Oh virtù che dà Christo a chi gli crede!" ("Oh, the power Christ gives to those who believe in Him!") echoes his earlier exclamations following Charlemagne's prayers and Astolfo's miraculous actions.

After Sobrino witnesses the miraculous healing, he immediately converts to Christianity:

> Tosto che vide del Monacho santo
> il miracolo grande et evidente,
> si dispose Machon poner da canto,
> E Christo confessar vivo e potente:
> e dimandò, con cor di fé contrito,
> iniciarsi al nostro sacro rito. (*OF* 39.190 A)

> On seeing the clearly miraculous cure

wrought by the holy man,
he decided to renounce Mahomet
and confess Christ, living and powerful.
His heart touched with faith,
he asked to be initiated in our sacred rite. (*OF* 43.193 C)

Thus Brandimarte's failed effort to convert Agramante before the battle is countered by the spontaneous conversion of Sobrino at its conclusion. Whereas persuasive rhetoric could not succeed in swaying the former, the sight of a miracle immediately convinces the latter. This final signal of God's presence in the poem complements and completes the earlier metamorphoses of stones into horses and leaves into ships. Moreover, like these more visually spectacular miracles, the healing of Sobrino evokes religious precedents, in this case the many instances of healing in the Gospels and hagiographic literature.[8]

With the destruction of Biserta and definitive Christian victory, the time for miracles is over, and within a few stanzas Ariosto dispenses with all the divine aids accumulated along the way. The ships are transformed back into leaves, which blow away in the breeze (*OF* 40.28 A; 44.20 C). Prester John will release the raging bag of winds once his troops reach Ethiopia (*OF* 40.30 A; 44.22 C). As the Nubians make their way over the Atlas mountain range, their horses turn again to stone, and they are forced to continue on foot (*OF* 40.31 A; 44.23 C). They are left to their own devices and out of the narrative at this point, since neither God nor Ariosto has any more need of them. Astolfo, once back in Provence, sets the hippogriff free following the orders of St John (*OF* 40.33 A; 44.25 C). Ariosto adds, moreover, that Logistilla's horn had already lost its power on the moon.

The Contemporary Relevance of Agramante's War

By recounting a story purportedly true but hidden by Turpin, Boiardo had offered an alternative to a literary tradition of Christians battling Saracens that supported the crusades. Ariosto, in contrast, renders concrete one of the most persistent fantasies of Christian Europe: a military victory over Muslims with the help of a Christian sovereign residing in Africa. But did he really subscribe to the crusading ideology so clearly outlined in the final phase of Agramante's war? The systematic degradation of Saracen heroes and the progressive development of the plot towards a holy war narrative would seem to indicate that he did. Nonetheless, from the highest geographical point we reach in the poem – offering a perspective from beyond the earthly realm – Ariosto warns us not to take literary or historical narrative at face value. Indeed, a figure no less authoritative than St John, who acts in the poem as the revelation of divine truth, warns that authors who are obliged to serve a patron provide accounts that are more often than not contrary to fact.[9] The saint therefore admonishes Astolfo, and by extension the reader, to transform the events of Greek and Roman epic into the opposite of what they appear: "se tu vuoi ch'el ver non ti sia ascoso, / tutta al contrario l'historia converti" ("if you want to know what really happened, invert the story") (*OF* 32.27 A; 35.27 C).

St John's revelation that fiction contradicts history may serve to undercut Astolfo's lavish praise of his Estense patron, but it may also help us to understand the geographical and ideological significance of the war between Agramante and Charlemagne in the *Furioso*. One way to read the saint's advice, I would propose, lies within the episode involving Senapo. In an unambiguous political allegory, the Ethiopian emperor ravished by the harpies represents none other than Italy depredated by its European neighbours:

Oh famelice, inique e fiere Harpie
ch'alla acciecata Italia e d'error piena,
per punir forse antique colpe rie,
in ogni mensa alto giudicio mena!
Innocenti fanciulli e madri pie
cascan di fame, e veggion ch'una cena
di questi monstri rei tutto divora
ciò che del viver lor sostegno fôra.

Troppo fallò chi le spelonche aperse
che già molti anni erano state chiuse;
onde il fetore e l'ingordigia emerse,
che ad amorbar Italia si diffuse.
La Pace allhora e il buon viver si perse;
e la Quïete in tal modo se excluse,
ch'in guerre, in povertà, sempre in affanni
è dopo stata, et è per star molti anni. (*OF* 31.1-2)

O ravenous, baneful harpies! How ruthlessly
you wreak divine vengeance at every table in purblind,

wayward Italy, to punish her (maybe) for faults of old.
Innocent children and devoted mothers succumb
to starvation as they watch these evil monsters make
one meal of everything on which they have expected to live.

That man perpetrated the worst of crimes who opened
the cave which had been closed for many a year:
out came the stench and gluttony to pervade Italy
and corrupt her. Happy days were at an end,
and peace driven out. Ever since has Italy
been steeped in wars, in poverty, and trouble (*OF* 34.1–2 C)

Continuing the parallel, the assumption is that Italy, once liberated from the rapacious harpy-states devouring it, could help in a war against the infidel just as the Nubian army did in that against Agramante.

Whereas on this occasion Italy's plight is evoked in the context of a fictional religious war, Ariosto also decries the plunder of Italy by its neighbours in the poem's most direct and lengthy call for a renewed crusade effort in the historical present, cited in chapter 13 (*OF* 15.74–7 A; 17.74–7 C). Prompted by these narrative asides, if we follow St John's advice to ascertain the truth behind the fiction by inverting the story, we might find that if in the poem the Franks and their western European allies are the defenders of Latin Christendom, their contemporary counterparts are in actuality the invaders against whom the Italian states are helpless to defend themselves.

Ariosto's persistent references to historical reality embedded within the epic plot of Agramante's war remind the reader of the striking contradictions between fictional past and historical present.[10] Rodomonte's ferocious attack on Paris, for example, prompts a condemnation of "le man rapaci e ladre / che sore e frati, e bianchi, neri e bigi, / vïolati hanno, e sposa e figlia e madre; / gettato in terra Christo in sacramento / per tôrgli il tabernaculo d'ariento" ("the thieving rascals who have violated wives, daughters, mothers, monks, and nuns – be they white, black, or grey – and thrown Christ in the Sacrament onto the floor to take from Him a silver tabernacle") (*OF* 12.8 A; 14.8 C). The perpetrators of the crimes referred to in the above-cited passage are not, however, the Africans besieging Paris or even the Ottoman Turks ravaging Constantinople but rather the French troops at the sack of Ravenna in 1512.

After alluding as well to the 1512 sack of Brescia, Ariosto goes on to link the current king of France to both Marsilio and Agramante, who are, however, more adept in the organization of their troops (*OF* 12.10 A; 14.10 C). A few cantos later, after lamenting that God, "a noi, greggi inutili et mal nati, / ha dato per guardian lupi arrabbiati" ("to guard us, unprofitable and ill-born flock, [...] has appointed vicious wolves for keepers") (*OF* 15.3 A; 17.3 C), Ariosto expresses the thought that one day the tables will be turned: "Tempo verrà che a depredar lor liti / andaren noi, se mai saren migliori" ("The time will come when we shall go to ravage their shores / if ever we grow better") (*OF* 15.5 A; 17.5 C). He then goes on explicitly to link Italy's current plight to that of the poem's unfortunate Christians whose lands were overrun by "il Turco e il Moro / con stupri, uccisïon, rapine et onte" ("the Turks and Moors [...], committing rape and murder, pillage and outrage") (*OF* 15.6 A; 17.6 C). Readers are thus repeatedly invited to equate the poem's Turks and Moors with Italy's present-day European Christian invaders with whom Ferrara was nevertheless careful to maintain an alliance.

Nor did the contemporary invaders evoked originate exclusively beyond the Italian peninsula. Openly branding the neighbouring Venetians as "i nemici" ("our enemy") (*OF* 13.2 A; 15.2 C), Ariosto links them to the Saracen armies throughout the poem. In the midst of an account of the poem's climactic naval battle, the Christian triumph over the African forces recalls Ippolito's victory over the Venetians (*OF* 36.5 A; 40.5 C). In this light, the final defeat and destruction of Biserta may be read as a wish-fulfilment fantasy not simply of western Europe triumphing over Ottoman aggressors but of Italy over European invaders, and of Ferrara over neighbouring enemies on the peninsula.

As the epic thread of the poem comes to an end, the narrative moves to the celebrations in Paris that take place, without any joy, because of the death of Brandimarte. One may in fact wonder why God (i.e., Ariosto) did not intervene to save this hero just as he did to orchestrate the Christian victory and to cure Orlando, Senapo, and Oliviero. Although there are many possible answers, I believe that for a fuller picture it is necessary to understand what this character represents in both the *Innamorato* and the *Furioso*. In the final two chapters I argue that Ariosto not only eliminates Brandimarte from the world of his poem but rewrites and inverts episodes that the character had undergone in Boiardo's poem in order to present a radically different view of the world both beyond and within the confines of western Europe.

PART FIVE

From Cosmopolitanism to Isolationism

Chapter Sixteen

Boiardo's Brandimarte across the Continents

After leaving Charlemagne's court in righteous anger and reaching Asia, Astolfo comes upon a Saracen whose perfection is not equalled in all the earth and whose excellence has already been recognized throughout Pagandom (*OI* 1.9.49–50).[1] Although his name literally means "Sword of Mars," Brandimarte has gained his reputation not in war but in tournaments and jousts ("torniamenti e giostra"), and the character traits that most distinguish him are his courteous, humane nature and the noble love ("gentil amore") that inflames his heart (*OI* 1.9.50).[2] Born in the *Isole Lontane* (Far Away Islands), Brandimarte was kidnapped as a boy and grew up at the *Roca Silvana* (Castle Wild). The general direction of both imaginary sites can be deduced via their distance from other locations. Brandimarte's birth city of Damogir is half a month's sail northeast of Balisardo's outpost (*OI* 2.10.51, 2.13.30), in turn a five-day trip by foot from Morgana's lake (*OI* 2.10.51), identified by Murrin as the Caspian Sea (*Allegorical Epic*, 228n), thus putting it somewhere above the vast Russian land mass.[3] The Roca Silvana is later said to lie about a thousand miles beyond Syria, past Samarkand (*OI* 2.27.27). While both invented locations are marked by their remoteness, the Roca Silvana's stated proximity to Samarkand (in today's Uzbekistan) could also have elicited concrete associations among Estense readers. Conquered by Alexander the Great in 329 B.C.E., the former Persian city subsequently became a meeting point between China and the Mediterranean. The Arabs took it over in the eighth century, and Genghis Khan captured and devastated it in 1220, but Marco Polo still refers to it as "una nobile cittade" ("a noble city") inhabited by both Saracens and Christians (*Mil.* 51.1, 60). Timur (or Tamerlane) made it the capital of his empire in 1370 and rebuilt it in accordance with its new prominence.[4] To Boiardo's early readers, therefore, Samarkand would have represented a crossroads of various civilizations in the East.

Brandimarte professes a chivalric calling that knows of no regional or national boundaries: "Brandimarte dapoi per suo valore / Cercato ha il mondo per monte e per piano" ("Then Brandimarte toured the world, / its hills and plains, to prove himself") (*OI* 2.13.12). In the course of the poem he covers more ground than any other character in the poem, whether alone or in the company of his beloved Fiordelisa – born in Laodicea (today the Syrian city of Latakia) but likewise kidnapped at a young age and raised at the Roca Silvana. His trajectory takes him, in fact, across the known world of the time, from an island situated in the outermost reaches of northern Russia to Uzbekistan and back, as well as to Cathay, Syria, and northern Africa, before he ultimately arrives in France in the final cantos of the unfinished poem. It is therefore with good reason that Boiardo selects this global knight errant *per eccellenza* to undergo an ordeal that requires coming face to face with an unknown other.

At Phebosilla's palace, Brandimarte must navigate his way through a world in which things are not always as they seem. While the source of harm may be difficult to identify, it can also happen that behind an outwardly intimidating guise one finds a benevolent individual offering the possibility of reciprocal kindness and friendship. The challenge is thus to avoid judging others according to their outer appearance or one's own inner fears and to penetrate through to the reality beneath the surface. Bringing to bear literary sources, symbolism, and contemporary events that would have been relevant to the poem's early readers, I argue that Boiardo develops this episode as an illustration of the flexibility of mind necessary when encountering all that is foreign.

Phebosilla's Palace

As Brandimarte and Fiordelisa travel together across Asia, a damsel signals them to avoid the palace ahead on their path. The intrepid knight, on the contrary, rushes forward and comes upon a battle underway between a giant and a serpent-dragon.[5] As soon as the giant spies Brandimarte, he attacks the newcomer using as a weapon "né spada né maza, / Né piastra o malia, o d'altre arme nïente" ("neither sword nor club / nor armaments – no plate or mail") but rather the "serpente" he was holding by the tail (*OI* 2.25.25). Even though the giant initially succeeds in knocking down both Brandimarte and his horse, in the end the knight manages to defeat him. Victory, however, is shown to be illusory, given that at this point a double metamorphosis takes place in which the giant and the snake transform into each other and resume the battle against him in the same manner as before.

After six rounds of this mutual transformation, the exhausted knight tries striking not the giant but his weapon – and the serpent dies instantly. When the giant then tries to flee, Brandimarte easily defeats him. Nevertheless, this time, too, his victory is merely provisional. A knight who had been mentioned earlier as apparently guarding a tomb in an adjacent room now abruptly approaches and begins to attack Brandimarte. Although our hero kills him after a brief battle, we do not learn his identity until much later, when Brandimarte has already left the palace. What we can surmise at this point is that the real source of the violence against Brandimarte was neither the giant nor the serpent – common symbols of wickedness – but a fellow knight who initially appeared to be uninvolved until the moment of his attack.

Yet before Brandimarte can leave the palace, the door suddenly disappears. The damsel who had earlier tried to turn him away now mysteriously appears and explains that Brandimarte must open the tomb and kiss what comes forth from it. The knight initially boasts that "Non ha l'Inferno un demonio sì fiero / Ch'io non gli ardisca il viso acostare!" ("No devil lives in hell so fierce / that I won't dare to press his face") (*OI* 2.26.5), but he quickly changes his mind and draws his sword when a ferocious-looking serpent emerges (*OI* 2.26.7). Although Brandimarte's response is understandable, the damsel explains that it is the wrong course of action to take, since his violence would cause everyone to fall to the bottom of the tomb. Unconvinced, Brandimarte begins to suspect that the damsel is deceiving him and imagines that "quela falsa" ("that false one") (as he now thinks of her) wants to vindicate the death of the still unidentified knight who attacked him (*OI* 2.26.11).

When he finally kisses the snake despite his fears (*OI* 2.26.13), the hideous creature is suddenly transformed into Phebosilla, the fairy who had built the palace, the garden, and the tomb. Boiardo explains that she had remained for a long time in torment ("in pena dura") in the form of a serpent and could only regain her true form when kissed (*OI* 2.26.14–15). In recompense for having been liberated, Phebosilla uses her magic to enchant Brandimarte's armour and resuscitate his dying horse.

The Literary Context

Brandimarte's ordeal at Phebosilla's palace can first of all be read against an earlier episode in the *Innamorato* itself, Orlando's adventure in Falerina's garden in Orgagna (*OI* 2.4.4–2.5.24). Thematically, both narratives critique an indiscriminate use of violence by warning of dire consequences. In the earlier episode, Orlando remains trapped within a travesty of the Garden of Eden after he has killed the serpent-dragon blocking its entrance, and he successfully battles its various monsters with the help of a book of instructions. For dealing with the giants at the final gate, however, the book only warns that two would rise up to replace each single one killed but does not offer a solution to the problem. Confirming through experience that these giants do indeed multiply upon death, Orlando's new strategy is to bind them so as to render them harmless. Thus the episode suggests that extreme measures cannot become an automatic response to every threatening situation.

In their respective adventures, both Orlando and Brandimarte receive some assistance from a knowledgeable female who initially attempts to keep the knight from entering the enchanted space. Yet whereas Orlando receives a book of detailed instructions for overcoming the garden's perils, Brandimarte must act principally on his own: in the first ordeal he thinks strategically in the face of a seemingly unavoidable defeat, and in the second he musters up the courage to follow advice that appears to lead to certain death.

Beyond the issue of when and how to use violent means in the face of danger, both knights are forced to question the relation between appearance and reality. In the garden of Orgagna, we are initially led to believe that the fairy Falerina is the primary culprit, and she herself claims as much, yet Boiardo gives us sufficient clues to deduce that Orgagna's absent king, Poliferno, is ultimately the one to blame for the death trap.[6] In Brandimarte's first ordeal at Phebosilla's palace, the one responsible is the seemingly innocuous knight who, as we later come to realize, had occupied the palace and engaged the services of the giant and serpent. While both episodes thus remind us that evildoers often remain behind the scenes, only Brandimarte's adventure will go on to present the second possibility – that an unknown other with a threatening demeanour may prove instead to be benevolent.

Boiardo constructs Brandimarte's double ordeal in dialogue not only with an earlier adventure from his own poem but also with prior narratives involving metamorphoses that would have been familiar to his readers. The first ordeal is set against the recurring reciprocal transformation of thief and serpent in *Inferno* 25, which in turn calls the reader's attention to Ovid's precedent. In Book Four of the *Metamorphoses*, the gods, after afflicting Cadmus for many years with unmitigated adversity for having killed a serpent sacred to Mars, eventually transform him into a snake. His wife, Harmonia, the daughter of Venus and Mars, caresses him despite his strange new form and is herself turned into a serpent during their passionate embrace. While Cadmus's transformation was the punishment for a transgression, that of Harmonia is due to a love so strong as to transcend all outer appearance. In contrast to Ovid's double metamorphosis, Dante imagines a reciprocal one in which the shades of a thief and a serpent join in a grotesque embrace and then change form simultaneously (*Inferno* 25.70–2). Making use of the negative stereotype of serpents as symbols of fraud following the Genesis story of Adam and Eve, Dante turns a single event into an indefinitely replaying occurrence.

Like Dante in the infernal circle of thieves, Brandimarte also witnesses a recurring reciprocal metamorphosis of man and serpent. Yet whereas the pilgrim simply looked on in amazement as he learned a general truth about theft, the knight must pierce through the veil of perception and change strategies in order to avert his own death. Yet Boiardo's final point lies elsewhere. The fact that an unknown knight takes up the battle after the defeat of the giant and the serpent reminds us that one who has the power to do harm, in practising it, often uses instruments that cannot be readily traced back to him or her. Thus visible opponents – even easily recognizable stereotypes such as giants and serpents – may be only an instrument rather than the source of evil.

Brandimarte's second ordeal is developed in contrast to both Ovid's and Dante's precedents. In the *Metamorphoses*, Cadmus serves as a negative example: because he killed a sacred serpent, he is beset by hardship until he is eventually transformed into the shape of the beast whose life he took. Boiardo's knight, by contrast, serves as an example to imitate: by kissing the serpent, he effectuates a metamorphosis in a positive sense when the fairy regains her original form. Brandimarte himself evokes Dante's infernal scene by noting how the serpent gnashes its teeth ("e denti digrigna"; *OI* 2.26.9), yet the maiden corrects his mistaken assumption of harm by replying that the serpent is only trying to show the knight how to kiss.[7] And whereas in the *Inferno* metamorphosis is the result of divine retribution, the transformation of Phebosilla into a serpent is simply a natural phenomenon that occurs about once every millennium in the life of a fairy (*OI* 2.26.15). In addition, whereas Dante's thieves continually lose their identity as they are transformed into serpents, Brandimarte acts to restore the fairy to her true self. Indeed, it is thanks to the knight's brave act that the mysterious damsel and his own beloved Fiordelisa also regain their identities in a very real sense, as discussed below.

If Brandimarte's first ordeal warns that the individual ultimately responsible for violence to others may be difficult to identify, the second one shows that it can be just as tricky to recognize a benevolent figure behind a frightening appearance. In developing the latter point, Boiardo evokes most directly a story of metamorphosis from medieval romance: the "fier baiser." Roger Sherman Loomis considers various renditions of this episode in which a knight must kiss a serpent who is thereby transformed back into her original human female form. In Ulrich von Zatzikhoven's *Lanzelet*, for example, the serpent speaks directly to Lancelot and facilitates his task by explaining the advantages of kissing her: not only would she recover her maidenly form but he would receive both material rewards and knightly glory.[8]

In the version related in Mandeville's *Travels*, the daughter of Hippocrates assures two would-be rescuers on successive occasions that she will regain her womanly shape if they kiss her in serpent form (115–20; tr. 53–4).[9] In the latter case, she explicitly explains that she was the victim of a spell and offers the young man her treasure, her hand in marriage, and indeed her entire realm in return for his kiss.[10] Nevertheless, both attempts fail tragically: a Knight Hospitaller is killed after his horse flees in terror; then a young man who is knighted in order to undertake the adventure loses his courage and dies during his attempt to escape. Reading the Mandeville episode as "an indirect critique of the knightly estate," Iain Macleod Higgins investigates the socio-ideological reasoning behind each failure: "The Knight Hospitaller's fate, after all, shows how individual desire and bravery alone are insufficient to win possession of promised territory: good planning and proper *matériel* are also needed. By the same token, the young man's fate reveals what can happen when commoners are too readily allowed into the knightly ranks" (86, 88). In Brandimarte's case, by contrast, there is no hint that the teeth-baring serpent might actually be a lovely maiden. His ability to disregard the other's frightening outer appearance thereby requires even greater courage and resolve.

Snakes, Knowledge, Women, and Sexuality: Countering Genesis

In the Judaeo-Christian tradition, serpents are routinely depicted in a negative fashion, in part owing to the biblical story in which a diabolical serpent is associated with deceit and disobedience.[11] Yet positive connotations of these reptiles can also be found across cultures. In her study of myths, Wendy Doniger notes that snakes can represent a series of polarities: "wisdom and evil, rebirth (sloughing) and death (poison), masculinity (the phallus) and femininity (the coiled power), water (the element of many serpents) and fire (the flame of its tongue)" (90). If the snake in Brandimarte's first ordeal is an instrument of evil associated with death, in the second case it is linked instead to benevolence and healing. Mandeville's "fier baiser" episode provides a direct precedent for the theme of healing, since the maiden assuming the dragon's form is after all the daughter of Hippocrates, the most famous of ancient Greek physicians. Perhaps drawing on this precedent, Boiardo further links his fairy to the curative powers ascribed to the serpent in Greek mythology.[12] The name Phebosilla (also spelled Phoebosilla in the critical edition) recalls the god Phoebus Apollo, who was often portrayed with a serpent and whose attributes included healing and medicine.[13] Fittingly, the fairy's magic is associated with health and the curative arts – she uses preventive medicine in enchanting Brandimarte's armour and intensive care when reviving his moribund horse.

In the second ordeal, it is not only the positive connotations of the serpent but the related theme of knowledge that cuts against the grain of the Genesis narrative. In the biblical account, God explicitly forbids Adam and Eve to taste from the Tree of Knowledge. Since, as the serpent explains, the wisdom gained from eating of that tree would make them similar to God by knowing good and evil, their transgression stems from a desire to elevate themselves to a divine state. In the adventure at Phebosilla's palace, knowledge entails instead the movement from erroneous supposition to accurate perception, thus enabling one to recognize the other as he or she really is.

Boiardo's female characters in this episode are likewise contrasted with the biblical Eve. While Genesis depicts the first woman negatively because she gives ill-fated advice to Adam leading to their mutual downfall, the mysterious maiden provides positive advice and guidance to Brandimarte. She not only knows what steps the knight must take to save all of their lives but also succeeds in persuading him to act against his own instincts. Moreover, whereas Eve is beguiled and brought down by a duplicitous serpent, the fairy Phebosilla is transformed into a wise one. Boiardo playfully alludes to her wisdom when the maiden tells Brandimarte that her gesture of apparently gnashing her teeth was actually her attempt to teach him how to kiss her: "Anci, [...] ela te insegna / Come dèi far" ("[Rather, she is showing] you what / you have to do") (*OI* 2.26.9). At the conclusion of the episode Phebosilla, restored to her female form, uses her knowledge of magic to extend Brandimarte's life by enchanting his armour and to revive his horse. Finally, although Fiordelisa is not active during this episode, she is the poem's ultimate figure of knowledge. Referred to as Brandimarte's "sagia dongiella" ("clever girlfriend") (*OI* 1.14.34) and "mastra in tutte l'arte" ("mistress of / all sciences") (*OI* 3.7.56), she is the one who consistently guides others since she has the most understanding of the various territories and their dangers.

Both Brandimarte's "fier baiser" and his ongoing relationship with his beloved Fiordelisa also run counter to the implications of the Genesis story regarding sexuality. After tasting thc forbidden fruit, the biblical couple move from unconscious bliss to a shamed awareness of their naked bodies. Medieval Christian artists and interpreters regularly imbued this story with negative sexual overtones. Brandimarte and Fiordelisa, on the contrary, are the unabashed protagonists of the poem's most elaborately described love scene. As the comrades Marphisa and Ranaldo are fighting their opponents outside the fortress of Albracà, the lovers move to a secluded locus amoenus for a passionate reunion.[14] The playful tone of Boiardo's language accentuates the positive connotations of their lovemaking, which is also evoked through metaphors of play ("gioco"), battle or sport ("assalto"), and dancing ("danzare"). Indeed, the happiness ("allegrezza"), joy ("gioia"), and pleasure ("diletto") they experience through physical union (*OI* 1.19.58–63) are pointedly juxtaposed to the graphic disintegration of body parts in the concurrent battle: the "foriösa" Marphisa "speza la gente in ogni banda" ("hack[s] men, cutting right and left"), while Ranaldo "braze con teste e gambe a tera manda" ("chopped off / no fewer arms and legs and heads") (*OI* 1.19.52).

After describing the lovers' ardent embrace, Boiardo acknowledges his inability to relate the sweetness of their sighs and moans while teasingly suggesting that the lovers themselves tell of it: "Lor lo dican per me, poi che a lor toca, / Che ciascaduno avìa due lengue in boca" ("I leave it up to them to tell, / since each one's mouth possessed two tongues") (*OI* 1.19.61). Boiardo's humorous play on the tongue as an instrument of both speaking and kissing merges the spheres of knowledge and sexuality in a positive way. This attitude, although counter to the Genesis story, accords instead with many pre-modern societies in which sexuality, in the words of Mircea Eliade, "like all the other functions of life, is fraught with sacredness [and] is a way of participating in the fundamental mystery of life and fertility" (25). If in Genesis contact with a snake leads to expulsion from the original paradisiacal setting and a future composed of exile, labour, pain, and death, in the *Innamorato* Brandimarte's act of kissing a serpent brings about various benefits associated with life: liberation from an enclosed space, the promise of bodily protection through enchanted armour, restored health for his horse, and eventually, as discussed below, reunion with family, marriage, and even immortality (symbolized by conversion). Indeed, in opposition to the biblical account of the Fall, Brandimarte's test can be viewed as a successful initiation into a higher state of "chivalric" grace.[15]

Current International Events

Thus far I have argued that in the Phebosilla episode Boiardo creatively imitates Mandeville and medieval romance as well as the canonical poets Ovid and Dante as he overturns basic assumptions of the Genesis story regarding snakes, knowledge, women, and sexuality. I would now like to suggest that the Phebosilla episode has added relevance in the light of the most pressing current events of the period.[16] Given the ongoing Ottoman aggression culminating in an attack on Italian soil, it could have seemed natural for the Kingdom of Naples and the allied Ferrarese state to fear anyone in a foreign guise. Brandimarte's second adventure demonstrates, however, that an undiscriminating hostile approach to an unknown other would be akin to striking the good fairy who happened to be in serpent form. From his earliest writings, in fact, Boiardo not only differentiates the aggressive Ottoman Empire from the rest of the East but also distinguishes the real threat of military invasion from the equally concrete possibilities of commercial and diplomatic contacts around the globe.[17] Considered especially in the context of the Turkish invasion of Otranto and the Venetian attack on Ferrara, the Phebosilla episode recognizes the need to defend oneself from violent onslaughts from all quarters while warning against the instinctive tendency to demonize the other.

Geopolitical Reflections on Phebosilla's Palace Walls

Boiardo also brings a geopolitical dimension directly to the romance adventure through an ekphrasis placed between Brandimarte's two ordeals. Confined within the palace after the doors have mysteriously vanished, the knight and his lady gaze upon four frescoed walls that depict unnamed members of the Este family against the backdrop of European and Italian history.[18] Unlike the anonymous illustrated manuscript *Genealogia dei principi d'Este* (c. 1471–9), which comprises medallion-like portraits of Este family members with brief captions containing factual information, Boiardo imagines knights as large as giants in action, with words written in gold above some of their heads both to identify them and to celebrate their personal virtues.

The ekphrasis begins in the context of the mid-twelfth-century German invasion of northern Italy. Boiardo's reference to the "bataglia a gran roina" ("ruinous fight") by the Adda River allows readers to identify the painted scene as the 1158 Battle of Cassano d'Adda in which northern Italian city-states defeated "li Alemani" ("the Germans") (*OI* 2.25.43–5). It is telling that although Boiardo was writing during a period of intensified Ottoman aggression, he chose to draw our attention not to any prior account of Christian and Muslim hostilities but rather to the onset of a period in medieval history in which the Italian peninsula was under attack from a northern European Christian state.[19] Murray N. Rothbard's succinct appraisal cuts to the core of this protracted conflict: "By the mid-twelfth century, the Italian city-states were the most prosperous countries in Europe. Prosperity meant the standing temptation of wealth to loot, and so the German emperors, beginning with Frederick Barbarossa in 1154, began a two-centuries-long series of attempts to conquer the northern Italian cities" (179). According to Rothbard, moreover, the Italian response to this aggression helped develop a sense of autonomy: "In the course of this chronic struggle, legal and political theorists arose in Italy to give voice to an eventually successful Italian determination to resist the encroachment of the German monarchs. They evolved the idea of the right of nations to resist imperial attempts at conquest by other states – what would later be called the right of national independence, or 'self-government' or 'national self-determination' " (179). The ekphrasis's underlying theme is precisely the destructiveness of this encroachment and the necessity of resolute defensive action to protect one's homeland from foreign aggression.

The description of the fresco covering the second wall focuses on the continued threat to northern Italy caused by the allied forces of Frederick Barbarossa's grandson, Frederick II (1194–1250), and the latter's Ghibelline son-in-law, Ezzolino III da Romano (1194–1259). After briefly evoking an unnamed Este hero who dies after facing Ezzolino, decried as worse than any other Italian or barbarian, Boiardo goes on to condemn both Ezzolino and his father for their atrocious actions: the elder Ezzolino, commonly believed to be a "butcher" born in hell rather than a human being, was guilty of slaughtering women and children (*OI* 2.25.47), while the younger, fighting alongside Germans and Ghibellines ("Boemi et ogni gibilino"), set fire to eleven thousand Paduan citizens

(*OI* 2.25.47-8).[20] The segment concludes with Ezzolino III's eventual defeat and death in the battle that occurred at Cassano in 1259.[21] This example of the combined forces of imperial Germany and the Ghibellines wreaking havoc in Italy but eventually defeated by the Este and their allies could be read as a historical parallel to the situation in contemporary Italy in which another foreign force, the Ottomans, had allied with the Venetians against Neapolitan and Ferrarese territories.

Moving forward to the more recent past, the third wall celebrates the accomplishments of Ercole's father, Niccolò. His political enemies are referred to allegorically as dangerous animals: the two lions are Florence and Venice; the dragon and panther represent other nearby states; and the other eagle is a treacherous member of Niccolò's own family. After commending Niccolò's resolution of conflicts within Italy, Boiardo outlines his travels beyond the peninsula not to wage war but in the role of a pilgrim to the Holy Land and Spain and a welcome visitor to France. The larger thematic nexus between Brandimarte's double adventure within Phebosilla's palace and the frescoed scenes on its walls is encapsulated by the two phases of Niccolò's career: defensive warfare against a range of perilous enemies gives way to the possibility of non-aggressive interaction (as pilgrim and visitor, in this case) with those outside one's homeland.

The final wall is dedicated to the background, character, and actions of Ercole d'Este himself. As Brandimarte stands admiring the image of the Ferrarese duke, Boiardo creates a strange reversal of perspective. Whereas in the rest of the poem the Este are treated as the public listening with pleasure to the exploits of Boiardo's heroes, in this instance one of the poem's characters is gazing through the lens of future history to witness the exemplary actions of the poem's dedicatee. Ercole's biography, moreover, suggests an ideal association with Brandimarte. First of all, he too is said to have grown up "fuor de sua casa" ("far from home") (*OI* 2.25.54). If Boiardo's knight was kidnapped, Ercole as a child was "hounded" by Fortune ("essendo fanciulin, Fortuna il caza"). In the next stanza, Ercole is credited with having exhibited wisdom, valour, and renown in his youth where "Hor con arme turbate et hor da gioco / Mostrar palese il generoso core" ("in arms, in tournaments, in wars / one could observe his noble heart") (*OI* 2.25.55). Brandimarte, likewise, "Di torniamenti e giostra sapìa l'arte" ("knew the ways of jousts and tournaments") (*OI* 1.9.50) before distinguishing himself in the war of Albracà. Boiardo's subsequent assertion that "'n diverse regione e tere tante / Sempre e nemici a lui fugino avante" ("through many [lands] and different regions / this man pursued his enemies") obliquely celebrates Ercole's military valour across the Italian peninsula (*OI* 2.25.55), suggesting a historical parallel to Brandimarte's successful adventures around the globe.

Brandimarte's Extended Family: Leodila and Doristela

If the interlude between the hero's two trials drew attention to members of the Este family in the context of European and Italian history, the narrative sequences on both sides of the Phebosilla episode develop the connection between our featured couple and their extended families and homelands. Earlier in the poem Brandimarte rediscovered his family when he was revealed to be the long-lost brother of the damsel Leodila and son of the king and queen of the Far Away Islands. The frame will be completed symmetrically following the Phebosilla episode when Fiordelisa is found to be the sister of the palace's mysterious damsel, whose name is Doristela, and daughter of the king and queen of Laodicea, situated on the coast of Syria (*OI* 2.26.17). If the challenge of kissing the serpent showed how a fearsome other might turn out to be a benevolent fairy, these discoveries demonstrate that a complete stranger may actually be one's closest relative.

Before their ties of kinship are revealed, both Leodila and Doristela give autobiographical accounts of how they duped their impotent old husbands by taking handsome young lovers. In vividly illustrating why marriages (and thus families) should stem from mutual love and desire and not socio-economic factors, the two tales contain the only scenes of consummated love in the poem apart from Brandimarte and Fiordelisa's forest rendezvous noted above. Yet beyond their shared celebration of sexuality, each tale is linked to a distinct theme developed in the Phebosilla adventure: while Leodila's novella highlights various conceptions of wisdom and knowledge, Doristela's turns the focus to international relations.

Leodila's Tale

Brandimarte encounters Leodila after having temporarily lost Fiordelisa, who was abducted by a necromancer while asleep. When the desperate knight says that he would prefer never to have been born than to live without his beloved, Leodila recounts her story in order to illustrate that he is not the only victim of misfortune. Although her tale is meant to offer the consolation of storytelling and not of philosophy, she frequently alludes to various forms of knowledge, sometimes even peppering her speech with maxims evoking ancient wisdom.

Leodila's opening declaration on the difficulty of attaining happiness – "Che anci ala morte alcun non è beato" ("no man is happy till he's dead") (*OI* 1.21.50) – recalls an episode involving the celebrated figure of wisdom in Herodotus's *Histories*, King Solon. In Boiardo's translation of that work, Solon explicitly tells the Lydian king Croesus that "ne beato si puo dire alcuno se non ha buon fine" ("no man can be called happy if he does not have a good ending to his life") (1.3, 10v). Croesus realizes the truth of Solon's assertion only after he has lost his kingdom and faces imminent death: "Essendo lui adunque sopra a legni gli venne in mente quello che gli havea già detto Solone, che *beato non si potea alcuno appellare fino al ultimo giorno della vita*" ("Being then on the pyre, he remembered what Solon had told him, that *no man could be called happy until the last day of his life*") (emphasis added, 1.8, 22r). The final verse of Leodila's statement evokes the moment in which Croesus realizes the truth of Solon's insight in order to imply that suffering is synonymous with life itself.

Although Leodila has recourse to proverbs to justify her actions, especially those prompted by love (*OI* 1.22.29), she also warns that ancient wisdom, even that of the biblical king Solomon, may not be applicable to the present. She takes issue, for example, with a misogynistic saying concerning the cunning of women:

> Neli antichi proverbi dir se sòle
> Che malicia non è che donna avancie:
> Salamon disse già queste parole,
> Ma al nostro tempo se ritrovan ciance.
>
> The age-old proverbs used to claim
> women succeed by wily ways –
> King Solomon himself said this –
> although no longer true these days. (*OI* 1.21.54)

Such a view is based on Leodila's experience of having been outsmarted by the older male Folderico in the context of a footrace designed to select a husband for her.

Folderico is presented alternately as crafty and foolish throughout the tale. The spectators of the footrace express this contradiction in the following terms:

Il *sagio* perderà la testa,
Ché qua non gioverà esser *scaltrito*:
Di tanta *astucia* al mondo era tenuto,
Hor per amor egli ha il *senno* perduto.

The *sage* has lost his head.
His *cleverness* can't help him here.
He was thought *wisest* in the world,
but love has made him lose his *mind*. (Emphasis added; *OI* 1.21.60)

As it turns out, Folderico has lost his wisdom (*senno*) but not his cleverness (*astuzia*), since he succeeds in tricking Leodila into losing the contest. Although his ruse of tossing three golden apples is derived from Atalanta's footrace in the *Metamorphoses*, here the suitor devises the strategy on his own without the aid of Venus. Despite his cunning on this occasion, Folderico is subsequently outwitted by Leodila's young lover, Ordauro, whose rhetorical question to God retains the focus on Folderico's proverbial wisdom: "Come hai costui del'*intelleto* tratto, / Che fo de tal *prudentia* e *senno* pieno?" ("Why have you taken this man's *wits*? / He had such *wisdom*, was so *prudent*!") (emphasis added; *OI* 1.22.35).

If Folderico's folly demonstrates that wisdom can be divorced from learning, Leodila herself links it to a philosophy of pleasure. Recalling her sexual experience with Ordauro, the princess proclaims: "Ciascun che è sagio el suo piacer apreza / E il viver diletoso, e star iocondo" ("The smart ones want their pleasure first, / to live delightful, happy lives") (*OI* 1.22.27). This personal manifesto is a twist on the association between wisdom and sexuality that emerged in the extended episode of Brandimarte and Fiordelisa. Before further exploring Leodila's relation to this couple, however, we turn our attention to the novella related by Fiordelisa's sister.

Doristela's Tale

Following his successful completion of the adventure at Phebosilla's palace, Brandimarte accompanies Doristela to her homeland on the sea of Syria (*OI* 2.26.17). Along the way there, she gives an account of her own trials and tribulations in which, like Leodila, she managed to meet secretly with her young lover despite her jealous old husband's extreme preventive measures. The aspect of Doristela's tale most relevant to the current study, however, is the viewpoint that it provides of Turkish events affecting Europe.[22]

Doristela recounts that her father betrothed her to an elderly Turk named Hosbego on the very same day that her true love, the Armenian prince Theodoro, asked for her hand in marriage. In addition to portraying Hosbego as the quintessential jealous, impotent husband in this *mal maritata* tale, Boiardo grounds him in a particular geographical and historical setting. First of all, he is from Bursa, "the political and commercial centre of the Ottoman Empire, [...] the most important trading city of Anatolia and an entrepôt for east-west trade" (Inalcik 121).[23] Second, his name is typically Turkish, recalling both Boccaccio's fictional Osbech, the Turkish king who was said to be constantly at war with the Byzantine emperor in the tale of Alatiel (*Decameron* 2.7), and the historical Uzbek, a fourteenth-century khan of the Golden Horde.

Doristela explains that she was able to encounter her beloved when her nominal husband left to join the Turkish invasion of Greece:

Ch'al mio marito fo forza d'andare
Con l'altri Turchi ch'han passato il mare.
Passarno e Turchi contra a Vatarone
Ch'avea de' Greci el domìno e l'imperio.

And soon my husband had to go
with other Turks across the sea.
The Turks attacked Avatarone,
who ruled the kingdom of the Greeks. (*OI* 2.26.32–3)

This bellicose scenario would have reminded Boiardo's early readers of recent and even contemporary events. In the course of the fifteenth century, the Ottoman Turks had conquered not only most of western Asia Minor, but also much of the Balkan Peninsula, including Greece. If we take into account that this episode could have been written in the late 1470s or early 1480s, then the Turkish attack on Avatarone's kingdom would directly evoke the concurrent Ottoman aggression in the Mediterranean, possibly on the eastern coastline of Italy itself.

Given the episode's explicit backdrop of Turkish military expansion, it is worth noting that Boiardo does not use the occasion to employ derogatory terms commonly used of Turks in the writings of his day or to conjure up scenarios of hostility between Christians and non-Christians. Furthermore, unlike his above-mentioned namesakes, Boiardo's Hosbego is depicted as completely uninterested in politics or warfare. Doristela specifies that her husband joined the war only because he was constrained to do so: "E mio marito con molte persone / Convien andar, non già per desiderio" ("And duty, not desire, made / my husband join this large invasion") (*OI* 2.26.33). Earlier in the poem, in the context of the war at Albracà, the Turkish king Torindo had sent out word to his various dominions, including Bursa, that "ciascun che può venir ne venga armato" ("every able man in Turkey / should arm and come forth instantly") (*OI* 2.2.33). We now get a glimpse of how an individual Turk might view warfare not as a chance for epic glory but rather as an unwelcome distraction from more pressing personal worries. The attitude of Hosbego thus stands as a reminder that the expansionist policies of rulers do not necessarily correspond to the personal interests of their subjects.

While Hosbego is forced to obey higher orders to fight on foreign soil, he in turn exercises a despotic command over those in his control. He locks his wife in an inaccessible tower and charges his slave Gambone with the task of guarding her day and night. Theodoro nevertheless succeeds in entering Doristela's bedchamber by bribing Gambone with a large quantity of gold. When Hosbego arrives unexpectedly at the tower and discovers the cloak Theodoro had inadvertently left behind as he fled, he does not hesitate to order his other slaves to execute Gambone, who is only saved thanks to Theodoro's ruse of pretending that his cloak had been stolen (*OI* 2.26.36–50).

Doristela goes on to relate that Hosbego eventually imprisoned her in Phebosilla's enchanted palace, specifying that although the fairy had constructed the palace and the tomb, a necromancer had placed the giant and serpent in the courtyard (*OI* 2.26.52). Although Doristela's tale is interrupted at this point, Boiardo has already provided enough information for us to imagine that this anonymous necromancer would have been acting at the request of Hosbego who, given the failure of the earlier arrangement and the proven existence of a rival, would have deemed it necessary to guard Doristela through supernatural means. Hosbego is, after all, the previously unidentified knight who takes up the battle as soon as Brandimarte has killed the giant and the serpent.

Family, Marriage, Conversion

The journey to Doristela's Syrian kingdom leads directly to the discovery that Fiordelisa is her long-lost sister. Having suspected the truth based on Doristela's remark that her older sister had been kidnapped and on his fortuitous encounter with none other than the kidnapper himself, Brandimarte asks the king if his missing daughter had any birthmarks.

When the queen interrupts to describe a dark spot she remembered seeing below her child's right breast, Brandimarte immediately confirms that Fiordelisa is indeed her daughter (*OI* 2.27.29). It is thus Brandimarte's intimate knowledge of his beloved's body that makes the recovery of her identity possible in this scene. This further underscores the extended episode's positive link between knowledge and sexuality. The circle closes with the double wedding of Fiordelisa and Doristela to the men they love.[24]

In the agnition scenes framing the narrative sequence, Boiardo not only creates a sense of community through the characters' reunion with their families but adds another level of union when the population is brought together in the same religious faith – which for the poet's circle of readers is perforce their own. These are the only instances of collective conversion in the entire poem. Ponte is therefore essentially correct when he says that the "mass conversion of infidels by Christian heroes are few, and over quickly" (*La personalità*, 19). At the same time, however, these rare, brief scenes are far from meaningless, since they convey the same model of conversion by persuasion rather than force that we have already seen at work in the Agricane episode.[25] In the present case, Boiardo specifically states that it is the graciousness (or grace) of the two sisters that induces their people to convert: "La gratia dele dame fo cotanta / Che dai monti d'Harmenia ala marina / Corse ciascuno ala legie divina" ("The damsels were so full of grace / that from the mountains to the sea, / all of Armenia joined the faith") (*OI* 2.27.35).

The fact that the poem's only group conversions occur specifically in the realms of Brandimarte and Fiordelisa is significant for two additional reasons. First, Boiardo has chosen to respect geographical reality rather than adopt a crusading ideology by staging these scenes in two territories known to have Christian populations – northern Russia and Armenia – rather than in Muslim regions or the Holy Land. Second, these collective moments are presented as the natural consequence of the individual conversions of Brandimarte and Fiordelisa themselves. Like Agricane's conversion – the only other one in the poem – these are completely voluntary. Moreover, they occur spontaneously rather than through proselytizing. Brandimarte is inspired by Orlando's sincere devotion when the two friends are facing death in King Manodante's dungeon, and Fiordelisa, along with Iroldo and Prasildo, is moved by Ranaldo's heroic effort to save their lives outside the treacherous garden of Orgagna. In both cases, conversion is a consequence of – and not a prerequisite for – friendship and aid.

Brandimarte at Biserta

Brandimarte's itinerary following his departure from Phebosilla's palace continues to develop his character as the representative of a truly universal knighthood. His marriage to Fiordelisa does not obstruct his quest to locate Orlando, and the couple soon head to France. Consistent with the greater factual detail provided for Mediterranean settings, Boiardo notes that after their boat passes Rhodes and Crete "col vento in popa" ("with a following breeze"), a gale from the north stirs up the Greek wind – "ch'è mala mistura / A cui di Creti vòl gir in Ciciglia" ("a bad mix / for trips from Crete to Sicily") (*OI* 2.27.39–40). Having spent the poem travelling effortlessly across Asia, Brandimarte and Fiordelisa are now blown off course on their way to Europe. Although the helmsman prays to reach Sardinia, they are swept directly to the shores of Biserta. This suggests the proximity of the various peoples of the Mediterranean – whether European, Middle Eastern, or North African – while it serves to bring Brandimarte into direct contact with Agramante and his entourage.

Brandimarte identifies himself through the name of his father and his homeland (*OI* 27.47–8), not by his new religion, because a prophecy that an Italian king would put the countryside to the torch had led to a death sentence against all Christians (*OI* 2.27.46).[26] Brandimarte accordingly tries to convert Agramante not from Islam to Christianity (as he will attempt to do near the end of the *Furioso*) but from imitating Alexander of Macedonia (with his unbridled ambition to conquer other states) to emulating Hector of Troy (representing the dutiful care of one's homeland). Brandimarte's address to the king not only reminds the reader that Christianity and Islam share the same classical cultural heritage but further suggests that the ideals of courtesy and chivalry cut across all boundaries. Although Agramante is not willing to replace Alexander with Hector as an epic model, he does welcome Brandimarte as a guest to his court.

For their stay the couple erect a colourful tent, said to have been embroidered by a sibyl in Cumae, near the Bay of Naples, a fact that evokes both Virgilian epic and Eleonora d'Aragona's birthplace (*OI* 2.27.51). Like the frescoed walls of Phebosilla's palace, the tent is illustrated with scenes combining European events and ducal family history; now, however, the images privilege the Aragonese side. Among the many "Gran fatti, en degne historie e peregrine, / E presenti, e futuri, e de' passati" ("worthy stories and great deeds / of past, present, and future times") are those of twelve heroes with the name of Alfonso (*OI* 2.27.52). After briefly alluding to the first nine (Spanish) figures in general terms, Boiardo focuses more closely on the tenth, Alfonso the Magnanimous (Alfonso V of Aragon), who became King Alfonso I of Naples from 1442 until his death in 1458. Although Alfonso conquered this region of Italy, Boiardo phrases it to claim that it was instead Italy which captured his heart: "Cossì a lui prese Italia vinta il core, / Onde scordosse la sua tera ispana" ("he lost his heart to Italy / and he forgot his kingdom, Spain") (*OI* 2.27.55).[27] He is described as "Pacifico, guierero e triomphante, / Iusto, benigno, liberal e pio" ("a peaceful but triumphant warrior, / generous, pious, just, and kind") (*OI* 2.27.54). The Alfonso who receives the most attention, however, is not Eleonora's grandfather but her brother. Although Boiardo credits this eleventh Alfonso with many victories, the two moments singled out are very current events: the battle of Poggio Imperiale against the Florentines in 1479 and the liberation of Otranto in 1481. In the latter case it was "per sua prodecia sola e suo valore" ("[by his] valor and strength [alone]") that Italy was delivered from the Turks (*OI* 2.27.56bis).[28] The twelfth and final figure is Alfonso d'Este (b. 1476), the first-born son of Ercole and Eleonora, who thereby unites the Este and Aragonese into a single family (Harris 1: 20n).

The use of embroidered tapestries for dynastic purposes had become fashionable among European royalty by the late fifteenth century. Noting "the ongoing but increasingly competitive ways in which the imperial courts of Renaissance Europe defined their political pre-eminence through their possession and display of narrative tapestry cycles," Jardine and Brotton point out that in the 1470s the Portuguese king Alfonso V commissioned extensive tapestries depicting his 1471 invasion of Morocco (79, 117). The encomiastic function of this art form was recognized in Italy as well, and the first two Italian courts to regularly employ weavers in situ were the Gonzaga in Mantua and the Este in Ferrara. Hillie Smit, in fact, finds that "in the 1480s in Ferrara under Ercole I d'Este (1471–1505) there were several master weavers active with their various workshops at the court of the Este" (122).[29] Through his ekphrasis depicting the tapestried pavilion, Boiardo thus acknowledges a popular encomiastic art form of his day and celebrates the virtues of Eleonora's side of the family.

Another moment in Brandimarte's African sojourn that would have had a special resonance for Boiardo's courtly readers is the hunt that interrupts his joust with Agramante. The popularity of hunting at the Este court is documented through historical data as well as Ferrarese art.[30]

During the Council of Ferrara (1438), it was one of the principal leisure activities shared by individuals from Byzantium and Latin Europe. When Ercole later expanded the family's hunting grounds, the new site was "a considerably larger hunting preserve where the duke, his courtiers, and his guests rode and hunted rabbits, deer, and game birds" (Rosenberg 111). The fact that the poem's only hunting expedition occurs at a Saracen court reminds readers that the sport was not only practised by European nobility but was also "a favored pastime of Islamic court life symbolizing princely values and authority" (Hess 11). At the same time, Boiardo alerts his readership to the fact that in Africa they are pursuing not prey common to western Europe but lions, panthers, and elephants (*OI* 2.28.20) as well as leopards, tigers, and a giraffe (*OI* 2.28.29–36), thus underscoring the nature of the geographical region in which Brandimarte finds himself.

This particular hunt, moreover, is not envisioned as a form of recreation but rather as the response to a call for help from locals pursued by wild animals: "Fugie la gente trista e sbigotita: / Tuti venìan cridando: 'Aita! Aita!'" ("People were in distress and fleeing, / shouting for help, and terrified") (*OI* 2.28.14). Thus when Brandimarte and Agramante quickly abandon their private joust to engage in a joint undertaking for the collective good, they demonstrate the potential for collaboration between individuals from diverse cultures. Rugiero joins them as all three "Baron soprani" ("bold barons") rush forth "Per dar aiuto ove facea mestiero" ("to help where others were in danger") (*OI* 2.28.19). After the poem's various suggested links between Brandimarte and Rugiero, this is the first time that the two knights work in tandem.

Following the successful outcome of the hunt, Agramante's entire court and its honoured guests continue to focus on the joys of social life until a musician admonishes the king for feasting while his soldiers await his command to invade France (*OI* 2.28.44–7). Thus ends the peaceful interlude of Brandimarte in Biserta as the poet announces his intention to relate "La più stupenda guera e la magiore / Che racontasse mai prosa né verso" ("the largest, most amazing war / attempted yet in prose or rhyme") (*OI* 2.29.1). While Agramante heads to France to wage war, Brandimarte and Fiordelisa go there instead to rescue Orlando from the enchanted Laughing Stream. Interestingly, Boiardo later notes that it was a seer on the North African coast who revealed to them their friend's whereabouts. The fact that this information comes from a non-Christian, non-European source is yet another reminder that valuable knowledge may be found in any corner of the globe.

Brandimarte in France

The search for Orlando brings Brandimarte and Fiordelisa into western Europe for the first time in the poem. In this initial romance adventure undertaken after their marriage, it is the female damsel Fiordelisa who instructs and coaches the male knight Brandimarte at every step through to the liberation of Orlando (*OI* 3.7.12–36). It is also at this site that the knight meets up again with Rugiero, further developing the association between the two heroes. Brandimarte subsequently travels to Paris in the company of Orlando and Fiordelisa. When they arrive outside the city at dawn and find it assailed from all sides by Agramante's army, Orlando falters in desperation and cries that all hope is lost, while Brandimarte takes charge in word and deed, leading his companion in a courageous defence of the city that begins to turn the tide of the battle (freeing prisoners, *OI* 3.8.17–23; fighting valiantly and unhorsing Rodamonte, *OI* 3.8.36–41). At the moment of the poem's interruption, it is clear that Brandimarte, even as he moves from romance adventure to the epic arena, would have continued to play a prominent role in the action.

Ariosto's Brandimarte

Ariosto keeps Brandimarte on the sidelines for most of the poem. In the only two instances in which he does appear prior to the final cantos, he no longer figures as a hero who saves others but on the contrary is first trapped within Atlante's enchanted palace in France (*OF* 20.21 A; 22.21 C) and later defeated by Rodomonte and sent as a prisoner to Africa (*OF* 35.44 A; 39.33 C). Moreover, whereas in the *Innamorato* it was thanks to Brandimarte that Astolfo was freed at the Isole Lontane, it is now Astolfo who liberates Brandimarte on the two latter occasions. Although this represents a role reversal of sorts, Ariosto avoids any reference to the earlier episode featuring Boiardo's hero. Indeed, Astolfo simply mentions to Ruggiero *en passant* that he had returned from "quelle isole estreme / che da Levante il mar Indico lava" ("those distant isles washed on the East by the Indian Sea") (*OF* 6.34 AC). Readers are hard pressed to recall that Astolfo's previous location was the capital of the Isole Lontane because Ariosto has relocated the islands to the Indian Ocean.[31]

Brandimarte's two brief encounters with Fiordelisa, renamed Fiordeligi, conspicuously omit the kind of joyous passion expressed in the forest outside Albracà. On each occasion there is the more urgent matter of helping Orlando; yet ironically, both times it is Brandimarte's loyalty to

Orlando that proves be to his undoing. In the first, it leads him to Rodomonte's bridge, where Phebosilla's gifts are annulled (his armour is left at the bridge as a trophy and his horse is drowned) and Brandimarte himself is sent in chains to Africa. In the second instance, Brandimarte places his commitment to Orlando above not only the sweetness of Fiordeligi's embrace but also the duties and joys of governing his own realm. Immediately following his liberation, he discovers that King Manodante is dead and that his brother and all the people of the kingdom call him to the throne, yet he chooses to remain in the war to assist Charlemagne. Ariosto draws attention to Brandimarte's choice first by evoking the beauty and prosperity of his homeland and then by commenting that "quando / si disponesse di voler gustarlo, / havria poi sempre in odio andare errando" ("should he be disposed to taste its sweetness, he would have no further appetite for foreign travel") (*OF* 35.74 A; 39.63 C).

One is subsequently left regretting that Brandimarte did not return home to tend to his own kingdom, since his decision to put his friendship to Charlemagne and Orlando first proves fatal. Although he is a character invented by Boiardo and not one of the traditional Carolingian paladins, he represents Christendom along with Orlando and Oliviero in the battle of Lipadusa. Brandimarte is especially vulnerable, however, since his loss to Rodomonte at the perilous bridge deprived him of both his armour enchanted by Phebosilla and his sword forged by Solomon. Even when an unmanned boat mysteriously arrives at the shores of Lipadusa laden with Hector's armour, the sword Balisarda, and the horse Frontino, the first two magical gifts go to Oliviero and Orlando while Brandimarte is simply left with the horse. Zanette questions Orlando's division of these goods, which puts Brandimarte at a notable disadvantage vis-à-vis his two companions (336–8); indeed, without the protection of his enchanted armour, he dies when Gradasso strikes him from behind. It is a terrible irony that while in the final cantos of Boiardo's poem Brandimarte had saved Orlando from death at the hands of Gradasso as the two knights fought over Durindana (*OI* 3.7.52–3), Orlando is now unable to save his friend in turn as Gradasso pierces him with the very same sword.[32]

Although throughout the poem Ariosto refrained from building upon the implications of the Phebosilla episode with respect to Brandimarte, at the moment in which the character lies dead upon the ground ("morto in terra"; *OF* 38.6 A; 42.6 C), the poet alludes to the earlier adventure – albeit with a negative twist. Orlando's reaction upon seeing his friend stricken by Gradasso is compared to that of a nomadic shepherd who has seen "fuggir strisciando il squalido serpente / che il figliuol che giocava ne la sabbia / ucciso gli ha col venenoso dente" ("the horrible snake slither away once its poisonous fangs have slain his child playing in the sand") (*OF* 38.7 A; 42.7 C). Brandimarte is thus reduced to the figure of a little boy who was naively oblivious to the very real danger of death which threatened him. Dennis Looney, in tracking serpent similes in the two poems, points out that in this final instance "for the first time, the serpent actually bites the unsuspecting human" (139). Brandimarte's experience with serpents in Phebosilla's palace, obliquely referenced in this simile, proves to be of no avail here. Ariosto thus has the last word: the (Saracen) other is as deadly as a poisonous serpent after all.

The *Furioso*'s treatment of Fiordeligi reveals an analogous pattern of ironic reversals. As in Boiardo's poem, the maiden attempts to enlist a champion to liberate Brandimarte and save Orlando. Whereas in the *Innamorato* both knights are confined together at Dragontina's garden and later Orlando is trapped at the Fonte del Riso, in the *Furioso* Brandimarte is a prisoner at Rodomonte's bridge and Orlando is a victim of his own madness. With respect to the rescue of her beloved, while in the first case she led Ranaldo to Dragontina's garden, in the latter poem she escorts Rinaldo's sister Bradamante to Rodomonte's bridge. Although in both poems they arrive too late to rescue Brandimarte, in the first instance he was already liberated and fighting alongside Orlando at Albracà, while in the second he had been sent to Africa as a prisoner. Both poems present scenes in which Ranaldo/Rinaldo learns of Orlando's predicament from Fiordelisa/Fiordeligi, but his response is remarkably different. In the *Innamorato*, Ranaldo states his readiness to help Fiordelisa even before finding out that his cousin Orlando is trapped by Dragontina:

Cortesemente quel Baron la chiama,
E prega lei per ogni suo disire,
Per quela cossa che più nel mondo ama,
E per lo Dio de il Ciel e per Macone,
Che de il suo duol li dica la cagione.

The gallant baron called to her
and conjured her – by her desires,
by what she loved the most on earth,
by God in heaven, by Mohammed –
to tell him why she worried so. (*OI* 1.11.47)

Ranaldo's reference to both God and Mohammed in his appeal to

Fiordelisa underscores his adherence to a universal chivalric code indifferent to religious creed. In the *Furioso*, on the contrary, Rinaldo refuses to heed Fiordeligi's plea to rescue the mad Orlando because he is involved in a matter he deems more important – the war against the Saracens (*OF* 31.42–9). The maiden's exceptional knowledge comes into play near the end of both poems, albeit with different results. Just as Fiordelisa guided Orlando's rescue at the Laughing Stream, Fiordeligi is the first to recognize the mad Orlando on the shores of Biserta. In the latter case, however, it is God's chosen instrument, Astolfo, who holds the magic means to break the spell, and Fiordeligi's role is thus reduced to that of a bystander.

In the *Innamorato*, Brandimarte and Fiordelisa's eventual marriage is followed not by their isolation from the world or their disappearance from the poem but by their successful joint liberation of Orlando at the Laughing Stream and their arrival in Paris to defend the city from invasion. In the *Furioso*, Ariosto keeps them mostly apart and backstage until he reintroduces them in order to play out their deaths.[33] In the end, Fiordeligi's intuitive knowledge allows her to foresee Brandimarte's demise but not to prevent it, and her unbounded love for him leads not to a new life together but to her own self-entombment near his corpse in Agrigento.

Chapter Seventeen

Ariosto's Rinaldo along the Po River

If, as I have argued in the previous chapter, Ariosto works against Boiardo's portrayal of Brandimarte, he does not do so through any lack of understanding of this character's importance in his predecessor's poem. Indeed, in this final chapter I aim to show that Ariosto carries out a systematic rewriting of Brandimarte's key *Innamorato* adventures, to an entirely different end. In a complex series of intertwining stories, Ariosto depicts Rinaldo undergoing two tests and listening to two novellas while he is in a moment of transition that involves traversing vast geographical spaces. Despite the abundance of shared features between the extended episodes of Brandimarte at Phebosilla's palace and Rinaldo along the Po River, to be fleshed out in the following pages, Ariosto rearranges and inverts various elements of the earlier sequence in order to overturn its optimistic assumptions and present a dramatically different picture of the world on both a global and a local level.

The Two Tests

In the *Innamorato*, Brandimarte's trajectory had taken him from ignorance of his origins to a reunion with his family and marriage to Fiordelisa, to whom he was joined in a bond of reciprocal love. By contrast, in the *Furioso* Rinaldo undergoes his first test suffering from heartbreak because the woman he loves, Angelica, has not only rejected him but has given herself to an African infantryman. As Rinaldo approaches a wooded area with "tal pensier, ch'el cor gli straccia e parte" ("his heart torn by thoughts such as these") (*OF* 38.42 A; 42.45 C), his emotional state is therefore the exact opposite of that of Brandimarte, who was in the company of "la sua dama" ("his girl") as they neared Phebosilla's palace "in zoglia et in solazo" ("with joy and glee") (*OI* 2.25.23). Ironically, Rinaldo's intense jealousy aligns him not with his knightly counterpart but rather with the husbands of Leodila and Doristela who flew into a jealous rage when their beautiful wives abandoned them for younger lovers.

In their first trial, both knights must defend themselves from a fierce creature who uses a serpent as a weapon.[1] In Brandimarte's case, as outlined in the previous chapter, a giant wields a very long and large ("longissimo e grosso"; *OI* 2.25.29) snake that knocks the knight to the ground. The female monster who assaults Rinaldo has "serpi a gran torma" ("a great tangle of snakes") for hair as well as "un fiero e maggior serpe" ("a larger, savage snake") as a tail (*OF* 38.44 A; 42.47 C). From the onset of the battle, Rinaldo's uncharacteristic fear (*OF* 38.48 A; 42.51 C) is set against Brandimarte's steadfast courage (*OI* 2.25.33).[2] Earlier, Brandimarte had acted alone to defeat the giant, the snake, and an unidentified knight who attacked him following his victory. By contrast, Rinaldo not only fails to subdue the snaky monster but is not even able to escape on his own. An unidentified knight comes into the picture here as well, this time not to attack but rather to rescue the hapless Rinaldo. In both cases, the mysterious knight will be identified only after the ordeal is over.

As soon as the newcomer takes Rinaldo's place, the conflict begins to offer parallels rather than contrasts with Brandimarte's combat. In both cases, the opponent springs back up after being knocked to the ground. Ariosto's description of the snake's remarkable resilience echoes the repeated metamorphosis of the giant and snake in the Phebosilla episode (*OF* 38.52–3 A; 42.55–6 C). Moreover, even though an aggressive giant or monster figures as the official opponent, the snake is the deadly weapon that must be eliminated. Like Brandimarte, the knight achieves victory only after changing strategy, in this case attacking the snake-tail with a fiery mace. Rinaldo's infinite gratitude towards the knight echoes the thankfulness of Phebosilla towards Brandimarte (*OF* 38.57 A; 42.59 C).

The mysterious knight's battle against the snake-monster also recalls features of Brandimarte's second ordeal, in particular the evocation of an infernal underworld and the restorative use of magic following the knight's victory. The *Innamorato* episode first suggested hell as the possible origin of the creature that Brandimarte must kiss through the knight's initial boast that "Non ha l'Inferno un demonio sì fiero / Ch'io non gli ardisca il viso acostare" ("No devil lives in hell so fierce / that I won't dare to press his face") (*OI* 2.26.5). Boiardo then marks it as the potential destination of the characters when Doristela subsequently warns that if

Brandimarte strikes the serpent "caderemo a un trato in quel profondo" ("we will fall in the abyss") (*OI* 2.26.8). In the *Furioso* these infernal references are rendered concrete when the knight "in la scura buca / fece tornar il mostro dal inferno" ("drove the fiendish monster back to her dark hole") (*OF* 38.55 A; 42.58 C). Thus Ariosto's snake is not only identified as a monster from hell but meets the same fate that would have befallen Boiardo's characters had Brandimarte failed the second test.

Following the successful ending to the *Furioso* adventure, Rinaldo becomes, like Brandimarte, a beneficiary of magic that leads to a higher state. In the first case, as previously mentioned, Brandimarte's armour was enchanted and his horse resuscitated. In the second instance, the victorious knight – who identifies himself as Disdain now that he has killed the monster, in turn revealed to be a personification of Jealousy – leads Rinaldo to drink again from Merlin's magic fountain, where he regains his role as both Charlemagne's paladin and Clarice's husband. Brandimarte's physical freedom from the palace of Phebosilla becomes Rinaldo's emotional freedom from the allure of Angelica.

The frame story of Rinaldo's second test is likewise developed using several elements from Brandimarte's precedent. Both knights are met by figures who explain what they need to do even though they will not be apprised of the entire context until after passing the test. Whereas the maiden-hostess informs Brandimarte that he must kiss whatever emerges from the tomb and warns him of calamitous consequences should he refuse, a knight-host tells Rinaldo that he must drink from a goblet and warns of the infelicitous result that would ensue should the test fail. Moreover, both the maiden-hostess and the knight-host, whose identity is only subsequently revealed, go on to relate an autobiographical novella that explains how they arrived at the unfortunate situation in which they found themselves at the moment of the test.

The parallels and contrasts between the two tests are played out on a structural level as well. Both are divided between two cantos at the moment of highest suspense – when Brandimarte is told to open the tomb and as Rinaldo is getting ready to put the chalice to his lips. Both poets, in fact, directly address their readers at this point, Boiardo playfully imagining the desire of his courtly audience to hear the rest of the story and Ariosto asking his patron for permission to rest. They both then commence the following canto with a proem expressing a value judgment on the action.

The similarity of structure, however, lays bare a striking contrast in the theme of the respective poems. After wistfully evoking "Il vago amor che a sue dame soprane / Portarno al tempo antiquo e cavaleri" ("the longing love the knights of old / felt for their lovely ladies"), along with their battles, adventures, and jousts, Boiardo moves on to celebrate Tristano and "sua dama" ("his damsel") together with Lancilotto and "sua Regina bella" ("his lovely queen"), whose inspirational stories lead readers to love them and set the heavens ablaze with love (*OI* 2.26.1–3). He then invites "ogni dongiella, / Ogni Baron chi vòl portar honore" ("all you women then, / and every knight who seeks esteem") to listen to his tale about ladies and knights, suggesting that the most famous lovers of the Breton cycle, his own characters Brandimarte and Fiordelisa, and his worthy listeners all share in the uplifting emotion of love.

Ariosto also gets right to the point in his proem, but his position is a radically different one. He opens the canto with an exclamation about avarice and greed – "O execrabile Avaritia, o ingorda / fame d'haver" ("O detestable avarice! O greed for gain!") – which not only infect base souls but contaminate high-ranking citizens, from scientists, theologians, military commanders, and scholars to beautiful and noble ladies (*OF* 39.1–4 A; 43.1–4 C). Whereas in Boiardo's proem the lovers Tristan and Isolde found even death sweet and joyous, Ariosto asserts instead that noblewomen of his time are prostituting their bodies to old, ugly, and monstrous men out of sheer greed: "in un dì, senza amor (chi fia che 'l creda?) / a un vecchio, a un brutto, a un mostro le dà in preda" ("in one day she bestows them, incredibly, on some unloved, monstrous old dotard") (*OF* 39.4 A; 43.4 C). The stated association between his characters and the courtly aristocracy outside the poem is an emphatically negative one.

Turning to the specifics of the second test, we may note that the literary sources for both kissing a serpent and drinking from a goblet are to be found in the Breton cycle.[3] In the earlier episode, Lancelot had not only provided a precedent for the "fier baiser" adventure but was specifically evoked along with Tristan in the proem that introduced Brandimarte's successful completion of the test. Ariosto cites the same legendary knights – not, however, to celebrate their love or heroism but rather to brand them as adulterers. He explains that King Arthur's sister Morgana devised the magic goblet to prove Guinivere's infidelity (*OF* 39.28 A; 43.28 C), while the pun on "Cornovaglia" refers to the kingdom of Isolde's husband as well as his position as a cuckold. Interestingly, the situation in which Rinaldo finds himself once again aligns him with the figure of the betrayed husband rather than the courtly lover.

The nature of the test, moreover, yields striking similarities as well as contrasts with respect to Brandimarte's example. Rinaldo's act of drinking from a goblet echoes that of kissing a serpent in its emphasis on the sheer physicality of the deed. The focus, in fact, is not on the consumption of a certain liquid (as in the case of the *Innamorato*'s twin fountains or chalice of Dragontina) but on the gesture of placing one's mouth and lips to the goblet: "Fu presso di volerlo a bocca porse: / poi, quanto fosse periglioso il caso / di far tal prova, col pensier discorse" ("Rinaldo reached out, grasped the chalice and made to undergo the test. But then he considered the danger he might be incurring by setting it to his lips") (*OF* 38.101 A; 42.104 C),[4] and "alquanto pensar volle, / prima che a i labri il vaso s'appressassi" ("he wanted to think a little before setting the cup to his lips") (*OF* 39.6 A; 43.6 C). While Brandimarte fears that the serpent will bite his face, Rinaldo worries that the wine will spill all over his chest. Both knights make the correct choice within their respective situations, yet whereas Brandimarte believes he is in mortal danger and decides nonetheless to put his life at risk, Rinaldo is threatened merely with humiliation but nevertheless declines to take a chance. In the end, Brandimarte's courageous kiss permits him to know the true identity of Phebosilla, Doristela, and, ultimately, his beloved Fiordelisa. Rinaldo's refusal to drink, on the other hand, deprives him of the opportunity to uncover the true identity of Clarice as either a chaste or an unfaithful spouse. While the first knight saves others' lives by his action, the second saves his own reputation by his *in*action.

Ariosto also opposes the Phebosilla episode on the theme of wisdom. As the host offers Rinaldo the chalice, he underscores the separation between knowledge and belief: "Se vuoi saper se la tua sia pudica / (com'io credo che credi, et creder déi)" ("Should you wish to know whether your wife is chaste, as I believe you think her, and so you ought") (*OF* 38.99 A; 42.102 C). When after some deliberation Rinaldo realizes that ascertaining the truth in such a case could be dangerous, he explains his refusal as an acceptance of the limitations placed on human knowledge: "Io non so se mi sia saggio né stolto; / ma non vuo' più saper, che mi convegna" ("Whether in this I am being wise or foolish I know not, but I desire no further knowledge than is suitable") (*OF* 39.7 A; 43.7 C).

As noted in the previous chapter, Boiardo's celebration of knowledge runs counter to the account of the Fall in Genesis. Ariosto contests his predecessor on this score by returning to the same biblical narrative. In classifying the desire to verify a partner's marital fidelity as a form of transgression, Rinaldo has recourse to no less than God's prohibition to taste of the tree of life (albeit, strangely, not that of knowledge): "che tal certezza ha Dio più prohibita / ch'al primo padre l'arbor de la vita" ("God has proscribed this kind of certainty even more than he proscribed the Tree of Life to our first father") (*OF* 39.7 A; 43.7 C). Rinaldo's statement thereby equates wilful ignorance of his wife's virtue with the prelapsarian bliss of the Garden of Eden.[5] Ariosto underscores the wisdom of choosing ignorance not only in Rinaldo's explanation of his decision but also in the host's words of approbation: "Tu tra infiniti sol sei stato saggio, / che far negasti il periglioso saggio" ("You among countless men have alone been wise enough to refuse the perilous test") (*OF* 39.44 A; 43.44 C).

In order to validate the sagacity of Rinaldo's refusal to drink from the goblet, the Mantuan host goes on to explain how he had actually led his wife into adultery by testing her chastity. The moral that Rinaldo draws from his tale is the inevitability of corruption and thus the need to avoid putting virtue to the test. He responds to the story by doubting whether the host would have been any more steadfast in the same situation (*OF* 39.49 A; 43.49). We now turn our attention to this novella as well as the complementary one related to Rinaldo by the boatman who soon thereafter conveys him along the Po River. Both novellas not only rearrange narrative elements from the Leodila and Doristela tales but ultimately reverse the geopolitical perspective of Brandimarte's extended episode outlined in the previous chapter.

The Twin Tales

Like Boiardo's Brandimarte, Ariosto's Rinaldo listens to a pair of stories in which a beautiful young wife betrays her absent husband. Thematically, however, the novellas offer opposing perspectives: while the earlier two are told from the point of view of women who are *mal maritate*, the latter two express the position of men, first the betrayed husband and second a boatman who privileges the point of view of the lover. Ariosto enacts a reversal at the structural level as well: whereas Boiardo created a progression towards more positive characteristics in the second novella, Ariosto inverts the trajectory so that his second tale depicts the characters in a much more negative light. This reversal is especially poignant because his darker second novella uses several analogous plot elements from Boiardo's brighter second one, including a jealous husband who is forced by duty away from home, a lover who has gone to great lengths to enter his beloved's enclosed space, the husband's drastic response at the discovery of the adulterous union, and his ultimately unsuccessful attempt at containment and revenge. Like Boiardo's second tale, moreover, Ariosto's latter story is the final novella in the 1516 edition, conferring upon it a more definitive position as the last word.[6]

The reverse trajectory is most clearly developed in the female characters. Both *Innamorato* wives are married against their wishes to impotent, manipulative, and loathsome old men whose unwholesome desire for a young bride deprives the girls of the handsome young suitors who have asked for their hand the same day. Their marriages, moreover, are in name only, since Leodila and Doristela remain virgin brides due to the impotence of both Folderico and Hosbego. Their subsequent love affairs, despite their forced solitary confinement, thus assert the rights of the flesh in a manner worthy of Boccaccio's female protagonists, from Bartolomea (*Dec.* 2.9) to Ghismonda (*Dec.* 4.1) to Madonna Filippa (*Dec.* 6.7). At the same time, however, Leodila carries some of the blame for her misfortune, since she lets her desire for golden apples distract her in the footrace and ends up bound to Folderico. Although she later regrets her actions, acknowledging how this weakness befalls the majority of the human race (*OI* 1.21.63), she nevertheless makes a similar mistake when later escaping with Ordauro: their carriage is so laden with riches taken from Folderico that they must move slowly and are thus overtaken.[7] Doristela, by contrast, is purely a victim of circumstance, since her father does not allow her to choose her beloved Theodoro as a husband.

Picking up on the theme of avarice from Boiardo's first tale, Ariosto uses it to develop the concept of sex as a commodity in both stories, assigning increased culpability to the characters in the second. In the first case, the Mantuan host's father-in-law resembles Folderico, since he was likewise "un huom saggio, / di tutte l'arti oltre ogni creder dotto" ("a learned man, incredibly knowledgeable on every subject") (*OF* 39.13 A; 43.13 C) who sought a young maiden in his golden years. Yet whereas Folderico shows cunning to win Leodila as his bride in a contest, Ariosto's character simply purchases a woman for a price: "d'amor condotto, / con premio ottenne una matrona bella, / e n'hebbe di nascosto una citella" ("Love induced him to purchase a handsome woman by whom he secretly had a girl") (*OF* 39.13 A; 43.13 C). The old man subsequently secludes his daughter "per vietar che simil la figliuola / non sia alla matre, ch'a lui per mercede / vendé sua castità" ("to prevent his daughter taking after her mother, who for a price sold her chastity") (*OF* 39.14 A; 43.14 C). After the Mantuan host marries the old man's daughter, he sets a trap to test her virtue by disguising himself as her former suitor and offering her jewels. Although she is said to love her husband, she inevitably acquiesces.

In the second *Furioso* tale, Argia is also happily married to a doting spouse but accepts the advances of a suitor motivated principally by a desire for jewels. The difference is that while in the first case the wife does not technically commit adultery, since at that moment her husband reveals himself, in the second tale Ariosto painstakingly relates how the woman sells her body despite her professed love for her husband. Initially, Argia appears devoted to Anselmo and sincerely distressed by his departure:

De la dura partita ella si duole,
con che lachryme, oh dio! con che querele!
E giura che più presto oscuro il Sole
vedrassi, che gli sia mai sì crudele
che rompa fede; e che morir più presto
vorria, che haver solo un pensier di questo. (*OF* 39.81 A)

She grieved at their painful separation;
oh how she wept and lamented!
She swore that she would see the sun grow dark
before ever she were so cruel to him as to break faith:
she would sooner die than ever entertain such an idea. (*OF* 43.85 C)

Such an outpouring of emotion would put any subsequent extramarital affair in a bad light, but Ariosto censures Argia's ensuing actions even further by attributing her motivation to greed. When she first attempts to purchase a magical, jewel-producing dog from Adonio, his refusal includes a contemptuous claim about female cupidity:

S'havesti più thesor che mai sitire
potesse cupidigia feminile
(rispose), non saria giusta mercede
per comperar di questo cane un piede. (*OF* 39.105 A)

"If I were given more money than was required
to satisfy even a woman's greed," he replied,
"it would not pay for one foot of my dog." (*OF* 43.109 C)

Argia goes on to confirm this negative view of women when she is easily seduced by the jewels and riches that the animal is able to produce. Although Ariosto lists mitigating circumstances, he uses the same term (*mercede*) and rhyme scheme as the above-cited verses to treat her sexual acquiescence as a payment for the dog: "ch'ella accettò il bel cane, e per mercede / in braccio e in preda a l'amator si diede" ("she accepted the dog and in payment abandoned herself into her lover's arms") (*OF*

39.111 A; 43.115 C). Argia thus fulfils the prediction made by Anselmo's magician friend that she would be corrupted by the promise of profit and gain: "non da beltà né lunghi prieghi indotta, / ma da guadagno e gran prezzo corrotta" ("neither beauty nor entreaties would sway her, but greed for gain would corrupt her") (*OF* 39.84 A; 43.88 C). Although the fairy Melissa will instil love for Adonio in Argia, it is telling that this occurs only through magical means and only after the onset of their adulterous union (*OF* 39.113 A; 43.116 C).

This process of degradation affects the male characters as well. Rather than contrast the husbands and lovers as Boiardo had done, Ariosto implicates all the men depicted in the novellas. At the same time, the second novella takes their moral decrepitude to an all-time low. First, Adonio purchases the sexual favours of his would-be sweetheart. Not able to win Argia in any other way, he tempts her with a magic dog that produces infinite wealth, thus iconographically symbolizing Avarice.[8] Although Adonio does thereby attain Argia, their relationship leads not to his happiness but rather to his demise: he wears himself out through such frequent intercourse that within four months he falls ill and dies. Ariosto's description of his fatal overindulgence puts the emphasis on physical lust without any hint of a romantic attachment:

E tanto se gli diede, et egli tanto
De superchio ne tolse e notte e giorno,
Parendogli avanzarlosi per quanto
Bramarà poi se fa il dottor ritorno,
Ch'in men de quattro mesi in doglia e in pianto
Volti li risi e le allegrezze forno:
Ne cadde infermo, e fu il suo mal sì rio,
Che non ne sorse mai, fin che morio. (*OF* 39.112 A)

And so much did she give herself to him, and he so much
in excess took both night and day,
seeming to him to acquire a surplus for when
he would be in need if ever the doctor returned,
that in less than four months into pain and tears
were turned the laughter and mirth:
he fell ill from it, and his illness was so terrible
that he never recovered, until he died.[9]

While the lover thus ends up dead, the husband undergoes an even more precipitous fall – into a moral abyss – when he agrees to prostitute his own body for gain. Anselmo is introduced as a man "di famiglia degna" ("of good family") who studied law and then sought a wife in accordance with his station (*OF* 39.68 A; 43.72 C). Like the Mantuan host of the former tale, at the outset he is portrayed as a solicitous partner tied to his wife in a reciprocal bond of love. By the end of the novella, however, he is willing to be sodomized by an ugly Ethiopian in return for a sumptuous palace in the forest. Ariosto's choice of verb ("inchinare" ["to stoop"]) naughtily gives both the figurative and literal sense of the judge's acquiescence: "fe' inchinarlo al suo voler malvagio" ("the judge [stooped] to his depraved desire") (*OF* 39.136 A; 43.139 C).

Throughout this final novella, in fact, sex is consistently envisioned not as an expression of passionate love but rather as a degrading service to be bartered. When Argia attempts to purchase the dog with gold, Adonio explicitly tells her nurse that the price tag is a night of sex: "se vuol ch'una notte seco io giaccia, / abbiasi il cane, e il suo voler ne faccia" ("on her agreeing to sleep one night with me, she may keep the dog to do her bidding") (*OF* 39.107 A; 43.111 C). In encouraging Argia to consent, the nurse characterizes sexual intercourse as a form of currency that incurs no loss: "acquistarlo / per prezzo può, che non si perde a darlo" ("it would cost her nothing to part with the price of its purchase") (*OF* 39.108 A; 43.112 C). By referring to the nurse as a whore ("puttana") simply for her corrupting words (*OF* 39.111 A; 43.115 C), Ariosto establishes a frame of reference for Argia's subsequent actions. The language of prostitution surfaces again when Anselmo fears the fate of his escaped wife: "Forse ancho verrà d'alcuno in mano, / che ne fia insieme adultero e ruffiano" ("She might even fall into the hands of a man who would prove to be both adulterer and procurer") (*OF* 39.126 A; 43.129 C). Moreover, Ariosto states that the Ethiopian's proposal to Anselmo is identical in nature to Adonio's earlier proposition to Argia: "E gli fa la medesima richiesta / c'havea già Adonio alla sua moglie fatta" ("And he made the same request to the judge that Adonio had made to his wife") (*OF* 39.136 A; 43.139 C). Indeed, the Ethiopian seeks Anselmo's submission by making the same point as Argia's nurse: "pagar lo può quel che vi costa meno" ("it may be bought with what costs you least") (*OF* 39.135 A; 43.138 C).

Thus, while the two *Innamorato* novellas illustrate the need for marriage to be based on love and desire rather than social advantages or wealth, the *Furioso* casts doubt on any woman's – or man's – capacity for marital fidelity, because of avarice. Boiardo's Virgilian dictum that love conquers all is thus replaced with Ariosto's presentation of greed as the most powerful human desire, a shift rendered explicit in their contrasting proems.

The Twin Tales and Phebosilla's Palace

Ariosto's two novellas also incorporate and transform several features from Brandimarte's adventure at Phebosilla's palace, notably the presence of a fairy along with the related themes of disguised identity, magic, and metamorphosis. The first novella's fairy, Melissa, is a decidedly negative one. It is out of her own desire for the Mantuan host that she induces him to test his wife's fidelity. She then gives him the outer appearance of his wife's prior suitor while she disguises herself as his servant. The second fairy, Manto, provides a more direct comparison with Phebosilla, since she is likewise periodically transformed into a snake as part of a law governing her nature.[10]

Adonio's introduction to Manto directly recalls Brandimarte's encounter with Phebosilla in the form of a snake. The "cavalliero" ("knight") arrives at a site where a "villan" ("peasant") is attempting to bludgeon to death a large but non-threatening garden snake (*OF* 39.70–4 A; 43.74–8 C). He saves the snake's life by convincing the peasant to stop beating the animal, which turns out to be the fairy Manto. After regaining her natural form, she shows her gratitude by reciprocating with an action that benefits her liberator. Like Brandimarte, in sum, Adonio acts benevolently towards a huge snake, which, as one finds out only a posteriori, is actually a fairy. At the same time, however, the register in the second case is far from heroic. While Brandimarte's act was one of great courage, since he believed that the snake intended to kill him, Adonio is never in danger of being harmed by either the peasant or the snake itself.

Ariosto also follows Boiardo's precedent in evoking Ovid's Cadmus, but he once again shifts the emphasis. As noted earlier, Boiardo suggests Brandimarte's greater wisdom with respect to Cadmus, who by killing a sacred snake brought calamity upon himself and his family until he was transformed into a serpent himself. Ariosto recalls instead the creation of the men of Thebes from a serpent's teeth. In the first tale, Rinaldo's host refers to Mantua obliquely as the city founded "quando a ruina / le mura andâr de l'Agenoreo draco" ("at the time when Thebes fell to ruin – the city of Agenor and the men born of a serpent's teeth") (*OF* 39.11 A; 43.11 C). In the second tale, Ariosto makes additional references to the founding of Thebes and to Cadmus when asserting a direct connection between Manto and Adonio through their common ancestry. On the first occasion, the boatman claims that both Adonio and Manto descended from the serpent's teeth that Cadmus had planted in the field:

> Che discendea da quell lignaggio altiero
> ch'uscì d'una mascella di serpente
> onde già Manto, e chi con essa fêro
> la patria mia, disceser similmente. (*OF* 39.70 A)

> He was descended from the proud line sprung
> from the same serpent's teeth which gave birth
> also to Manto and to those who with her
> founded Mantua, my homeland. (*OF* 43.74 C)

He then repeats the information five stanzas later to reinforce Adonio's ancestry:

> Sempre solea le serpi favorire;
> che per insegna il sangue suo le porta
> in memoria ch'uscì sua prima gente
> de' denti seminati di serpente. (*OF* 39.75 A)

> [...] he always championed snakes:
> the family-emblem was a serpent,
> to commemorate the serpent's teeth, sown in the ground,
> from which his forbears had issued. (*OF* 43.79 C)

Manto later proclaims their common descent not from the serpent's teeth but from Cadmus himself: "Parente son, perché da Cadmo fiero / scende d'amendue noi l'alto lignaggio" ("We are related because we both trace our proud ancestry back to mighty Cadmus") (*OF* 39.93 A; 43.97 C).[11] If in Boiardo's episode Brandimarte and Fiordelisa discover that their parents are kings, Adonio learns that his lineage goes back to the mythological founder of an ancient city. Yet such a heritage for Mantua may have been a questionable tribute: beyond the violence of its foundational myth, Thebes was known in literature for internecine warfare and familial misfortune.

Given their different associations – Phoebus Apollo in Boiardo, Cadmus in Ariosto – it is not surprising that the two serpent-fairies use their magical power in distinct ways. Whereas Phebosilla acts to preserve

Brandimarte's life and to heal his horse, Manto aims instead to produce an infinite supply of riches. Her "mercede" ("reward") (*OF* 39.99 A; 43.103 C) to Adonio is sheer wealth, both as an end in itself and as a means to seduce Argia. Adonio had initially attempted to attain Argia by spending recklessly over the course of two years until he dissipated his inheritance. Now, seven years later, Manto assumes (correctly, as it turns out) that Adonio will finally seduce her through a greater abundance of material goods.

Manto's ability to conjure up even sumptuous buildings leads to the climactic scene of the novella and the culmination of the extended sequence's ironic reversals with respect to Boiardo's precedent. Like Brandimarte's challenge in Phebosilla's palace, Anselmo's encounter with the Ethiopian consists of a test involving physical contact with a revolting figure in a palace built by magic. Brandimarte's active gesture of kissing a fearsome serpent has been replaced, however, by Anselmo's passive "stooping" to being sodomized by an ugly and licentious foreigner. Whereas Brandimarte acted courageously to keep his promise even at the risk of his life, Anselmo acts shamefully to acquire wealth even at the loss of his integrity. This scene thus represents the fourth and final variation on Brandimarte's experience in Phebosilla's palace, following (1) Rinaldo's initially unsuccessful bout with the formidable snake-lady representing jealousy, (2) Rinaldo's refusal to test his wife's faithfulness by putting the goblet to his lips, and (3) Adonio's actions to save the life of a snake that turns out to be the fairy Manto. While in the first and third cases Ariosto's characters fall short of Brandimarte's heroism, in the second and fourth the terms of the test are drastically altered.

The climactic scene of the final novella, moreover, with its description of a lecherous Ethiopian, brings us back to the very start of this extended sequence when Rinaldo voiced his disgust over Angelica's choice of an African mate. In the earlier case, however, Ariosto had first fashioned Medoro as a Greek Adonis, thus allowing readers to dismiss Rinaldo's projections as a product of his angry imagination. Now, however, Ariosto expects his audience to be revolted by the figure he describes:

> Nanzi alla porta vede uno Ethïòpo
> con naso e labri grossi; et ègli aviso
> che non vedesse mai, prima né dopo,
> un così sozzo e dispiacevol viso;
> poi de fattezze qual si pigne Esopo,
> d'attristar, se vi fusse, il paradiso;

bisunto e sporco, e d'habito mendico:
né a mezo anchor di sua brutteza i' dico. (*OF* 39.132 A)

Before the gate he saw an Ethiopian
with broad nose and thick lips.
Never before or since, he was convinced,
had he set eyes upon so hideously repulsive a face.
For the rest, he shared the deformities attributed to Aesop –
enough to depress a saint in paradise.
He was greasy, dirty, dressed like a beggar,
and I have gone but half-way towards describing his ugliness. (*OF* 43.135 C)

The Ethiopian is never given an individual identity but is referred to generically and pejoratively as "il negro" ("the negro") (*OF* 39.133 A; 43.136 C) and "il brutto Moro" ("the ugly Moor") (*OF* 39.135 A; 43.138 C). His licentious proposal explicitly exposes his nature as "bestiale" ("brute") rather than human (*OF* 39.136 A; 43.139 C).

Ariosto's disparaging depiction of the Ethiopian indirectly deprecates Senapo, the emperor who put hundreds of thousands of troops under Astolfo's command.[12] In the context of the present argument, moreover, it goes against the deepest implications of the extended Phebosilla episode. Brandimarte's "fier baiser" symbolized the piercing through the veil of appearance to *know* the other through direct, intimate contact. As a result, a ghastly serpent revealed itself to have an individual identity in the form of the fairy Phebosilla. In Ariosto's perverse transformation of Brandimarte's ordeal, the individual being tested agrees to allow himself to be "possessed" by the other in return for profit. The foreign other not only retains his gruesome outer form but succeeds in convincing Anselmo to serve as a vehicle for his sexual debauchery. Contact with the unknown other thus brings about not increased knowledge of the world beyond one's horizon but rather the debasing of one's own self by contamination.

In challenging us to question our preconceived notions, Boiardo chose a non-human icon certain to instil an initial horror in his reader. As Ariosto's Manto will later say: "Non è sì odiato altro animale in terra, / come la serpe" ("No creature on earth is so loathed as the snake") (*OF* 39.96 A; 43.100 C). It is precisely because we understand Brandimarte's hesitation that we can more fully appreciate the heroism required for him to overcome his fears. Ariosto's depiction of the other as a repulsive black African is not a universal symbol but a culture-specific and xenophobic image. Moreover, the superiority that Argia gains over her husband is increased by the degree of repulsion that the reader is made to feel towards the Ethiopian stranger. Rajna, associating him with the dwarf in the Giocondo novella, refers to him as "that horrible Ethiopian, introduced evidently to aggravate all the more the culpability of the husband, to the total benefit of the feminine sex" (*Le fonti*, 582).[13]

Mantua and Ferrara: A Local Perspective

While the Ethiopian stands out because of his diversity, this scene is not the only moment in the narrative sequence in which geography takes on thematic significance. The world of Ariosto's two novellas is vastly different from Boiardo's precedent not only with regard to the motivations and actions of the characters but also by its location on the map. All characters in Boiardo's extended episode – both the frame story and the two novellas – were born and had lived thus far beyond the confines of Christian Europe. Ariosto replaces Boiardo's global range with a very restricted local vista. The boatman specifies to Rinaldo that both he and the host are from the same homeland (*OF* 39.66 A; 43.70 C). In fact, not only the storytellers themselves but virtually all the characters are from Mantua and its environs. Those noted to have come from outside Mantua in the first novella are the suitor, who is from nearby Ferrara (*OF* 39.32 A; 43.32–3 C), and Argia, who comes from "una terra quindi non lontana" ("a neighbouring city") (*OF* 39.68 A; 43.72 C). The fairy Manto, unlike all the other (good and evil) fairies who populate the two poems, also has a local provenance. Indeed, as noted earlier, she is designated as the founder of the city that bears her name. The boatman tells Rinaldo that even the circulation of his story is local, since it is unknown on the other side of the Alps. This is confirmed by the fact that Rinaldo only hears it when he himself is travelling along the Po River.

In Ariosto's second tale, moreover, departure from the restricted city space is viewed as negative since it is the result either of a failure (Adonio's exile after squandering all his capital in a vain attempt to win over Argia) or of forced duty (Anselmo's compulsory service as orator to the pope). Although Adonio is away for seven years and Anselmo for one year, the reader learns nothing about their destinations. The place where Adonio lives during this seven-year period is identified simply through its quality of being "fuor de la patria" ("outside his homeland") (*OF* 39.76 A; 43.80 C). Although the reader is told that Anselmo leaves to serve the pope, Ariosto never specifies that his duty takes him to Rome. Rather, he chooses the same two terms to describe Anselmo's involuntary departure that he employed to characterize Adonio's voluntary exile: Anselmo will move from his homeland ("patria"; *OF* 39.78 A; 43.82 C) to an outside space ("fuore"; *OF* 39.79 A; 43.83 C). In these instances the greater world has no reality of its own, serving merely to indicate absence, and the two characters return to their native city in the same frame of mind that characterized their departure (unrequited love in the first case, extreme jealousy in the second).

When the world beyond Mantua or Ferrara does take on more specificity, it is the cause of moral decadence. Ariosto's first novella views India and Africa as loci of luxury and corruption. When the husband pretends to have left for the East (Levante) and then returns disguised as the Ferrarese suitor, the equally disguised Melissa produces "le più ricche gemme [...] / che mai mandasson l'Indi o li Erythrei" ("jewels as rich as ever came out of the Indies or Ethiopia") (*OF* 39.35 A; 43.35 C). In the second novella, the Ethiopian's splendid alabaster palace – where even the stables were decorated "di tapeti e di razzi, e di cortine / tessute e riccamate a varie foggie" ("with finest-quality draperies, richly woven in various fabrics"), along with countless objects made of gold, silver, and precious gems – is of an opulence far beyond buildings found locally, exemplified by the host's palace (*OF* 39.129–30 A; 43.132–3 C). This contributes further to the overall negative view of a luxuriously corrupt world outside the Po Valley.

The extreme localism of the setting, combined with the sense of realism inherent in the novelistic genre, invites the reader to wonder about the extent to which the society depicted in these tales can be linked to Ariosto's Ferrarese patrons. The ties between Ferrara and Mantua were very close during the period of the poem's composition, not only through geographical proximity but through political alliance as well. Although Ariosto does not (and could not) state that the sordid characters of the novellas were meant to mirror his own society, the exclusively local setting of the two tales raises questions about referentiality to a greater degree than epic or romance episodes occurring in faraway or imaginary places.

Ariosto actually draws us outside the poem's fiction at more than one point to behold exponents of contemporary courtly society. Among the magnificent works of art within the Mantuan knight's "gran palazzo" ("great palace") (*OF* 38.70 A; 42.73 C) one can find eight statues of prominent women, including Isabella d'Este, the marchioness of Mantua through her marriage to Francesco Gonzaga. Just as earlier Boiardo included male members of the Estense family in the context of Brandimarte's test through their representations on Phebosilla's palace walls, Ariosto constructs an ekphrastic setting for the Este women and their admirers.[14] Although the unmitigated praise of this encomiastic parenthesis is in sharp contrast with the squalid view of humanity depicted in the Mantuan novellas, the juxtaposition may have been more than a little disconcerting to Ariosto's circle of courtly readers.

Historical reality mixes with the poem's fiction in a more insidious manner as Rinaldo himself makes a speech about Ferrara's future. As his boat sails by, he enumerates some of the wonders of both the city itself and its patrons that he remembers having heard from his wizard cousin Malagigi (*OF* 39.55–7 A; 43.55–61 C).[15] Yet Rinaldo's stanza-long prayer that concludes the encomium causes the reader to pause, since it assumes Ferrara's adversarial position with respect not only to its declared enemies but to every one of its neighbours as well: "del tuo contento ogni vicino arrabbi, / più presto che tu invidia ad alcuno habbi" ("May your neighbours chafe at your happiness before ever you feel envy towards any of them") (*OF* 39.58 A; 43.62 C). In contrast to the openness evidenced in the extended Phebosilla episode, in which foreign strangers were potential friends and relatives, this isolationist comment depicts even one's closest neighbours as latent enemies.

Brandimarte and Rinaldo

Ariosto also develops a meaningful contrast between Boiardo's Brandimarte and his own Rinaldo as a reader and auditor of tales. Boiardo's hero, it should first be noted, has different reactions after hearing the two novellas. In the first case, he is too distraught over Fiordelisa's disappearance to pay attention to Leodila's vicissitudes and therefore leaves before she completes her story (*OI* 1.21.70). He had, however, already brought about a happy conclusion by intervening to save her from the giant who had abducted her, the note upon which she eventually interrupts her narration. In the case of Doristela's tale, Brandimarte's role is even more pronounced. If, prior to hearing her story, he defeats a knight who turns out to have been the jealous husband holding her hostage, after hearing her tale he delivers her safely to her homeland and puts an end to the war that had broken out between her beloved Theodoro and her father. His intervention not only brings about the young couple's happy reunion but also leads to the discovery of Fiordelisa's true identity and their own subsequent marriage. This agency on the part of Brandimarte in bringing about a resolution to a dire situation disclosed through a novella links him to Boiardo's Ranaldo, who, as I have argued elsewhere, plays an active role as a reader and auditor of novellas and an upholder of justice.[16]

In the early cantos of the *Furioso* Rinaldo continues to act in this guise when he listens to the story of Ginevra and Ariodante and then brings about a just conclusion to their drama. He does not hear any further tales, however, until this episode in the final cantos of the poem. Although Rinaldo is once again designated as the privileged reader and listener, he no longer carries out his previous function but is characterized instead by his very lack of action. Even before hearing the first novella he refuses to act by drinking from the goblet. After listening to each tale he restricts himself to wry comments, first questioning the Mantuan knight's integrity if tested and later praising Argia's "aviso" ("wit") for having caught her husband in the same kind of trap he had set for her (*OF* 39.141 A; 43.144 C). This is a far cry indeed from Ranaldo's reaction in the *Innamorato* after hearing the tale of Tisbina, Iroldo, and Prasildo. In that episode Ranaldo not only expresses admiration for the knights' reciprocal benevolent actions but is ready to risk his life to share in their ideal friendship (*OI* 1.17.21). Here, having relinquished his role of a civic-minded individual who seeks justice, Rinaldo conveys only bemused cynicism.

The reversal in Rinaldo's attitude from civic-minded engagement to pessimistic passivity nullifies his role as a reader who interprets a story and then acts on his knowledge. Yet Ariosto does not blame the knight himself. Indeed, the idea of bringing about a change for the better in a world motivated by greed seems hardly a viable one, and we are at a loss to find an alternative response to Rinaldo's sense of resignation. The intervention of heroes is out of the question, since the tainted universe described by the storytellers has moved forward on its own, with its own internal solutions. The morally corrupt society of the novellas may indeed contain knights (both the Mantuan host and Adonio are specifically designated as such), but it is utterly devoid of chivalric values.[17]

In the course of this narrative sequence the moral virtues that had sustained Boiardo's poem have disappeared. Prudence, as the Po River journey's first novella and surrounding narrative context show, no longer means acting according to the dictates of reason but rather choosing to remain ignorant of an unpleasant truth. Wisdom, in the second novella, has lost its ethical purpose and is turned into the cunning that allows one to get the better of one's opponent (or spouse). Finally, justice is no longer attained by combating evil but simply by proving that one's accuser (or spouse) is more degenerate than oneself. This redefinition of failings as virtue reveals a profoundly negative view of human nature without offering any hope for its improvement.

In the final cantos of the poem, Ariosto devises a trajectory for Rinaldo that parallels that of Boiardo's Brandimarte. As noted in the previous chapter, in addition to recovering his identity, Brandimarte eventually moves from romance adventure to epic warfare, and from the expanse of Asia to the outskirts of Paris. Rinaldo's recovery of his Carolingian identity also leads to both a shift away from romance and a change in geographical direction: whereas he had set out to seek Angelica in India, he now travels instead to the site of the poem's epic endpoint, the island of Lipadusa. It is at these outer contours of his counter-sequence that Ariosto brings Rinaldo and Brandimarte together in a more direct way. The tests and novellas related in the context of Rinaldo's travels from France to Lipadusa are framed by nothing less than Brandimarte's death and burial. Shortly after recounting Brandimarte's demise at the hands of Gradasso (*OF* 38.14 A; 42.14 C), Ariosto returns to France where Rinaldo is still in love with Angelica (*OF* 38.28 A; 42.28 C). Following an uncharacteristically long continuous narrative sequence comprising Rinaldo's two tests and the two Mantuan novellas, the paladin arrives on the island of Lipadusa, where he immediately hears the news of Brandimarte's death (*OF* 39.149 A; 43.152 C). At the start of the sequence, the epic battle at Lipadusa and the romance enchantment at Merlin's fountain are worlds apart. Yet Rinaldo's experience at Merlin's fountain is precisely what leads him to the island – too late to save Brandimarte's life but in time to attend his funeral. Thus it seems that the world that emerges by the poem's conclusion finds space for the cynical-minded Rinaldo but not for the ideal knight Brandimarte and his beloved Fiordeligi.

As I hope to have shown in this chapter, Ariosto goes to great lengths to rearrange the elements surrounding the Phebosilla episode in order to present a vastly different, and substantially dimmer, worldview. A detailed comparison of the two extended episodes reveals a thick web of shared narrative elements, including (1) metamorphosis; (2) the inclusion of the Este family in a privileged way through ekphrasis and encomium; (3) a knight who undergoes two tests during and following a period of transition, the first of which involves being attacked by a snake used as a weapon; (4) a knight who intervenes on behalf of a serpent who unbeknownst to him is a benevolent fairy; (5) the gratitude of the fairy who reciprocates by bestowing her favours through magic; (6) an explanation that fairies periodically transform into serpents as part of their nature;

(7) the immortality of fairies whether in snake or human form; (8) references to Cadmus; (9) allusions to the Garden of Eden in Genesis; (10) the discovery that two strangers are part of the same family; (11) a magic test involving physical contact with a particularly revolting creature in a fabulous palace; and (12) the association of wisdom with both supernatural and human female characters.

At the same time, however, these elements are reworked almost beyond recognition. In Ariosto's poem not only does false opinion masquerade as knowledge, but even in cases in which objective knowledge is possible, it is deemed undesirable. The world is so ruled by avarice, and human nature responds so destructively to unpleasant realities, that it is sometimes better not to know the truth at all. Even though this courtly culture is thus debased, the world outside one's "patria" is even more dangerous: it is no longer an infinitely open site of adventure and discovery waiting beyond the threshold, but it barges in with precious jewellery and luxurious palaces that would corrupt even the most faithful wife and the most stalwart judge. Whether Ariosto intended to portray human nature with resigned cynicism or to criticize the flaws of his society through moral censure, Rinaldo's final sequence is conspicuously bereft of the love and courtesy celebrated in the corresponding *Innamorato* episodes. As a result, the 1516 *Furioso* breaks the *Innamorato*'s link between knowledge and ethical action and offers little hope to its readers for a better future.

Conclusion

The lives of our two poets overlap both temporally and spatially. Boiardo was thirty-three when Ariosto was born in Reggio Emilia in 1474, and Ariosto had just turned twenty when Boiardo died in that same city two decades later. At the age of ten Boiardo moved with his mother from Ferrara back to his birthplace in Scandiano, a few miles from Reggio; Ariosto made a reverse journey with his family, arriving in Ferrara in time for his tenth birthday.[1] The poets themselves not only alternated between the same cities during their lifetimes, but both served the Estense family in various capacities. In 1482–3 Boiardo dedicated his romance epic to Duke Ercole I d'Este, whose service Ariosto entered for a brief period (1498–1503) before joining the entourage of Ercole's son Ippolito, to whom he dedicated his continuation. Both poets read aloud from their works in progress to Ercole's exceptionally cultivated daughter, Isabella. Nevertheless, as this study has argued, their respective poems offer distinct and opposing visions of the world.

Boiardo

Marco Villoresi has called attention to Boiardo's virtually unlimited "cultural syncretism," noting his seamless combination of themes and styles, sources, and genres taken from "the entire literary universe" (*La letteratura cavalleresca*, 151, 157–8). This all-inclusive approach to past literary traditions can be extended to his treatment of geographical space as well, given that his knights and damsels originate from every corner of the globe, which they then proceed to traverse in a variety of directions for a host of different motives. Newly invented Asian, African, and Middle Eastern characters join traditional Carolingian figures in embodying a code of chivalry that transcends national, religious, ethnic, and linguistic barriers. At the same time, however, Boiardo does not underestimate the capacity for evil on the part of powerful individual characters within the poem, just as he does not minimize the threats to Ferrara in the real world – whether from other Italian states such as Venice and the papacy or, more indirectly, from the Ottoman Turks.

The world depicted in the *Orlando innamorato*, in fact, is teeming with injustices both within and beyond Latin Christendom. Nonetheless, the narrative outcomes often suggest that communication and increased knowledge can lead to the enlightenment of the individual and the improvement of human society at large. As Charles S. Ross notes, "set in the realistic context of Ferrara, the *Innamorato* more than ever looks like a supreme effort to create a better world" (*Orlando innamorato*, xlv). Despite all the dangers to be found both within and outside one's homeland, Boiardo does not encourage an attitude of either isolationism or aggression but, on the contrary, advocates interpenetration at all levels. This attitude of openness corresponds to an interest on the part of Boiardo's early readers in the vast world lying beyond the confines of western Europe. Indeed, without negating Boiardo's individual vision as a poet, the *Innamorato* can be viewed as encapsulating a moment in which, according to Guido Ruggiero, "European encounters with other worlds [...] reflected an original confidence that meeting and understanding others was ultimately a project that was valuable and doable" (10).

The extent of Boiardo's literary and global interpenetrations, perhaps unprecedented in a work of fiction, suggestively parallels the exceptional religious syncretism exemplified by his younger cousin, Giovanni Pico della Mirandola, during the same period. In 1486, just a few years after the publication of the *Innamorato*, Pico published nine hundred propositions containing ideas drawn from various Egyptian, Greek, Arabic, Hebrew, Chaldean, Aramaic, and Roman thinkers, and invited a discussion of them at a public disputation in Rome. The introductory oration for this projected debate gives an immediate sense of Pico's range: he opens by citing Abdala the Saracen from "the records of the Arabians" and the Egyptian Hermes Trismegistus from the esoteric *Asclepius*, and then refers to both the Persians and the Psalms to support his assertion about the position of man in the universe (223). Kristeller writes that Pico "was able to absorb many different ideas and traditions that most of his contemporaries would have considered incompatible" (215, 216).[2]

Boiardo and Pico would not have lacked occasions for encountering each other since both were grandsons of Feltrino Boiardo (Pico through the latter's daughter Giulia). Both were in contact with Guarino da Verona's son Battista, the former as a fellow humanist and poet of eclogues and the latter as a student in Ferrara.[3] I am not positing, however, that either Boiardo or Pico was influenced by the other, nor would I minimize the differences between the metaphysical postulations of Neoplatonic philosophy and the fictional scenarios of romance epic. I would like to suggest, rather, that the embracive outlook implicit in their methods of incorporating a wide range of sources to conceive a more comprehensive and original whole is a departure from conservative and dogmatic thinking in both philosophical and epic writing. This shared propensity towards inclusiveness may have been fostered by their humanist education. Kristeller, in fact, views Pico's syncretism as a philosophical justification of the humanists' procedural eclecticism: "In their opposition to the exclusive Aristotelianism of the medieval philosophers, the Humanists liked to quote and make use of the teachings of all the different ancient thinkers and schools accessible to them" (221–2).

The freedom exercised by both Boiardo and Pico to draw from diverse literary genres and religious beliefs corresponds, moreover, to the open-mindedness intrinsic to their respective works: whereas Pico viewed humans as not confined to the centre of a cosmic ladder (as was the case in Ficino's philosophy) but capable of moving from the vegetative to the angelic mode of being, for Boiardo human freedom was epitomized by the imaginary wanderings of Charlemagne's paladins across the globe in the company of non-European and non-Christian knights and ladies who often shared their chivalric ideals.

Higher powers and historical circumstances prevented the completion of both intrepid projects: Pico's plans were squelched by Pope Innocent VIII; Boiardo's poem was suspended during the invasion of Charles VIII, and his death a few months later rendered the poem's interruption permanent. It is impossible to imagine either how Boiardo would have assessed the contemporary historical situation or how he would have concluded his fictional universe if he had lived to complete his work. A similar crisis was recorded at the end of Book Two when the offenders were not French but Venetian troops. In this case, the opening proem of Book Three proclaimed a revival of Ferrarese court life, while the narrative found room once again for romance adventures that brought together Christians and Saracens outside war – from Mandricardo's serendipitous rescue of all those imprisoned at the Fountain of the Fay to Fiordispina's futile passion for a Christian stranger. As it stands now in its unfinished but final state, a poem celebrating the global adventures of both Charlemagne's paladins and newly invented foreign protagonists ends with a chilling evocation of the modern day "Galli" ("Gauls") setting all of Italy ("la Italia tutta") aflame. In the poem's concluding stanza the French army has been transformed from the defending heroes within the epic plot to the invading enemies who have taken away the voice of the poet.

Ariosto

Noting that "northerners fought a war quite as ruthless as the Turks," Murrin considers the terror of massacre used against the Italian population as a factor in the different depiction of battle tactics in the two poems: "The north brought these tactics to Italy. In their campaigns of 1494 and 1495 the French made mass killing an Italian reality. [...] Other nations soon emulated the French example: first the Spaniards (1503), then the Germans (1509). Ruthlessness now could characterize tactics anywhere, and the change can be seen in Ariosto, who continued Boiardo's poem" (*History and Warfare,* 202).[4] These historical invasions may have influenced not only the poem's battle scenes but its overall outlook as well. In fact, against a longstanding tendency of critics to emphasize the lighter motifs of the *Furioso*, recent studies have looked to the crisis overtaking Italy at the time as a factor darkening its composition.[5] As Mario Santoro has put it: "Between Boiardo and Ariosto there's 1494; there is the growing recognition, in the consciousness of contemporaries, of a reality marked by irrationality and violence, in the face of the urgent and upsetting events of political and social reality" (*L'anello di Angelica*, 65).

Charles VIII's descent into Italy with 90,000 troops was followed by a wave of invasions on the part of French, Spanish, Swiss, and German-Austrian armies, which successively reduced Italy to a possession of its European neighbours in the course of a few decades – the same period in which Ariosto was composing his poem. By the time Machiavelli wrote *The Prince* in 1513, he refers to Italy as "più stiava che li ebrei, più serva che' persi, più dispersa che gli ateniesi: sanza capo, sanza ordine, battuta, spogliata, lacera, corsa, e avessi sopportato d'ogni sorte ruina" ("more enslaved than the Hebrews, more oppressed than the Persians, more widely scattered than the Athenians; leaderless, lawless, crushed, despoiled, torn, overrun; she had to endure every kind of desolation") (*Il principe*, 169; tr., 82). Murrin aptly reminds us of Guicciardini's anguished statement that particularly after 1509 civilians "saw nothing but scenes of infinite slaughter, plunder and destruction of multitudes of towns and cities, attended with the licentiousness of soldiers no less destructive to friends than foes" (*History and Warfare*, 83).[6]

Italy's position as a land overrun by more powerful states may help explain Ariosto's virtual silence regarding maritime discoveries in the first edition of his poem, despite his extensive historical references regarding other European events. Doroszlaï, noting that the only direct reference to recent global discoveries is the fact that Angelica returned to Cathay with Portuguese ships (*OF* 38.35 A), concludes that, "Clearly, [America] does not exist as a new continent in the eyes of the poet at the time of the composition of the first *Orlando Furioso*" (57).[7] Yet Ariosto would have had little reason to celebrate the conquest of new "pagan" territories at the farthest reaches of the known world when his countrymen were yearning for the liberation of their own soil from European invaders.

It was not only forces outside the Italian peninsula, however, that threatened Ferrara during the years preceding the poem's publication. Alfonso d'Este came under fire from Pope Julius for his excessively close ties to the French and other alleged offences. From 1510 until his death in May 1513, the pope viewed the duke as an enemy, to the point of declaring his fiefs forfeit and annexing Ferrara to the Papal States. Ippolito had also managed to provoke Julius's ire, and Ariosto's diplomatic missions to the pope on behalf of both excommunicated brothers did not produce any positive results. On the contrary, his attempt to mediate in favour of Ippolito led to his flight back to Ferrara in fear for his own life.[8] Nor did the election of Giovanni de' Medici as Pope Leo X bring more than a temporary reprieve to the Ferrarese state. Dorigatti aptly refers to both popes as "ferocious enemies" of the Estense ("La favola," 54). Ariosto's criticism of the papacy may be veiled, but as Albert Ascoli has shown ("Ariosto's 'Fier Pastor'"), it is no less piercing for that.[9]

The most virulent criticism is reserved, perhaps, for Venice. Ariosto not only compares the Venetians to the poem's Saracen invaders, as noted in chapter 15, but states outright that offences committed by Venice's mercenaries were more inhuman than anything undertaken by the historical Mongols, Turks, or Moors:

Tutti li crudeli atti et inhumani
ch'usasse mai Tartaro o Turco o Moro;
credo contra 'l voler de' Venetiani,
[…]
usaron l'empie e scelerate mani
de li soldati mercenarii loro.

Io non dico hor de tanti accesi fuochi
che le ville arse e nostri ameni luochi;
[...]
Io non parlo di questo nè di tanti
altri lor discortesi e crudeli atti;
ma sol di quel che trar da' sassi i pianti
devrai poter [...] (*OF* 33.3 A)

Every cruel, inhuman deed ever practised
by Tartar, Turk, or Moor was perpetrated,
if not by will of the Venetians
[...]
by the criminal hand of their mercenaries.
I say nothing of all the fires they started,
which burned down our farms and country retreats –
[...]
I speak not of this, or of so many
other villainous deeds of cruelty. (*OF* 36.3 C)[10]

The heart-wrenching deed that Ariosto does go on to describe in all its horror is the decapitation of the young Ercole Cantelmo in sight of the Estense army, including his own father, in nearby Padua in 1509.[11] In terms of cruelty, according to Ariosto not even the infamous Scythians, often cited as the ancient ancestors of the ferocious Turks, could compare with the "Barbar crudel" ("Cruel barbarians") inhabiting the Italian peninsula in his own day (*OF* 33.9 A; 36.9 C). Indeed, how could Ariosto have felt anything other than pessimism regarding the human race in the face of such inhumanity? Boiardo's vision of global interpenetration under the banner of a universal chivalric code looks naively optimistic when it comes up against the reality of a Ferrarese youth beheaded by the Venetian mercenaries to whom he had surrendered in good faith, while his father can only look on in utter helplessness.

While the narrative episodes featuring Boiardo's Brandimarte challenge the reader to consider the most frightening stranger as a potential friend, it is perhaps after all not surprising that Ariosto's extended sequence of Rinaldo along the Po River should alert us instead to the possibility that even a close neighbour could turn into a mortal foe. Addressing Ippolito and Alfonso d'Este in a proem, Ariosto stresses the frequency with which even one's dearest friends act like enemies in their deeds due to political circumstance: "quanti n'havete, o gloriosi nati / d'Hercole invitto, a questi dì veduto / che vi son stati e son di cor amici, / e ne li effetti poi come nemici!" ("How many, oh glorious ones born of invincible Hercules, have you seen in our day that were and still are your close friends, but who in their deeds are like enemies") (*OF* 35.5A).[12] Tellingly, Ariosto's final words, in the form of the Latin motto "pro bono malum" that accompanied all three editions, caution readers not to expect anything other than evil in return for the good they may do for others.

Names and Origins of Fictional Characters

Since several characters have variant spellings, especially in Boiardo's poem, the choice of names is partially arbitrary. In the present study I have adopted names found in the critical edition of the *Innamorato* for Boiardo's characters and the 1516 edition of the *Furioso* for Ariosto's characters. I have tried not to force discrepancies, however, when a single name could be used (e.g., given that Boiardo uses both Marphysa and Marphisa whereas Ariosto uses Marfisa and Marphisa, I have chosen the name common to both). The slightly different spelling does not, in any case, affect meaning or make the characters any less recognizable.

Adonio – Mantuan knight, seduces Argia with the help of the fairy Melissa (*OF*)
Agolante – North African king who invaded Calabria in the *Aspramonte*, grandfather of both Agramante (via his son Troiano) and Rugiero (via his daughter Galaziella)
Agramante – King of Biserta (Tunisia); commands rulers of other African states
Agricane – khan of Tartary (Mongol Empire); father of Mandricardo
Alceste – Lidia's hapless suitor (*OF*)
Alcina – enchantress; Boiardo locates her north of the Caspian Sea, Ariosto on an East Asian island
Alda – Orlando's wife
Almonte – Agolante's son and Galaziella's brother
Amone – father of Ranaldo/Rinaldo, Bradamante, and Ricciardetto
Angelica – princess of Cathay
Anselmo – Argia's husband in the novella a boatman tells Rinaldo along the Po River (*OF*)
Aquilante – brother of Grifone, raised in Constantinople

Argalìa/Argalia – brother of Angelica, from Cathay

Argia – Anselmo's wife in the novella a boatman tells Rinaldo along the Po River (*OF*)

Astolfo – son of the king of England; serves Charlemagne; cousin of Orlando and Ranaldo/Rinaldo

Atalante/Atlante – North African wizard and guardian of Rugiero/Ruggiero

Baiardo – horse belonging to Ranaldo/Rinaldo, coveted by Gradasso

Balugante – brother of Marsilio, Saracen king of Spain, and of Galerana, Charlemagne's wife

Basaldo – Turkish ruler from Anatolia, allied with the Greek Costanzo (*OI*)

Beatrice – Amone's wife; Bradamante's mother (*OF*)

Beltramo – treacherous brother of Rugiero/Ruggiero II (di Risa, i.e., Reggio Calabria)

Bradamante – beloved of Rugiero/Ruggiero and sister of Ranaldo/Rinaldo

Brandimarte – beloved of Fiordelisa/Fiordeligi; born in the Far Away Islands (northern Russia); kidnapped and raised at Castle Wild, near Samarkand (Uzbekistan)

Branzardo – North African king

Brunello – North African thief; originally serves king of Fez, becomes king of Tingitana

Caligorante – giant terrifying pilgrims in Egypt, becomes slave in Jerusalem (*OF*)

Clarice – wife of Ranaldo/Rinaldo

Costanzo – son of Varatone, king of Greece (*OI*)

Dolistone – king of Laodicea (today's Latakia), on the coast of Syria (*OI*)

Doralice – princess of Granada, beloved of Rodamonte/Rodomonte; becomes Mandricardo's lover (*OF*)

Doristela – sister of Fiordelisa (*OI*)

Dragontina – enchantress from Media (northern Iran)

Falerina – enchantress in charge of the Garden of Orgagna (possibly, Turkmenistan)

Fata della Fonte – fairy of an enchanted fountain located in or near Syria

Phebosilla – fairy freed from serpent form by Brandimarte (*OI*)

Falcirone/Falsirone – brother of Marsilio and Balugante

Feraguto/Ferraù – nephew of Saracen King Marsilio of Spain (Ferragù in the *Entrée d'Espagne*; Feraù in the *Spagna ferrarese*; Ferraù in the *Spagna maggiore*)

Fiordelisa/Fiordeligi – beloved of Brandimarte; from the Syrian city of Laodicea (Latakia); kidnapped and raised at Castle Wild, near Samarkand, Uzbekistan

Fiordespina/Fiordispina – Spanish princess, King Marsilio's daughter

Folderico – Leodila's nominal husband (*OI*)
Galaciella – daughter of an Amazon warrior and the African king Agolante (Galiziella in Andrea da Barberino's *Aspramonte*; Galicielia in Niccolò degli Agostini's *Orlando innamorato*, Book Four)
Galafrone – Angelica's father, ruler of Cathay
Galerana – King Marsilio's sister, Charlemagne's wife
Gano – Charlemagne's treacherous adviser who betrayed the Christians at Roncevaux because of personal hatred for his stepson Orlando (Ganelon in the *Chanson de Roland*)
Garamanta, king of – North African king and astrologer (*OI*)
Gradasso – king of Sericana (southeast Asia)
Grandonio – king of Morocco
Grifone – brother of Aquilante, raised in Spain
Helidona – Egyptian beloved of Alexander of Macedonia, gives birth to triplets at Tripoli (*OI*)
Hosbego – Turk from Bursa, Doristela's nominal husband (*OI*)
Iroldo – courteous knight from Babylonia, rival then friend of Prasildo
Isolieri/Isoliero – brother of Ferraguto/Ferraù
Leodila – King Manodante's daughter, Brandimarte's sister (*OI*)
Lidia – princess of Lydia (ancient kingdom in Anatolia), currently a shade Astolfo encounters in the otherworldly inferno located on the African continent (*OF*)
Logistilla – virtuous stepsister of Morgana and Alcina (*OF*)
Lucina – daughter of Tibiano, king of Cyprus; beloved, then wife, of Noradino/Norandino
Malagise/Malagigi – Carolingian counterpart to the Arthurian wizard Merlin; cousin of Ranaldo/Rinaldo
Mandricardo – son and heir of Agricane of Tartary
Manodante/Monodante – Brandimarte's father, king of the Isole Lontane (far-northern Russia)
Manto – fairy from Mantua in the novella a boatman tells Rinaldo along the Po River (*OF*)
Mantuan host – tells autobiographical novella to Rinaldo (*OF*)
Marphisa – female warrior from the East; identified as Ruggiero's sister by Niccolò degli Agostini and Ariosto
Marsilio/Marsiglio – King of Spain
Medoro – North African foot soldier in Agramante's army, marries Angelica and becomes ruler of Cathay (*OF*)
Melissa – fairy; Merlin's helper, also appears in novella by Rinaldo's Mantuan host (*OF*)

Morbeco – a Turkish ruler from Anatolia, allied with the Greek prince Costanzo (*OI*)
Morgana – enchantress, Alcina's sister
Mulabuferso – North African king (*OI*)
Noradino/Norandino – King of Syria in love with Cypriot princess Lucina
Oliviero – Frankish knight, close friend of Orlando
Ordauro – Leodila's lover (*OI*)
Orlando – Charlemagne's nephew, in Italian tradition born in Sutri (north of Rome)
Orilo/Horrilo – Egyptian wizard
Poliferno – king of Orgagna, ally of Agricane in the war at Albracà (*OI*)
Prasildo – courteous knight from Babylonia, rival then friend of Iroldo
Ranaldo/Rinaldo – Frankish knight from Montalbano (Montauban, Provence)
Ricciardetto – Bradamante's brother; Ariosto makes them identical twins
Rodamonte/Rodomonte – King of Sarza (Algeria)
Rugiero/Ruggiero – son of Rugiero/Ruggiero II (of Reggio) and Galaciella, raised in the Atlas Mountains (northern Africa)
Rugiero/Ruggiero II (of Reggio) – knight from Reggio Calabria, marries Galaciella (Riccieri in Andrea da Barberino's *Aspramonte*)
Sacripante – King of Circassia (in the Caucasus)
San Giovanni (St John) – author of the Gospel of John, inhabits the Earthly Paradise, located on the African continent (*OF*)
Sansonetto – neophyte Christian, governor of Jerusalem (*OF*)
Senapo – Christian ruler of Ethiopia, also called Nubia; the legendary Prester John (*OF*)
Sobrino – North African king and advisor to Agramante
Tibiano – king of Cyprus, Lucina's father
Theodoro – prince of Armenia, Doristella's beloved and second husband (*OI*)
Torindo – king of Turkey (*OI*)
Troiano – King Agramante's father
Trufaldino – treacherous king of Baghdad and ruler of all of Babylonia (*OI*)
Turpino –archbishop and warrior in Charlemagne's army, purported author
Varatone – king of Greece (*OI*)

Notes

Introduction

1 Although, as Antonia Tissoni Benvenuti has pointed out, *Inamoramento de Orlando* was the poem's original general title, the additional title *Orlando innamorato* was already placed at the opening of each book in the earliest extant edition (1487) and was used as the general title as early as the Venetian edition of 1506. The latter publication, which contained Boiardo's unfinished poem along with Niccolò degli Agostini's Book Four continuation, served as the basis for successive sixteenth-century editions likewise entitled *Orlando innamorato* (Harris 1: 34–5). Dorigatti argues based on textual evidence that Ariosto used the 1505 or 1506 edition when composing his own poem ("La favola," 50–1). I therefore prefer to retain the title that Ariosto deliberately echoed and by which Boiardo's poem has been known for centuries. My consideration of the *Furioso*, unless otherwise stated, concerns the original 1516 edition (ed. Marco Dorigatti). It should be noted that none of the episodes added in the 1532 edition take place outside the European arena.

2 Ross's maps trace the trajectories of Orlando, Gradasso, and the various armies led by other characters (*Orlando in Love*, lxxxii–lxxxiii). See Murrin, "Trade and Fortune," 90n67, for the specific caravan routes Boiardo's heroes follow on their way East and back.

3 "L'*Orlando innamorato* del Boiardo," 330–1, and *Le fonti*, 59. Unless otherwise stated, English translations from non-English sources are my own.

4 *L'opera dei pupi*, 111. These statements are echoed by Alexandre-Gras, who provides further examples of this phenomenon (301–10).

5 A few studies move in this direction, albeit with a limited focus: see Serra, "La sublimazione del grottesco," for the character of Brunello, Benedetti

for Atlante, and Zanette for brief references to Gradasso (346–7) and Rodomonte (352–4 and 363). For the *Innamorato*'s anti-crusading spirit, but without reference to Ariosto's alterations, see Ponte, *La personalità*, 80; Franceschetti, *L'*Orlando innamorato *e le sue componenti tematiche e strutturali*, 30 and 103; Bruscagli, *Studi cavallereschi*, 20, and *Orlando innamorato*, 1: xx; and Alexandre 141. My own previous work examines Ariosto's revision of Boiardo's poem, including various non-Christian characters and settings, but without fully addressing the implications of the poems' global features ("Denying Closure," "The Pathways of Knowledge in Boiardo and Ariosto," and *The Romance Epics of Boiardo, Ariosto, and Tasso*, 82–125).

6 It is not clear how familiar Calvino actually was with the *Innamorato* given that he makes various errors recounting its basic plot line in his brief summary of the poem (xxxi–xxxii) and cites as the poem's best passage one of the few scenes routinely included in anthologies (i.e., the dialogue between Orlando and Agricane). Alas, even Umberto Eco readily admits to never having read the *Orlando innamorato,* while asserting that he could nonetheless lecture on it for twenty minutes ("How to Talk about Books You Haven't Read"). I thank Charles S. Ross for bringing Eco's interview to my attention.

7 Caramella's detailed study, "L'Asia nell'*Orlando innamorato*," aimed to redress the scarce treatment of Boiardo's geography in Vernero's *Studi critici sopra la geografia nell'* Orlando furioso; it does not, however, compare geographical usage in the two poems. Ponte (*La personalità*, 87–94) and Murrin ("Trade and Fortune," and *History and Warfare*, 63–75) also offer detailed accounts regarding Boiardo's use of geography in the *Innamorato*, but not in comparison to the *Furioso.*

8 Serra ("Da Tolomeo alla Garfagnana"), Bontempelli, and Mac Carthy, likewise overlook the importance of Boiardo's precedent for Ariosto's poem.

9 Meserve, "From Samarkand to Scythia," 14.

10 For interest in geography on the part of both Borso and Ercole, see Vernero 7n2, 130n1, and Caramella 47–9. For geographical texts in the Este library 1467 inventory, see Murrin, "Trade and Fortune," 278n59.

11 Serra calls Ferrara "the major centre of geographic and cartographic studies of the peninsula" ("Da Tolomeo alla Garfagnana," 155).

12 To be precise, Guarino translated the first ten books of Strabo's *Geography* while his fellow humanist, Gregorius Tifernas, covered the remaining seven (Jones 1: xl). Donnus Nicholas Germanus's dedication of Ptolemy's *Geography* to Borso d'Este can be found in Edward Luther Stevenson's English translation of the work.

13 Milano 19–20, 68, and 80. For Ptolemy and Strabo in the Estense library inventory, see Bertoni 237, no. 69, and 250, no. 447.

14 *Trading Territories*, 32. In 1463 Borso made a payment for "unum mapamundi secundum tabulas Ptholomei" (Milano 88).

15 Remarking that "it is hard [...] to think of a historical work that is more multicultural than that of Herodotus," Knox recalls Plutarch's comment that the Greek historian was *philobarbaros,* "too fond of foreigners" (20).

16 The only part of the *Lives of Famous Captains* still extant is that dedicated to non-Roman captains, including a fairly positive entry on Hannibal.

17 For Books 1 and 2 of the *Historia imperiale* I refer to the first volume of Rizzi's edition (by volume and page number). However, because the second volume covering Books 3 and 4 is still forthcoming, I refer to Rizzi's dissertation (by page number) for Book 3, and Muratori's edition, entitled *Istoria imperiale*, for Book 4 (by column number).

18 In the preface, Boiardo explains that he has taken his history of the Saracens from "lo Alchorano de Maumeth e li cinque libri de le historie de Arabia" ("the Koran of Mohammed and the five Books of the Histories of Arabia") (1: 4), and he later cites Bernard the Treasurer and the Archbishop of Tyre as his sources when summarizing the first three crusades. Although the Koran was in fact available in three different translations in late fifteenth-century Italy (see Burman), Boiardo's insertions focus on historical events rather than religious creed. For an in-depth discussion of Boiardo's probable sources, see Andrea Rizzi's introduction and notes to his recent edition of the *Historia imperiale.* For copies of Riccobaldo's work available at the Estense court, see Rizzi, "Riccobaldo da Ferrara e Matteo Maria Boiardo."

19 Unless otherwise noted, all Italian citations of the *Milione* are from the version edited by Gabriella Ronchi. Citation references provide the chapter and sentence number, followed by the page number.

20 Matteo, "Marco Polo." For a selection of recent essays on Marco Polo in historical and literary context, see Akbari and Iannucci. Although I have not had the opportunity to read Ganim and Legassie's *Cosmopolitanism and the Middle Ages*, forthcoming in November 2012, this volume promises to be a useful resource in this regard as well.

21 One finds a "Marcho Polo de Veneciis" and a "Libro uno chiamado Marco Polo, in membrana, in vulgare" in 1436 (Cappelli 16, no. 52, and 23, no. 180), a "Marcus Paulus de Venetijs de conditionibus et consuetudinibus de Orientalium Regionum" in 1467 (Bertoni 218, no. 62), and a "Marcopollo in latino" in 1495 (Bertoni 246, no. 319). In 1457 "madama Contessa Strozzi" borrowed a "marco pollo" (Bertoni 56; Bezzola 396n), while in

1467 a courtier received a book of Marco Polo's travels directly from Borso d'Este (Lach, vol. 2; bk 2, 49). Moreover, Ercole requested "un Marco Polo" for his private study (Bertoni 19), where a copy was indeed present (as "Marcus Paulus Venetus") in 1489 (Bertoni 262).

22 Guzman notes that there are several extant manuscripts of the *Speculum historiale*, which was also "printed at least three times in the fifteenth century" (287). Milano describes a still-extant fifteenth-century manuscript of this work from the ancient Estense collection (50). Pistarino finds numerous editions of Mandeville in the last quarter of the fifteenth century, especially in Italian translation (106–7). For the composition history and reception of this work, see Higgins. For additional works on the East incorporated by both Vincent and Mandeville, see Voorbij and Deluz 428–91, respectively. For a succinct account of papal envoys and merchants in Mongol territory, see Abu-Lughod 161–70.

23 This work was dictated in French in 1307 and translated into Latin for Pope Clement V the same year (Larner 124). Its popularity is attested to by the large number of extant manuscripts and translations, including one into Spanish, *La flor de las ystorias de Orient.* Other medieval works with a geographical flavour represented in the Estense library include Brunetto Latini's *Livres dou tresor* ("Brunetto Latino in francese," Bertoni 237, no. 17) and Fazio degli Uberti's *Dittamondo* (Bertoni 224, no. 130; 230, no. 15; 241, no. 172). In addition, an otherwise unidentified work listed as "India per Ludovico de Mario de le sue cose mirabile" appears in the 1495 inventory (Bertoni 244, no. 251).

24 Referring to the period of Columbus's voyages, Edson goes on to say that "there had been little European travel in Asia since the early fourteenth century, and the two-hundred-year-old information of Marco Polo remained the most authoritative source" (210). Indeed, when Columbus consulted Toscanelli's 1474 letter envisioning a westward route to Asia, the information he found on China and Japan was derived from Marco Polo's travels (Edson 209–10). For Columbus's own marginal notes to *Il milione*, see Polo, *Il milione: Con le postille di Cristoforo Colombo.*

25 Pedani 78, 260. See also Gundersheimer for a brief account of Venice's substantial role in Ferrara's political history (31–3).

26 In this passage Pedani is referring specifically to the 1460s, but she also provides extensive examples of Middle Eastern, Mongolian, and North African ambassadors and messengers in Venice from the fourteenth to the sixteenth centuries (112–48).

27 Greppi, "Una carta per la corte." For "mappamundi" at the Este court, see Milano 88–90.

28 The translation of Columbus's letter to Gabriel Sánchez, printed in Rome in

May 1493, is still extant in the Biblioteca Estense (Greppi, "Luoghi e miti," 459).

29 Inalcik notes that "until 1569 the Italian states, primarily Venice, handled Ottoman trade with the western Christian world" (133). According to Schwoebel, moreover, between the mid-fourteenth century and the end of the fifteenth century, "all the major Italian powers at one time or another cultivated Ottoman friendship for commercial and political purposes" ("Coexistence, Conversion, and the Crusade against the Turks," 166).

30 Isabella d'Este's husband, Francesco Gonzaga, would later send his agents to the Ottoman Empire to acquire prestigious horses.

31 Examples from inventories show an abundance of Oriental carpets in Venice between the late fifteenth and early sixteenth centuries (Erdmann 538). For their circulation throughout Italy during this period, see also Aslanapa 61–101.

32 Boralevi notes that the carpets in the fresco, with their stylized geometric designs, have the classic structure of those typical of Anatolia (217).

33 The shop remained active until about 1530. See also Boralevi 217–20 and Rogers 73. For the extensive flow of material goods into Italy from the Islamic world, see, in particular, Brotton, *The Renaissance Bazaar*, Jardine, and Mack.

34 Cachey 7–8, 52–3. Petrarch's work is listed in the ducal library in both Italian and Latin: *Libro chiamado lo itinerario de Messere Francesco Petrarcha al sepolcro* (Cappelli 13, no. 15) and *Itinerarium Francisci Petrarce ad Sepulcrum* (Bertoni 218, no. 50).

35 Sanseverino's *Viaggio in Terra Santa* also notes that Borso repaid the visit by reaching him in Venice the day before his ship set sail (14 and 23). For a list of fifteenth-century pilgrimage accounts in Italian, see Rossebastiano, "La vicenda umana," 20.

36 Copies of his travelogue are documented in the 1467 inventory of the ducal library (Bertoni 225, no. 144, no. 145, and no. 147). I cite from the publication edited by Giovanni Ghinassi, entitled *Viaggio a Gerusalemme di Nicolò da Este.*

37 Rossebastiano and Fenoglio, the editors of Don Domenego's travelogue, maintain that Milliaduse measured his trip against that of Niccolò in an attempt to outdo his father. They also recall his sojourn in Florence in 1434 in the company of Feltrino Boiardo, a veteran of the earlier trip (10).

38 According to Pedani, the turbans in Italian paintings from the late fifteenth and early sixteenth centuries are designed "with great accuracy without leaving anything to fantasy" (176). Ricci notes, moreover, that "in Ferrara turbans and Turkish clothes circulated in abundance, whether authentic or

imitation," and "were used for masquerade parties, theatrical plays, and picturesque ambience" (*I turchi alle porte*, 158).

39 Pedani, however, finds him returning to Italy in 1480 "full of honours" (174). The point, in any event, is Ercole's interest in this artistic collaboration between the Neapolitan Kingdom and the Ottoman Empire.

40 A "Guerre del turcho in vulgare" listed in the Estense library inventory is not otherwise identified (Bertoni 242, no. 198), but a selection of poems about the Turkish invasions can be found in *Guerre contro i turchi (1453–1470)*. Meserve, recalling that "the Turkish 'problem' was a topic that occupied Italians of every social station," finds that particularly in the aftermath of the fall of Negroponte "an enormous amount of information circulated via oral reports, private letters, ambassadorial dispatches, and official government pronouncements" and "printing presses further disseminated stories of the doleful event by publishing both popular vernacular ballads and humanist Latin compositions" ("News from Negroponte," 472, 446). See also Pertusi; Bisaha, *Creating East and West*; and Hankins, "Renaissance Crusaders."

41 For contemporary accounts of this invasion, see Gualdo Rosa, Nuovo, and Defilippis; for a collection of essays on various aspects of this historical event, see Fonseca.

42 Hankins, "Renaisance Crusaders," 125. Hankins remarks, in fact, that during the Venetian-Turkish war "the other Italian powers looked on gleefully" (127). The *Diario ferrarese* reports that Genoa and Florence actually assisted the Turks in seizing Negroponte: "In ajuto de li quali Turchi erano le galee de Zenovisi et de Fiorentini, chè altramente non l'haveriano avuto mai" ("Helping the Turks were galleys of Genoese and Florentines, since otherwise they would have never taken it") (64).

43 For the probable complicity of Venice, see Ricci, *I turchi alle porte*, 71. The Florentines also welcomed the Turkish invasion of Otranto because it resolved their problems with the Neapolitan king, and "it was widely believed that [Lorenzo de' Medici] had been responsible for inviting the Turk into Italy in 1480" (Hankins, "Renaisance Crusaders," 125–6).

44 Alfonso did not have much success with the Turkish troops, however; three hundred of them escaped with Venetian help, given that Venice was once again on good terms with the Ottomans (Ricci, *Ossessione turca*, 36).

45 In the Ottoman-Venetian war of 1499–1502, for example, Milan and Naples were allied with the sultan Bayezid II against Venice.

46 Both Bayezid II (ruled 1481–1512) and his successor Selim I (ruled 1512–20) directed their resources mainly against non-Christian states (Housley, *The Later Crusades*, 124). See Schwoebel, *The Shadow of the Crescent*, for a detailed account of the complex relations between Latin Christendom and the Ottoman Empire extending from 1453 to 1517.

47 The Ottomans took over Jerusalem from the Mamelukes in 1517, the year following the *Furioso*'s publication. Selim's death in 1520, however, put an end to any concerted military effort before it got off the ground.

48 Ricci reminds us, for example, how the bellicose pope Julius II had talked about an expedition against the Turks yet in the end preferred to instigate a Holy League against neighbouring Venice, almost destroying it in 1509. Ironically, as Ricci goes on to note, faced with this onslaught, "the youngest and most pragmatic Venetian senators proposed calling in the Turks as allies" (*I turchi alla porta*, 74–5).

49 A "Homerus de Bello Troiano" and an "Inventio Troyane historie" were listed in the 1467 ducal library inventory (Bertoni 215, no. 24, and 216, no. 2).

50 Borso purchases a "Quinto Curtio de gestis Alexandri" (Bertoni 42); the 1467 inventory includes an "Alexandri Maximi gesta" (Bertoni 215, no. 24), a "Liber de Sestis Alexandri Imperatoris" (Bertoni 220, no. 82), and a "Liber Alexandreydos" (Bertoni 221, no. 102); the 1495 list documents an "Ariano in vulgaro di gesti de Alexandro" (Bertoni 235, no. 5), a "Guere de Alixandro" (Bertoni 242, no. 210), a "Plutarco de la fortuna de Alexandro" (Bertoni 249, no. 406), and a "Vita Lixandri in latino" (Bertoni 252, no. 501).

51 Sharon Kinoshita has brought to light the complex, and often positive, depictions of Christian-Saracen encounters in these medieval French epics, in accordance with the multicultural social reality of the Mediterranean world (*Medieval Boundaries*). See also Kay and Akbari.

52 Sberlati cites this assertion by Folena in his own exposition of the poem (177). See also the essays by Limentani collected in "*L'Entrée d'Espagne*" *e i signori d'Italia*.

53 Gritti and Montagani have recently produced a critical edition of this *Spagna ferrarese* from the only extant copy, preserved at the Biblioteca Ariostea of Ferrara. My references to the *Spagna* refer to this edition unless otherwise noted.

54 The ducal inventory had various copies of this epic, and the *ottava rima* version is still extant in the Biblioteca Estense of Modena.

55 He finds, moreover, "a definite improvement in the attitude of Italian writers towards the Saracens" over the course of the fifteenth century ("On the Saracens," 207–8).

56 In addition, "just as reason and order are associated with the great Christian hope Guerrino, so the Saracens – in this case the Persians, Arabs, and Turks – are all labeled lustful sodomites" (Vitullo 76).

57 The bibliography on the *Morgante* is rather vast. Of recent studies, see especially Polcri for the poem's moral-allegorical elements and Perrotta, "Lo spazio della corte," for its more political-ideological aspects. Although the

Morgante never appears in the Estense inventories, Ercole requests a copy of the poem in November 1478 (Tissoni Benvenuti, intro., *Inamoramento de Orlando*, 1: xii). For signs of Boiardo's awareness of the *Morgante* in the later cantos of his own poem, see Tissoni Benvenuti, intro., *Inamoramento de Orlando*, 1: xii.

58 The above paragraphs can hardly do more than note the few key Carolingian works that are most relevant to the present study. For an informative panorama of the chivalric genre with relevant bibliography, see especially Villoresi, *La fabbrica dei cavallieri* and *La letteratura cavalleresca*, 47–145. For the contemporary political relevance of select fifteenth-century chivalric works, see Perrotta, "Rifare secondo la norma" and "Alleanze necessarie." Muslim characters are also found in the novella tradition: for Boccaccio's *Decameron*, see Smarr; for Masuccio Salernitano's mid-fifteenth century *Novellino*, see Papio, "Il pericolo che viene dal mare," and Attar. The depiction of non-Christians in Italian literature predating the *Innamorato* presents a fruitful area for future study, especially given the Italian peninsula's complex relation to the Ottoman Empire traced briefly above.

59 I have not included in this study various secondary Eastern characters and sites covered in my earlier work. For the negligent King Sacripante of Circassia, the guileful King Poliferno of Orgagna, and the treacherous King Truffaldino of Baghdad, see Part One of *The Romance Epics of Boiardo, Ariosto, and Tasso.* For the courteous Tisbina, Iroldo, and Prasildo, also from Baghdad, as well as the Pleasure Palace, Castle Cruel, the Garden of Orgagna, Morgana's Lake, and the Fountain of Narcissus in India, see *Boiardo's* Orlando innamorato: *An Ethics of Desire.*

60 For the limitations of Said's critique of European orientalism for the field of medieval and Renaissance studies, see especially Kinoshita, "Deprovincializing the Middle Ages," 61–75, and Rubiés x–xiv.

61 Much, in fact, has been written over the past few decades investigating the complexity and dynamics of multicultural encounters during the Renaissance. The burgeoning field of Mediterranean studies provides a particularly relevant frame of reference for the present study by outlining economic, artistic, technological, intellectual, and cultural interaction across ethnic and religious boundaries. For an excellent overview of recent scholarship in this field, see O'Connell, "The Italian Renaissance in the Mediterranean or between East and West."

1. Angelica of Cathay

1 Quotations from Boiardo's poem refer to Tissoni Benvenuti and Montagnani's critical edition and Ross's translation. For a contemporary description

of a three-day joust decreed by Borso d'Este in May of 1464, see the *Diario ferrarese*, 45.

2 Scholarly studies have addressed Boiardo's familiarity with various versions of these narratives. Luciano Serra, for example, notes that Boiardo combines Grandonio's origin in Morocco following the *Entrée* with his link to Saracen Spain found in the *Spagna* ("Letture boiardesche," 155, 160). Limentani (141) and Sberlati (194) argue that in the poem's opening sequence Boiardo drew more on the Franco-Venetian *Entrée* than on Italian versions. Franceschetti, while finding it plausible that Boiardo also knew the popular forty-canto *Spagna maggiore*, cites specific textual allusions to the thirty-four canto *Spagna ferrarese* ("*La Spagna in rima*," 323). For additional allusions to this latter version, see Montagnani 20–8; for the character of Grandonio in the literary tradition, see Tissoni Benvenuti, "Intertestualità cavalleresca," 60–78. My intention here is not to determine which versions contained the details used by Boiardo but rather to argue that the poet deliberately presented characters familiar to his own readership in order to work against their expectations.

3 The fifteenth-century prose *Storia di Rinaldino di Montalbano*, which like the *Innamorato* opens at Pentecost ("la Pasqua pentecosta"), depicts Charlemagne holding a council to announce his intention to attack Spain (3).

4 According to Giuseppe Pardi, seating jousters at a round table was also "a very ancient custom" in Ferrara, aimed to "prevent disputes over preference" (*Diario ferrarese*, 89n).

5 Tissoni Benvenuti notes that the "barbaric" table manners of Saracens were proverbial in medieval epic (*Inamoramento de Orlando*, 1: 14n). For Saracens lying on carpets as per their custom in earlier romance epics, see Andrea da Barberino, *I reali di Francia*, VI.xx, 316, and the *Storia di Rinaldino di Montalbano*, 220. Saracens are commonly referred to as dogs in the Italian epic tradition; see, for example, *Spagna* 6.37, 8.9, and 29.45. In the *Innamorato*, Angelica shortly thereafter calls the Christian Malagise "quel can musorno" ("that old dog") (*OI* 1.2.13).

6 *Orlando innamorato*, liv. For Ross's reading of this exchange, see liii–lvi.

7 The name echoes that of Baligant, the emir of Babylon and Marsile's lord in *La chanson de Roland*. The negative depiction of Balugante is part of the Italian literary tradition. In the forty-canto *Spagna maggiore*, while Balugante is seeking allies in Persia, he also wrests Jerusalem from Christian rule (37.37), then chases Ansuigi's Christian troops towards Spain, where he arrives with the king of Persia and 160,000 troops (38.3); he kills many Christians at Roncevaux until he is in turn deprived of life by Charlemagne thanks to divine aid (38.40–3). In Pulci's *Morgante*, he is likewise killed by Charlemagne at Roncevaux (28.231).

8 My citations of the *Reali* refer to Vandelli and Gambarin's 1947 edition, but I have included book and chapter numbers in Roman numerals for easy reference to other editions.

9 As was customary, Boiardo uses "Saracen" and "pagan" interchangeably. Tolan points out that the words "Islam" and "Muslim" were virtually unknown in western European languages prior to the sixteenth century (*Saracens*, xv).

10 Identifying the capital city of Cathay as Beijing, Caramella notes that, according to estimates made by medieval European merchants and other travellers, the trip between the Don River and Beijing lasted approximately eight months (51). He suggests that the relative brevity of Angelica's (less than seven-month) trek to the Don could be due to the restriction of the size of Asia in the Catalan-Estense and Fra Mauro world maps (51–2), which he considers the most probable sources for Boiardo's geography (48–9).

11 During this period "India" was commonly referred to as both the vast expanse of Asia and, more specifically, the Far East (Silverberg 57). In the poem's first reference, Cathay would be east of Tartary and north of India in the restricted sense, thus lying between both states, whereas in the second case Cathay is simply considered to be part of a greater India.

12 Citing Ponte, Ross notes that although Boiardo placed Cathay within Media in his translation of Cornelius Nepos, in the poem he locates it in the more distant India in accordance with world maps of the time (*Orlando innamorato*, 603). Pointing to the precedent of Cornelius Nepos, Tissoni Benvenuti would situate Galafrone's Cathay inside Media, although she does acknowledge at least one of the problems that result from this placement (*Inamoramento de Orlando*, 1: 331n). Angelica's opening statement alerts us to the fact that her homeland at the "fin del mondo" ("ends of earth") (*OI* 1.1.24) is at a much greater distance from Europe than Media (western Iran).

13 All citations unless otherwise noted are from Deluz's critical edition, *Le livre des merveilles du monde,* and Moseley's translation, *The Travels of Sir John Mandeville.*

14 Lach confirms Cathay's magnificence during this period, calling it "the largest, wealthiest, and most populous land of the thirteenth century" (vol. 1; bk 1, 36).

15 Columbus refers to Cathay various times in his writings. In his 1493 letter to Luis de Santángel about his voyage to "India," he remarks that one of the islands was so large that he believed it to be part of the mainland in the "provincia de Catayo" ("province of Cathay") (*Textos y documentos completos*, 220). The Latin translation of Columbus's letter that circulated

in Italy similarly reads, "ut non insulam: sed continentem Chatai provinciam esse crediderim" (*La scoperta*, 61).

16 This is not a case of erased alterity connected to an espousal of empire building, as De Weever detects in medieval epics in which a French knight acquires a Saracen kingdom when its princess falls in love with him (xxv–xxvi). Here it is Angelica who is in control. As Kinoshita notes, "In the conventional language of epic [...] the Saracen queen is indistinguishable from any beautiful woman of high station" (*Medieval Boundaries*, 184). As Ross points out, moreover, "like Boiardo, Marco Polo does not describe the people he visits in physical terms that would suit what we see in modern China" ("From Asia," 226). For Angelica in relation to previous Saracen females in fifteenth-century Italian literature, see especially Villoresi, "Le donne e gli amori."

17 Ross notes that Ranaldo's unmanned ship took him not only beyond the strait of Gilbraltar but around the southern tip of Africa, even though Vasco da Gama's historic voyage did not take place until 1497 (*Orlando innamorato*, 573n). See Bruscagli (*Orlando innamorato*, 1: 162n) and Tissoni Benvenuti (*Inamoramento de Orlando*, 1: 256–60) for various classical and medieval precedents for the description of the sumptuous palace.

18 In this she distances herself from the treacherous character Marchino and his wife, who commit heinous deeds motivated by unrequited and jealous passions. As she explains to Ranaldo: "Ben ti confesso che io son tanto acesa / Che io potrebe ussir for de ogni ragione: / Ma che nocer potesse a tua persona, / Questo pensier al tutto lo abandona!" ("I feel, I must confess, such flames, / I've lost my grip, I'm half insane. But I / could never do you harm: / that is a thought you must discard") (*OI* 1.9.15). For more on the Pleasure Palace and Castle Cruel episodes, see my *Boiardo's* Orlando innamorato*: An Ethics of Desire*. These two fictitious sites, in any case, are placed far from inhabited land and not related to any geopolitical realities, recalling the medieval tendency to place strange creatures and monsters outside the reaches of the known world.

19 The narrator's explanation that each year one hundred women are captured and rounded up for transport at Circassia (*OI* 1.14.29) may be geographically determined. Circassians made up a large part of the slave population from the Ottoman Empire to Egypt, sometimes with the involvement of Italian trading cities (Abu-Lughod 214).

20 See, for example, Fahy's "Three Early Renaissance Treatises on Women."

21 Quotations from Ariosto's poem refer to Marco Dorigatti's critical edition, *Orlando furioso secondo la princeps del 1516*, while for the English I have used Guido Waldman's translation of the 1532 edition whenever possible.

My own translations are in brackets. According to standard practice, the 1516 and 1532 editions are designated by the letters A and C, respectively.

22 Many readers of the poem have noted Angelica's role as "prey to be conquered," as Santoro puts it (*L'anello di Angelica*, 61). Finucci writes: "Running away in fright from erotic and erratic pursuits is, after all, Angelica's most recurrent activity. [...] The possibility that she could be self-confident and self-reliant is unimaginable within the libidinal economy that permeates her presence in the text" (111). At the same time, Finucci notes that her reading of Angelica "as a narcissistic, indifferent woman would not work for Boiardo's Angelica, who is both pursuer and pursued" (274).

23 The friar is nonetheless punished through his later imprisonment. Rajna points out this episode's resemblances to another *Innamorato* moment in which a palmer attempts to rape Fiordelisa by the same method and with the same failed result (*Le fonti*, 196–7).

24 As Finucci writes regarding this scene, "Ariosto does not fail to eroticize and aestheticize each detail in his description. With no veil to cover her, as he coyly reminds his readers, Angelica becomes a spectacle; her body – carefully constructed by combining parts – is described as nude rather than naked, and thus open to possession and ready to claim" (123). The voyeuristic nature of these episodes has found expression in the visual tradition. The painting *Angelica and the Hermit* by Peter Paul Rubens is taken up mostly by Angelica's naked body sprawled across its diagonal, with her pubis featured in the foreground. In *Ruggiero Delivers Angelica* by Jean Auguste Dominque Ingres, Angelica's upright naked body – wrists tied together above her shoulders so as to expose her breasts – emerges from the darkness of the surrounding rocks. Crossing over her leg is Ruggiero's lance as it penetrates the mouth of the sea-monster below. These illustrations can be found in Lee 14 and 16. Other artists inspired by Ariosto's poetic rendition of Angelica's naked body in these scenes include Tiepolo and Andrea de Chirico. For their illustrations, see Prampolini 159 and 231.

25 In the 1532 edition, Ariosto changes "peregrina" to "vagabonda."

26 Referring to this thirty-eight-line soliloquy, Diana Shemek remarks, "If Angelica is Ariosto's figure for femininity in the poem, then it is significant that these are virtually the only words she utters in all forty-six cantos of the *Furioso*" (60).

27 For Ariosto's textual allusions to this latter couple in *Thebaid* 10, see Rajna, *Le fonti*, 253–6, and Cabani 23.

28 Lee notes that the text does not make clear whether both or only one did the carving, but points out that "it was Angelica who carried the tool kit" (43).

29 Although previous studies of the *Furioso* have pointed out classical allu-

sions in these scenes, they have not taken notice of Ariosto's systematic and ideologically charged geographic doubling of Medoro. Sacchi, however, examines the ambivalence towards the character in later chivalric works: "The judgment on Medoro always oscillates between class and ethnic-religious disdain, all however complicated by the fact that Angelica herself is a pagan (but a queen) and by way of compensation Medoro is very beautiful and therefore not a 'Moor' to the core" (167). He notes that Medoro is denigrated for his provenance, whether simply as "un vil Moro" ("a vile Moor") in Bartolomeo Horiuolo's *Di Ruggero* or as a vile *white* Moor ("un vil moro bianco") in Aretino's *Astolfeida* (167). For the varying depiction of Medoro in later works, see also Bruscagli, *Studi cavallereschi*, 86–101.

30 Cabani refers more generally to the "nullity of the character of Medoro, object of a bizarre erotic choice" (20). Yet whereas Cabani attributes the contradictory depiction of Medoro to the romance genre that does not require coherent characterization, I have been arguing instead that Ariosto deliberately presents Medoro through two different prisms, effectively Hellenizing the African character.

31 Various critics have taken issue with this conventional ending. Lee, for example, maintains that Angelica's role already comes to a close with her enamourment: "With her love settled on Medoro, her characteristic, autonomous life vanishes and her generative force in the poem's action is finished" (30). See also Finucci 142–3.

32 After all, Ippolito d'Este obtained the archbishopric of Esztergom in Hungary thanks to the marriage of his aunt Beatrice d'Aragona to Hungary's king Matthias Corvinus, and he later became the archipresbyter of St Peter's in Rome thanks to the marriage of his brother Alfonso to Lucrezia Borgia, daughter of the Valencian pope Alexander VI.

2. Gradasso of Sericana

1 Caramella points out that Fra Mauro's world map places Sericana in the Far East, in southern China (58). Citing Galafrone's subsequent reference to Sericana as located past India (*OI* 2.5.55), Bruscagli suggests that Boiardo deliberately keeps the location of the region imprecise (*Orlando innamorato*, 1: 79n). Notwithstanding the realm's lack of specificity, Ross points out that "Boiardo offers, through his character King Gradasso, perhaps the earliest reference in Western literature to the coastal waters of China" ("From Asia," 222).

2 William of Rubruck, for example, maintained that the inhabitants of Cathay were originally the Seres (119).

3 As Tissoni Benvenuti notes, Gradasso's plan to fight Charlemagne and all the knights of Christendom (*OI* 1.1.7) is "only an accidental consequence of the fact that the possessors of the things he desires are Christians" (*Inamoramento de Orlando*, 1: 8n).

4 Caramella points out that Boiardo affirmed the possibility of circumnavigating Africa through Gradasso's voyage from India to France – as well as Ranaldo's later journey in the opposite direction (136–7). Ross suggests that Gradasso's sea route is based upon Marco Polo's return voyage to Venice in 1290 ("From Asia," 222–3).

5 Ross has recently proposed that the King of Sericana's Far Eastern origin, sophistication, and love for horses were inspired by Marco Polo's depiction of the Mongol Kublai Khan ("From Asia," 230). Although it is plausible that Boiardo had the Mongols in mind when creating Gradasso, Kublai's sedentary style of rulership is at odds with this character's unbounded ambition. In any event, I would argue that resemblances between *Innamorato* characters and historical figures remain nebulous at this early stage of the poem and are only developed beginning with the appearance of Agricane (chapter 3).

6 Although Boiardo is not interested in describing the attire of his actual Eastern protagonists, in this scene he depicts the orientalizing look of the demon impersonating Gradasso's messenger by noting the rings in his ears, his turban, and his long gown with gold stripes, likening him to a Persian emir (*OI* 1.5.34).

7 Noting the ridiculous figure that Astolfo cuts in various versions of this episode, Ferrero examines in particular *Li fatti di Spagna* where he "conducts himself and speaks like an authentic buffoon" (524). For more on the figure of Astolfo/Estous prior to the *Innamorato*, see also Santoro, "L'Astolfo ariostesco," 195–201; Cossutta 463–83; Limentani 117–19; and Sberlati.

8 Since the *Spagna ferrarese* does not develop this comic scene, I cite from the forty-canto version edited by Catalano, commonly referred to as the *Spagna maggiore*. Scholars have pointed out that Catalano's edition presents a "hybrid" text because it incorporates variants from different manuscripts (see, most recently, Gritti 65n), but it is still useful in that it offers a testimony of the figure of Astolfo circulating at the time.

9 Andrea Canova points out a similarly comic portrayal of Astolfo in the late fifteenth-century *Vendetta di Falconetto* (101–6). After being captured by Saracens the knight professes a desire to convert to Islam and fight against his former companions, yet once released he claims that he was simply playacting in order to deceive the Saracens. Contrasting this episode with Astolfo's actions in the *Innamorato*, Canova remarks, "here too it is all a joke, only that this time Astolfo is the prankster and not the butt" (106).

10 Indeed, Tissoni Benvenuti notes, "The main action of the first seven cantos of the *Innamorato* creates a sort of enclosed poem that – following the clear intention of the author to overturn traditional stereotypes – sees Astolfo as the absolute protagonist: a poem that could also be entitled *Astolfeide*. We find in these cantos the beginning of the paradoxical revaluation of Astolfo, which will have its apotheosis in the *Furioso*" ("Intertestualità cavalleresca," 72).

11 The verse was modified in 1532 to: "Abbial chi aver lo vuol con lite e guerra: / io d'averlo con pace più disio" ("Let him who wants to pick a fight to win the steed do so – I prefer to win him peacefully") (*OF* 33.94 C).

12 *Le fonti*, 59 and 422. Gradasso's action and attitude blatantly contradict even Ariosto's prior avowal of his courtesy and magnanimous heart (*OF* 29.100 A; 31.101 C).

13 See Praloran 127–42 for an extended discussion of this combat.

14 Zanette sees this as a deus-ex-machina solution that ultimately diminishes Orlando's heroism as much as it offends Gradasso. Orlando, however, at least has the motivation of avenging the treacherous murder of his friend.

3. Agricane of Tartary

1 Referring to the *Spagna* as "perhaps the most important of all" the chivalric works available to Boiardo as a point of departure for his new stories, Bruscagli suggests that even the poet's anti-Carolingian move to avoid Roncevaux and portray Orlando uncharacteristically as *innamorato* can be best appreciated when set against this work – "not only as a refusal to retrace the well-known moments in the life of the paladin, but above all as an echo and allusive distortion of that very familiar text" (*Orlando innamorato*, 1: ix–x). Tissoni Benvenuti considers cantos XIII–XIV of the *Spagna ferrarese* as one of the models "most present" in the Albracà episode (*Inamoramento de Orlando*, 1: 321n).

2 In the *Entrée*, Orlando experiences a twinge of desire for the sultan's daughter before his thoughts return to his Christian fiancée (v. 12562–4, 2:166), but this hint of a potential romance not only remains undeveloped in the Italian *Spagna* narratives but is completely eliminated.

3 In the *Spagna maggiore*, the sultan's daughter requests a Christian husband and is promptly married off to Ansuigi (*Sp. magg*. 20.20–1).

4 Upon occupying Spanish cities, the Frankish troops customarily give the inhabitants the choice of conversion or death (*Spagna* 5.30, 23.40).

5 Tellingly, while Galafrone's alliances stretch across vast areas, including Circassia, Media, Turchia, and Babilonia (the rough equivalents of the Caucasus, western Iran, Turkey, and Iraq), western Europe remains completely out

of the picture (*OI* 1.10.39–40). Although Angelica's messenger tells Orlando that he is traversing the entire world ("tuto il mondo") looking for help for his queen, he only mentions travelling through Media and Circassia (*OI* 1.6.40).

6 Although Agricane's status as the ruler of Tartary has been routinely noted, the implications of his identity as a Mongol khan have not been taken into consideration.

7 The Armenian monk Hayton similarly writes, "Only in the west is Cathay bordered by another kingdom, that of Tars [Tartars]" (*The Flower of Histories of the East,* bk 1, ch. 1). Ponte maintains that Giovanni da Pian del Carpine's *Historia Mongalorum* was known to Boiardo, citing a detail from the earlier work that Boiardo included in his *Historia imperiale* (*La personalità*, 89n48). Boiardo's probable sources for Mongol history and custom, as well as their availability at the Estense court, are noted in the introduction of this study.

8 See Lomantsov for descriptions and images of these early Mongol flags.

9 Caramella, while locating Orgagna in northern Iran (44), notes references to variants of the name in medieval maps and travellers' accounts (146–7). The point is that early readers of the poem could have associated the realm of Orgagna with a region of central Asia under Tartar-Mongol domination (Falchetta 606).

10 The horse, sun, and moon symbols have survived in Mongolian heraldry until today: the official Mongolian coat of arms includes the horse (the national symbol), while their national emblem, the *soyombo*, is an abstract design representing a flamed sun together with the moon, the earth, and water.

11 Boiardo may have invented Agricane's name based on that of Marco Polo's Argon Khan, the "signore di tuttutto i Levante" ("ruler of the entire East") (*Mil.* 18.11, 19–20).

12 While the attempt to win a bride by force is a motif common to the literature of many cultures, Olschki notes that it was particularly prevalent in tales elaborated by Mongol story-tellers and singers in various centres of Tartar expansion in Asia (*L'Asia di Marco Polo*, 54n35).

13 This map, listed in the 1488 inventory, can still be found at the Biblioteca Estense in Modena. Edson notes that the Catalan Atlas of 1375, a fragment of which can also be found in Modena (82), depicts an elaborate caravan of Tartars (198). This atlas is the first surviving world map to make extensive use of Marco Polo's travels (Edson 86).

14 See Caramella 54–5, Ponte, *La personalità*, 89n; Bruscagli, *Orlando innamorato*, 1: 121n; Murrin, *The Allegorical Epic*, 75.

15 While Boiardo uses Cathay to refer to both the region and its capital, in this instance it can only mean the latter since Angelica would not have fled beyond the western borders of her father's vast realm in order to escape from a suitor arriving from that same direction.

16 It is suggestive, moreover, that incidents from this siege find parallels in Boiardo's poem. Just as "military and political leaders retreated into fortress-villages outside" Beijing (Man 139), Angelica fled to the nearby fortress of Albracà. Subsequently, as "Beijing held out, isolated" (Man 136), the Jin emperor's general betrayed him from within the city, staging a coup and declaring himself regent; in Boiardo's poem Trufaldino betrays his allies and takes command of Albracà. In time the treacherous general was assassinated by an army commander (Man 138) just as Trufaldino is killed by Ranaldo.

17 *Chronica Majora*, cited in Komroff xiii. See Komroff for more on the European perception of the havoc wreaked by the Mongols.

18 Although Gradasso had earlier led a destructive march on his way to France, once Boiardo links this kind of excess to the Tartars, he refrains from describing it elsewhere in the poem.

19 Vitullo traces this recurring episode from its French origins to its Italian rewritings, noting that Roland first uses rhetoric to try to convert Saracens in the *Entrée d'Espagne* (81). In the various *Spagna* narratives, the Christians and Saracens find numerous occasions to deride each other's faith and to attempt to convert the other to their own. For additional chivalric works in which warring knights argue for their respective religions, see Bruscagli, "L'*Innamorato*, la *Spagna*, il *Morgante*," 120.

20 Reichenbach compares the conversion scene in the *Innamorato* and the *Spagna in rima*, noting that Ferraù does not convert in either the *Entrée* or the *Spagna in prosa* (22–32). See also Franceschetti, "*La Spagna in Rima*," and L'Orlando innamorato *e le sue componenti tematiche e strutturali*, 107–9 and 244–55.

21 Alexandre also points out this episode's departure from its Carolingian precedent: "If their duel owes much to that famous one between Orlando and Ferraù in *La Spagna*, as is well known, nevertheless it is worth insisting on the vast difference in the motivation of the action: Agricane dies because of love, whereas Ferraù for his faith and fatherland" (132).

22 When in a fierce duel prior to their final combat both knights ask for divine aid – "De il suo Dio si ricorda ognon di loro" ("Each one recalled to mind his God") (*OI* 1.16.11) – Boiardo does not say exactly which god Agricane has in mind.

23 Nor, despite this "pagan" aura, can Agricane be likened to the figure of the

pagan king who in some medieval epics converts to Christianity in the midst of a crusade and subsequently "attacks and defeats the pagan armies and destroys the idols he once worshipped" (Tolan, *Sons of Ishmael*, 67; for Tolan's discussion of such examples, see 66–78).

24 For his more extended comments and notes, see *Orlando innamorato*, x–xvi and 341–52. Montagnani has also recently argued that the "profound structural similarities [...] draw greater attention to the ideological divergence, the deliberate distancing on Boiardo's part from his literary source" (25).

25 On the theme of jealous love-struck rivals, Tissoni Benvenuti notes echoes from Boccaccio's *Teseida* (*Inamoramento de Orlando*, 1: 527n–42n).

26 Paratore has argued for a deeper thematic affinity as well: "Studying carefully to appropriate the technique of epic narrative as it came to him from the Iliadic books of the *Aeneid*, Boiardo found in these books that miraculous illumination of humanity in the soul of the warriors, and he let himself be controlled by it, following its revealing power at least in the episode of Agricane" (364).

27 According to Silverberg, "Genghis himself had no strong religious convictions but was content to observe the simple pagan shamanism of his forefathers" (79–80).

28 Chambers writes, "The story of Kuyuk's baptism was almost certainly true since it is recorded by the Moslem historian Juvaini, but it is more likely to have been motivated by self-interest than by profound conviction" (130).

29 Kublai's mother was among the prominent Mongols who converted to Nestorian Christianity; her sons subsequently built a "temple of the cross" in her honour (Jagchid and Hyer 189).

30 Bedrosian (in Hayton) notes the Armenian monk's "tendency to emphasize (or overemphasize) Christian currents among the Mongols" in an attempt to portray them as potential allies of western Europe.

31 He reports having replied on this occasion, "Our Scriptures teach that the servant of God must not dispute, only be kind to all. I am thus ready to explain, without hatred, the faith and hope of the Christians to who ever wishes to question me" (173).

32 As Nederman puts it, William of Rubruck's account, "however unwittingly, illustrates how a devout medieval Christian might learn, in the face of circumstance, to conduct himself with a measure of tolerance, without surrendering his certainty about the ultimate rectitude of his own convictions" (55).

33 Man notes further that faith in "the supreme power, Blue Heaven," which "watched over events below with a remote benevolence [...] was common to all Central Asian peoples" (52–3). For the Mongol concept of an "abstract"

heaven (i.e., not personified or anthropomorphized), see Jagchid and Hyer 163–5. Mongolia is still called the land of "the Eternal Blue Sky" (Robinson).

34 During the course of their previous battle, Orlando at one point wished to himself that Agricane were a Christian (*OI* 1.16.9) but never engaged in proselytizing. Moreover, as Alhaique Pettinelli notes, "his desire to convert the pagan does not derive, as in the tradition, from a generic impulse of all Christians toward all pagans, but is tied to the individual merit of the person, to his 'virtù,' that makes the count wish that Agricane would enter the group of the chosen ones" (*L'immaginario cavalleresco*, 28).

35 The debate over the proper activities of the knight was familiar enough in medieval and Renaissance Europe and continued well into the sixteenth century. In Castiglione's *Libro del cortegiano*, arms constitute the courtier's first duty, but he must have many other interests as well (1.17–2.41). See Cossutta 91–169 for these contrasting positions in the context of Ferrarese humanism.

36 Cossutta writes that Orlando's words "re-propose the concepts expressed by Pico" in the *De hominis dignitate* (126–7), yet it is worth noting that Boiardo's poem predates the oration.

37 For increasingly intolerant attitudes towards Muslims in late fifteenth-century Spain, see Echevarría.

38 Cardini remarks that here "the Turks and the other infidels, rather than armies of the Antichrist, carry out the role of Gentile candidates destined for final conversion" (143). For a fuller discussion of this treatise, see Nederman 85–97. For Nicholas of Cusa's Christian humanism and method of "concordance," see Cassirer. For the proposed peaceful conversion of Saracens during this period, see Schwoebel, "Coexistence, Conversion, and the Crusade against the Turks," 174–9.

39 That challenge will be effectively taken up instead by Torquato Tasso, who refashions the episode as the tragic climax of the unrequited love story between the Italo-Norman crusader Tancredi and the Ethiopian-born female warrior Clorinda (*Gerusalemme liberata* 12.2–70).

40 Her reference to Galafrone as the "Great Khan," moreover, is confusing, since it would have made him a Mongol himself rather than a victim of Mongol expansion.

4. Mandricardo, Son of Agricane

1 The only other khan to seriously threaten the West, Tamerlane, has been referred to as the "sword of Islam" (Marozzi).

2 Marco Polo also notes that there are some who adore fire (*Mil.* 74.31, 95) and that Kublai Khan was interested in receiving "olio de la làmpana ch'arde al sepolcro <di Cristo> in Gerusalem" ("oil from the lamp that burns in the Holy Sepulchre at Jerusalem") (*Mil.* 7.7, 9). For additional references to the Mongol worship of fire, see Odorico 217; for fire in purification ceremonies, see Giovanni da Pian del Carpine (11) and William of Rubruck (182–3). According to Heissig, "The idea that fire is holy and to be worshipped is one of the oldest religious conceptions of the Mongols" (69).

3 Jagchid and Hyer note, moreover, that the importance of fire as an object of worship for Shamanistic Mongols is sometimes attributed to the influence of Zoroastrianism (169).

4 As ducal commissioner in the Garfagnana under Duke Alfonso, Ariosto upholds the fairness of returning contested goods until a dispute is resolved (letter of June 9, 1523). Ariosto's letters are available in Stella's edition and Looney's translation.

5 Whereas Praloran goes on to view this "ethical perspective" as "an inheritance of the classical epic world" (117), I find it in keeping with Ariosto's systematically negative depiction of non-Christian heroes.

5. Marphisa, Eastern Queen

1 For the common practice of demonizing Saracen women in medieval French epic by depicting them as ugly or monstrous, see De Weever 53–109. Tomalin writes that with Marphisa "Boiardo created the prime example of the independent woman: [...] she is tough, dedicated to a life of martial activity and still allowed to be beautiful" (16).

2 Citation references for *Il Guerrin Meschino* provide the book and chapter number, followed by the page number.

3 Ariosto's contemporary Lodovico Dolce had already linked Marphisa (and Bradamante) to Penthesilea and Camilla (Rajna, *Le fonti*, 49n1). Noting the variant spellings of Marpesia and Marthesia in Boccaccio and his sources, Baldan argues that Boiardo had this particular Amazon in mind when choosing a name for his warrior queen. The links between the two characters, however, do not go beyond their generic role of female warrior and ruler.

4 Roche notes this structural containment of Marphisa's classical counterparts, albeit in comparison to Ariosto's character only: "Penthesilea and Camilla are sports in the epic game; noble and valiant they are, but defeated, killed, got rid of" (114).

5 This connection makes her likewise the brother of Rugiero, who recounts the circumstances of his birth in Book Three of the *Orlando innamorato* (discussed in the following section). Since I only had access to a later edition

of Agostini's continuation (1545), I am grateful to Marco Dorigatti for transcribing the characters' names and verses cited in this study from the earliest extant edition of Book Four (Venice: Georgio de Rusconi, 1506), available in a single copy held at the Biblioteca Nazionale Marciana, Venice.

6 Although Galiziella is not present in the earlier French *Aspremont* narratives (Rajna, *Le fonti*, 49), Allaire has located her in six extant Italian texts, noting that she is most fully developed in Andrea da Barberino's version ("The Warrior Woman," 35).

7 Franceschetti disagrees with Rajna, arguing that Marphisa appears in the poem much earlier than Rugiero and participates in comic scenes that would hardly be fitting for an ancestor of the Estense ("L'*Orlando innamorato* e la tradizione dell'*Aspremont*," 520).

8 For *donne guerriere* in Italian chivalric literature, see Rajna, *Le fonti*, 45–53; Bendinelli Predelli, "La donna guerriera"; Allaire, "The Warrior Woman" and "Babes in Arms"; Tomalin 33–52; Pasqualino, "Dama Rovenza"; Alhaique Pettinelli, "L'*Orlando innamorato* e la tradizione cavalleresca in ottave," 395–6; and Villoresi, "Le donne e gli amori," 19–20, 23–7. For Amazonian themes in popular epic productions, travel accounts, and fifteenth-century fresco cycles, see Stoppino 61–71.

9 Previous critical studies have not addressed this startling transformation in Marphisa's character. Roche, for example, maintains that in the second half of the poem she "serves as a double for both Bradamante and her twin brother Ruggiero and mediates the marriage that will occur in canto 46" (133). Wiggins views her as "a loner, an isolated being, whose outrage remains unmitigated to the last" (186). Stoppino maintains that "it is Marfisa's stability, almost her inflexibility, that identify her throughout the poem" (82).

10 Troiano, in fact, did not even participate in the expedition against Calabria (*Asp.* 1.12.1–9, 14).

11 Even though later Ariosto seems to acknowledge that Almonte was acting alone (*OF* 34.5 A; 38.5 C), this passing thought is not sufficient to reverse the previous multiple assertions of Troiano's guilt.

12 By contrast, as noted above, Marphisa's conversion for love of her brother in Niccolò degli Agostini's fourth book contains no hint of animosity against either her maternal ancestors or Saracens in general.

6. Agramante of Biserta (Tunisia)

1 Comparing the *Innamorato* to both the prose version by Andrea da Barberino and a late fifteenth-century anonymous *cantare*, Franceschetti posits that Boiardo was gleaning his information from prior accounts that served as sources to both narratives but are now lost ("L'*Orlando innamorato* e la

tradizione dell'*Aspremont*," 531). Tissoni Benvenuti notes that the *Aspremont* is the Carolingian title most represented in the Estense library between 1436 and 1488, but that it is impossible to determine which versions it held ("Rugiero," 69–70). In this study I refer to Andrea da Barberino's prose *Aspramonte*, which Tissoni Benvenuti finds the version closest to Boiardo's retelling ("Rugiero," 71). As in the case of the *Spagna* narratives, my intention is not to compare variants among extant versions, but to investigate the use that Boiardo makes of the storyline.

2 In a letter calling for Charlemagne's submission, Agolante refers to himself as "re delle due parti maggiori del mondo, cioè Asia e Africa, per la virtù di Maometto che à fatto crescere e' venti africani [per modo che la nostra forza] è giunta nel Farro di Messina, e tutte le forze di Puglia e di Calavria sottomettiamo alla nostra singnoria" ("king of the two major parts of the world, i.e., Asia and Africa, for the virtue of Mohammed who caused the winds of Africa to grow so that our force has reached the port of Messina, and we have placed all the forces of Apulia and Calabria under our dominion") (*Asp.* 2.5.3–6, 50).

3 The actual dates for these rulers of Italy are 825–75 and 905–66, respectively. Robert Bartlett reminds us that in fact "at the beginning of the tenth century [Rome] was located on the edge of Latin Christendom, within a hundred miles of Saracen bases and Greek churches, its port prey to Muslim pirates" (294). For recent studies of this turbulent period, see Arnaldi, Kreutz, Pryo, and Tolan, *Saracens*, especially 71–7.

4 "E, giunto a Roma, <là pose campo> e prese <dal ponte di Adriano oltro al Tebre> tuta la citade, e tene per dispregio e' soi cavalli ne la chiesia di Sancto Pietro, <dove egli anchora sceleratissime cose in obrobrio di nostra religione fece publicamente fare" ("And, having reached Rome, they set up camp there and took over all of the city from the bridge of Hadrian across the Tiber, and in contempt kept their horses in the Church of Saint Peter's, where they publicly carried out further wicked deeds in the disgrace of our religion") (119r). In citing from the *Historia imperiale*, I have maintained Rizzi's use of triangular brackets to indicate text for which there is no known source.

5 This is part of the historical account by Boiardo's Turpino that opens Book Two, discussed below.

6 Fazio degli Uberti also writes that Charlemagne "in Aspramonte / fece a gli African sentir tristizia" ("made the Africans suffer in Aspramonte") (*Dittamondo* 2.21.17–18), although his subsequent reference to Orlando as the one who killed Ferraù and Don Chiaro indicates that the author had in mind the epic narrative.

7 Although rigid divisions between epic and history were not always made during this period, Boiardo clearly states that in this work he is interested exclusively in the latter. In concluding his section on Charlemagne, for example, he remarks that "di lui sono molte cose favolegiate" ("many things are fabled about him") without deigning to mention any details (116v). Indeed, discrediting the Carolingian epic tradition that depicted Saracens attacking Christians at the pass of Roncevaux, he follows Charlemagne's biographer Einhard in asserting that the Frankish rear guard was routed by local Basques. Rizzi notes that Boiardo even omits the legends and myths about Charlemagne included by Riccobaldo (*The "Historia imperiale,"* 1: 166n). Tristano also characterizes him as "a conscientious and critical historian" in this section of the work (145–51).

8 See, for example, *Aspramonte* 2.10.20–1, 55 and 3.33.26–7, 145–6. The genealogical tie between Agolant and Alexander is also present in the French *Chanson d'Aspremont* where it likewise serves to justify his ambition for imperial rule (vv 459–61).

9 Ercole d'Este was said to have "believed in the thaumaturgic properties of histories such as Rufus's *Gestae Alexandri*" (Rizzi, *The "Historia imperiale,"* 1: xxxix). In addition to the various titles concerning Alexander listed in the ducal library, noted in the introduction, a copy of "Le historie di Alexandro Macedonio" was documented in Ercole's private wardrobe closet (Bertoni 51n3). See also Bruscagli, "Prove di commento."

10 Moreover, Boiardo's claim that Alexander saw the sea and sky "per sua arroganza" reads like a correction of the *Entrée*'s ekphrasis in which it is said that Alexander "conquist por largeçe la tere e le marin" ("conquered the earth and sea through his largesse") (v. 10431). For Alexander in the *Entrée*, see Limentani 180–9.

11 Ponte, *La personalità*, 81, and Murrin, *History and Warfare*, 59–63. For links to Statius's *Thebaid* as well, see Zampese 193–9.

12 Heckel observes that Curtius Rufus had earlier enhanced his biography of Alexander through allusions to Livy and Herodotus (7–9).

13 Although Searles suggests Roxane as a possible source, he nevertheless concedes that she "is not credited with any of the adventures which befell Elidonia" (45). On the contrary, Plutarch recounts how a pregnant Roxane murders Stateira and her sister after Alexander's death (*Life of Alexander*, 72). In Thomas de Kent's *Roman d'Alexandre*, Alexander is tricked by the oriental queen Candace into becoming her lover for a short period, but the moral of this inserted episode is the unparalleled astuteness of women, not the overwhelming power of love. Dronke also refers to Henri d'Andeli's *Lai d'Aristote* (c. 1220) in which Alexander falls in love with an Indian princess,

but the focus is on the contrast between the latter's defence of natural love and the recriminatory arguments of Aristotle (lvi).

14 Curtius Rufus 8.4.23–5, 10.3.11–12; Plutarch, *Life of Alexander*, 46, 66.

15 When justifying his marriage to Roxane, Alexander purportedly tells his men that "Achilles [...] had also shared his bed with a captive" (8.4.26). He later stresses the women's concubine status even as he explains his program of consolidation to his newly trained Asian troops: "That is why I married the daughter of the Persian Oxyartes, feeling no hesitation about producing children from a captive. Later on, when I wished to extend my bloodline further, I took Darius' daughter as a wife and I saw to it that my closest friends had children by our captives, my intention being that by this sacred union I might erase all distinction between conquered and conqueror. [...] Asia and Europe are now one and the same kingdom" (10.3.11–13).

16 Davis Hanson notes that in these two essays Plutarch lauds Alexander's "promises to craft a new hybrid inclusive culture devoted to ideals that transcended race, religion, or nationalism" (*Life of Alexander*, xiii). For the uniqueness of Alexander's policy, see Fredricksmeyer.

17 This idea of intermixing was also, after all, at the basis of Virgil's *Aeneid*, which imagines the Roman people as descendants of the peninsula's native inhabitants and displaced Trojans.

18 Even Turpino's telegraphic summary – "Fo d'amor preso nel regno de Egypto / D'una dongiella, et ebela per manza" ("[He] was grasped in Egypt's realm by Love. / He took a maiden as his [lady love]") (*OI* 2.1.5) – might also be said to contain a trace of love poetry. Bruscagli points out the Provençal origin of the term "amanza" (*amansa*) when earlier in the poem Feraguto tells Orlando that Angelica "prima fu mia che la tua manza" ("belongs to me, not you") (*OI* 1.3.73) (*Orlando innamorato*, 1: 73n). The term can be found in Boccaccio's *Teseida* ("amanza"; 5.40) as well as Italian Renaissance love lyrics (e.g., the anonymous "O occhi, manza mia" and "La manza mia si chiama").

19 See also the oracle's pronouncement to Alexander (53–5). This popularizing work was translated into several languages. I cite from a translation of the Armenian version, considered by the editor as the most faithful to the earliest manuscript tradition of the work (Wolohojian 3–5). Ten of the forty extant manuscripts in Armenian are located on Italian soil, in Venice (Wolohojian 21).

20 Strabo died in 20 C.E., and Ptolemy worked at the library there between 127 and 150 C.E.

21 Balard notes that "in the last decades of the fifteenth century Venice sent an average of seven galleys each year to Alexandria and Beirut" (209).

22 For Alexander's links to Rollant in the *Entrée d'Espagne*, see Sturm-Maddox; for his links to Guerrino in Andrea da Barberino's prose romance, see Allaire, *Andrea da Barberino*, 17–18. For positive as well as negative views of Alexander in the medieval period, see Cary, Frugoni, and Dronke.

23 Inalcik writes: "With the possession of Constantinople, the capital of the Eastern Roman Empire, Mehmed regarded himself as the only legitimate heir of the Roman Empire. [...] The Greek scholars and Italian humanists at his court instructed him in Roman history" (56). Babinger likewise writes of him, "All our informants agree that the young sultan took an interest in the heroes of classical antiquity. Alexander the Great, whose life and exploits were probably familiar to him from the Islamic legends, struck him as a shining example, which he was determined to emulate" (499). For contacts between Italians (especially Venetians and Neapolitans) and the Ottoman court, see especially Babinger, Inalcik, Pedani, Howard, and Ricci, *I turchi alle porte*.

24 A Venetian informant from the period depicts the Ottoman ruler in the following way: "In his unconfined ambition to emulate and indeed to outdo Alexander the Great and Julius Caesar, he aspired to create an empire, a stable world power [...]. His drive to rule, to reduce the whole world to his power, knew no bounds. Alexander of Macedonia, so he said, had marched into Asia with a smaller army; now the times had changed, for he was marching from East to West" (Babinger 410).

25 Ciarambino posits that the invasion recounted in the *Aspramonte* was already a response to the growing Turkish menace (60–2), and Limentani has found references to the contemporary Turks in the *Entrée* (358–78). This is clearly an area that begs further study.

26 For Tissoni Benvenuti's dating of the poem, see her introduction, *Inamoramento de Orlando*, 1: xi–xxi. The *Diario ferrarese* entry for 31 July 1470, relates the Ottoman conquest of Negroponte in chilling terms: "se dise che, intrati che furno dicti Turchi in Negroponte, amazorno tutti universalmente li Cristiani che ivi se ritrovorno, et maschi et femine, da otto anni in suso [...]: et questa nuova è molto damnosa a tutti li Christiani" ("it is said that these Turks, having entered Negroponte, killed universally all the Christians that they found there, both male and female, from eight years old and above [...]: and this news is very harmful to all Christians") (64). The *Diario ferrarese* later records that in December 1470 Borso joined with several other Italian states in a defensive league against the Turkish empire "lo qualle non cessa ogni altro giorno di pigliare qualche paese de Christiani" ("which continues every couple of days to take over some Christian country") (66).

7. Rugiero (Atlas Mountains, Northern Africa)

1 See Cavallo, *The Romance Epics*, 37–8, 41–2.

2 See Dorigatti, "Rugiero and the Dynastic Theme," 96, for a diagram of his family tree.

3 Dorigatti notes in passing that Rugiero's name is reminiscent of Roger I and II but does not develop the association ("Rugiero and the Dynastic Theme," 98).

4 I have used Kenneth Baxter Wolf's translation of Malaterra, *The Deeds of Count Roger of Calabria and Sicily and of His Brother Duke Robert Guiscard*. For more on Malaterra and the Italo-Normans, see Wolf, *Making History*, 143–71. The other two contemporary chroniclers of this period in southern Italian history, Amatus of Montecassino and William of Apulia, pay greater attention to Roger's brother Robert.

5 Betumen/Bethumi (in Arab writings Ibn at-Tumna), the emir of Catania and Syracuse, travelled to Calabria in February 1061 to enlist Roger's aid against his rival (Houben 14; Wolf, *Making History*, 22).

6 Rizzi notes that Boiardo's coverage of the Normans "seems to depend partially on Malaterra, but [his immediate] source is certainly using other sources still to be identified" ("M.M. Boiardo's Version of Riccobaldo Ferrarese," 200n).

7 Wolf argues that Malaterra had implicitly questioned the Normans' fixation with extending their power: "Considering what Sallust and especially Augustine had to say about the role of such motivations in the world of politics, it would seem that Geoffrey's *De rebus gestis Rogerii et Roberti* represents something of a cross between a specific glorification of the Norman achievement and a generic Augustinian critique of any and all state-building endeavors" (*Making History*, 173). In the *Innamorato*, Rugiero is pointedly free of the overreaching ambition that characterizes instead his cousin Agramante.

8 For more extensive accounts of early Estense history, see Chiappini 15–81, Panini 1–17, Dean, and Bestor 559–69.

9 Moreover, Bestor later points out that the "preservation of fraternal unity, despite intervening difficulties, had enabled the unity of the patrimony to be preserved for the forty-one years of the brothers' combined rulership" (568).

10 Recalling that "it was thanks to a partly Arab administration and army that Roger II had been able to seize control of mainland southern Italy," Arnaldi writes that during his tenure "Islam and Judaism continued to be practiced regularly" (95). Roger II had his detractors as well, but Boiardo would logically have been more interested in aspects that corresponded to the image he was creating for his own Rugiero.

11 Ricci points out the alarming fact that with the invasion of Otranto Christians were forced into slavery by the Turks right on Italian soil (*I turchi alle porte*, 45).
12 As noted above, Roger I was called duke of Calabria; Roger II became duke of Apulia and Calabria in 1127.
13 He also included a stanza in the *Innamorato* celebrating Alfonso for his military exploits, the first being that of saving Italy from the Turks: "Sì com'è Italia da' Turchi diffesa / per sua prodecia sola e suo valore" ("Here, he defended Italy / from Turks, by valor and by strength") (*OI* 2.27.56bis in the critical edition, but 2.27.57 in Bruscagli's and other modern editions). Although Tissoni Benvenuti dates this stanza to the period following the poem's initial publication in two books and after the conclusion of the war against Venice (*Inamoramento de Orlando*, 2: 1496n), Riccucci's account of Ercole's resentment towards Alfonso after the war for agreeing to Ferrara's definitive loss of the Polesine to Venice makes it more likely that the stanza was written before the Treaty of Bagnolo (7 August 1484) that brought the war to a close (239–40, 246–7).
14 Her brother Rinaldo was linked to Clermont through his grandfather, Bernardo of Chiaramonte, in Andrea da Barberino's *Reali di Francia*.
15 Levi argues that Boiardo honoured Eleonora by taking Rugiero's recurring family saga of "slaughtered fathers and brave, valorous mothers" from narratives in Aragonese chronicles present in Ferrara (462). Although most of the parallels noted by Levi are too generic for these chronicles to be considered as a primary source – especially since events surrounding Rugiero's birth are drawn directly from the *Aspramonte* narrative – any possible allusions to Aragonese history would add yet another layer of historical specificity to the construction of the dynastic couple.
16 "Rugiero and the Dynastic Theme," 101. Dorigatti returns to this topic in "La favola"; see especially 43–4.
17 Hankins points out, moreover, that "the kings of France, England, Castile, and their humanist courtiers were busily elaborating Trojan ancestries as a way of suggesting that these kingdoms had as fair a claim to be considered empires as did ancient Rome" ("Renissance Crusaders," 139).
18 Although Bradamante's lineage is encapsulated in one verse, her naming of Chiaramonte and Mongrana was sufficient to link her to this family tree. Citing Panizzi's edition, Ross explains how Buovo d'Antona's sons established the two houses (*Orlando innamorato*, index, "Mongrana").
19 See Rajna, *Le fonti*, 136–7.
20 Looking beyond Ferrara, in the second half of the fifteenth century there existed marriages between Venetian nobles and the dynastic family ruling

western Persia, both states allied against the Ottomans until the Persian ruler's death in 1477 (Pedani 113–15).

21 In Rajna's summary of the episode, the Saracens are responsible for the ensuing battle (*Le fonti*, 594–7). Regardless of which side is to blame, the idea of a marriage between a Frankish maiden and a non-European suitor is treated as inconceivable.

22 Even when such romances lead to marriage, most famously that between Mainetto (the young Charlemagne) and Marsilio's sister Galerana, whom he met while living in Saracen Spain (*Reali di Francia*), the union does not typically give rise to a dynastic family. For additional relations between Christian knights and Saracen maidens in fifteenth-century Italian chivalric literature, see Villoresi, "Le donne e gli amori," and *La letteratura cavalleresca*, 74–7. For mixed marriages, along with their eventual offspring, in French medieval epic, see Kinoshita, *Medieval Boundaries*; Kay 25–48; and Akbari 173–99. For examples of marriage and conversion in late medieval romance, see Goodman.

23 For Rugiero's exemplary treatment of Oliviero and the Bishop Turpino, see *OI* 3.4.22–3 and 3.4.44.

24 See Cavallo, *The Romance Epics of Boiardo, Ariosto, and Tasso*, 82–92, and accompanying footnotes for further bibliography.

25 Taking into consideration the early sixteenth-century belief that Columbus's voyage had brought him to islands off the eastern coast of Asia, some scholars have attempted a more precise designation. Following Fornari, Vernero argues that Alcina's island corresponds to Marco Polo's Zipagu (Japan), which Columbus mistakenly thought he had reached upon arriving on the island known today as Cuba (87, 116). For the island's location, see also Doroszlaï 48–53 and Rossi 106–7.

26 For the scene's classical precedents, see Giamatti 141–64.

27 Although Waldman translates "cedri" as "cedar," the context suggests that Ariosto is referring to the citron. Train explains why "cedro" is used in Italian to indicate both kinds of trees (7). Boiardo had placed "verdi cedri" and "palme" in Dragontina's dangerous garden (*OI* 1.6.48) and "cedri, aranci e palme" in the hills of Provence (*OI* 2.14.16). Tissoni Benvenuti remarks that "cedri" and "palme" would have been the appropriate vegetation for "an undefined exotic, Middle Eastern place" (*Inamoramento de Orlando*, 1: 216n). Ariosto later imagines that "cedri" are growing in Africa along with "lauri e myrti, olive e palme" ("laurel [and myrtle], olive, and palm") (*OF* 35.37 A; 39.26 C).

28 Train briefly traces the introduction of citrus into southern Europe at various stages, principally by Alexander of Macedonia in ancient times, the

Arabs during the Middle Ages, and the Portuguese in the Renaissance (7–8). He also notes more specifically the presence of oranges in the life and literature (13–14) as well as art (36–42) of the Italian Renaissance.

29 In the *Innamorato* they are simply sisters (*OI* 2.13.55).

30 Such a transformation has sparked substantial critical debate. See, in particular, Benson; Finucci 229–53; Jordan; Shemek 77–125; Rajna, *Le fonti*, 54; and Sacchi 171.

31 Rajna laments this new characterization of Bradamante: "I don't like to see this *donna guerriera* held by her family in Montalbano like the least important little girl" (*Le fonti*, 54). Carrara likewise complains that she is thus "transformed into a housewife and pathetic fiancée, who cries, writes, and stays home to wait" (281).

32 Rajna considers this alteration more likely due to deference towards his patrons than to ignorance of literary tradition: "To have descended from an illegitimate progenitress would not have been pleasing to the Estense" (52).

8. Rodamonte of Sarza (Algeria)

1 Ulieno is one of the four principal lords who accompany Agolante in his invasion of southern Italy, and he is subsequently singled out as "il più franco barone di tutta l'oste" ("the most valorous knight of the army") (*Asp.* 3.42.116, 160).

2 Tissoni Benvenuti also points to the characterization of Nimrod in the medieval *Dittamondo* (*Inamoramento de Orlando*, 2: 1164–5n).

3 Brunetto Latini also notes that Noah's son Cam "tient toute Afrique" ("holds all of Africa") (1.21) and is the grandfather of Nenbrot (*Li livres dou tresor* 1.23). For the diffusion of this belief, see Relaño 35.

4 Dorigatti discusses this character in greater detail in "Sobrino ariostesco e misconosciuto," noting too that he is the only member of Agramante's entourage who survives the ensuing war (1).

5 The king of Garamanta is linked to the Greek god Apollo through his designation as a prophet of the god Apollino as well as through the location of his realm. Writers of medieval epic sometimes added Apollino to the "gods" Mohammed and Trivigante in order to create a Saracen trinity; here Boiardo features the Greek-sounding Apollino at the expense of the other two names. Murrin refers to a 1367 portulan in which the Garamantes are said to be named after Garat, a son of Apollo (*History and Warfare*, 275n23).

6 In this analogy, characterizing flame by the light ("lume") it supplies and by its gradual dimming ("se oscura"), Rodamonte links the diminished faculty

of sight ("vista") in humans to a loss of both wisdom ("senno") and courage/spirit ("animo").

7 Although Boiardo did not need to have read the *Theaetetus* in order to express a similar position, it is worth recalling that Marsilio Ficino translated Plato's dialogues in the 1460s. For Plato in late fifteenth-century Italy, see Hankins, *Plato in the Italian Renaissance.*

8 He first expounded this trajectory in *De docta ignorantia* (*On Learned Ignorance*, 1440), and later developed the concept in his other speculative works, especially *De coniecturis* (*On Conjectures*, c. 1443), *Apologia doctae ignorantiae* (*Apology of Learned Ignorance*, 1449), and *De visione dei* (*On the Vision of God*, 1453). For Nicholas of Cusa in Italy, see Cassirer 46–72.

9 As Garin explains: "His *De magnis coniunctionibus* argued that planetary conjunctions in general, and in particular those of Saturn, Jupiter and Mars, are to the world what the horoscope is to man: they are the signs and the causes of great historical events" (21). For Arabic planetary theories, see Saliba.

10 Ricci, *Ossessione turca*, 31. Milano also notes that Ercole gathered to his court "men versed in geography and astronomy" (88). For the importance of astrology at the courts of Borso and Ercole, see also Bertoni 192–4 and Micocci 35–65.

11 For Albumasar and the decans in the Sala dei Mesi, see Lippincott and Bertozzi, "Il talismano di Warburg." An additional source of the decans cited by historians is the *Picatrix*, an eleventh century Arabic text known in Italy in Latin translation (Bertozzi, "Il talismano di Warburg," 202–3). For another use of Arab astrology in Ferrarese art, see Toniolo 121.

12 Warburg originally published this 1487 letter, cited in Bertozzi, "Il talismano di Warburg," 204–5. De Armas notes that Albumasar's "popularity and authority remained virtually unchallenged until the end of the fifteenth century" (158).

13 Said has made a similar point with regard to the ever ongoing intermingling of cultures in history: "Partly because of empire, all cultures are involved in one another; none is single and pure, all are hybrid, heterogeneous, extraordinarily differentiated, and unmonolithic" (*Culture and Imperialism*, xxv).

14 Although Tissoni Benvenuti and Montagnani choose "senno" in their critical edition, their note to this verse lists various editions that use "viso," including the earliest extant edition (Venice, 1487). Bruscagli comments that "il viso" refers to "la vista" or, in this case, discernment, thus referring to Rodamonte's inability to see with the mind's eye (*Orlando innamorato*, 2: 574n).

15 Alexandre notes Rodamonte's positive transformation, although she does

not discuss it in terms of increasing knowledge but attributes it instead to a general civilizing process that Boiardo's pagan knights experience in the course of the poem (136–41).

16 Indeed, Sarzano was also the name of a castle located within Estense territory, in the hills outside Reggio Emilia.

17 Ariosto's repeated references to Rodomonte as "barbarian" may correspond to an increasing tendency on the part of humanists to apply this label to contemporary Turks rather than to the various invaders who swept through the late Roman Empire. See Bisaha, *Creating East and West*, 60–87.

18 Boiardo used the former term twice when referring generically to the African troops invading France (*OI* 2.6.46 and 3.5.16) and once to depict Hannibal (*OI* 2.29.2). The latter term is used only once in the earlier poem, to describe an unnamed African soldier riding a "gianeto bianco / Che coda e chioma avìa tinto de alchena" ("jennet, / whose mane and tail were henna-tinted") (*OI* 3.6.7). Ross draws attention to this verse as an example of the greater realistic detail found in the battles of Book Three (*Orlando innamorato*, 581).

19 Zanette notes Rodomonte's ugliness in the *Furioso* (349–40).

20 *Boiardo e altri studi cavallereschi*, 173. One could find a vestige of his ideology, refashioned in a comic vein, in Brunello's desire not only to steal the moon from the sky and the pitchfork from the devil but also, in order to "spregiar la gente christïana" ("spite the Christians"), rob the sound of the bell from the pope (*OI* 2.3.42).

21 Although Benson develops her argument along different lines, her following comment regarding Rodomonte is apropos here: "Experience corrects his opinion of women and leads him to appreciate the truth of the old man's concept" (107). It is a truth, however, that he learns too late, and at the price of Isabella's death. See also Weaver 396–8.

22 Here Zanette is alluding to his earlier statements: "It was, for the fierce hero, a true misfortune to pass from the hands of the romantic Count of Scandiano to those of his continuer who bears the entire responsibility of his atrocious calamities" and "the king of Sarza is truly a victim of his poet, and not of others" (352 and 354, respectively).

9. Saracen Spain

1 Montagnani likewise notes that Boiardo's Feraguto is "uprooted from the original epic context and inserted with full force among the 'comic' protagonists" (21).

2 For the record, in the *Spagna ferrarese* Grandonio kills Astolfo directly

while in the longer version the English knight is killed by a Turk sent by Grandonio to attack the Christians (Serra, "Letture boiardesche," 151). Tissoni Benvenuti reads Astolfo's defeat of Grandonio as a form of anticipatory revenge: "For the Ferrarese public, which remembered as well as Boiardo the massacre perpetrated by Grandonio in Borso's *Spagna*, it was well-deserved, and therefore also an occasion for great satisfaction" ("Intertestualità cavalleresca," 74–5).

3 *Diario ferrarese*, 45–6. See also Ricci, "Una nicchia d'Oltralpe," 66.

4 For Boiardo's classical and medieval sources in devising the diverse African troops who comprise Agramante's army, see Murrin, *History and Warfare*, 63–8; Alhaique Pettinelli, "L'*Orlando innamorato* e la tradizione cavalleresca in ottave," 405–6; and Tissoni Benvenuti, *Inamoramento de Orlando*, 2: 1349–52n.

5 Ross points out that apart from the warriors cited above, who previously appeared in the *Spagna*, Boiardo derives his names from other sources or invents them "to form a list inspired by geographical considerations, a list of the most famous cities and regions of the Iberian peninsula" (*Orlando innamorato*, 579). In addition, one of Boiardo's Spanish kings is said to be originally from the Levant ("di Levante") and wears a turban (*OI* 2.23.71–2 and 2.24.31), suggesting interactions between the East and Saracen Spain.

6 For the poem's publication, see Harris 1: 15–17 and 2: 20–8.

7 In the *Furioso*, in fact, he will continue to alternate between romance and epic episodes until he is unhorsed by Bradamante at Arles thanks to none other than Argalia's magic lance.

8 In the 1532 edition, he emphasizes the pleasure principle even further by adding the general precept that one should always pursue whatever gives delight (*OF* 25.51 C).

9 For Saracen maidens loved and then left behind by Christian heroes in the Italian literary tradition, see Pasqualino, *Le vie del cavaliere*, 187–9.

10 Di Cesare finds, moreover, a "baptismal overtone" in Isabella's death scene, noting its combination of classical and scriptural allusions (322). Concurring with Di Cesare, Finucci remarks that Isabella's "self-immolation is bathed in liturgical, baptismal overtones" (178).

10. Boiardo's Noradino in Cyprus

1 The Lestrigons perhaps most immediately call to mind the *Odyssey*, especially given the presence of other Homeric adventures in the poem, but Tissoni Benvenuti points out that Boiardo would have found "historical"

precedents as well in both classical and medieval texts, namely Pliny's *Natural History* and the *Dittamondo* (*Inamoramento de Orlando*, 2: 1267n).

2 Even when Circassia is not specifically "in conquasso" ("a shambles") caused by the passage of Agricane's troops (*OI* 1.9.38) or set on fire by Mandricardo (*OI* 2.3.10), it is still described as "quel diserto inhospite e silvano" ("this unwelcome, barren land") (*OI* 1.10.8).

3 Rossebastiano notes that fifteenth-century pilgrimage writers often remark on the material decay of the region's cities ("La vicenda umana," 25–6).

4 Tissoni Benvenuti explains that the 1487 Venice edition containing the first two books (P) spells the king's name Noradino, whereas sixteenth-century editions derived from a lost subarchetype (y) use instead Norandino, the variant later adopted by Ariosto (*Inamoramento de Orlando*, 2: 1297n).

5 The fourteenth-century Damascene chronicler Ibn al-Qalanisi speaks of Nur ad-Din in majestic terms, frequently referring to his exemplary leadership and conduct (v. 293, 294, 297, 300, 305–6, 308, 309, 319, 321, 345). For more on Nur ad-Din's twenty-eight-year reign, see Maalouf 141–58.

6 Nur ad-Din's reputation has persisted even among recent historians. Tyerman, for example, writes that he "cultivated a reputation as a just ruler and judge, a knowledgeable jurist and theologian, educated, literate, orthodox, although, in the words of an Iraqi panegyrist, Ibn al-Athir, 'not a fanatic'" (344). Runciman calls him "a great ruler and a good man, who had loved above all things justice" (2: 398).

7 He may have had in mind a passage like the following one from an Old French continuation of William of Tyre: "For the men of France hold those of Italy in scorn. However rich a man may be, he will not be so noble that they will not regard him as a peasant, since most of the men of Italy are usurers, corsairs, merchants or seafarers, and because the men of France are knights they treat them with contempt" (*The Conquest of Jerusalem and the Third Crusade*, 39).

8 Such an attitude is not uncommon in crusading chronicles, beginning with William of Tyre's assertion that God made Christians suffer at the hands of Muslims because of their sins (1: 77). Both the Old French and Latin chronicles of the Third Crusade matter-of-factly treat Muslim victories as the will of God. Ambroise's *Estoire de la guerre sainte* states, "The anger of God was so great against the Christian host because of their sins that Saladin vanquished them quickly" (47). The anonymous *Itinerarium peregrinorum et gesta regis Ricardi* explains, "The Lord saw that the land of His Nativity, the place of His Passion, had fallen into the filthy abyss. Therefore He spurned His Inheritance, permitting the rod of His fury, Saladin [...], to rage and exterminate the obstinate people" (23).

9 Saladin made his appearance in the novella tradition as well. Boccaccio refers to his "grandissime […] magnificenze" ("extraordinary acts of munificence") in *Decameron* 1.3 (61; tr. 42) and then goes on to depict reciprocal exemplary actions on the part of both Saladin and an Italian nobleman in the midst of the Third Crusade (*Decameron* 10.9). For an overview of Saladin in the medieval European imagination, see Tolan, *Sons of Ishmael*, 79–100.

10 Rajna was apparently referring to this figure when he called Nur ad-Din "a courteous and pious son of Saladin, who left an excellent reputation also among the Christians" (*Le fonti*, 281n).

11 Knights were also known to disguise their identity in Saracen territory, but this was only a temporary measure until they gained the upper hand. The use of this ruse in the *Spagna* is discussed below.

12 Murrin notes the precision of Boiardo's Middle Eastern geography (*History and Warfare*, 285n45).

13 The text goes on to celebrate its fountains, fruit gardens, and architecture (*Le livre* 255; tr. 99). For the singular beauty of Damascus in Italian fifteenth-century pilgrimage accounts, see Rossebastiano, "La vicenda umana," 30–1.

14 Although Beirut was not the only city linked to the legend of St George and the dragon, the designation can also be found in Mandeville (*Le livre* 257; tr. 100). For the cult of St George in the fifteenth century, see Brotton and Jardine 17–20.

15 In the murky waters of Italian dynastic politics, the widowed Caterina almost ended up marrying a son of the king of Naples (Cardini 132).

16 See Perkins for a succinct overview of the musical culture in Ferrara during this period. Don Domenego refers to "pifare stranie" ("strange flutes") as well as "tamburi grandissimi et trombaze" ("very large drums and trumpets") in Damascus (74).

17 This Breton motif had entered earlier Carolingian works, but the opportunity for Christian knights to use such an occasion to win territory in the East and engineer mass conversions was generally looming in the background (as in the *Storia di Rinaldino*, discussed below).

18 As Ross has commented: "In praising Arthur over Charlemagne, as in praising his patron, Duke Ercole d'Este, for following peace not war (II xxi 59), Boiardo turns a harder eye on military conflict than might be expected of a poet who spends so much time describing sword strokes and the tidal movement of armies on a battlefield" (*Orlando in Love*, xxiv). Donnarumma suggests that these verses may contain a polemic against Andrea da Barberino, who proclaimed the superiority of Carolingian over Breton narratives precisely for their focus on Holy War (228n).

19 This Turkish-Greek alliance is only temporary, however, since six cantos later we find that the Turks have invaded Vatarone's Greek kingdom (discussed in chapter 16).
20 Echoing these sentiments, Boiardo writes in his *Historia imperiale* that the crusades began in Nicea "per la malizia de' Greci" ("due to the malice of the Greeks") who acted "per propria utilità" ("out of self-interest") and "per aggrandire l'Imperio di Constantinopoli" ("in order to enlarge the empire of Constantinople") (col. 333).
21 This negative attitude carries over into depictions of ancient Greek heroes in Italian literature, including Dante's condemnation of Odysseus to hell as a fraudulent counsellor (*Inferno* 26). The *Innamorato*'s own treatment of epic Greek characters follows in this vein: it is by treachery that Achilles and Aegisthus are said to have killed Hector and his son Astyanax (*OI* 3.1.27 and 3.5.22, respectively).
22 Rossebastiano and Fenoglio aptly describe Milliaduse's attitude as that of a "curious explorer who approaches a new world in order to learn, determined to understand its substance, composed of words and things, of customs, including the different mentality, to be respected" (18).
23 Pugliese notes, moreover, that earlier versions of this passage also referred to the diverse customs practised in various other courts, including those of the sultan of Alexandria and Prester John (176).

11. Egypt: From Damietta to Cairo

1 The brothers apparently left Cyprus at some point after Orlando's precipitate departure; prior to their arrival in Egypt they appeared as prisoners at the enchanted Fountain of the Fay where they were freed by Mandricardo.
2 In the only study to date devoted to this episode, Kathleen Egan has proposed that the magician's ability to reconnect limbs evokes, in dialogue with Pico della Mirandola, the ancient Egyptian religion in which Osiris was dismembered and then restored. The present chapter will be investigating the episode's historical rather than mythical associations, thus more in the spirit of Murrin's pioneering essay "Trade and Fortune," which used the extended episode of Morgana's realm as a test case for asserting that Boiardo's poem was concerned with international issues and social values.
3 Boiardo could have read about crocodiles in various sources, beginning with the ancient texts of Herodotus and Strabo, but he also had confirmation through at least one near contemporary account closer to home. Don Domenego notes that in 1440 Milliaduse d'Este purchased the head of a crocodile while travelling through Egypt on his return from Jerusalem (118). Although it is not clear what became of this unusual souvenir, the chronicler provides

a description of Nile crocodiles based on both first-hand observation and information gleaned from the locals. When crocodiles previously made their way into chivalric narratives, they were not depicted with such attention to biological detail (cf Andrea da Barberino, *Il Guerrin Meschino*, 3.28.17–24, 223–4, *Ugone d'Avernia*, 1: 317, and Pulci, *Morgante* 19.108–10).

4 While it is not possible to determine the extent of the crusading chronicles known to Boiardo, we can glean some idea from the summaries of crusading history that he inserts in his *Historia imperiale*, which covers up to the year 1201. According to Rizzi, Boiardo's immediate Latin source would have combined material from one of the many French rewritings of the early crusades known as the "Estoires d'Eracles" and the composite work by Ernoul and Bernard the Treasurer (see Morgan) which relates events up to 1231 (*The "Historia imperiale,"* 1: xlii). For the Fifth Crusade, Boiardo would also have known the work of two eyewitnesses, Oliver of Paderborn's *Historia Damiatina* and Jacques de Vitry's *Histoire orientale*, if not independently, certainly inscribed in another work. Oliver's account of the expedition at Damietta was incorporated into Francesco Pipino's *Chronicon* (Mas-Latrie 413n1), while Jacques de Vitry's narrative was used by a number of authors, including Vincent of Beauvais (*Speculum historiale*), Mandeville, Poggibonsi, and various continuers of William of Tyre (Bird 63, 73n58). In addition to the medieval chronicles, I have also consulted recent crusade historians, in particular Runciman and Tyerman (especially 346–50 and 628–49) for the successive Egyptian campaigns, and Powell specifically for the Fifth Crusade.

5 Tyerman notes that one of the most detailed proposals came from the Venetian Marino Sanudo Torsello "who based his plan (*c.* 1306–21) on a long historical study of the eastern campaigns, including Louis IX's" (802).

6 Runciman accounts for the city's importance by describing it as "the rich fortress that commanded the main branch of the Nile" (2: 386).

7 Since Boiardo's translation breaks off at the beginning of the thirteenth century, its references to Damietta are limited to this first Egyptian expedition.

8 For the centrality of the tower and chain, see Powell 140–3, who refers to the latter as Damietta's "most striking feature"; see also Runciman 2: 387 and 3: 152.

9 Although the *Historia imperiale* refers to the deliverance of the Holy Land as a magnanimous and glorious undertaking, Ponte points out Boiardo's condemnation of the crusaders' excessive violence as well as his harsh judgment of religious fanaticism in general (*La personalità*, 18–19). As Hankins notes, "The arguments in favor of a policy of crusade could be stated, the arguments against it could not. Nonetheless, there are numerous hints and

indirect evidence that many humanists, like other members of the public, had deep reservations about the feasibility and utility of crusading" ("Renaissance Crusaders," 124).

10 Wiggins briefly reviews previous interpretations of the character Astolfo, including those by sixteenth-century commentators, as a symbol of literature or the poet, the contemplative man, the *homo fortunatus*, and reality itself (140–2), while treating him as a figure of lucidity and "detachment from oneself" (150). Whereas Wiggins reads Astolfo simply as "an apparent deus ex machina" (153), it would be more accurate to say that he is an instrument of the Christian God.

11 The allegorical summary introducing Canto 15 in the 1553 Valvassori edition, for example, designates the horn as "giustitia" ("justice") and the book as "prudenza" ("prudence"). The allegories from these early editions are available on-line via Lina Bulzoni's project, *L'*Orlando Furioso *e la sua tradizione in immagini*. See also the resulting volume edited by Bulzoni, Pezzini, and Rizzarelli, *"Tra mille carte vive ancora": Ricezione del* Furioso *tra immagini e parole*.

12 Edson notes that the Catalan atlas, which is otherwise "almost devoid of Christian content" (81), nevertheless contains an illustration of "the three wise men" in Persia on their way to Bethlehem (82).

13 Although Caligorante will remain a minor character, the following aspects from Orvieto's characterization of Morgante could also apply here: "a horrible and savage giant who assumes a Western mask [...], but who conserves the unerasable characteristics of an Oriental who, if domesticated, is transformed into something grotesque, something diverse that fascinates, attracts, and diverts because of his deformity: if before he was a threat, now he provides a spectacle" (169).

14 Roberto da San Severino, for example, reports that twenty thousand Mamelukes were in Cairo "o per propria voluntate, o per forza, quando fussero stati prexi, o che essendo puti, siano stati venduti" ("either of their own will, or by force when they were captured, or having been sold into slavery when young boys") and later simply equates "cristiano renegato" with "schiavo venduto" ("bought slave") (quoted in Rossebastiano, "La vicenda umana," 32 and 45).

15 I have not been able to determine whether Ariosto would have had reason to believe this to be the case. According to Pedani, "Among those who chose to convert, whether in Europe or in Muslim territory, there were mostly prisoners and slaves who wanted to purchase for themselves a different life, specialized artisans in search of higher remuneration, political opponents of the regime in power, or criminals fleeing from punishment" (179). Scaraffia's

study of renegades, both forced and otherwise, focuses mainly on the period that postdates the *Furioso*.

16 In the 1532 edition Ariosto will make a slight adjustment to the insistently repetitive use of "pilgrim" by removing it in this one instance (*OF* 15.68 C).

17 When serving as the ducal commissioner of the Garfagnana, Ariosto has a similar response to the problem of unsafe roads closer to home. He repeatedly beseeches Duke Alfonso to send armed forces to rid the area of bandits, especially in letters written between May 1523 and January 1524.

18 The brothers end up as prisoners in many of the poem's traps: Dragontina's garden, the Bridge of Roses that supplies victims for the Garden of Orgagna, Manodante's Far Away Islands, and the Fountain of the Fay.

12. Jerusalem

1 For the dissemination of legendary accounts depicting Charlemagne in Jerusalem as both pilgrim and crusading hero, see Bisaha, *Creating East and West*, 34–41. For Jerusalem in medieval narrative, see Yeager.

2 The latter hero is also commonly called Ugo d'Alvernia, but for consistency I use the name as it appears in the title of the edition from which I cite.

3 For similar scenes of bloodbath in early accounts of the sack of Jerusalem, see William of Tyre 1: 370–2, Raymond of Aguilers (in Foss 177), and the *Gesta Francorum*, 92.

4 Precedents for the piety of Saladin upon entering Jerusalem are found in chronicles of the Third Crusade. An Old French continuation of William of Tyre, for example, states, "When Saladin had the keys [to Jerusalem], he was very happy and rendered thanks to Our Lord and to his Mohammed" (*The Conquest of Jerusalem and the Third Crusade*, 61).

5 William of Tyre, for example, branded Mohammed as "this first-born son of Satan [who] falsely declared that he was a prophet sent from God and thereby led astray the lands of the East" (60). In the Italian literary tradition, Mohammed is condemned to hell not only in Dante's *Inferno* (28.31–3) but in Andrea da Barberino's *Guerrin Meschino* and *Ugone d'Avernia*. Indeed, in the latter work the protagonist discovers him among the "porci Saraini, pieni d'avarizia e di lussuria" ("Saracen pigs, full of avarice and lust") and does not hesitate to spit at him (2: 115). For Christian anti-Islamic polemic in historical context, see especially Daniel, Southern, and Tolan, *Saracens*.

6 Dal Campo's journal reports, in fact, that the group left Ferrara on 6 April 1413 and landed in Syria after a month's navigation.

7 Rajna notes this discrepancy between the *Furioso* and the *Spagna* narratives (*Le fonti*, 266). Perhaps Ariosto belabours the point because in the *Spagna*

Sansonetto did not remain in Jerusalem but rather accompanied Orlando to Spain.

8 The 1532 version replaces "asini o muli" ("donkeys or mules") with the more generic "bestie da soma."

9 *The Pilgrimage of Charlemagne*, 37. Mandeville also devotes substantial attention to holy relics found in Jerusalem and elsewhere.

10 For fifteenth-century humanist publicists of the holy war, see especially Black (226–40) and Bisaha (*Creating East and West* and "Pope Pius II and the Crusade"). Casadei notes that sixteenth-century poets sometimes echoed Ariosto's plea that rulers stop fighting each other and shift their military arena to the East (*La strategia delle varianti*, 54–5).

13. Ariosto's Norandino in Damascus

1 We already know from the *Innamorato* that Mandricardo and Gradasso rescued the damsel, who was last seen aboard her father's ship at the French coastline (*OI* 3.4.10). A knight from Damascus relates additional components of the story to Astolfo and the brothers, including the arrival of Norandino and Lucina in the ogre's territory after a storm blew their ship off course, Norandino's unsuccessful attempt to free his bride, and his eventual return home after her departure (*OF* 15.26–65 A; 17.26–65 C).

2 For Poggibonsi's description of Damascus, see his *Libro d'Oltramare*, ch. 153, 2: 9–18.

3 Describing life in Outremer, Runciman notes that "the clothes of the settlers soon became as Oriental and luxurious as their furnishings. When a knight was not in armour he wore a silk burnous and usually a turban. On campaigns he wore a linen surcoat over his armour, to protect the metal from the heat of the sun, and a *kefieh* in the Arab style over his helmet" (2: 317). Pedani notes, moreover, that between 1490 and 1530 oriental, specifically Mameluke, fashion was in vogue in Venice, inspired by Alexandria, Damascus, and Cairo (175). For other examples of cross-cultural dressing, see Ricci, *I turchi alle porte*, 105–34.

4 In the final edition Ariosto substitutes "le ricchezze d'Asia" with the more specific "ricchezze del Turco" (*OF* 17.77 C).

5 Murrin goes on to say that "Ariosto accordingly represents the Levant benignly, as a Damascus of tournaments and chivalric enterprise." Bezzola also describes Ariosto's Middle East as fascinating, while bypassing its more troubling aspects (397). In my reading, Norandino's Damascus is much less benign than it appears to be, especially when compared to the Middle East depicted in the *Innamorato*.

14. From Ethiopia to the Moon

1 Silverberg (41–231) is especially informative for both the figure of Prester John and the historical context. See also Relaño 51–72, Milanesi, Pistarino, and Zaganelli, *La lettera del Prete Gianni*, 7–42. I have drawn mainly from the above works for the historical context provided in this chapter. For the historical Chinese ruler who may have given rise to the Prester John legend, see Edson 97.

2 Edson notes that there is no trace of a purportedly original letter to the Byzantine emperor Manuel Comnenos, only Latin versions to Pope Alexander III and Frederick Barbarossa (97). Although the letter circulated extensively in the late fifteenth century in various languages, it is not possible to know which copies were familiar to Ariosto. For the Latin version, I cite from Zaganelli's recent edition, which contains inserted material not present in the text reconstructed by Friedrich Zarncke but commonly found in the various subsequent accounts, including a late fifteenth-century version in Italian ("Lettera del Presto Giovanni"). Silverberg provides an English translation of Zarncke's reconstruction (41–5), followed by a summary of the various interpolations (63–8); where possible, I cite from this translation.

3 The late fifteenth-century Italian version likewise notes that upon entering the palace one feels satiated "siccom'egli avesse mangiate tutte le buone vivande del mondo" ("as if he had eaten all the choice meals in the world") ("Lettera del Presto Giovanni," 258).

4 The interchangeability of the geographical designations during the Middle Ages is continued into the *Furioso* where Astolfo originally arrives in Ethiopia (*OF* 33.100) but later returns to Nubia (*OF* 38.24, 26, 31). For the record, Nubia comprised southern Egypt and northern Sudan, lying north of the modern state of Ethiopia.

5 In addition to Silverberg's broader account (163–92), see Pistarino 121–9 for the years 1316–1483.

6 For the presence of Ethiopians at the Council of Florence, see Cerulli, "Eugenio IV e gli Etiopi."

7 Silverberg 179, 187–8; Pistarino 122. Pistarino notes the repeated efforts of Alfonso to establish relations with this African state (131).

8 Breazeale 100–9; Silverberg 180–5.

9 While a summary of the earlier work was contained in the first edition of 1483, the latter text was included as a *Treatise* on the "Most High Pope of the Christian Indians and Ethiopians" beginning with the second edition of 1485 (Silverberg 222). The *Supplementum chronicarum* (Venice, 1483) was very popular in the late fifteenth century, with numerous subsequent editions, including an Italian translation published in 1491.

10 For the various works concerning Prester John that circulated in Italy, see Milanesi 44–7; Zaganelli, *La lettera del Prete Gianni*, 25–31; and Relaño 51–8.

11 The *Ugone d'Avernia* circulated in Franco-Italian verse before Andrea da Barberino's Italian prose romance. See Meregazzi for excerpts containing the Prester John episode from three extant Franco-Italian versions composed between 1341 and 1441. The *Guerrin Meschino* was especially popular, existing in seventy manuscripts and fragments, with fifteen incunabula and at least sixteen sixteenth-century print editions (Allaire, *Andrea da Barberino*, 10).

12 The *cantare* is reprinted in Neri 145–65. For the dating of the poem, see Olschki, "I 'Cantari,'" 294, who also notes that Dati wrote a *Secondo cantare dell'India* between August 1494 and August 1495. For Dati's sources, see also Olschki, "I 'Cantari,'" 293–300.

13 Silverberg 200–5; Pistarino 120–1; Milanesi 49; Relaño 60–1. For a detailed summary of the ongoing Portuguese effort, see especially Silverberg 193–231.

14 According to Silverberg, "Albuquerque dreamed of using the Ethiopian port of Massawa, on the Red Sea, as a staging base for an invasion of Arabia: aided by the legions of Prester John, he would capture Mecca, carry off the coffin of Mohammed, and use it to ransom the Holy Land" (209).

15 For the depiction of Prester John in world maps, see Doroszlaï 95–119 and Relaño 55–62. Cerulli argues that Ariosto relied primarily on the Genoese maps ("Il volo di Astolfo").

16 According to Pistarino, the news that a Portuguese ambassador had penetrated the land of Prester John in 1521 elicited in the West the same level of emotion as the voyage of Columbus (137).

17 Rinaldo's eastern adventures in the *Morgante* prior to his arrival in Egypt provide a closer precedent in terms of plot, even though they are condensed into a summary of just a few stanzas. As Astaroth explains to Malagise, after visiting Cairo, Damascus, and the sepulchre of Christ, among other biblical sites, Rinaldo and his companions "trascorson fino in India al prete Ianni, / e combatteron là molti e molti anni, / tanto che sol v'era un signor rimaso / il qual non si voleva battezzare / e redurre alla fede di Tommaso" ("went through Indian lands, as far as Prester John, / and there they combated more years than one, / till not a single lord was left around / who still refused to be baptized and yield / to Thomas's faith") (*Morg*. 25.128–9).

18 Rajna states, "Lodovico's Senapo is a Prester John only on the outside. The former one was a saintly and holy pontiff, cultivator of every virtue, enemy of every vice, lord of populations unaccustomed to falsehood. [...] By contrast Senapo when young was arrogant just like Alexander – and, let us also add, in imitation of him" (*Le fonti*, 533–4).

19 See Silverberg 46–8 and 66; Zaganelli, *La lettera del Prete Gianni*, 11 and 45. Olschki calls Prester John the "last heir of all the marvels that the fantasy of the Hellenistic Greeks had gathered and invented regarding Alexander the Great and the fabulous India" ("I 'Cantari,'" 308). Orvieto cites Alexander and Prester John as "apotropaic heroes" whose function was "to hold subjugated, under control, the otherwise devastating 'oriental malignity'" (168).

20 The Cantino Plantisphere likewise mentions continuous local warfare between the Nubian Christians under Prester John and a nearby province ruled by the king of Nubia (Milano 64).

21 Additional sources are noted in Relaño 54–5 and Zaganelli, *La lettera del Prete Gianni*, 29.

22 Edson notes that in this world map, which presents an enlarged Africa compared to Europe and Asia, the earthly paradise sits on the equator in East Africa surrounded by six mountains; Ptolemy's Mountains of the Moon are on the north shore of the Gulf of Guinea; and Prester John is pictured "in splendor" inside a royal tent (197–8).

23 *La lettera del Prete Gianni*, 158, 162. Bendinelli points out that Italian translations stemming from the letters in Old French contain references to these animals ("Volgarizzamenti italiani," 59). The late fifteenth-century Italian "Lettera del Presto Giovanni" contains the birds with razor-edged wings (247), rivers flowing from paradise (249, 250, 251), and birds that attack a Christian people twice a year during harvest (249).

24 This interpolated material is also present in the Italian "Lettera del Presto Giovanni" (249, 255).

25 Hercules takes the place of the Boreades in many accounts of the Phineus story, including the one found in Pietro Andrea de' Bassi's *Fatiche d'Ercole*, written at the request of Niccolò d'Este. After shooting his arrows to drive the harpies from the table, Hercules likewise pursues them as far as the Strophades (Bassi, *The Labors of Hercules*, 82). To date, the only published edition of this work is Thompson's abridged English translation.

26 Ovid's story of Anaxarete, the haughty Cypriot noblewoman who remained unmoved by her suitor's suicide and was subsequently turned into stone by Venus (Ovid, *Met.* 14.698–758), was also evoked in Boccaccio's *Decameron* (5.8) and incorporated into Machiavelli's "Serenade." For Lidia's novella in relation to the Italian tradition of the prose romance *Palamedès*, see Stoppino 98–104.

27 *Le fonti*, 531. It is possibly the fact that Astolfo replays the journeys of these two knights to both hell and the earthly paradise that led Rajna to assume that for Ariosto the Prester John figure was limited to his characterization in these chivalric works.

28 Ariosto's choice of guide could have been prompted by Guerrino's question to Enoch and Elijah whether St John the Evangelist ("'l santo vangelisto santo Giovanni el profeta") was also present (*Guerrino* 6.27, 431).
29 Mandeville tells of the fate of Senapo's predecessors in the same foolhardy attempt: "Meintz grantz seignurs et de grant volunté ount assaiez plusors foiz a aler par celles riveres vers Paradiz et as grantz compaignies. Mes unques ne poaient espleiter lour voie ancys moroient pusours de lasser pur vager, contre les undes et plusours autres qe deviendrent aveogles, et plusours sourdz pur la noise del eawe, et plusours sont suffoqués et perduz dedeinz les undes, si qe nul mortel ne poet approcher si ce n'estoit d'especial grace de Dieu" ("Many great lords have tried at different times to travel by those rivers to Paradise, but they could not prosper in their journeys; some of them died through exhaustion from rowing and excessive labour, some went blind and deaf through the noise of the waters, and some were drowned through the violence of the waves. And so no man, as I said, can get there except through the special grace of God") (*Le livre,* 470; tr. 185).
30 The 1532 edition increases Orlando's culpability by calling his desire incestuous (*OF* 31.64 A; 34.64 C). Rajna takes issue with Ariosto's new twist on the story, declaring that Boiardo "certainly would not have made madness a divine punishment, inflicted on Orlando to punish him for the blind love for a pagan woman" (*Le fonti*, 56).
31 For additional precedents locating the Garden of Eden near Prester John's realm or on a mountain approaching the circuit of the moon, see Delumeau 39–96.
32 Ariosto foretells that this state will not last indefinitely, however, and indeed the *Cinque canti* recount his later "fall" caused by his unruly sexual appetite.
33 Monteverdi shows the extent to which Ariosto draws from the *Chanson de Roland* and the *Chanson d'Aspremont* for the conclusion of his epic plot. See also Villoresi, *La fabbrica dei cavalieri*, 344, and Moretti, *L'ultimo Ariosto*, 15–16.

15. The Destruction of Biserta

1 In an editor's note, Caretti uncritically cites an explanation for Ariosto's choice that actually validates the orientalizing stereotype: "Ariosto has placed it (the House of Sleep) in an Oriental country, where in fact the softness of the climate encourages indolence and often living in a state of drowsiness" (1: 368). This view was not only prevalent in medieval epic, but can be found, for example, in Petrarch's description of "Turchi Arabi et Caldei" ("Turks, Arabs, and Chaldeans") as a "popolo ignudo paventoso et lento" ("naked, cowardly, and lazy people") (*Rime sparse*, 28.54 and 28.58).

2 For the episode's epic and chivalric precedents, see Rajna, *Le fonti*, 549.

3 The present argument seeks to gauge not the extent of Ariosto's irony but the presence of his crusading rhetoric. See Gregory for a reading of divine intervention in the poem as a "latent subversion of conventional piety" (113–19).

4 For a similar exclamation in a pious context, see Petrarch's "Trionfo della Fama" (2.67–9).

5 In the 1532 edition Ariosto removed the adjective "infinite" referring to the incalculable number of rapes committed on the part of the paladins and their allies; at the same time, however, he added that Orlando himself knew about a great many of these crimes and a thousand other acts of injustice but was nevertheless unable to prevent them.

6 Tasso, in turn, will echo the destruction of Biserta when describing that of the Holy City in the *Gerusalemme liberata* (Cavallo, *The Romance Epics*, 205–6). Of course, Ariosto would have encountered scenes of horrendous deeds elsewhere as well, from humanist accounts of the fall of Constantinople in 1453 (see Bisaha, *Creating East and West*, 60–9) to the sacks of Italian cities during the poet's lifetime. I would therefore view Ariosto's graphic description not as an attempt to undermine the Christian victory at Biserta (and, by extension, the crusaders' conquest of Jerusalem) but rather as a statement on the utter inhumanity that unchecked violence in warfare can unleash.

7 Rajna looks to Carolingian epic, including the *Spagna* narratives, for the scene's precedents (*Le fonti*, 558–9). This dialogue may also echo Brandimarte's failed attempt to "convert" the bandit Barigaccio to a more honest way of life in the *Innamorato* (*OI* 2.19.22–46).

8 Considering Ariosto's source to be "sacred legends," Rajna remarks on the anomaly of this kind of scene in the romance epic: "Healing by way of simple prayers had not been used, as far as I know, for the benefit of chivalric heroes" (*Le fonti*, 564).

9 For the radical implications of this provocative claim attributed to the Gospel author, see especially Zatti, *Il* Furioso *fra epos e romanzo*, 142–9, and "Dalla parte di Satana," 148–50. For Zatti's studies in English translation, see *The Quest for Epic*.

10 The frequent intrusion of historical reality has not passed unobserved by Ariosto critics, who have accounted for this practice in various ways. Brand finds contemporary military allusions to be not only "flattering reminders of Estense brillance" but also reflections on the horrors and widespread suffering brought about by war – especially due to the modern practice of sacking cities, slaughtering prisoners, and employing firearms – as well as on other

issues such as problems of leadership and the hatred of tyranny (90–1). For a closer investigation of Ariosto's allusions to current political events in all three editions, see Casadei, *La strategia delle varianti.*

16. Boiardo's Brandimarte across the Continents

1 Boiardo gives a sense of the distance between France and Circassia by listing the various countries he passes before reaching the Don River, the traditional frontier of Asia (*OI* 1.9.37).

2 Alexandre writes that Brandimarte "personifies, better than any other, the new ideal of equilibrium, strength, and prudence cherished by our poet" (135). Although Lorch stresses Brandimarte's noble characteristics in the context of various episodes, she does not address his pivotal adventure at Phebosilla's palace.

3 Islands can exist in the extreme north because Boiardo equates the Russian Sea with an ocean (*OI* 1.16.38). Caramella notes that Marco Polo had also envisioned an ocean bordering Russia on the north (148n). Edson finds that fifteenth-century maps differed in their representation of the northernmost reaches of the globe, with some depicting an ocean with islands (125–7). In Fra Mauro's world map, the land mass is surrounded on all sides by water and islands.

4 Abu-Lughod calls Samarkand "perhaps the quintessential caravan city" (178). For the city's prominence and strategic location at the intersection of trade routes, see Abu-Lughod 178–81.

5 Boiardo uses the terms "serpente" and "drago(ne)" interchangeably in describing the creature (*OI* 2.25.25–37), but he also specifies that this "serpente" is winged (*OI* 2.25.37).

6 Cavallo, *The Romance Epics*, 25–31.

7 In her note to this verse, Tissoni Benvenuti cites *Inferno* 21.131 and 22.91.

8 Loomis 106–8. His essay focuses on early versions and refers to Boiardo only in passing (112). Bregoli Russo considers the *Lanzelet* to be Boiardo's most probable source (65–72). According to Rajna, Boiardo may have also been familiar with the *Cantari di Carduino*, in which the eponymous knight successfully undertakes a "fier baiser" adventure thanks to instructions from a dwarf who explains that the diverse animals he encounters are the city's inhabitants. Rajna finds it more likely, however, that the episode was suggested to Boiardo from an earlier French source (introduction, *I cantari di Carduino*, xxxv–xxxvi).

9 Rossebastiano Bart demonstrates that the *Innamorato* episode has more features in common with Mandeville than with *Lanzelet* ("Alle fonti del

Boiardo," 20). She also provides a transcription of the episode from the *Livre de Johann de Mandeville* manuscript housed in the Biblioteca Estense of Modena ("Alle fonti del Boiardo," 22–3).

10 "Et conbien que il vous sainblera que je soye hydeuse a veoir, cest par enchantement, car je suis telle comme vous veez et se vous me baisiez, vous aurés tout cest tresor et serez mon mary et sire de ceste ysle" ("however hideous I may seem to your sight, it was done by enchantment, since I am just as you see me, and if you kiss me, you will have all that treasure and be my husband and lord of this island" (*Livre de Johann de Mandeville*, in Rossebastiano Bart, "Alle fonti del Boiardo," 23).

11 This negative connotation carries over into medieval chivalric epic as well. In the *Storia di Rinaldino da Montalbano*, for example, Rinaldo slays a serpent who has killed his travelling companion in the Holy Land, but its foul smell renders him unconscious (21). He later dies from the odour of another serpent that his son Rinaldino has managed to defeat. Examining bouts between Christian knights and serpents located in the Orient, Orvieto finds that "the terrifying battle between the paladin and the serpent-dragon-basilisk also signifies, allegorically, the battle between the Christian and the devil, Mohammed the Muslim; between Christ and the Antichrist, the monstrous being also diabolical" (176).

12 La Barre notes that "the snake played an important role in the worship of the Great Mother, Magna Mater or Demeter, and snakes were an attribute of Athene, Erichthios, Hermes, Asklepios, Dionysos, and many other Greek gods" (70).

13 These attributes are sometimes transferred to his son, Asclepius, "the father of medicine," who was popular in late fifteenth-century Italy thanks to the circulation of the hermetic *Asclepius*.

14 At this point in the narrative, Fiordelisa has just led Ranaldo from Dragontina's garden in Circassia (in the Caucasus), past the Caspian Sea, and along the (fictitious) river Drada to Albracà, in order to reach Brandimarte. See Ross's map (*Orlando innamorato*, lxxxii) for a visual sense of the vast distance traversed in this quest.

15 Eliade, in fact, finds "a considerable number of initiatory motifs in the literature that, from the twelfth century, grew up around the 'Matière de Bretagne,' especially in the romance giving a leading role to Arthur, the Fisher King, Percival, and other Heroes pursuing the Grail quest" (124–5).

16 Tissoni Benvenuti surmises that the Estense ekphrasis must have been written before 1476 because Ercole's son Alfonso (born in 1476) is not mentioned (*Inamoramento de Orlando*, 1: xx), but there is no reason the child would have had to be included in this particular encomium, especially if the

poet already had in mind a parallel ekphrasis dedicated to the Aragonese (*OI* 2.27.51–61). Bruscagli suggests that Alfonso d'Aragona's crucial aid to Ferrara in the course of its war against Venice could have occasioned the insertion of the stanzas celebrating Aragonese virtue as the poem was approaching publication (*Orlando innamorato*, 1: 1004–5n). Contemporary historical vicissitudes might have also occasioned the prior celebration of Estense virtue on Phebosilla's palace walls. In the absence of an exact date of composition, it remains suggestive that the extended Phebosilla episode (2.25.23 to 2.27.35) features Estense family history as it invites a reflection on the various guises of the foreign other.

17 For example, in the opening eclogue of his first extant work, *Pastoralia* (1463–4), he alludes to the Turkish invasion of the Morea as the reason for which the god Pan was forced to abandon Arcadia (I.4–8); however, when Pan goes on to offer Poeman (Boiardo) a reed-pipe, the poet replies that even the incense and cinnamon imported from the East would be insufficient repayment for such a priceless gift (I.59–61).

18 Bruscagli's study of this segment focuses not on "the content of such digressions" but rather on "the narrative modality with which Boiardo's dynastic ekphrasis is fitted into the fabric of the poem" ("L'ecfrasi dinastica," 270–1).

19 As Ponte notes, in the *Historia imperiale*, Boiardo considers Frederick Barbarossa as the "barbarico" ("barbarian") enemy in antithesis to the descendants of Rome (*La personalità*, 87).

20 This fiercely negative characterization accords with medieval chronicle and legend: Villani reputed Ezzolino III to be the "most cruel and feared tyrant who ever existed among Christians," Salimbene of Parma considered him "truly of the body of the devil and a son of inquity," while legend identified him as the devil's son (Benfell 366). Dante condemned his soul to a river of boiling blood in the seventh circle of hell along with tyrants who committed violence and cruelty against their neighbours (*Inferno* 12.109–10).

21 Although Boiardo does not name his victorious opponent, the Estense family would have known that the successful leader of this battle was none other than Azzo VII d'Este (1205–64).

22 For a fuller comparison of the Leodila and Doristela episodes, see Cavallo, *Boiardo's* Orlando innamorato, 130–6.

23 Inalcik notes specifically that after 1468 "for European traders such as the Venetians, Genoese and Florentine merchants in Constantinople and Galata, the two most important centres of Levantine trade, Bursa was the closest market in which to purchase eastern goods and sell European woolens" (124). Citing Ponte, Ross notes that "the limits Boiardo imposes on Turkey

[...] show that he was acquainted with maps of his day" (*Orlando innamorato*, 632).

24 McMichaels considers this to be among the various benefits derived from Brandimarte's courageous kiss (202).

25 It is thus perhaps fitting that Brandimarte should end up with Agricane's sword, originally belonging to Solomon, and his helmet, which he removes from the king's uncorrupted corpse in order to protect Fiordelisa from a gang of thieves (*OI* 2.19.26–8).

26 This cryptic allusion to North Africa's foretold destruction is sometimes seen as a reference to King Roger's campaign, but it could also have been a reference to the impending destruction of Biserta in Boiardo's epic plot. In any event, we may note that the Africans' decree against Christians stems from a perceived threat of danger to themselves rather than from an a priori hostility toward other faiths.

27 He also softens the conquest in Italy by contrasting it to Alfonso's invasion of northern Africa: "L'Affrica vinta a lui stava davante / Ingienochiata col suo popul rio, / Ma lui de Italia avìa preso un gran limbo, / Standosi a quela con amor in grembo" ("Before him, beaten Africa / and all its abject people kneeled. / He conquered much of Italy / and held it to his heart with feeling") (*OI* 2.27.54). This reference to Alfonso's domination of Africa also serves as a historical reversal of both Agramante's ill-advised invasion of Europe and the recently thwarted Ottoman offensive in the Neapolitan kingdom.

28 This verse is given as 2.27.56bis in the critical edition, but 2.27.57 in other editions. As noted earlier, Riccucci demonstrates that Boiardo's praise of Alfonso would most logically correspond to the period between the spring and autumn of 1482 (239–40, 246–7).

29 For the popularity of tapestries in Ferrara at the time of Leonello and Borso, see Forti Grazzini 29–50 and Smit 119.

30 Sabadino degli Arienti's late fifteenth-century description of the Este palaces includes scenes of dancing, hunting, and other representations of exotic or wild animals. See also Venturi 388–9 and Manca 269.

31 Ariosto's relocation of the Isole Lontane was not due to the geographical impossibility of situating islands north of Russia since he elsewhere alludes to the possibility of travelling across a northern sea from eastern Asia to western Europe (*OF* 13.12 A; 15.12 C). Caramella was most likely conditioned by Ariosto in situating the Isole Lontane in Indonesia (130–3).

32 Indeed, Boiardo explicitly makes the point that Gradasso would have killed Orlando had it not been for Brandimarte's intervention: "Pur (nela historia el ver si convien dire!) / A suo dispetto li dava de piglio; / Ma Brandimarte non puòte soffrire / Vedere Orlando posto in tal perilio, / Onde correndo sel

puose a seguire" ("In history, truth must be told. / He would have overcome Orlando, / but Brandimarte could not stand / to see the Count in danger, so / he followed after him") (*OI* 3.7.53).

33 See Quint for a different, but in my view not incompatible, reading of this latter episode.

17. Ariosto's Rinaldo along the Po River

1 Serpents are clearly on Ariosto's mind since just prior to this scene Angelica is said to loathe Rinaldo more than a serpent (*OF* 38.34 A; 42.37 C). Ascoli notes several additional references to serpents in the ensuing narrative segment (*Ariosto's Bitter Harmony*, 337n, 347n, 348).

2 It corresponds, rather, to the fear that Brandimarte exhibits in the second test (*OI* 2.26.9–12).

3 For a close reading of this episode see Santoro who, however, reads Rinaldo's refusal to drink as a warning of the limits of the possibility of knowledge in the face of an ever-changing reality ("La prova del 'nappo,'" 16). See also Martinez 25, Sherberg 43–89, and Weaver 400. The latter reads Rinaldo's refusal to know too much about his spouse as a counter-example to the *pazzia* that Rodomonte and Orlando undergo upon learning an unpleasant truth about the woman they love. In the latter case, Weaver points out that the simile comparing Orlando to a farmer coming upon a snake in the grass evokes the Genesis story's warning against excessive knowledge (395).

4 In the 1532 edition, Ariosto becomes even more explicit by shifting the focus from Rinaldo's mouth to his lips ("li labri"; *OF* 42.104 C).

5 Benson writes: "Rinaldo develops the analogy to draw a parallel between the consequences of knowledge in Adam's case and in the case of the inquiring husband and reveals the misogynist audacity of his analogy and the particular limits of his own philosophy. […] He suggests that, in both the case of the apple and of the wife, God forbade knowledge to man because it would bring man unhappiness" (112).

6 Casadei notes that in the first *Furioso* these novellas functioned as two *exempla* coming as they do near the very end of the poem (*Il percorso*, 81).

7 For the theme of avarice in the Leodila story, see Gragnolati.

8 Carlo Delcorno writes: "the animal (usually a monkey) that produces gold rather than excrements represents in medieval iconography Avarice, an obsessive theme, as one has seen, of the entire canto" (325).

9 Ariosto removes this passage from the final edition where, although Adonio does not die from excessive fornication, he is nevertheless conspicuously absent when Anselmo aims to have Argia put to death.

10 Sangirardi notes that Ariosto had Boiardo's Phebosilla in mind in fashioning his own serpent-fairy (170–1 and 199n).

11 Virgil (*Aen.* 10.275–80) and Boccaccio (*Famous Women*, 60–1) had also linked Manto to both Thebes and Mantua. Ariosto, however, links her directly to Cadmus rather than presenting her as the daughter of the Theban seer Tiresias.

12 Ariosto had access to a range of sources depicting black Africans in a negative fashion, from patristic and medieval writings (De Weever xiii–xvi), to the exemplum tradition, which specifically associated Ethiopians with the devil and fornication (Delcorno 327–30), to the novella (Papio, *Keen and Violents Remedies,* 104–24, and Attar). Said's reflection on the general tendency to demonize the foreign other as "unutterably corrupt, degenerate, irredeemable" (*Culture and Imperialism,* xix) seems especially pertinent here.

13 Santoro likewise writes, "The culpability of the judge turns out to be much more serious and unforgivable, for the absolute lack of any other motive besides avarice, for the intrinsic repugnance of the sordid deal, for the repulsion of the ugly and filthy appearance of the Ethiopian" ("La prova del 'nappo,'" 182).

14 Both combine a description of the figure's personal characteristics with captions providing further information (*OI* 2.25.45 and *OF* 38.79 A; 42.82 C). Whereas Boiardo's ekphrasis culminates with an inscription in which the unknown artist confesses the inability of images to capture the virtues of Ercole d'Este's soul (*OI* 2.25.56), Ariosto concludes with a tribute to his own lady love in which he turns to the same topos of impossibility, now claiming the inadequacy of words to convey her greatness (*OF* 42.94 C).

15 The four additional stanzas of encomium contained in the 1532 edition include praise for Alfonso's walled defences that made the city safe from the entire world ("tutto il mondo"; *OF* 43.59 C).

16 This occurs in the episodes of Castle Cruel; Tisbina, Iroldo, and Prasildo; Albarosa and Polindo (see Cavallo, *Boiardo's* Orlando innamorato, 54–73, 79).

17 Given Rinaldo's new cynical attitude in contrast to his former role as a civic-minded reader, I disagree with Martinez who sees Rinaldo's vicissitudes from the stream of *disamore* up to Anselmo's tale as a process of "reeducation" (25).

Conclusion

1 Incidentally, both Boiardo and Ariosto's father, Nicolò, held the post of military governor in the two most important Estense cities outside of Fer-

rara itself, Modena and Reggio Emilia. Boiardo was Reggio's governor from 1487 to 1494, a role that Ariosto's father had exercised earlier (1472–81), whereas in 1488 Nicolò took over the same post in Modena that Boiardo had held at the beginning of the decade (1480–3).

2 See also Farmer's discussion of Pico as "among the most extreme syncretists in history" (211). For Pico's library, see Kibre.

3 Pico went to Ferrara to study humanities with Battista Guarino in 1479 following his mother's death (Folin, "Studio e politica," 76). Carrai notes that the Ferrarese poet Lodovico Pittorio wrote an epigram expressing his agreement with Pico's judgment of Boiardo as "the only one among contemporary poets worthy of being compared to the ancients" as well as an elegy also addressed to Pico in which he portrays Boiardo together with other proponents of Guarino's humanism, including his son Battista Guarini, and assigns him "the crown of pastoral poet" (*Pastoralia*, viii).

4 Murrin suggests that the horrors of the French invasion of Italy provided a real-life precedent for Rodomonte's assault on Paris: "Virgil's Turnus and Boiardo's Agricane, the heroes in the scenes that served as models for Ariosto, fight other soldiers. Rodomonte slaughters civilians. The French had shocked the Italians in 1494, when they killed all their prisoners" ("Trade and Fortune," 83). See also *History and Warfare*, 80–92, 280–1n.

5 Ascoli traces this evolution in critical readings of the poem (*Ariosto's Bitter Harmony*, 4–12). His "Ariosto's 'Fier Pastor'" provides an exemplary case study for the poem as (among other things) "a response to and a product of extreme historical pressures – above all the threat to Italy generally from the violent incursions of European nation-states and from its own foolish and ambitious leaders and the threat to Ferrara specifically from the imperial papacy that emerged in the early Cinquecento" (190–1).

6 For other writings of the period exposing the crisis ushered in with France's 1494 invasion, see especially Martines 249–63 and Fiorato 179–225. Shaw provides an overview of recent studies dealing with the impact of war in Italy during this period, while noting that "much work remains to be done before even the main features of the Italian Wars and their consequences for Italy and for the European powers can be mapped out with confidence" (viii).

7 The ships belong to the Catalans in the 1532 edition (*OF* 42.38 C), acknowledging the ascendance of Spanish over Portuguese seafaring vessels by that time.

8 The pope reportedly threatened to have him thrown into the Tiber. He alludes to this incident in *Satira* 1.152–3. For Ariosto's trips to Rome on behalf of both Alfonso and Ippolito, see Catalano, *Vita di L. Ariosto*, 1: 322–30.

9 Although my analysis has followed a different path, I agree with Ascoli's assessment of the 1516 poem as the "more direct product and representation of historical crisis" ("Ariosto's 'Fier Pastor,'" 219).

10 In the 1532 edition, Ariosto substitutes an ambivalent verse from this stanza – "forse con sdegno ben del Leon d'oro" ("perhaps with the disdain of the Golden Lion") (*OF* 33.3 A) – with the disclaimer that the Venetians "sempre esempio di giustizia fôro" ("have always been of exemplary justice") (*OF* 36.3 C); however, given the historical vicissitudes between Venice and Ferrara as well as the negative references to Venice elsewhere in the poem, this is likely an ironic comment.

11 For further historical details, see Catalano, *Vita di L. Ariosto*, 1: 315–18. Brand, who notes that "all come in for their share of criticism," including the French, Spanish and Jewish mercenaries, the Ferrarese, and Venetian mercenaries, draws attention to this event for the "outburst of indignation" it occasions on the part of the poet (91).

12 In the next stanza, Ariosto singles out Venice and the papacy. For a consideration of this proem, excised after the first edition, see Casadei, *La strategia delle varianti*, 73–5.

Works Cited

Primary Works

Agostini, Niccolò degli. *Orlando innamorato del S. Matteo Maria Boiardo, Conte di Scandiano insieme co i tre libri di Nicolo de gli Agostini, nuovamente riformato per M. Lodovico Domenichi.* Venice: Girolamo Scotto, 1545.

Ambroise. *The History of the Holy War: Ambroise's Estoire de la guerre sainte.* Ed. Marianne Ailes and Malcolm Barber. Trans. Marianne Ailes. Woodbridge, UK; Rochester, NY: Boydell Press, 2003.

Andrea da Barberino Mangabotti. *L'Aspramonte: Romanzo cavalleresco inedito.* Ed. Marco Boni. Collezione di opere inedite o rare. Bologna: Antiquaria Palmaverde, 1951.

Andrea da Barberino Mangabotti. *Il Guerrin Meschino: Edizione critica secondo l'antica vulgata fiorentina.* Ed. Mauro Cursietti. Medioevo e Umanesimo 109. Rome-Padua: Antenore, 2005.

Andrea da Barberino Mangabotti. *I reali di Francia.* Ed. Giuseppe Vandelli and Giovanni Gambarin. Bari: Laterza, 1947.

Andrea da Barberino Mangabotti. *Storia di Ugone d'Avernia volgarizzata nel sec. XIV.* Ed. F[rancesco] Zambrini and A[lberto] Bacchi della Lega. Scelta di curiosità letterarie inedite o rare dal secolo XIII al XIX, dispense 188–9. 2 vols. Bologna: Romagnoli, 1882. Repr. Bologna: Commissione per i testi di lingua, 1968.

Ariosto, Ludovico. *Lettere.* Ed. Angelo Stella. Verona: Mondadori, 1965.

Ariosto, Ludovico. *"My muse will have a story to paint": Selected Prose of Ludovico Ariosto.* Trans. Dennis Looney. Toronto: University of Toronto Press, 2010.

Ariosto, Ludovico. *Orlando furioso.* Trans. Guido Waldman. Oxford: Oxford University Press, 1974.

Ariosto, Ludovico. *Orlando furioso secondo la princeps del 1516*. Ed. Marco Dorigatti. Città di Castello: Olschki, 2006.

Ariosto, Ludovico. *The Satires of Ludovico Ariosto: A Renaissance Autobiography*. Trans. Peter DeSa Wiggins. Athens: Ohio University Press, 1976.

Arrian. *History of Alexander and Indica*. Trans. E. Iliff Robson. Loeb Classical Library. 2 vols. Cambridge: Harvard University Press, 1966–7.

Bassi, Pietro Andrea de'. *The Labors of Hercules*. Translation of *Le fatiche d'Ercole*. Trans. W. Kenneth Thompson. Barre, MA: Imprint Society, 1971.

Bessarion, John. [Communication of August 24, 1463]. In *Documents on the Later Crusades, 1274–1580*. Ed. and trans. Norman Housley. New York: St Martin's Press, 1996. 147–54.

Boccaccio, Giovanni. *Amorosa visione*. Trans. Robert Hollander, Timothy Hampton, and Margherita Frankel. Hanover and London: University Press of New England, 1986.

Boccaccio, Giovanni. *Decameron*. Ed. Cesare Segre. c1966. Milan: Mursia, 1974.

Boccaccio, Giovanni. *The Decameron*. Trans. G.H. McWilliam. 1972. New York: Penguin, 1995.

Boccaccio, Giovanni. *Famous Women*. Trans. Virginia Brown. Cambridge, MA: Harvard University Press, 2003.

Boccaccio, Giovanni. *Teseida*. *Opere minori in volgare*. Ed. Mario Marti. Vol. 2. Milan: Rizzoli, 1970. 247–658.

Boiardo, Matteo Maria. *Inamoramento de Orlando*. Ed. Antonia Tissoni Benvenuti and Cristina Montagnani. *Opere*. 2 vols. Milan: Riccardo Ricciardi, 1999.

Boiardo, Matteo Maria. *Orlando in Love*. Trans. Charles S. Ross. West Lafayette, IN: Parlor Press, 2004.

Boiardo, Matteo Maria. *Pastorali*. Intro. Stefano Carrai; comment and textual notes Marina Riccucci. Milan: Fondazione Pietro Bembo; Parma: U. Guanda, 2005.

Boiardo, Matteo Maria. *Pastoralia*. Ed. and trans. Stefano Carrai. Padua: Antenore, 1996.

Boiardo, Matteo Maria. *Tarocchi*. Ed. Simona Foà. Rome: Salerno, 1993.

Boiardo, Matteo Maria, trans. *Ciropedia*. By Xenophon. Modena: Biblioteca Estense, MS Ital. 416.

Boiardo, Matteo Maria, trans. *Delle guerre de greci & de persi*. By Herodotus. Venice: Bernardino de Bindoni, 1539.

Boiardo, Matteo Maria, trans. *The* Historia imperiale *by Riccobaldo Ferrarese translated by Matteo Maria Boiardo (1471–1473)*. Vol. 1. Ed. Andrea Rizzi. Rome: Istituto Storico Italiano per il Medio Evo, 2008 [contains Books 1 and 2].

Boiardo, Matteo Maria, trans. *Istoria imperiale*. In *Rerum italicarum scriptores*. Vol. 9. Ed. L.A. Muratori. Città di Castello: S. Lapi, 1900 [contains Books 3 and 4].

Boiardo, Matteo Maria, trans. "M.M. Boiardo's version of Riccobaldo Ferrarese: The *Historia Imperiale* (1471–73)." Ed. Andrea Rizzi. Diss. University of Kent at Canterbury, 2000 [contains Book 3].

Boiardo, Matteo Maria, trans. *Le vite degli eccellenti capitani*. By Cornelius Nepos. Bologna: Zanichelli, 1908.

I cantari di Carduino giuntovi quello di Tristano e Lancielotto quando combattettero al petrone di Merlino. Ed. Pio Rajna. *Scelta di curiosità letterarie inedite o rare dal secolo XIII al XVII*. Vol. 135. Bologna: Gaetano Romagnoli, 1873.

La canzone d'Aspromonte: Poema epico del XV secolo. Ed. Carmelina Sicari. Vibo Valentia: Qualecultura, 1991.

Castiglione, Baldassare. *The Book of the Courtier*. Trans. Charles S. Singleton. New York: Doubleday, 1959.

Castiglione, Baldassare. *Il libro del cortegiano*. Ed. Walter Barberis. Turin: Einaudi, 1998.

La chanson d'Aspremont: Chanson de geste du XIIe siècle. Ed. Louis Brandin. 2 vols. Paris: Librairie Ancienne Honoré Champion, 1923.

Chronique d'Ernoul et de Bernard le Trésorier. Ed. M.L. de Mas-Latrie. Paris: J. Renouard, 1871.

Colonne, Guido delle. *Historia destructionis Troiae*. Trans. Mary Elizabeth Meek. Bloomington: Indiana University Press, 1974.

Columbus, Christopher. *La scoperta del nuovo mondo: La divulgazione in Italia dell'impresa attraverso due testi del 1493*. Intro. Martin Davies. Florence: Olschki, 1992.

Columbus, Christopher. *Textos y documentos completos*. Ed. Consuelo Varela, and Juan Gil. Madrid: Alianza, 1992.

The Conquest of Jerusalem and the Third Crusade: Sources in Translation. Ed. Peter W. Edbury. Aldershot, UK; Brookfield, VT: Ashgate, 1998.

Conti, Niccolò. "The travels of Nicolò Conti, in the East, in the early part of the fifteenth century, as related by Poggio Bracciolini, in his work entitled 'Historia de Varietate Fortunae,' lib. IV." In *India in the Fifteenth Century, Being a Collection of Narratives of Voyages to India, in the Century Preceding the Portuguese Discovery of the Cape of Good Hope*. Ed. R.H. Major. London: The Hakluyt Society, 1857. 1–39.

Curtius Rufus, Quintus. *The History of Alexander*. Trans. John Yardley. Intro. Waldemar Heckel. 1984. London: Penguin, 2001.

Dal Campo, Luchino. *[El viaggio al santo Sepolcro del nostro Signor Gesù Cristo in Jerusalem, el qual fece lo illustrissimo signor marchese Nicolò da Este con altri gentiluomini suoi compagni.] Viaggio a Gerusalemme di Nicolò da Este*. Ed. Giovanni Ghinassi. Turin: UTET, 1861.

Dante Alighieri. *Divina Commedia*. Ed. Natalino Sapegno. Florence: La Nuova Italia, 1976.

Dati, Giuliano. "*La gran magnificentia de Prete Janni, signore dell'India maggiore & della Ethiopia*. Ed. Achille Neri." *Il Propungatore* 9.1 (1876): 145–65.

Dati, Giuliano. "Lettera delle isole che ha trovato il re di Spagna." In *La scoperta del nuovo mondo: La divulgazione in Italia dell'impresa attraverso due testi del 1493*. Intro. Martin Davies. Florence: Olschki, 1992.

Diario ferrarese dall'anno 1409 al 1504 di autori incerti. Ed. Giuseppe Pardi. *Rerum italicarum scriptores* 24, pt 7, nos 1–4. Ed. L.A. Muratori. Bologna: Zanichelli, 1928–33.

Don Domenego. *Viaggio in Oriente di un nobile del Quattrocento: Il pellegrinaggio di Milliaduse d'Este*. Ed. Alda Rossebastiano and Simona Fenoglio. Turin: UTET, 2005.

Einhard. *The Life of Charlemagne*. In *Charlemagne's Courtier: The Complete Einhard*. Ed. and trans. Paul Edward Dutton. c1998. Peterborough, ON: Broadview Press, 2003. 15–39.

L'Entrée d'Espagne, chanson de geste franco-italienne, publiée d'après le manuscrit unique de Venise. Ed. Antoine Thomas. 2 vols. Paris: Firmin-Didot, 1913.

Erasmus. *Consultatio de bello Turcis inferendo*. 1530. In *Documents on the Later Crusades, 1274–1580*. Ed. and trans. Norman Housley. New York: St Martin's Press, 1996. 178–83.

[Ernoul and Bernard the Treasurer.] *Chronique d'Ernoul et de Bernard le Tresorier*. Paris: J. Renouard, 1871.

[*Genealogia dei principi d'Este*] *Commentario al codice Genealogia dei principi d'Este*. Ed. Ernesto Milano and Mauro Bini. Modena: Il bulino edizioni d'arte, 1996.

[*Gesta Francorum et aliorum Hierosolimitanorum*.] *The Deeds of the Franks and the Other Pilgrims to Jerusalem*. Trans. and ed. Rosalind Hill. London: Thomas Nelson and Sons Ltd, 1962.

Giovanni da Pian del Carpine. [*Historia Mongalorum*.] "The Journey of Friar John of Pian de Carpini to the Court of Kuyuk Khan 1245–1247 as Narrated by Himself." In Komroff, ed., *Contemporaries of Marco Polo*, 3–50.

Guerre contro i turchi (1453–1470). Ed. Marina Beer and Cristina Ivaldi. *Guerre in ottava rima*. Vol. 4. Ferrara: Istituto di Studi Rinascimentali, 1988.

Guicciardini, Francesco. *History of Italy*. Trans. Sidney Alexander. New York: Macmillan, 1969.

Guicciardini, Francesco. *Storia d'Italia*. Ed. Ettore Mazzali. 3 vols. Milan: Garzanti, 1988.

Hayton of Cocyrus (Het'um). *The Flower of Histories of the East*. Trans. Robert Bedrosian. http://rbedrosian.com/hetumint.htm. Accessed 12 November 2009.

Herodotus. *Delle guerre de greci & de persi*. Trans. M.M. Boiardo. Venice: Bernardino de Bindoni, 1539.

Homer. *The Odyssey*. Trans. Richmond Lattimore. 1965. New York: Harper and Row, 1975.

Ibn al-Qalanisi. *The Damascus Chronicle of the Crusades. Extracted and Translated from the Chronicle of Ibn Al-Qalanisi*. Ed. H.A.R. Gibb. London: Luzac and Company, 1967.

[Itinerarium peregrinorum et gesta regis Ricardi] *Chronicle of the Third Crusade: A Translation of the* Itinerarium peregrinorum et gesta regis Ricardi. Trans. Helen J. Nicholson. Aldershot: Ashgate, 1997.

Jacques de Vitry. *Histoire orientale*. Trans. Marie-Geneviève Grossel. Paris: Honoré Champion, 2005.

John of Segovia. [Letter of 2 December 1454.] *Documents on the Later Crusades, 1274–1580*. Ed. and trans. Norman Housley. New York: St Martin's Press, 1996. 144–7.

Latini, Brunetto. *Li livres dou tresor*. Ed. Spurgeon Baldwin and Paul Barrette. Tempe, AZ: MRTS, 2003.

[Letter of Prester John, late fifteenth-century Italian version.] "Lettera del Presto Giovanni." In "Documenti," appendix to *Cronica di Giovanni Villani a migliore lezione ridotta*. Ed. F. Gherardi Dragomanni. Florence, 1844. 245–59.

[Letter of Prester John, Latin and Old French versions.] *La lettera del Prete Gianni*. Ed. Gioia Zaganelli. Milan: Luni, 2000.

Machiavelli, Niccolò. *The Prince*. Intro. Anthony Grafton. Trans. George Bull. 1961. New York: Penguin, 2003.

Machiavelli, Niccolò. *Il principe*. Ed. Giorgio Inglese. Turin: Einaudi, 1995.

Machiavelli, Niccolò. "Serenade." In *The Chief Works and Others*. Vol. 2. Trans. Allan Gilbert. Durham: Duke University Press, 1989. 1016–21.

Malaterra, Goffredo [Geoffrey]. [*De rebus gestis Rogerii, Calabriae et Siciliae comitis, et Roberti Guiscardi ducis, fratris ejus*.] *The deeds of Count Roger of Calabria and Sicily and of his brother Duke Robert Guiscard*. Trans. Kenneth Baxter Wolf. Ann Arbor: University of Michigan Press, 2005.

Mandeville, John. *Le livre des merveilles du monde*. Ed. Christiane Deluz. Paris: CNRS, 2000.

Mandeville, John. *The Travels of Sir John Mandeville*. Trans. C.W.Rd.D. Moseley. London: Penguin, 1983.

More, Thomas. *Utopia*. Ed. George M. Logan and Robert M. Adams. c1989. Cambridge: Cambridge University Press, 2005.

Nicholas of Cusa. *Of Learned Ignorance: A Translation and Appraisal of the* De docta ignorantia. Trans. D.J.B. Hawkins. New Haven: Yale University Press, 1954.

Nicholas of Cusa. *On the Peace of Faith (De pace fidei)*. Trans. William F. Wertz. Reprinted from *Toward a New Council of Florence: "On the Peace of Faith" and Other Works by Nicolaus of Cusa*. http://www.schillerinstitute.org/transl/cusa_p_of_f.html. Accessed 4 June 2010.

Odorico da Pordenone. *The Journal of Friar Odoric*. In Komroff, ed., *Contemporaries of Marco Polo,* 213–50.

Oliver of Paderborn. *The Capture of Damietta*. Trans. John J. Gavigan. In *Christian Society and the Crusades 1198–1229*. Ed. Edward Peters. Philadelphia: University of Pennsylvania Press, 1971. 49–139.

Ovidius Naso, Publius. *Metamorphoses*. Trans. David Raeburn. Intro. Denis Feeney. New York: Penguin, 2004.

Petrarca, Francesco. [*Itinerarium ad sepulchrum domini nostri Yehsu Christi.*] *Petrarch's Guide to the Holy Land: Itinerary to the Sepulcher of Our Lord Jesus Christ*. Ed. and trans. Theodore J. Cachey, Jr. Notre Dame, IN.: University of Notre Dame Press, 2002.

Petrarca, Francesco. *Petrarch's Lyric Poems: The* Rime sparse *and Other Lyrics*. Trans. Robert M. Durling. Cambridge, MA: Harvard University Press, 1976.

Petrarca, Francesco. *Rime e trionfi*. Ed. Raffaello Ramat. c1957. Milan: Rizzoli, 1971.

Pico Della Mirandola, Giovanni. "Oration on the Dignity of Man." Trans. Elizabeth Livermore Forbes. *The Renaissance Philosophy of Man*. Ed. Ernst Cassirer, Paul Oskar Kristeller, John Herman Randall, Jr. Chicago: Phoenix, c1948. 223–54.

Plato. *Theaetetus*. Trans. John McDowell. Oxford: Clarendon Press, 1973.

Plutarch. [De Alexandri Magni fortuna aut virtute, I & II.] "On the Fortune or the Virtue of Alexander." *Moralia*. Cambridge, MA: Loeb, 1936. Vol. 4, 363D–351B. 379–487.

Plutarch. *The Life of Alexander the Great*. Trans. John Dryden. Ed. Arthur Hugh Clough. Intro. Victor Davis Hanson. New York: The Modern Library, 2004.

da Poggibonsi, Niccolò. *Libro d'Oltramare*. Ed. Alberto Bacchi della Lega. 2 vols. Bologna: Commissione per i testi di lingua, 1968.

da Poggibonsi, Niccolò. *Voyage beyond the Sea (1346–1350)*. Trans. T. Bellorini and E. Hoade. Jerusalem: Franciscan Printing Press, 1945.

Polo, Marco. *Milione. Le divisament dou monde. Il milione nelle redazioni toscana e franco-italiana*. Ed. Gabriella Ronchi. Intro. Cesare Segre. 1982. Milan: Mondadori, 2006.

Polo, Marco. *Il milione: Con le postille di Cristoforo Colombo*. Ed. Luigi Giovannini. Turin: Paoline, 1985.

[Pseudo-Callisthenes] *The Romance of Alexander the Great by Pseudo-Callisthenes*. Ed. Albert Mugrdich Wolohojian. New York: Columbia University Press, 1969.

Ptolemy. *Geography of Claudius Ptolemy*. Trans. Edward Luther Stevenson. Intro. Joseph Fischer. New York: New York Public Library, 1932; New York: Dover, 1991.

Pulci, Luigi. *The Epic Adventures of Orlando and His Giant Friend Morgante*. Trans. Joseph Tusiani. Intro. Edoardo A. Lèbano. Bloomington: Indiana University Press, 1998.

Pulci, Luigi. *Morgante*. Ed. Franca Ageno. Milan: Ricciardi, 1955.

Riccobaldo da Ferrara. *Compilatio chronologica*. In *Rerum italicarum scriptores*. Vol. 9. Ed. L.A. Muratori. Città di Castello: S. Lapi, 1900-.

Sagundino, Niccolò. "Oratio ad serenissimum principem et novissimum regem Alfonsum." *Notes et extraits pour servir à l'histoire des Croisades au XVe siècle*. Ed. N. Jorga. 3rd series. Paris, 1902. 316–23.

Sanseverino, Roberto da. *Viaggio in Terra Santa*. Bologna: Commissione per i testi di lingua, 1969.

La Spagna, poema cavalleresco del secolo XIV [*Spagna maggiore*]. Ed. Michele Catalano. Collezione di opere inedite o rare, vols 111–13. 3 vols. Bologna: Commissione per i testi di lingua, 1939–40.

Spagna ferrarese. Ed. Valentina Gritti and Cristina Montagnani. Novara: Interlinea, 2009.

Statius, Publius Papinius. *The Thebaid: Seven against Thebes*. Trans. Charles S. Ross. Baltimore: Johns Hopkins University Press, 2004.

Storia di Rinaldino da Montalbano. Ed. Carlo Minutoli. Bologna: Gaetano Romagnoli, 1865.

Strabo. *The Geography of Strabo*. Trans. Horace Leonard Jones. 8 vols. London: William Heinemann; New York: Putnam, 1917–32.

Thomas de Kent. *Le roman d'Alexandre, ou, Le roman de toute chevalerie*. Trans. Catherine Gaullier-Bougassas and Laurence Harf-Lancner. Ed. Brian Foster and Ian Short. Paris: Champion, 2003.

Uberti, Fazio degli. *Il Dittamondo e Le rime*. Ed. Giuseppe Corsi. Scrittori d'Italia, no. 207. Bari: G. Laterza, 1952.

Virgil. *The Aeneid*. Trans. Robert Fitzgerald. New York: Vintage Classics, 1990.

[Voyage de Charlemagne à Jérusalem et à Constantinople] *The Pilgrimage of Charlemagne*. Trans. Glyn S. Burgess. Intro. Anne Elizabeth Cobby. New York: Garland, 1988.

William of Rubruck. The Journal of Friar William of Rubruck. In Komroff, ed. *Contemporaries of Marco Polo*, 53–209.

William of Tyre. *A History of Deeds Done beyond the Sea*. 2 vols. Trans. Emily A. Babcock and August C. Krey. New York: Columbia University Press, 1943.

Secondary Works

Abu-Lughod, Janet. *Before European Hegemony: The World System AD 1250–1350*. New York: Oxford University Press, 1989.

Akbari, Suzanne Conklin. *Idols in the East: European Representations of Islam and the Orient, 1100–1450*. Ithaca: Cornell University Press, 2009.

Akbari, Suzanne Conklin, and Amilcare Iannucci, eds. *Marco Polo and the Encounter of East and West*. Toronto: University of Toronto Press, 2008.

Alexandre, Denise. "Tre figure boiardesche di eroe saraceno: Ferraguto, Agricane, Rodamonte." *Annali d'Italianistica* 1 (1983): 129–43.

Alexandre-Gras, Denise. *L'héroisme chevaleresque dans le* Roland amoreux *de Boiardo*. Saint-Etienne: Institut d'études de la Renaissance et de l'Age Classique, 1988.

Alhaique Pettinelli, Rosanna. *L'immaginario cavalleresco nel rinascimento ferrarese*. Rome: Bonacci, 1983.

Alhaique Pettinelli, Rosanna. "L'*Orlando innamorato* e la tradizione cavalleresca in ottave." *La Rassegna della Letteratura Italiana* 71 (1967): 383–418.

Allaire, Gloria. *Andrea da Barberino and the Language of Chivalry*. Gainesville: University of Florida, 1997.

Allaire, Gloria. "Babes in Arms." In *Medusa's Gaze: Essays on Gender, Literature, and Aesthetics in the Italian Renaissance, in Honor of Robert J. Rodini*. Ed. Paul A. Ferrara, Eugenio Giusti, and Jane Tylus. Boca Raton, FL: Bordighera Press, 2004. 9–29.

Allaire, Gloria. "Portrayals of Muslims in Andrea da Barberino's *Guerrino il Meschino*." In *Medieval Christian Perceptions of Islam: A Book of Essays*. Ed. John Victor Tolan. New York: Garland, 1996. 243–69.

Allaire, Gloria. "The Warrior Woman in Late Medieval Prose Epics." *Italian Culture* 12 (1994): 33–43.

Arnaldi, Girolamo. *Italy and Its Invaders*. Trans. Antony Shugaar. Cambridge, MA: Harvard University Press, 2005.

Ascoli, Albert Russell. *Ariosto's Bitter Harmony: Crisis and Evasion in the Italian Renaissance*. Princeton: Princeton University Press, 1987.

Ascoli, Albert Russell. "Ariosto's 'Fier Pastor': Structure and Historical Meaning in *Orlando furioso*." In *Phaethon's Children: The Este Court and Its Culture in Early Modern Ferrara*. Ed. Dennis Looney and Deanna Shemek. Tempe, AZ: Arizona Center for Medieval and Renaissance Studies, 2005. 189–224. More recently published as chapter 6 of *A Local Habitation and a Name: Imagining Histories in the Italian Renaissance*. New York: Fordham University Press, 2011.

Aslanapa, Oktay. *One Thousand Years of Turkish Carpets*. Trans. William A. Edmonds. Istanbul: EREN, 1988.

Attar, Karina F. "Muslim-Christian Encounters in Masuccio Salernitano's *Novellino*." In *Medieval Encounters: Jewish, Christian and Muslim Culture in Confluence and Dialogue*. Leiden: Brill Academic Publishers, 2005. 71–100. http://dx.doi.org/10.1163/157006705775032825

Babinger, Franz. *Mehmed the Conqueror and His Time*. Ed. William C. Hickman. Trans. Ralph Manheim. Bollingen Series XCVI. Princeton: Princeton University Press, 1978.

Balard, Michel. "A Christian Mediterranean: 1000–1500." In *The Mediterranean in History*. Ed. David Abulafia. Los Angeles, CA : The J. Paul Getty Museum, 2003. 183–218.

Baldan, Paolo. "Marfisa: Nascita e carriera di una regina amazzone." *Giornale storico della letteratura italiana* 158 (1981): 518–29.

Bartlett, Robert. *The Making of Europe: Conquest, Colonization and Cultural Change 950–1350*. Princeton: Princeton University Press, 1993.

Bedrosian, Robert, pref. *The Flower of Histories of the East*. By Hayton of Cocyrus (He'tum). Trans. Robert Bedrosian. http://rbedrosian.com/hetumint.htm. Accessed 12 November 2009.

Bendinelli, Maria Livia. "Volgarizzamenti italiani della *Lettera del Prete Gianni*." *Testi e interpretazioni. Studi del Seminario di Filologia Romanza dell'Università di Firenze*. Milan-Naples, 1978. 37–64.

Bendinelli Predelli, Maria. "La donna guerriera nell'immaginario italiano del tardo medioevo." *Italian Culture* 12 (1994): 13–31.

Benedetti, Laura. "I paradossi dell'amore. Atlante e Ruggiero dall'*Innamorato* al *Furioso*." *Quaderni d'Italianistica* 21.2 (2000): 113–26.

Benfell, V. Stanley. "Ezzelino III da Romano." In *The Dante Encyclopedia*. Ed. Richard Lansing. New York: Garland, 2000. 365–6.

Benson, Pamela Joseph. *The Invention of the Renaissance Woman*. University Park, PA: Pennsylvania State University Press, 1992.

Bertoni, Giulio. *La biblioteca Estense e la cultura ferrarese*. Turin: Ermanno Loescher, 1903.

Bertozzi, Marco. "Il talismano di Warburg. Considerazioni sull'impianto astrologico di Palazzo Schifanoia." In *Alla corte degli Estensi: Filosofia, arte e cultura a Ferrara nei secoli XV e XVI. Atti del Convegno Internazionale di Studi, Ferrara, 5–7 marzo 1992*. Ed. Marco Bertozzi. Ferrara: Università degli Studi, 1994. 199–208.

Bestor, Jane Fair. "Bastardy and Legitimacy in the Formation of a Regional State in Italy: The Estense Succession." *Comparative Studies in Society and History* 38.3 (1996): 549–85. http://dx.doi.org/10.1017/S0010417500020053.

Bezzola, Reto. "L'Oriente nel poema cavalleresco nel primo Rinascimento." *Lettere Italiane* 15 (1963): 385–98.

Bird, Jessalynn Lea. "The *Historia Orientalis* of Jacques de Vitry: Visual and Written Commentaries as Evidence of a Text's Audience, Reception, and Utilization." *Essays in Medieval Studies* 20.1 (2003): 56–74. http://dx.doi.org/10.1353/ems.2004.0002.

Bisaha, Nancy. *Creating East and West: Renaissance Humanists and the Ottoman Turks*. Philadelphia: University of Pennsylvania Press, 2004.

Bisaha, Nancy. "Pope Pius II and the Crusade." In *Crusading in the Fifteenth Century: Message and Impact*. Ed. Norman Housley. Basingstoke and New York: Palgrave Macmillan, 2004. 39–52.

Black, Robert. *Benedetto Accolti and the Florentine Renaissance*. Cambridge and New York: Cambridge University Press, 1985. http://dx.doi.org/10.1017/CBO9780511562525

Bontempelli, Massimo. "L'Ariosto geografo." In *L'ottava d'oro*. Ed. A. Baldini. Milan: Mondadori, 1933.

Boralevi, Alberto. "I tappeti." In *Atlante di Schifanoia*. Ed. Ranieri Varese. Modena: Panini, 1989. 217–20.

Brand, C.P. *Ludovico Ariosto: A preface to the* Orlando furioso. Edinburgh: Edinburgh University Press, 1974.

Breazeale, Kennon. "Editorial Introduction to Nicolò de' Conti's Account." *SOAS Bulletin of Burma Research* 2.2 (2004): 100–9.

Bregoli Russo, Mauda. *Studi di critica boiardesca*. Naples: Federico and Ardia, 1994.

Brotton, Jerry. *The Renaissance Bazaar: From the Silk Road to Michelangelo*. Oxford: Oxford University Press, 2002.

Brotton, Jerry. *Trading Territories: Mapping the Early Modern World*. Ithaca, NY: Cornell University Press, 1998.

Bruscagli, Riccardo. "L'ecfrasi dinastica nel poema eroico del Rinascimento." *In Ecfrasi: modelli ed esempi fra Medioevo e Rinascimento*. Ed. Gianni Venturi and Monica Farnetti. Roma: Bulzoni, 2004. Vol. 1. 269–92.

Bruscagli, Riccardo. "L'*Innamorato*, la *Spagna*, il *Morgante*." *Intertestualità e smontaggi*. Roma: Bulzoni, 1998. 111–26.

Bruscagli, Riccardo. "Prove di commento all'*Orlando innamorato*." *Studi italiani* 1 (1989): 5–29.

Bruscagli, Riccardo. *Studi cavallereschi*. Florence: Società Editrice Fiorentina, 2003.

Bruscagli, Riccardo, intro. and notes. *Orlando innamorato*. By Matteo Maria Boiardo. Turin: Einaudi, 1995.

Bulzoni, Lina, ed. "L'*Orlando furioso* e la sua tradizione in immagini." Centro Elaborazione Informatica di Testi e Immagini nella Tradizione Letteraria. Scuola Normale di Pisa. http://www.ctl.sns.it/furioso. Accessed 11 November 2010.

Bulzoni, Lina, Serena Pezzini, and Giovanni Rizzarelli. *"Tra mille carte vive ancora": Ricezione del* Furioso *tra immagini e parole*. Lucca: Maria Pacini Fazzi, 2010.

Burman, Thomas E. *Reading the Qur'an in Latin Christendom, 1140–1560. Material Texts*. Philadelphia: University of Pennsylvania Press, 2007.

Cabani, Maria Cristina. *Gli amici amanti: Coppie eroiche e sortite notturne nell'epica italiana*. Naples: Liguori, 1995.

Cachey, Theodore J., Jr, intro. and appendix I. *Petrarch's Guide to the Holy Land: Itinerary to the Sepulcher of Our Lord Jesus Christ*. By Francesco Petrarca. Ed. and trans. Theodore J. Cachey, Jr. Notre Dame, IN.: University of Notre Dame Press, 2002. 1–56.

Calvino, Italo. [Presentation.] *Orlando furioso*. By Ludovico Ariosto. Ed. Lanfranco Caretti. c1966. Turin: Einaudi, 1992. xxv–xlvi.

Canova, Andrea. "*Vendetta di Falconetto* (*e Inamoramento de Orlando*?)." In *Boiardo, Ariosto e i libri di battaglia*. Ed. Andrea Canova and Paola Vecchi Galli. Novara: Interlinea edizioni, 2007. 77–106.

Cappelli, Adriano. "La biblioteca Estense della prima metà del secolo XV." *Giornale storico della letteratura italiana* 14 (1889): 1–30.

Caramella, Santino. "L'Asia nell'*Orlando innamorato*." *Bollettino della Società geografica italiana*. Series 5, Vol. 12 (1923): 44–59, 127–50.

Cardini, Franco. *In Terrasanta: Pellegrini italiani tra Medioevo e prima età moderna*. Bologna: Il mulino, 2005.

Caretti, Lanfranco, ed. *Orlando furioso*. By Ludovico Ariosto. c1966. Turin: Einaudi, 1992.

Carrai, Stefano, intro. *Pastorali*. By Matteo Maria Boiardo. Milan: Fondazione Pietro Bembo; Parma: U. Guanda, 2005.

Carrai, Stefano, intro. and comments. *Pastoralia*. By Matteo Maria Boiardo. Padua: Antenore, 1996.

Carrara, Enrico. "Alcune 'storie' del *Furioso*." *Studi petrarcheschi ed altri scritti: Raccolti a cura di amici e discepoli*. Turin: Bottega d'Erasmo, 1959. 277–315.

Cary, George. *The Medieval Alexander*. Cambridge: Cambridge University Press, 1956.

Casadei, Alberto. *Il percorso del* Furioso*: Ricerche intorno alle redazioni del 1516 e del 1521*. Bologna: Il Mulino, 1993.

Casadei, Alberto. *La strategia delle varianti: Le correzioni storiche del terzo* Furioso. Lucca: Pacini Fazzi, 1988.

Cassirer, Ernst. *The Individual and the Cosmos in Renaissance Philosophy*. Trans. and intro. Mario Domandi. Chicago: University of Chicago Press, 2010.

Catalano, Michele. *Vita di Ludovico Ariosto. Ricostruita su nuovi documenti*. 2 vols. Geneva: Olschki, 1930–1.

Cavallo, Jo Ann. *Boiardo's* Orlando innamorato*: An Ethics of Desire*. Rutherford, NJ: Fairleigh Dickinson Press; London: Associated University Presses, 1993.

Cavallo, Jo Ann. "Denying Closure: Ariosto's Rewriting of the *Orlando innamorato*." In Cavallo and Ross, eds, *Fortune and Romance*, 97–134.

Cavallo, Jo Ann. "The Pathways of Knowledge in Boiardo and Ariosto: The Case of Rodamonte." *Italica* 79.3 (2002): 305–20. http://dx.doi.org/10.2307/3656094.

Cavallo, Jo Ann. *The Romance Epics of Boiardo, Ariosto, and Tasso: From Public Duty to Private Pleasure*. Toronto: University of Toronto Press, 2004.

Cavallo, Jo Ann, and Charles Ross, eds. *Fortune and Romance: Boiardo in America*. Tempe, AZ: Medieval and Renaissance Texts and Studies, 1998.

Cerulli, Enrico. "Eugenio IV e gli Etiopi al concilio di Firenze nel 1441." *Atti dell'Accademia dei Lincei*. Series 6, Vol. 9 (1933): 347–68.

Cerulli, Enrico. "Il volo di Astolfo sull'Etiopia nell'*Orlando furioso*." *Atti dell'Accademia dei Lincei*. Series 6, Vol. 8 (1932): 19–38.

Chambers, James. *The Devil's Horsemen: The Mongol Invasion of Europe*. Chicago: Phoenix, 1979.

Chiappini, Luciano. *Gli estensi*. Modena: Dall'Oglio, 1967.

Ciarambino, Gerardo C.A. *Carlomagno, Gano e Orlando in alcuni romanzi italiani del XIV e XV secolo*. Pisa: Giardini, 1976.

"Cina." *Il Milione: Enciclopedia di tutti i paesi del mondo*. Novara: Istituto Geografico de Agostini, 1962. Vol. 8. *Asia*. 13–352.

Cossutta, Fabio. *Gli ideali epici dell'Umanesimo e l'*Orlando innamorato. Rome: Bulzoni, 1995.

Cremante, Simona. "Entra Angelica (*Orlando innamorato*, Ii)." *Studi italiani* 1.2 (1995): 5–17.

Daniel, Norman. *Islam and the West: The Making of an Image*. c1960. Edinburgh: Edinburgh University Press, 1962.

Davis Hanson, Victor, intro. *The Life of Alexander the Great*. By Plutarch.

Trans. John Dryden. Ed. Arthur Hugh Clough. New York: The Modern Library, 2004. ix–xvi.

Dean, Trevor. *Land and Power in Late Medieval Ferrara*. New York: Cambridge University Press, 1988. http://dx.doi.org/10.1017/CBO9780511523144

De Armas, Frederick A. *Saturn from Antiquity to the Renaissance*. Ed. Massimo Ciavolella and Amilcare A. Iannucci. University of Toronto Italian Studies 8. Ottawa: Dovehouse Editions, 1992. 151–72.

Delcorno, Carlo. *Exemplum e letteratura: Tra Medioevo e Rinascimento*. Bologna: Mulino, 1989.

Delcorno Branca, Daniela. "Orlando e Agricane alla fontana." *Tristano e Lancilotto in Italia. Studi di letteratura in Italia*. Ravenna: Longo, 1998. 165–73.

Delumeau, Jean. *History of Paradise: The Garden of Eden in Myth and Tradition*. Trans. Matthew O'Connell. New York: Continuum, 1995.

Deluz, Christiane. *Le livre de Jehan de Mandeville: Une "géographie" au XIVe siècle*. Textes, Etudes, Congrès 8. Louvain-la-Neuve: Institut d'Etudes Médiévales de l'Université Catholique de Louvain, 1988.

De Weever, Jacqueline. *Sheba's Daughters: Whitening and Demonizing the Saracen Woman in Medieval French Epic*. New York: Garland, 1998.

Di Cesare, Mario. "Isabella and Her Hermit: Stillness at the Center of the *Orlando furioso*." *Mediaevalia* 6 (1980): 311–32.

Dionisotti, Carlo. *Boiardo e altri studi cavallereschi*. Ed. Giuseppe Anceschi and Antonia Tissoni Benvenuti. Novara: Interlinea, 2003.

Dionisotti, Carlo. "La guerra d'Oriente nella letteratura veneziana del Cinquecento." In *Venezia e l'Oriente fra Tardo Medioevo e Rinascimento*. Ed. Agostino Pertusi. Venice: Sansoni, 1966. 471–93.

Doniger, Wendy. *The Implied Spider: Politics and Theology in Myth*. New York: Columbia University Press, 1998.

Donnarumma, Raffaele. *Storia dell'*Orlando innamorato. *Poetiche e modelli letterari in Boiardo*. Lucca: Pacini-Fazzi, 1996.

Dorigatti, Marco. "La favola e la corte: Intrecci narrativi e genealogie estensi dal Boiardo all'Ariosto." In *Gli dèi a Corte. Letteratura e immagini nella Ferrara estense*. Ed. Gianni Venturi and Francesca Cappelletti. Florence: Olschki, 2009. 31–54.

Dorigatti, Marco. "Reinventing Roland: Orlando in Italian Literature." In *Roland and Charlemagne in Europe: Essays on the Reception and Transformation of a Legend*. Ed. Karen Pratt. London: King's College London Centre for Late Antique and Medieval Studies, 1996. 105–26.

Dorigatti, Marco. "Rugiero and the Dynastic Theme from Boiardo to Ariosto." In *Italy in Crisis: 1494*. Ed. Jane Everson and Diego Zancani. Oxford: Legenda, 2000. 92–128.

Dorigatti, Marco. "Sobrino ariostesco e misconosciuto." *Belfagor* 65.4 (2010): 401–14.

Doroszlaï, Alexandre. *Ptolémée et l'hippogriffe: La géographie de l'Arioste soumise à l'épreuve des cartes*. Alessandria: Edizioni dell'Orso, 1998.

Dronke, Peter, intro. *Alessandro nel Medioevo Occidentale*. Ed. Piero Boitani et al. Rome: Fondazione Lorenzo Valla; Milan: Mondadori, 1997. xv–lxxv.

Eboigbe, Delphia Robinson. "The Depiction of the Negro African in Three Old French Chansons de Geste and Two Renaissance Epico-Chivalric Poems." Diss. Indiana University, 1987.

Echevarría, Ana. *The Fortress of Faith: The Attitudes toward Muslims in Fifteenth Century Spain*. Leiden: Brill, 1999.

Eco, Umberto. "How to Talk about Books You Haven't Read: Pierre Bayard and Umberto Eco with Paul Holdengraber." *Live from the New York Public Library*, 17 Nov. 2007. http://www.nypl.org/audiovideo/how-talk-about-books-you-havent-read-pierre-bayard-umberto-eco-paul-holdengr%C3%A4ber. Accessed 23 November 2010.

Edson, Evelyn. *The World Map, 1300–1492: The Persistence of Tradition and Transformation*. Baltimore: Johns Hopkins University Press, 2007.

Egan, Kathleen. "On the Indignity of Man: The Quarrel between Boiardo and Pico della Mirandola." In Cavallo and Ross, eds, *Fortune and Romance*, 237–57.

Eliade, Mircea. *Rites and Symbols of Initiation: The Mysteries of Birth and Rebirth*. Trans. Williard R. Trask. New York: Harper Torchbooks, 1958.

Erdmann, Kurt. "Venezia e il tappeto orientale." In *Venezia e l'Oriente fra Tardo Medioevo e Rinascimento*. Ed. Agostino Pertusi. Venice: Sansoni, 1966. 529–45.

Fahy, Conor. "Three Early Renaissance Treatises on Women." *Italian Studies* 11.1 (1956): 30–55. http://dx.doi.org/10.1179/007516356790589324.

Falchetta, Piero. *Fra Mauro's World Map*. Trans. Jeremy Scott. Turnhout: Brepols, 2006.

Farmer, Stephen Alan. *Syncretism in the West: Pico's 900 theses (1486): The Evolution of Traditional, Religious, and Philosophical Systems: With Text, Translation, and Commentary*. Tempe, AZ: Medieval and Renaissance Texts and Studies, 1998.

Ferrero, Giuseppe Guido. "Astolfo (Storia di un personaggio)." *Convivium* 29 (1961): 513–30.

Finucci, Valeria. *The Lady Vanishes. Subjectivity and Representation in Castiglione and Ariosto*. Stanford: Stanford University Press, 1992.

Fiorato, Adelin Charles. "Complaintes, *cantari* et poésies satiriques inspirés par la campagne de 1494-1495." In *Italie 1494*. Ed. Adelin Charles Fiorato. Paris: La Sorbonne, 1994. 179–225.

Folin, Marco. *Rinascimento estense: Politica, cultura, istituzioni di un antico stato italiano*. Rome, Bari: Laterza, 2001.

Folin, Marco. "Studio e politica negli Stati estensi fra Quattro e Cinquecento: Dottori, ufficiali, cortigiani." In *Giovanni e Gianfrancesco Pico: L'opera e la fortuna di due studenti ferraresi*. Ed. Patrizia Castelli. Florence: Olschki, 1998. 59–90.

Fonseca, Cosimo Damiano, ed. *Otranto 1480. Atti del Convegno internazionale di Studi nel V Centenario della caduta di Otranto ad opera dei Turchi*. Lecce: Galatina, 1986. 2 vols.

Forti Grazzini, Nello. *L'arazzo ferrarese*. Milan: Electa, 1982.

Foss, Michael. *People of the First Crusade*. New York: Arcade, 1997.

Franceschetti, Antonio. "On the Saracens in Early Italian Chivalric Literature." In *Romance Epic: Essays on a Medieval Literary Genre*. Ed. Hans Erich Keller. 1987. 203–11.

Franceschetti, Antonio. "L'*Orlando innamorato* e la tradizione dell'*Aspremont*." *GSLI* 147 (1970): 518–33.

Franceschetti, Antonio. *L'*Orlando innamorato *e le sue componenti tematiche e strutturali*. Florence: Leo S. Olschki, 1975.

Franceschetti, Antonio. "*La Spagna in rima* e il duello di Orlando e Agricane." *Lettere Italiane* 21 (1969): 322–6.

Fredricksmeyer, Ernst. "Alexander the Great and the Kingship of Asia." In *Alexander the Great in Fact and Fiction*. Ed. A.B. Bosworth and E.J. Baynham. Oxford: Oxford University Press, 2000. 136–66. http://dx.doi.org/10.1093/acprof:oso/9780198152873.003.0005

Frugoni, Chiara S. *La fortuna di Alessandro Magno dall'antichità al medioevo*. Florence: La Nuova Italia, 1978.

Ganim, John M., and Shayne Aaron Legassie, eds. *Cosmopolitanism and the Middles Ages*. New York: Palgrave MacMillan, 2012.

Garin, Eugenio. *Astrology in the Renaissance: The Zodiac of Life*. Trans. Carolyn Jackson and June Allen; revised by Clare Robertson. London and Boston: Routledge and Kegan Paul, 1983.

Giamatti, A. Bartlett. *The Earthly Paradise and the Renaissance Epic*. Princeton: Princeton Universtiy Press, 1966.

Goodman, Jennifer R. "Marriage and Conversion in Late Medieval Romance." In *Varieties of Religious Conversion in the Middle Ages*. Ed. James Muldoon. Gainesville: University Press of Florida, 1997. 115–28.

Gragnolati, Manuele. "Love, Lust, and Avarice: Leodilla between Dante and Ovid." In Cavallo and Ross, eds, *Fortune and Romance*, 151–73.

Gregory, Tobias. *From Many Gods to One: Divine Action in Renaissance Epic*. Chicago: University of Chicago Press, 2006.

Greppi, Claudio. "Una carta per la corte: Il viaggiatore immobile." In *The Re-*

naissance in Ferrara and Its European Horizons / Il Rinascimento a Ferrara e i suoi orizzonti Europei. Ed. June Salmons and Walter Moretti. Cardiff: University of Wales Press; Ravenna: Mario Lapucci, c1984. 199–222.

Greppi, Claudio. "Luoghi e miti. La conoscenza delle scoperte presso la corte ferrarese." In *La tirannia degli astri: Aby Warburg e l'astrologia di Palazzo Schifanoia*. Ed. Marco Bertozzi. Bologna: Cappelli, 1985. 447–63.

Gritti, Valentina. "Un libro di Boiardo: La *Spagna* di Borso d'Este." In *Miscellanea Boiardesca*. Ed. Cristina Montagnani. Novara: Interlinea, 2010. 61–88.

Gualdo Rosa, Lucia, Isabella Nuovo, and Domenico Defilippis, eds. *Gli umanisti e la guerra otrantina: Testi dei secoli XV e XVI*. Bari: Dedalo, 1982.

Gundersheimer, Werner. *Ferrara: The Style of a Renaissance Despotism*. Princeton, NJ: Princeton University Press, 1973.

Guzman, Gregory G. "The Encyclopedist Vincent of Beauvais and His Mongol Extracts from John of Plano Carpini and Simon of Saint-Quentin." *Speculum* 49.2 (1974): 287–307. http://dx.doi.org/10.2307/2856045.

Hankins, James. *Plato in the Italian Renaissance*. New York: Brill, 1991.

Hankins, James. "Renaissance Crusaders: Humanist Crusade Literature in the Age of Mehmed II." *Dumbarton Oaks Papers* 49 (1995): 111–207. http://dx.doi.org/10.2307/1291712.

Harris, Neil. *Bibliografia dell'*Orlando innamorato. 2 vols. Modena: Panini, 1988–91.

Heckel, Waldemar, intro. *The History of Alexander*. By Quintus Curtius Rufus. Trans. John Yardley. 1984. London: Penguin, 2001. 1–15.

Heissig, Walther. *The Religions of Mongolia*. c1970. Trans. Geoffrey Samuel. Berkeley, Los Angeles: University of California Press, 1980.

Hess, Catherine. "Brilliant Achievements: The Journey of Islamic Glass and Ceramics to Renaissance Italy." *Arts of Fire: Islamic Influences on Glass and Ceramics of the Italian Renaissance*. Ed. Catherine Hess with Linda Komaroff and George Saliba. Los Angeles: J. Paul Getty Museum, c2004. 1–33.

Hibbert, Christopher. *Venice: The Biography of a City*. New York and London: W.W. Norton, 1989.

Higgins, Iain Macleod. *Writing East: The* Travels *of Sir John Mandeville*. Philadelphia: University of Pennsylvania Press, 1997.

Houben, Hubert. *Roger II of Sicily: A Ruler between East and West*. Trans. Graham A. Loud and Diane Milburn. Cambridge and New York: Cambridge University Press, 2002.

Housley, Norman. *The Later Crusades, 1274–1580: From Lyons to Alcazar*. Oxford: Oxford University Press, 1992.

Howard, Deborah. *Venice and the East: The Impact of the Islamic World on Venetian Architecture 1100–1500*. New Haven, CT; London: Yale University Press, 2000.

Imber, Colin. *The Ottoman Empire, 1300–1650: The Structure of Power*. Basingstoke: Palgrave Macmillan, 2002.

Inalcik, Halil. *The Ottoman Empire: The Classical Age 1300–1600*. c1973. London: Phoenix, 2000.

Jagchid, Sechin, and Paul Hyer. *Mongolia's Culture and Society*. Boulder, CO: Westview Press, 1979.

Jardine, Lisa. *Worldly Goods: A New History of the Renaissance*. New York: Doubleday, 1996.

Jardine, Lisa, and Jerry Brotton. *Global Interests: Renaissance Art between East and West*. Ithaca, NY: Cornell University Press, 2000.

Jones, Horace Leonard, intro. *The Geography of Strabo*. London: William Heinemann; New York: Putnam, 1917–32.

Jordan, Constance. "Writing beyond the *Querelle*: Gender and History in *Orlando furioso*." In *Renaissance Transactions: Ariosto and Tasso*. Ed. Valeria Finucci. Durham, NC: Duke University Press, 1999. 295–315.

Kay, Sarah. *The Chansons de geste in the Age of Romance*. Oxford: Clarendon Press, 1995. http://dx.doi.org/10.1093/acprof:oso/9780198151920.001.0001

Kibre, Pearl. *The Library of Pico della Mirandola*. New York: AMS Press, 1966.

Kinoshita, Sharon. "Deprovincializing the Middle Ages." In *The Worlding Project: Doing Cultural Studies in the Era of Globalization*. Ed. Rob Wilson and Christopher Leigh Connery. Santa Cruz: New Pacific Press; Berkeley: North Atlantic Books, 2007. 61–75.

Kinoshita, Sharon. *Medieval Boundaries: Rethinking Difference in Old French Literature*. Philadelphia: University of Pennsylvania Press, 2006.

Knox, Bernard. *The Oldest Dead White European Males and Other Reflections on the Classics*. New York: Norton, 1993.

Komroff, Manuel, ed. *Contemporaries of Marco Polo: Consisting of the travel records to the Eastern parts of the world of William of Rubruck (1253–1255), the journey of John of Pian de Carpini (1245–1247), the journal of Friar Odoric (1318–1330), and the Oriental travels of Rabbi Benjamin of Tudela (1160–1173)*. New York: Dorset, c1989.

Kreutz, Barbara M. *Before the Normans: Southern Italy in the Ninth and Tenth Centuries*. Philadelphia: University of Pennsylvania Press, 1996.

Kristeller, Paul Oscar, intro. "Oration on the Dignity of Man." By Giovanni Pico della Mirandola. Trans. Elizabeth Livermore Forbes. *The Renaissance Philosophy of Man*. Ed. Ernst Cassirer, Paul Oskar Kristeller, and John Herman Randall, Jr. Chicago: Phoenix, c1948. 215–22.

La Barre, Weston. *They Shall Take Up Serpents*. c1962. New York: Schocken, 1969.

Lach, Donald F. *Asia in the Making of Europe*. Vol. 2. Bk 2. Chicago: University of Chicago Press, 1965.

Larner, John. *Marco Polo and the Discovery of the World*. New Haven: Yale, 1999.

Lee, Rensselaer W. *Names on Trees: Ariosto into Art*. Princeton: Princeton University Press, 1977.

Levi, Ezio. "L'*Orlando furioso* come epopea nuziale." *Archivum romanicum* 17 (1933): 459–96.

Limentani, Alberto. *L'Entrée d'Espagne e i signori d'Italia*. Ed. Marco Infurna and Francesco Zambon. Padua: Antenore, 1992.

Lippincott, Kristin. "Gli dei-decani del Salone dei Mesi di Palazzo Schifanoia." In *La tirannia degli astri: Aby Warburg e l'astrologia di Palazzo Schifanoia*. Ed. Marco Bertozzi. Bologna: Cappelli, 1985. 181–97.

Lomantsov, Victor. "Early Mongol Flags." http://flagspot.net/flags/mn-early.html. Accessed 13 September 2008.

Loomis, Roger Sherman. "The Fier Baiser in Mandeville's Travels, Arthurian Romance, and Irish Saga." *Studi medievali* 17 (1951): 104–13.

Looney, Dennis. *Compromising the Classics: Romance Epic Narrative in the Italian Renaissance*. Detroit: Wayne State University Press, 1996.

Lorch, Maristella de Panizza. "*Ma soprattutto la persona umana / era cortese*: Brandimarte's *cortesia* as Expressed through the Hero's *loci actionis* in Boiardo's *Orlando innamorato*, Book 1." In *La corte e lo spazio: Ferrara Estense*. Ed. Giuseppe Papagano and Amedeo Quondam. Rome: Bulzoni, 1982. 739–81.

Maalouf, Amin. *The Crusades through Arab Eyes*. Trans. Jon Rothschild. New York: Schocken Books, 1985. Chapter 8, "Nur al-Din, the Saint-King," 141–58.

Mac Carthy, Ita. "Ariosto the Traveller." *MLR* 102.2 (2007): 397–409. http://dx.doi.org/10.2307/20467285.

Mack, Rosamond E. *Bazaar to Piazza: Islamic Trade and Italian Art, 1300–1600*. Berkeley, CA; London: University of California Press, 2001.

McMichaels, John. "Double Vision: Boccaccio's *Filocolo* in Boiardo's *Orlando innamorato*." In Cavallo and Ross, eds, *Fortune and Romance,* 193–203.

Man, John. *Genghis Khan: Life, Death, and Resurrection*. New York: St Martin's Press, 2004.

Manca, Joseph. "Boiardo and the Visual Arts in Ferrara: Comparisons and Convergences." In Cavallo and Ross, *Fortune and Romance,* 261–70.

Marozzi, Justin. *Tamerlane: Sword of Islam, Conqueror of the World*. Cambridge, MA: Da Capo, 2004.

Martines, Lauro. *Strong Words. Writing and Social Strain in the Italian Renaissance*. Baltimore: Johns Hopkins University Press, 2001.

Martinez, Ronald L. "Two Odysseys: Rinaldo's Po Journey and the Poet's

Homecoming in *Orlando furioso*." In *Renaissance Transactions: Ariosto and Tasso*. Ed. Valeria Finucci. Durham, NC: Duke University Press, 1999. 17–55.

Mas-Latrie, Louis de, ed. *The Chronicle of Ernoul and Bernard the Treasurer*. Paris: Société de l'histoire de France, 1871.

Matteo, Sante. "Marco Polo." *The Literary Encyclopedia*. http://www.litencyc.com/php/speople.php?rec=true&UID=3594. Accessed 1 June 2010.

Medvedev, Michael. "The Russian Ways of the Heraldic Lions and Eagles of Medieval Europe." http://the.heraldry.ru/text/russian_ways.html. Published 16 August 2006.

Meregazzi, Luisa A. "L'episodio del Prete Gianni nell'*Ugo d'Alvernia*." *Studi Romanzi* 26 (1935): 5–69.

Meserve, Margaret. *Empires of Islam in Renaissance Historical Thought*. Cambridge, MA: Harvard University Press, 2008.

Meserve, Margaret. "From Samarkand to Scythia: Reinventions of Asia in Renaissance Geography and Political Thought." In *Pius II "El più expeditivo pontefice."* Ed. Zweder Von Martels and Arjo Vanderjagt. Leiden and Boston: Brill, 2003. 13–39.

Meserve, Margaret. "News from Negroponte: Politics, Popular Opinion, and Information Exchange in the First Decade of the Italian Press." *Renaissance Quarterly* 59.2 (2006): 440–80. http://dx.doi.org/10.1353/ren.2008.0312.

Micocci, Claudia. "Appunti su magia e astrologia nel *Canzoniere* di Boiardo." In *Il Mago, il cosmo, il teatro degli astri: Saggi sulla letteratura esoterica del Rinascimento*. Ed. Gianfranco Formichetti. Rome: Bulzoni, 1985. 35–65.

Milanesi, Marica. "I regni del Prete Gianni." In *L'Africa. Storie di viaggiatori italiani*. Ed. Leopold Sedar Senghor. Milan: Nuovo Banco Ambrosiano, 1986. 42–55.

Milano, Ernesto. *La carta del Cantino e la rappresentazione della terra nei codici e nei libri a stampa della Biblioteca Estense e Universitaria*. Modena: Il Bulino, 1991.

Montagnani, Cristina, intro. *Spagna Ferrarese*. Ed. Valentina Gritti and Cristina Montagnani. Novara: Interlinea, 2009. 11–35.

Monteverdi, A. "A proposito delle 'fonti' dell'*Orlando furioso*." *Cultura Neolatina* 21 (1961): 259–67.

Morgan, Margaret Ruth. *The Chronicle of Ernoul and the Continuations of William of Tyre*. London: Oxford University Press, 1973.

Moretti, Walter. *L'ultimo Ariosto*. Bologna: Pàtron, 1977.

Murrin, Michael. *The Allegorical Epic: Essays in Its Rise and Decline*. Chicago: Chicago University Press, 1980.

Murrin, Michael. *History and Warfare in Renaissance Epic.* Chicago, London: University of Chicago Press, 1994.

Murrin, Michael. "Trade and Fortune: Morgana and Manodante." In Cavallo and Ross, eds, *Fortune and Romance,* 77–95.

Nederman, Cary J. *Worlds of Difference: European Discourses of Toleration, c. 1100–c. 1550.* University Park: Pennsylvania State University Press, 2000.

Neri, Achille. "La gran magnificenza del Prete Janni, poemetto di Giuliano Dati." *Il Propugnatore* 9.1 (1876): 138–65.

O'Connell, Monique. "The Italian Renaissance in the Mediterranean or between East and West. A Review Article." *California Italian Studies Journal* 1 (2010): 1–30.

Olschki, Leonardo. *L'Asia di Marco Polo. Introduzione alla lettura e allo studio del Milione.* Florence: Sansoni, 1957.

Olschki, Leonardo. "I 'Cantari dell'India' di Giuliano Dati." *La Bibliofilia* 40 (1938): 289–316.

Orvieto, Paolo. "La descrizione del difforme e del mostruoso nella letteratura cavalleresca del Quattrocento. Lettura postcoloniale." In *Ecfrasi: modelli ed esempi fra Medioevo e Rinascimento.* Ed. Gianni Venturi and Monica Farnetti. Roma: Bulzoni, c2004. 165–201.

Panini, Giuseppe. *La famiglia Estense da Ferrara a Modena.* Modena: Armo, 1996.

Papio, Michael. *Keen and Violent Remedies. Social Satire and the Grotesque in Masuccio Salernitano's* Novellino. New York: Peter Lang, 2000.

Papio, Michael. "Il pericolo che viene dal mare: Il *Novellino* di Masuccio Salernitano tra xenofobia e misoginia." In *Mediterranoesis: Voci dal Medioevo e dal Rinascimento Mediterraneo.* Ed. Roberta Morosini and Cristina Perissinotto. Rome: Salerno, 2007. 235–52.

Paratore, Ettore. "L'*Orlando innamorato* e l'*Eneide.*" In *Boiardo e la critica contemporanea.* Ed. Giuseppe Anceschi. Florence: Olschki, 1970. 347–75.

Pardi, Giuseppe, ed. *Diario ferrarese dall'anno 1409 al 1504 di autori incerti. Rerum italicarum scriptores* 24, pt 7, no. 1–4. Ed. L.A. Muratori. Bologna: Zanichelli, 1928–33.

Pasqualino, Antonio. "Dama Rovenza dal Martello e la leggenda di Rinaldo da Montalbano." In *I cantari, struttura e tradizione.* Ed. M. Picone and M. Bendinelli Predelli. Florence: Olschki, 1984.

Pasqualino, Antonio. *L'opera dei pupi.* Palermo: Sellerio, 1977.

Pasqualino, Antonio. *Le vie del cavaliere dall'epica medievale alla cultura popolare.* Milan: Bompiani, 1992.

Pedani, Maria Pia. *Venezia porta d'Oriente.* Bologna: Il Mulino, 2010.

Perkins, Leeman. "Musical Culture in Late Quattrocento Ferrara: Local Traditions and Foreign Influences." In Cavallo and Ross, eds, *Fortune and Romance,* 295–314.

Perrotta, Annalisa. "Alleanze necessarie: Cristiani, saraceni e persiani *nell'Altobello*." In *Il cantare italiano fra folklore e letteratura*. Ed. Michelangelo Picone and Luisa Rubini. Biblioteca dell'Archivium Romanicum. Florence: Olschki, 2007. 127–44.

Perrotta, Annalisa. "Rifare secondo la norma: Il *Falconetto* 1483 e il suo rifacimento in ottave." *Schifanoia* 34/35 (2008): 249–58.

Perrotta, Annalisa. "Lo spazio della corte: La rappresentazione del potere politico nel *Morgante* di Luigi Pulci." *Italianist* 24 (2004): 141–68.

Pertusi, Agostino. "I primi studi in Occidente sull'origine e la potenza dei Turchi." *Studi Veneziani* XII (1970): 465–552.

Pistarino, Geo. "I Portoghesi verso *l'Asia* del Prete Gianni." *Studi medievali* (1961): 75–137.

Polcri, Alessandro. *Luigi Polcri e la Chimera: Studi sull'allegoria nel* Morgante. Florence: Società Editrice Fiorentina, 2010.

Ponte, Giovanni. "La discordia nel campo di Agramante e la coscienza ariostesca dei limiti degli ideali umani." *Esperienze Letterarie* 20.2 (1995): 3–12.

Ponte, Giovanni. *La personalità e l'opera del Boiardo*. Genoa: Tilgher, 1972.

Powell, James M. *Anatomy of a Crusade 1213–1221*. Philadelphia: University of Pennsylvania Press, 1986.

Praloran, Marco. *Tempo e azione nell'*Orlando furioso. Florence: Olschki, 1999.

Prampolini, Giovanni. *Le "Storie di Orlando": Rappresentazioni pittoriche e sceniche* dell'Innamorato *e del* Furioso. Casalgrande (RE), Italy: Litostampa La Rapida, 2000.

Pryo, John. "The Mediterranean Breaks Up: 500–1500." In *The Mediterranean in History*. Ed. David Abulafia. Los Angeles: The J. Paul Getty Museum, 2003. 155–81.

Pugliese, Olga Zorzi. *Castiglione's* The Book of the Courtier*: A Classic in the Making*. Naples: Edizioni Scientiche Italiane, 2008.

Quint, David. "The Death of Brandimarte and the Ending of the *Orlando furioso*." *Annali d'Italianistica* 12 (1994): 75–85.

Rajna, Pio. *Le fonti dell'*Orlando furioso. 1900. Florence: Sansoni, 1975.

Rajna, Pio. "L'*Orlando innamorato* del Boiardo." In *Vita italiana nel Rinascimento*. Vol. 2. Milan: Fratelli Treves, 1893. 309–48.

Rajna, Pio, intro. *I cantari di Carduino giuntovi quello di Tristano e Lancielotto quando combattettero al petrone di Merlino*. Ed. Pio Rajna. *Scelta di curiosità letterarie inedite o rare dal secolo XIII al XVII*. Vol. 135. Bologna: Gaetano Romagnoli, 1873. v–lxxiii.

Reichenbach, Giulio. *L'Orlando* innamorato *di M.M. Boiardo*. Florence: La Nuova Italia, 1936.

Relaño, Francesc. *The Shaping of Africa: Cosmographic Discourse and Cartographic Science in Late Medieval and Early Modern Europe*. Aldershot, UK; Burlington, VT: Ashgate, 2002.

Ricci, Giovanni. "Una nicchia d'Oltralpe: Ferrara come Digione." In *Cosmè Tura e Francesco del Cossa: L'arte a Ferrara nell'età di Borso d'Este*. Ed. Mauro Natale. Ferrara: Ferrara Arte S.p.A., 2007. 61–73.

Ricci, Giovanni. *Ossessione turca: In una retrovia cristiana dell'Europa moderna*. Bologna: Il mulino, 2002.

Ricci, Giovanni. *I turchi alle porte*. Bologna: Il mulino, 2008.

Riccucci, Marina, comment and textual notes. Boiardo, Matteo Maria. *Pastorali*. Introduction by Stefano Carrai. Milan: Fondazione Pietro Bembo; Parma: U. Guanda, 2005. 227–64.

Richards, D.S., intro. *The Rare and Excellent History of Saladin, Being the al-Nawadir al-Sultaniyya wa'l-Mahasin al-Yusufiyya*. By Baha' al-Din Ibn Shaddad. Trans. D.S. Richards. Burlington, VT: Ashgate, 2001.

Rizzi, Andrea. "Riccobaldo da Ferrara e Matteo Maria Boiardo: Note preliminari." In *Gli Amorum Libri e la lirica del Quattrocento*. Ed. Antonia Tissoni Benvenuti. Novara: Interlinea, 2003. 137–55.

Rizzi, Andrea, ed. *The "Historia imperiale" by Riccobaldo Ferrarese Translated by Matteo Maria Boiardo (1471–1473)*. Vol. 1. Rome: Istituto Storico Italiano per il Medio Evo, 2008.

Rizzi, Andrea, ed. "M.M. Boiardo's Version of Riccobaldo Ferrarese: The *Historia imperiale* (1471–73)." Diss. University of Kent at Canterbury [contains Book 3].

Robinson, Carl. *Nomad Empire of the Eternal Blue Sky*. Mongolia: Odyssey Publications, 2010.

Roche, Thomas P., Jr. "Ariosto's Marfisa or Camilla Domesticated." *Modern Language Notes* 103 (1988): 113–33.

Rogers, J. Michael. "The 'Gorgeous East': Trade and Tribute in the Islamic Empires." In *Circa 1492*. Ed. Jay A. Levenson. New Haven: Yale University Press; Washington: National Gallery of Art, 1991. 69–74.

Rosenberg, Charles M. *The Este Monuments and Urban Development in Renaissance Ferrara*. Cambridge and New York: Cambridge University Press, 1997.

Ross, Charles S. "From Asia by Sea: Marco Polo, Boiardo, and the First Western Fantasy of the Chinese Maritime." In *Haiyang Wenxue Yanjiu Wenji*. Beijing: Ocean Press, 2009. 222–30.

Ross, Charles S., intro. and notes. *Orlando innamorato*. West Lafayette, IN: Parlor Press, 2004.

Rossebastiano, Alda. "La vicenda umana nei pellegrinaggi in Terra Santa del secolo XV." *La letteratura di viaggio dal medioevo al rinascimento: Generi e problemi.* Alessandria: Edizioni dell'Orso, 1989. 19–49.

Rossebastiano, Alda, and Simona Fenoglio, eds. *Viaggio in Oriente di un nobile del Quattrocento: Il pellegrinaggio di Milliaduse d'Este.* By Don Domenego. Turin: UTET, 2005.

Rossebastiano Bart, Alda. "Alle fonti del Boiardo: Il 'fier baiser' nell'*Orlando innamorato.*" *Studi e Problemi di Critica Testuale* 25 (1982): 19–23.

Rossi, Massimo. "La geografia del *Furioso.* Sul sapere geo-cartografico alla corte estense." In *Lucrezia Borgia: Storia e mito.* Ed. Michele Bordin and Paolo Trovato. Florence: Olschki, 2006. 97–138.

Rothbard, Murray N. *Economic Thought before Adam Smith: An Austrian Perspective on the History of Economic Thought.* Edward Elgar Publishing Ltd., 1995. 2 vols. Auburn, AL: Ludwig von Mises Institute, 2006.

Rubiés, Joan Pau. *Travel and Ethnology in the Renaissance: South India through European Eyes, 1250–1625.* Cambridge and New York: Cambridge University Press, 2000. http://dx.doi.org/10.1017/CBO9780511496608

Ruggieri, Ruggero M, intro. *Il milione.* By Marco Polo. Florence: Olschki, 1986.

Ruggiero, Guido. "Introduction: Renaissance Dreaming: In Search of a Paradigm." In *A Companion to the Worlds of the Renaissance.* Ed. Guido Ruggiero. Oxford; Malden, MA: Blackwell Publishers, 2002. 1–20.

Runciman, Steven. *A History of the Crusades.* 3 vols. Cambridge: Cambridge University Press, 1951.

Sacchi, Guido. *Fra Ariosto e Tasso: Vicende del poema narrativo.* Pisa: Scuola Normale Superiore, 2006.

Said, Edward W. *Culture and Imperialism.* New York: Alfred A. Knopf, 1993.

Said, Edward W. *Orientalism.* c1978. New York: Vintage Books, 1979.

Saliba, George. *A History of Arabic Astronomy: Planetary Theories during the Golden Age of Islam.* New York: New York University Press, 1994.

Sangirardi, Giuseppe. *Boiardismo Ariostesco. Presenza e trattamento dell'* Orlando innamorato *nel* furioso. Lucca: Pacini Fazzi, 1993.

Santoro, Mario. *L'anello di Angelica: Nuovi saggi ariosteschi.* Naples: Federico and Ardia, 1983.

Santoro, Mario. "L'Astolfo ariostesco: 'Homo fortunatus.'" *Ariosto e il Rinascimento.* Naples: Liguori, 1989. 185–236.

Santoro, Mario. "La prova del 'nappo' e la cognizione ariostesca del reale." *Esperienze letterarie* (1976): 5–24.

Sberlati, Francesco. "Dall'*Entrée d'Espagne* all'*Orlando innamorato*: Una genealogia non solo linguistica." In *Il Boiardo e il mondo estense nel Quattrocento.* Ed. Giuseppe Anceschi and Tina Matarrese. 2 vols. Padua: Antenore, 1998. 175–94.

Scaraffia, Lucetta. *Rinnegati: Per una storia dell'identità occidentale*. Rome and Bari: Laterza, 2002.

Schwoebel, Robert H. "Coexistence, Conversion, and the Crusade against the Turks." *Studies in the Renaissance* 12 (1965): 164–87. http://dx.doi.org/10.2307/2857073.

Schwoebel, Robert H. *The Shadow of the Crescent: The Renaissance Image of the Turk (1453–1517)*. Nieuwkoop: B. De Graaf, 1967.

Searles, Colbert. "Some Notes on Boiardo's Version of the Alexander-Sagas." *Modern Language Notes* 15.2 (1900): 45–8. http://dx.doi.org/10.2307/2918116.

Serra, Luciano. "Da Tolomeo alla Garfagnana: La geografia dell'Ariosto." *Ludovico Ariosto: Il suo tempo la sua terra la sua gente. Bollettino storico reggiano* 7 (Oct. 1974): 151–84.

Serra, Luciano. "Letture boiardesche." In *Il Boiardo e il mondo estense nel Quattrocento*. Ed. Giuseppe Anceschi and Tina Matarrese. 2 vols. Padua: Antenore, 1998. 143–74.

Serra, Luciano. "La sublimazione del grottesco: Brunello." In *Il Boiardo e la critica contemporanea*. Ed. Giuseppe Anceschi. Florence: Olschki, 1970. 489–97.

Shaw, Christine, ed. *Italy and the European Powers. The Impact of War, 1500–1530*. Leiden, Boston: Brill, 2006.

Shemek, Diana. *Ladies Errant: Wayward Women and Social Order in Early Modern Italy*. Durham, NC: Duke University Press, 1998.

Shemek, Diana. "Of Women, Knights, Arms, and Love: The *Querelle des Femmes* in Ariosto's Poem." *Modern Language Notes* 104 (1989): 68–97.

Sherberg, Michael. *Rinaldo: Character and Intertext in Ariosto and Tasso*. Stanford French and Italian Studies 75. Saratoga, CA: Anma Libri, 1993.

Silverberg, Robert. *The Realm of Prester John*. New York: Doubleday, 1972.

Smarr, Janet Levarie. "Altre razze ed altri spazi nel *Decameron*." In *Boccaccio geografo: Un viaggio nel Mediterraneo tra le città, i giardini e... il 'mondo' di Giovanni Boccaccio*. Ed. Roberta Morosini, with Andrea Cantile. Florence: Mauro Pagliai Editore, 2010. 133–58.

Smit, Hillie. "Flemish Tapestry Weavers in Italy c. 1420–1520. A Survey and Analysis of the Activity in Various Cities." In *Flemish Tapestry Weavers Abroad: Emigration and the Founding of Manufactories in Europe*. Ed. Guy Delmarcel. Leuven: Leuven University Press, 2002. 113–30.

Southern, R.W. *Western Views of Islam in the Middle Ages*. Cambridge, MA: Harvard University Press, 1962.

Stoppino, Eleonora. *Genealogies of Fiction: Women Warriors and the Dynastic Imagination in the* Orlando furioso. New York: Fordham University Press, 2012.

Sturm-Maddox, Sara. "Roland épigone d'Alexandre dans *L'Entrée d'Espagne.*" In *Plaist vos oïr bone cançon vaillant? Mélanges de Langue et Littératures Médiévales offerts à François Suard.* Ed. Dominique Boutet et al. Lille: Université Charles-de-Gaulle-Lille 3. 872–8.

Tangheroni, Marco. "Trade and Navigation." In *Italy in the Central Middle Ages, 1000–1300.* Ed. David Abulafia. Oxford: Oxford University Press, 2004. 127–46.

Tissoni Benvenuti, Antonia. "Intertestualità cavalleresca." *"Tre volte suona l'olifant ..." (La tradizione rolandiana in Italia fra Medioevo e Rinascimento).* Milan: Unicopli, 2007. 57–78.

Tissoni Benvenuti, Antonia. "Rugiero o la fabbrica dell'*Inamoramento de Orlando.*" In *Per Cesare Bozzetti.* Ed. S. Albonico, et al. Milan: Fondazione Mondadori, 1996. 69–89.

Tissoni Benvenuti, Antonia, intro. and notes. *Inamoramento de Orlando.* Ed. Antonia Tissoni Benvenuti and Cristina Montagnani. *Opere.* 2 vols. Milan: Riccardo Ricciardi, 1999. xi–vvviii.

Tolan, John V. *Saracens: Islam in the Medieval European Imagination.* New York: Columbia University Press, 2002.

Tolan, John V. *Sons of Ishmael. Muslims through European Eyes in the Middle Ages.* Gainesville: University Press of Florida, 2008.

Tomalin, Margaret. *The Fortunes of the Warrior Heroine in Italian Literature.* Ravenna: Longo Editore, 1982.

Toniolo, Federica. "La miniatura a Ferrara: Crogiolo dele arti." In *Cosmè Tura e Francesco del Cossa: L'arte a Ferrara nell'età di Borso d'Este.* Ed. Mauro Natale. Ferrara: Ferrara Arte S.p.A., 2007. 111–23.

Train, John. *The Orange.* Milan: M.T. Train/Scala Books, 2006.

Tristano, Richard M. "The *Istoria imperiale* of Matteo Maria Boiardo and Fifteenth-Century Ferrarese Courtly Culture." In *Phaethon's Children: The Este Court and Its Culture in Early Modern Ferrara.* Ed. Dennis Looney and Deanna Shemek. Tempe, AZ: Arizona Center for Medieval and Renaissance Studies, 2005. 129–68.

Tyerman, Christopher. *God's War: A New History of the Crusades.* Cambridge, MA: Belknap Press of Harvard University Press, 2006.

Venturi, Adolfo. "L'arte ferrarese nel periodo d'Ercole I d'Este." *Atti e memorie dell R. deputazione di storia patria per le provincie di Romagna* 7 (1889): 388–9.

Vernero, Michele. *Studi critici sopra la geografia nell'* Orlando furioso. Turin: Palatina di Bonis e Rossi, 1913.

Villoresi, Marco. "Le donne e gli amori nel romanzo cavalleresco del Quattrocento." *Filologia e critica* 23 (1998): 3–43.

Villoresi, Marco. *La fabbrica dei cavallieri: Cantari, poemi, romanzi in prosa fra Medioevo e Rinascimento*. Rome: Salerno, 2005.

Villoresi, Marco. *La letteratura cavalleresca: Dai cicli medievali all'Ariosto*. Rome: Carocci, 2000.

Vitullo, Juliann M. *The Chivalric Epic in Medieval Italy*. Gainesville: University Press of Florida, 2000.

Voorbij, J.B. "The *Speculum historiale*: Some Aspects of Its Genesis and Manuscript Tradition." In *Vincent of Beauvais and Alexander the Great. Studies on the Speculum maius and Its Translations into Medieval Vernaculars*. Ed. W.J. Aerts, E.R. Smits, and J.B. Voorbij. Groningen: E. Forsten, 1986. 11–55.

Weaver, Elissa Barbara. "Lettura dell'intreccio dell'*Orlando furioso*: Il caso delle tre pazzie d'amore." *Strumenti critici* 11.3 (1977): 384–406.

Wiggins, Peter DeSa. *Figures in Ariosto's Tapestry: Character and Design in the* Orlando furioso. Baltimore: Johns Hopkins University Press, 1986.

Wolf, Kenneth. *Making History: The Normans and Their Historians in Eleventh-Century Italy*. Philadelphia: University of Pennsylvania Press, 1995.

Wolohojian, Albert Mugrdich, ed. *The Romance of Alexander the Great by Pseudo-Callisthenes*. New York: Columbia University Press, 1969.

Yeager, Suzanne M. *Jerusalem in Medieval Narrative*. Cambridge: Cambridge University Press, 2008. http://dx.doi.org/10.1017/CBO9780511483400

Zaganelli, Gioia. *L'Oriente incognito medievale: Enciclopedie, romanzi di Alessandro, teratologie*. Soveria Mannelli (Catanzaro): Rubbettino, 1997.

Zaganelli, Gioia, ed. *La lettera del Prete Gianni*. Milan: Luni, 2000.

Zampese, Cristina. *"Or si fa rosa or pallida la luna": La cultura classica nell'*Orlando innamorato. Lucca: Pacini Fazzi, 1994.

Zanette, Emilio. *Conversazioni sull'*Orlando furioso. Pisa: Nismalaterratri-Lischi, 1958.

Zarncke, Friedrich. *Der Priester Johannes*. Des VII. Bandes der Abhandlungen der philologish-historischen Classe der Königl. Sächsischen Gesellschaft der Wissenschaften. Vol. 7, no. 8. Leipzig: S. Hirzel, 1876–9.

Zatti, Sergio. "Dalla parte di Satana." In *La rappresentazione dell'altro nei testi del Rinascimento*. Ed. Sergio Zatti. Lucca: Pacini Fazzi, 1998. 146–82.

Zatti, Sergio. *Il* Furioso *fra epos e romanzo*. Lucca: Pacini Fazzi, 1990.

Zatti, Sergio. *The Quest for Epic: From Ariosto to Tasso*. Ed. Dennis Looney. Trans. Sally Hill with Dennis Looney. Toronto: University of Toronto Press, 2006.

Index

www.ingramcontent.com/pod-product-compliance
Lightning Source LLC
LaVergne TN
LVHW041112090826
844660LV00061B/704/J
* 9 7 8 1 4 4 2 6 4 6 8 3 4 *